Chicago

GIFT RECEIPT

Barnes & Noble - DePaul Center
1 E. Jackson Boulevard
Chicago, IL 60604
312-362-8792

ORE:00850   REG:006   TRAN#:6598
ASHIER:JENNY Z

siders' Guide to
RADE*
780762760138   T
@ RL.HT)   RL.HT

203.65   12/12/2012 06:45PM

CUSTOMER COPY

TEXTBOOKS:

* A full refund will be given in your original form of payment if textbooks are returned during the first week of classes with original receipt.
* With proof of a schedule change and original receipt, a full refund will be given in your original form of payment during the first 30 days of classes.
* No refunds on unwrapped loose leaf books or activated eBooks.
* Textbooks must be in original condition.
* No refunds or exchanges without original receipt.

GENERAL READING BOOKS, SOFTWARE, AUDIO, VIDEO & SMALL ELECTRONICS

* A full refund will be given in your original form of payment if merchandise is returned within 14 days of purchase with original receipt.
* Opened software, audio books, DVDs, CDs, music, and small electronics may not be returned. They can be exchanged for the same item if defective.
* Merchandise must be in original condition.
* No refunds or exchanges without original receipt.

ALL OTHER MERCHANDISE

* A full refund will be given in your original form of payment with original receipt.
* Without a receipt, a store credit will be issued at the current selling price.
* Cash back on merchandise credits or gift cards will not exceed $
* No refunds on gift cards, prepaid cards, phone cards, newspapers or magazines.
* Merchandise must be in original condition.

Fair Pricing Policy

Barnes & Noble College Booksellers comply with local weights measures requirements. If the price on your receipt is above the advertised or posted price, please alert a bookseller and we will gladly refund the difference.

All photos licensed by Shutterstock.com.

Page 1: Chicago harbor lighthouse.

Page 2: (top left) The Wrigley building with flowers in the foreground; (top right) An ivy-draped building on Huron Street in Chicago; (bottom) The festive Navy Pier in Chicago.

Page 3: (top) The Chicago financial district along the river; (bottom left): The sign says it all; (bottom right, upper) Chicago's famous deep dish pizza ha a loyal following; (bottom right, lower) Chicago Cubs sign at Wrigley Field.

Page 4: (top) Stunning and elegant Buckingham Fountain against the Chicago skyline; (bottom) Ballooning is a great way to take in views of downtown Chicago and its surrounding area.

INSIDERS' GUIDE® TO
CHICAGO

HELP US KEEP THIS GUIDE UP TO DATE

We would love to hear from you concerning your experiences with this guide and how you feel it could be improved and kept up to date. Please send your comments and suggestions to:

editorial@GlobePequot.com

Thanks for your input, and happy travels!

INSIDERS' GUIDE® TO
CHICAGO

FIRST EDITION

ELISA DRAKE

INSIDERS' GUIDE

GUILFORD, CONNECTICUT
AN IMPRINT OF GLOBE PEQUOT PRESS

All the information in this guidebook is subject to change. We recommend that you call ahead to obtain current information before traveling.

To buy books in quantity for corporate use or incentives, call **(800) 962-0973** or e-mail **premiums@GlobePequot.com.**

INSIDERS' GUIDE ®

Editor: Kevin Sirois
Project Editor: Lynn Zelem
Layout: Mary Ballachino
Text Design: Sheryl Kober
Maps: Design Maps Inc. © Morris Book Publishing, LLC

ISBN 978-0-7627-6013-8

Printed in the United States of America
10 9 8 7 6 5 4 3 2 1

CONTENTS

Directory of Maps

ABOUT THE AUTHOR

When **Elisa Drake** attended college near Boston, she would tell people for simplicity's sake that she was from Chicago. Plus, it sounded cool. In fact, she's really from a suburb about 30 miles north of Chicago and didn't have a car in high school. So trips downtown were by train or with friends who did have their own wheels. In other words, she was as much a visitor then as you might be now—and going from quiet suburb to bustling city was always exhilarating and energizing.

It wasn't until a few years after college that Drake got her first apartment in Chicago. She worked as a freelance writer for several years, then got a job at Citysearch.com. Her work at the online city guide provided a great excuse to get out and explore the city even more. She also worked as an editor at Mobil Travel Guides, contributed to *Eyewitness Top Ten Chicago Guide, TimeOut Chicago,* and *TimeOut LA* (during a short time living out there), and wrote dozens of hotel reviews for Expedia.com (no, she didn't get to stay at all of them).

Her first book published by Globe Pequot Press was the recently released *Day Trips from Chicago,* and includes 25 drives outside of the city—a handful of the destinations are mentioned in this book too. With two young children, though, staying right here in the city is often best, presenting even more places to visit with her family than she did by herself—or at least different ones (i.e., more museums, fewer bars). She knows she's lucky to live in a city that's so easy to write about and even more fun to explore.

ACKNOWLEDGMENTS

In completing this book, I owe many thanks to several key people. Most importantly, my husband and daughters, my parents and my sister's family, but also Lindsey Jo White and Lisa Shames whose help was immeasurable, and my editor Kevin Sirois.

Chicago Overview

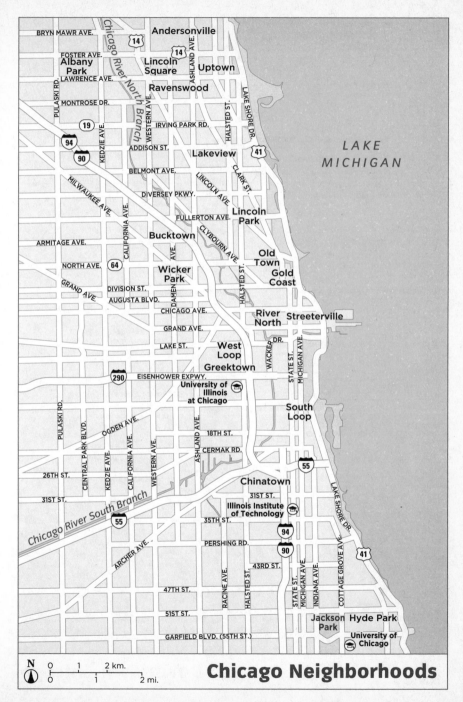

Chicago Neighborhoods

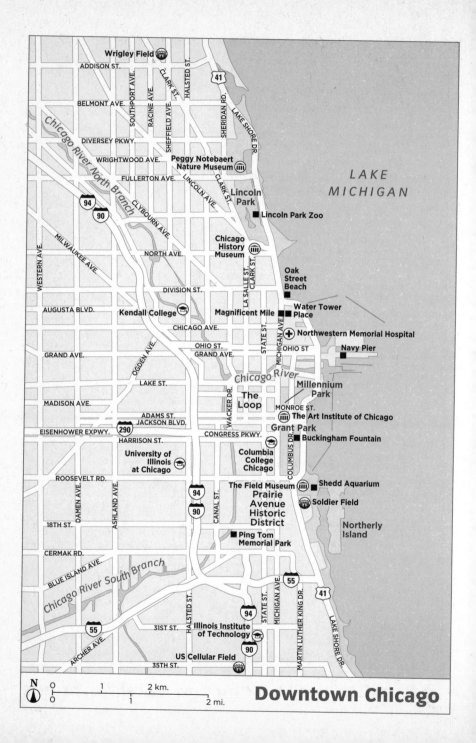

Wrigley Field

ADDISON ST.

BELMONT AVE.

Chicago River North Branch

DIVERSEY PKWY.

WRIGHTWOOD AVE.

Peggy Notebaert
Nature Museum

FULLERTON AVE.

Lincoln
Park

Lincoln Park Zoo

LAKE
MICHIGAN

SOUTHPORT AVE.
RACINE AVE.
SHEFFIELD AVE.
CLARK ST.
HALSTED ST.
SHERIDAN RD.
LAKE SHORE DR.
LINCOLN AVE.
CLYBOURN AVE.
CLARK ST.

NORTH AVE.

Chicago
History
Museum

DIVISION ST.

Oak
Street
Beach

WESTERN AVE.
MILWAUKEE AVE.

AUGUSTA BLVD.

Kendall College

Magnificent Mile

Water Tower
Place

Northwestern Memorial Hospital

CHICAGO AVE.

OHIO ST.
GRAND AVE.

GRAND AVE.

OHIO ST.

Navy Pier

LA SALLE ST.
CLARK ST.
STATE ST.
MICHIGAN AVE.

OGDEN AVE.

LAKE ST.

Chicago River

MADISON AVE.

The
Loop

Millennium
Park

MONROE ST.

The Art Institute of Chicago

WACKER DR.

ADAMS ST.
JACKSON BLVD.

EISENHOWER EXPWY.

Grant Park

Buckingham Fountain

COLUMBUS DR.

290

CONGRESS PKWY.

HARRISON ST.

University of
Illinois
at Chicago

Columbia
College
Chicago

ROOSEVELT RD.

The Field Museum

Shedd Aquarium

94

90

Prairie
Avenue
Historic
District

Soldier Field

DAMEN AVE.
ASHLAND AVE.
CANAL ST.

18TH ST.

Northerly
Island

Ping Tom
Memorial Park

CERMAK RD.

BLUE ISLAND AVE.

Chicago River South Branch

STATE ST.
MICHIGAN AVE.
MARTIN LUTHER KING DR.
LAKE SHORE DR.

55

41

55

31ST ST.

94

Illinois Institute
of Technology

90

HALSTED ST.

ARCHER AVE.

US Cellular Field

35TH ST.

N

0   1   2 km.
0   1   2 mi.

Downtown Chicago

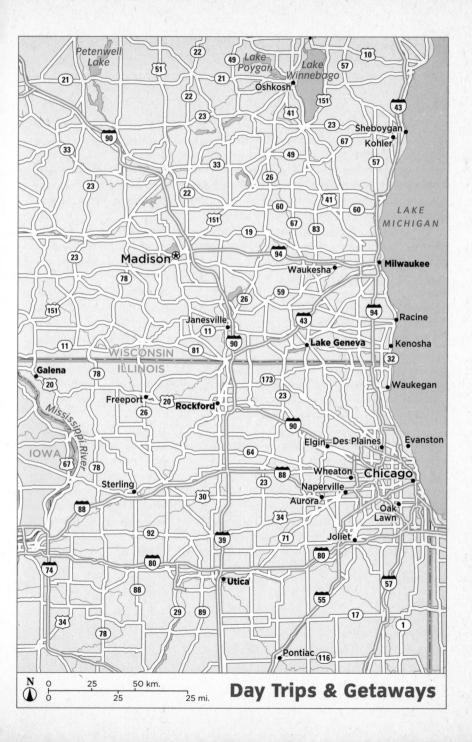

Day Trips & Getaways

INTRODUCTION

On a post–high school trip to Europe, I quickly learned what foreigners thought of Chicago: "You're from Chicago? Oh, gangsters, shoot 'em up, bang bang!" they'd exclaim, with an excited twinkle in their eyes. Well, yes, there used to be gangsters and there probably are some now, but . . . .Well, it was amusing, to say the least. But not surprising, given the prominent role the gangster era played in Chicago's history, with its popular images of glamour and wealth that were more entertaining than any movie.

These days, our image is no longer of a criminal nature (thank goodness), but rather a culturally dynamic, ethnically diverse, and economically solid metropolitan city that's both big and friendly. It's a city that equally cherishes its lakefront and its skyscrapers, its award-winning restaurants and its hole-in-the-wall eateries, its fashion-forward trends and its casual style. It's a city where artisans of all kinds find opportunities to express their individuality and their creativity—whether as chefs at innovative cafes or owners of funky clothing shops, brewing their own beer, or producing thought-provoking theater or controversial artwork. And in turn, Chicago has an eager audience that appreciates the results of their craft, a population open to new ideas and willing to try just about anything. We're an inclusive sort of city, too, where a gay pride parade and the St. Patrick's Day Parade are two of the most attended of any in the city. Where Fortune 500 companies fill the Loop, and independent businesses fill the neighborhoods. And we're a tough-get-going place where a dump of 24 inches of snow might be annoying, but sets us back only a day or two.

Speaking of that weather, though outdoor activity can be limited by our Midwestern four seasons, Chicago boasts an excellent walkability factor, and residents don't miss a moment to enjoy the fresh air. We take advantage of the many bike and jogging paths, boating and fishing spots, dozens of alfresco dining options, and its acres and acres of green space. Chicago has surprising natural beauty, in fact, from its lakeshore to the riverfront, and in its many parks sprinkled throughout the city, giving people space to breathe and a convenient break from the downtown bustle. While the gangsters of yesteryear may be gone, we know their stories live on, which is just fine with Chicagoans who relish the chance to chat up visitors about them and anything else they'd like to know. We're just that kind of place.

HOW TO USE THIS BOOK

Whether you're visiting or moving to Chicago, this book will be your handy reference and your go-to resource for everything you need to get the most out of your trip or feel comfortable in your new home.

While some books wow you with flashy photos, this one focuses on what's important—the information, the insider information, to be exact, and we've got lots of it. While websites are invaluable for timely additional research, books still win for their timeless, in-hand, no-battery-required, flip-through-ability. We hope you will, in fact, carry this around in your backpack or purse, refer to it, mark it up, and star your favorites. This book isn't a sacred tome; it's your traveling companion and trusty source to navigating the Windy City.

The chapters are organized to make it as easy as possible to find what you're looking for. They don't insist on a certain itinerary, because we know everyone has different ideas of what makes a perfect day. Zip through a few attractions in as many hours or spend one leisurely afternoon at a scenic park. Begin your food-loving Chicago fantasy with breakfast and don't stop till late-night cocktails. Or sleep in and start the day with brunch.

Some chapters include locations that are cross-referenced in another section. Like Millennium Park, which is as much an attraction as it is a green space, so it's listed in Parks & Recreation as well as Attractions & Museums. Or Lincoln Park Zoo, which has universal visitor appeal and is of special interest to kids, so you'll find it in Attractions & Museums, but also Kidstuff. You won't read identical reviews, either: Each one is targeted for that category, so you get the info you're looking for.

Chapters begin with a quick introduction that gives you an overall look at what's to come and some include a separate Overview if there are pertinent housekeeping-type details that help explain the chapter or guide you to a better experience when you're out and about.

For an even greater advantage, start by reading the Area Overview and History chapters. There's so much fascinating background to Chicago that it was hard to limit it to one chapter of history, but I'm confident that you'll find it a fast and interesting read. The Area Overview also includes descriptions of some of Chicago's many diverse neighborhoods, some you may have heard about and others you should hear about.

For both need-to-know and good-to-know info about traveling to and within Chicago, peruse the aptly titled chapter, Getting Here, Getting Around.

In the chapters that include reviews of places to go, stay, experience, and see, please know that each subject could practically be its own book, so I've tried to choose a wide variety of the best to appeal to all tastes and budgets.

If you've got some extra time on your visit or you're settling down in the area, check out the Day Trips & Getaways chapter, which includes a few destinations within a few hours' drive of the city.

HOW TO USE THIS BOOK

Throughout the book are **Insiders' Tips** (indicated by an ⬛i), which give you some tidbits gleaned from locals on things you might not otherwise find, as well as sidebars, which condense practical information and basic facts into an easy-to-read list. **Close-ups** go into more depth about particular aspects of Chicago.

You'll also find listings accompanied by the ✳ symbol—these are our top picks for attractions, restaurants, accommodations, and everything in between that you shouldn't miss while you're in the area. You want the best this region has to offer? Go with our **Insiders' Choice.**

Finally, if you're moving to the Chicago area or already live here, be sure to check out the blue-tabbed pages at the back of the book. There you will find the **Living Here** appendix that offers sections on relocation, media, child care, education, health care, and retirement.

AREA OVERVIEW

Being a metropolis in the Midwest gives Chicago the best of both worlds: friendly folks and an urban lifestyle. The type of place where if you stand on a corner with an open map, more than one passerby will stop to ask if you need help—really. The city's reputation as a gentler, cleaner option than our East Coast cousin is what brings people here—and keeps them here too. While New York may be the "city that never sleeps," Chicago is, as the famous song says, "my kind of town" where "people smile at you." L.A. may have its posh Hollywood hills and fancy red carpets, but Chicago has soaring skyscrapers and beachfront paths. Sure, the winters last too long, but Chicagoans tough it out and patiently explain to visitors and newcomers, "You just need to dress for it." Then, as soon as the thermometer inches over 60, Chicagoans dash outside to play until winter starts again. With its easy public transportation system, top-notch cultural institutions, shopping meccas, and stunning architecture, it's no wonder that Chicago has grown from its days as a swampy, stinky place in the middle of nowhere to a world-class city, boasting a booming economy and a bustling tourism industry that attracts more than 45 million people each year.

CHICAGO LIVING

Each fall, the Chicago Marathon brings nearly 34,000 runners to Windy City streets, making it the second largest marathon in the country, behind New York and ahead of Boston with about 10,000 more participants. Why the extraordinary turnout? Well, for one thing, novice marathoners appreciate that the course has just one slight incline. And that's Chicago for you: flat. But that merely describes its topography, because there's absolutely nothing monotonous about any other aspect of the city.

Thanks to former Mayor Richard M. Daley's concerted effort to bring people into the heart of the city over the past two-plus decades, Chicago's downtown area has blossomed into a desirable place not just to work, but also to live and to explore. Loop offices and crowded lunchtime hangs may go dark during non-business hours, but that's when downtown comes alive with a different feel—with theatergoers off to see everything from original dramas to brilliant Broadway musicals; with hordes of people making a beeline for the city's ever-expanding shopping options; and with couples, families, groups of friends, and visitors flocking to year-round activities at Millennium and Grant parks. The best part is that multiple buses and trains, plus a range of downtown hotels, offer convenient access to all of it.

And the locals know that these things are not just for tourists. They make the most of their city too. They head to the museums for indoor entertainment; they hit the beaches and city pools whenever weather permits; they meet at festivals throughout the city and throughout the year; they try the more than 7,300 eateries, from four-star restaurants to ethnic dives; they root for their home sports teams; and they live in more than 175 distinct neighborhoods that make up the multihued, multifaceted fabric of Chicago.

With so many neighborhoods, Chicago takes on fascinatingly distinct identities. It could be the quiet, suburblike quality of Hyde Park or the posh digs of the Gold Coast, the vibrant atmosphere near Lincoln Park's DePaul University, or the revitalized, artsy feel of Bucktown. Residents frequently relocate within the city, choosing locations depending on what they can afford and what they need. Families search for homes in school districts they prefer; young and single crowds tend to congregate in places that are walkable to shopping, bars, and restaurants; and those with strong religious affiliations select their church or synagogue first, then find nearby housing.

Though city promoters don't like to admit it, in a city with a population of more than 2.7 million, there are inevitable degrees of crime and poverty, but they certainly don't define this city whose alternative motto to "City in a Garden" is "I Will." As Chicago's first new mayor in more than two decades (taking office in 2011, following Daley's 22-year tenure), Mayor Rahm Emanuel may have some economic and social challenges ahead. But Chicago's "I Will" attitude continues to motivate and inspire, providing the backbone for many of this determined city's civic projects and civic pride.

WEATHER-WISE

It's a silly old joke, but it truly does apply to Chicago: If you don't like the weather, wait five minutes. The city's unpredictable climate stems partly from its location halfway between the equator and the North Pole, and in the center of the continent. Winters are particularly annoying for their crazy ups and downs; you wake up shivering to negative windchills and by the afternoon, it's pushing 40. One day it snows 6 inches, and the next day melts it all away (no complaining there). The best winter weather tip is to be prepared: Wear layers, and never underestimate the biting winds.

Which brings up the city's notorious nickname: the Windy City. It often seems perfectly suited, but Chicago actually ranks only about 75th on a nationwide list of the windiest cities. Although the term may have been used first to describe the gusts off Lake Michigan, the name stuck as a reference to city boosters who tooted Chicago's horn to win the 1893 World's Columbian Exposition. But that doesn't mean it isn't windy. Plenty of breezy days blow umbrellas inside out, and canyonlike wind tunnels between downtown buildings keep moms holding tight to little hands and can force even grown men to walk at an angle.

Despite grumbles from locals that Chicago has merely two seasons—"winter and road construction" (the city is, indeed, amok with road construction from May to October)—Chicago is a four-season town, however loosely interpreted by Mother Nature that may be. Spring, in particular, seems to laugh heartily at the calendar, usually shuffling in around mid-May, bringing rain showers and thunderstorms. Even into June, you'll still want to carry a light jacket, especially when attending an outdoor evening concert.

July tends to be Chicago's hottest month, and August surprisingly the wettest. Both are often accompanied by unpleasant Gulf of Mexico–born humidity, sending curly heads into a frizz and making straight-haired ones fight for their lives. That's why the lakefront is so cherished. Meteorologists talk about "lake-effect" breezes that typically result in cooler temps by the lake during warm months and warmer breezes on colder days. Thank goodness for the fall, often cited as Chicago's best season, when trees show off their rainbow of colors, humidity takes a dip, and temperatures still hover around 70. Come November, it's back to snow country and airflow from Arctic Canada. Silk long underwear helps.

When to Go

Every season gives Chicago a different air and appeal. Summer is the city's most popular, which means streets teeming with tourists, higher wait times at restaurants, and peak prices for most hotels. On the flip side, the wonderful weather brings alfresco dining; neighborhood and downtown festivals galore; flowers everywhere; twice-weekly fireworks at Navy Pier; splendid boat cruises along the Chicago River and Lake Michigan; beach-time fun, from sand volleyball to surfing to simply sunning; and the general vitality of a city that is sincerely grateful for the chance to toss coats, hats, gloves, and other cumbersome clothing. If you're visiting, be sure to ask hotels about any special summer packages, because tourist season also inspires special offers that can make the most of your budget.

The fall has its color-scape of changing leaves and the real feel of autumn, with breezy nights and lingering warm-weather days. Plus, hotels often begin off-peak rates after Labor Day, so the period before daylight savings time ends (usually the first weekend in November) can offer a perfect balance of pleasant weather and pleasing prices. Halloween is a big deal here, with a city-sponsored festival and pumpkin patches that pop up even around the city. It's also the time that theaters, sports teams, and dance companies often kick off their seasons. Just know that from September through November, there are often large conventions that fill up hotel rooms throughout the city.

From the moment Halloween wraps until after the New Year, Chicago is a whirlwind of holiday sparkle. From hot sales up and down the Mag Mile to tree-lightings to visits with Santa, there are plenty of reasons to bundle up and get out. Note, though, that this marks a different peak season for the hotel industry and prices tend to climb once again. Until Christmas Eve, which is so slow that great deals can be found for those who want them. And though we can't guarantee every Christmas is a white one, it's without doubt the most festive time of the year. In terms of hotel prices, New Year's Eve is yet a different story, with special packages making for sometimes pricey nights.

Spring takes a little while to appear—sometimes not until mid-May—and it never seems to last long enough, but it also presents fair temperatures and the pretty budding of flowers and trees. March and April can be a bit chilly still (it's even been known to snow), but the city can get busy with convention groups during these months as well, so be aware as you make plans. As Memorial Day hits, the beaches and pools open, and city fests begin in earnest. It also marks the beginning of peak tourist time as far as pricing goes.

NEIGHBORHOODS AT A GLANCE

Whether embarking on a beyond-downtown excursion or choosing a spot to unpack your boxes, Chicago offers dozens of neighborhoods (about 180, in fact). These are just a handful to get you started, with boundaries given in general terms, as some neighborhoods zig and zag a bit.

Albany Park

Boundaries—East: Chicago River, North Branch; west: Pulaski Avenue; north: Foster Avenue; south: Montrose Avenue
Proximity—8 miles northwest of the Loop
Public Transportation—Brown Line El: Francisco, Kedzie, and Kimball stops; #81 bus
Info—Albany Park Chamber of Commerce, (773) 478-0202, www.albanyparkchamber .org; Albany Park Community Center, (773) 583-5111, www.apcc-chgo.org

Named by real estate investor and Albany, New York, native DeLancy Louderback, this northwest-side community has a multiethnic past—and present. In the early 20th century, it was Germans and Swedes; then came Russian Jews; and later, a mix of Korean, Mexican, Thai, Indian, and Middle Eastern populations. A cruise down its central thoroughfare, Lawrence Avenue, reveals a fascinating mélange of Korean barbecues, Mexican bakeries, Middle Eastern restaurants, East Asian teashops, and more. Housing types and prices vary as well, with everything from large apartment buildings to single-family bungalows to brand-new condos.

Andersonville (Lakewood/Balmoral)

Boundaries—East: Magnolia Avenue; west: Ravenswood Avenue; north: Bryn Mawr Avenue; south: Ainslie Avenue
Proximity—5 miles north of the Loop
Public Transportation—Red Line El: Berwyn and Bryn Mawr stops; #22, #92 buses; Metra commuter train: Ravenswood stop
Info—Andersonville Chamber of Commerce, (773) 728-2995, www.andersonville .org

Anchoring this historically Swedish neighborhood is the Swedish American Museum, where an exhibit relates the tale of Swedish immigrants who sailed to Chicago and later headed north from the congested downtown to farm this 1-square-mile area. The Swedish population thinned over the years, giving way to singles, young families, gay and lesbian residents, and older retirees. Still, the original settlers left their mark. Find it in Swedish bakeries and restaurants; the Midsommarfest street festival; a Swedish Christmas market; and Clark Street's hand-carved Dala horse, a national symbol of Sweden. Despite its compact size, Andersonville boasts top-notch restaurants and shops, a whopping 95 percent of which are independently owned (many residents resisted a Starbucks), including a cluster of outstanding home decor stores. Well-preserved vintage homes along tree-lined streets have earned the neighborhood National Historic District status. The community also keeps its eye focused on the future with its own eco-Andersonville Sustainable Business Certification Program, awarding stars to businesses that demonstrate a commitment to environmental, social, and economic sustainability.

Bucktown-Wicker Park

Boundaries—East and north: Kennedy Expressway; west: Western Avenue; south: Division Street

Proximity—4 miles northwest of the Loop

Public Transportation—Blue Line (O'Hare) El: Damen and Western stops; #56, #70, #72 buses

Info—Wicker Park & Bucktown Chamber of Commerce, (773) 384-2672, www.wicker parkbucktown.com

Bucktown and Wicker Park get double billing because the six-way intersection that divides them—at North, Damen, and Milwaukee avenues—also happens to be the area's main drop-off point for El trains and buses. Start here and set out in any direction to explore this hipster hub of trendy restaurants, bars, and clothing boutiques. Both neighborhoods began as immigrant enclaves in the 19th and early 20th centuries—Bucktown took its name from the goats that Polish residents kept on their properties—but later fell into decline. In the late 1980s and '90s, artists spied bargains for studio space and moved on in. While Bucktown eventually gentrified to a wild extent, with million-dollar condos the norm, Wicker Park maintained more of its edgy feel, with old brick construction, resale shops, alt-music venues, and no-frills neighborhood bars.

Chinatown

Boundaries—East: Wentworth Avenue; west and south: Kennedy Expressway; north: Cermak Street

Proximity—5 miles south of the Loop

Public Transportation—Red Line El: Cermak/Chinatown stop

Info—Chicago Chinatown Chamber of Commerce, (312) 326-5320, www.chicago chinatown.org

Pass under the ornamental gold and red gateway to this 10-block area, and you enter a Chinese haven that has held tight to its identity while still welcoming visitors. Along Wentworth Avenue's vibrant commercial strip, you can take part in a traditional tea ceremony; pick up paper lanterns, exotic herbs and spices, woks, and moon cakes; and experience a delicious dim sum meal. In the other direction is Chinatown Square, a strip mall of divey eateries, Chinese groceries, and more shops. Delve a little deeper into the history and culture of Chinese Americans at the Chinese-American Museum. Outside the main-drag bustle is Ping Tom Memorial Park, a serene green space along the Chicago River.

Gold Coast

Boundaries—East: Lake Shore Drive; west: Clark Street; north: North Avenue; south: Oak Street

Proximity—1.5 miles north of the Loop

Public Transportation—Red Line El: Clark & Division stop: #22, #36, #151, #156 buses

Info—Gold Coast Neighbors Association, (312) 332-6122, www.goldcoastneighbors .org

In the 1880s, real estate mogul and hotelier Potter Palmer (of Palmer House fame) saw great potential in the vacant lakefront north of the city. Soon after erecting his home castle here, other wealthy elites followed, lending this neighborhood its fitting moniker. Today, a stroll along lush streets and past carefully tended gardens affords a glimpse into the lives of present-day, high-style

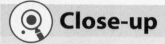 **Close-up**

Local Lingo

Study up on these common Windy City words and phrases, and you'll pass as a local in no time.

Bleacher Bums—If you buy the cheap seats for a Cubs baseball game at Wrigley Field, you'll probably be in the bleachers with the rest of the "bums." The name originated in 1967 with a group of about 10 young guys (including Mike Murphy, who went on to be a popular sports radio announcer) who hung out drinking beer and heckling the players. The posse even inspired a play written in 1977 that starred actors Joe Mantegna and Dennis Franz.

The Cell—Wrigley Field's South Side counterpart and home to the American League Chicago White Sox baseball club, "the Cell" is short for Cellular Field, the newfangled stadium that replaced old Comiskey Park in 1991.

Chicagoland—Because Chicago draws workers and visitors from so many nearby suburbs, everyone gets pulled together with this catchy name extension whose origin is attributed to a 1926 *Chicago Tribune* article. Precisely which towns fall under the category depends on whom you ask, though: According to the *Tribune*, it's the city of Chicago, the rest of Cook County, eight other Illinois counties, and two Indiana counties, whereas the Illinois Department of Tourism excludes the city itself.

Chicago-style dog—When in Rome...order the right frankfurter. In true Chicago style, you start with an all-beef hot dog (grilled, steamed, or boiled), cushioned in a steamed poppy seed bun; top it with sweet pickle relish, yellow mustard, a crunchy pickle spear, chopped onions, tomato wedges, whole sport peppers, and celery salt, and never, ever ketchup. It's said that the first hot dog was introduced at the 1893 Columbian Exposition in Chicago, while the toppings were added by street cart vendors during the Depression to add value to their product.

Deep-dish—Pizza, that is. And it was invented right here in Chicago in the early 1940s at Pizzeria Uno. Who exactly invented it is debatable—was it restaurateur Ric

Chicagoans. While the Palmer mansion has since been razed, remnants of the community's gilded beginnings can be spotted in structures like the 1885 Queen Anne–style Archbishop's Residence; Hugh Hefner's original Playboy mansion, now a seven-unit luxury condo building; and a 1917 French châteaulike home built by Howard Van Doren Shaw that now houses the fascinating International Museum of Surgical Science. But it's not just the old that's celebrated here.

It's also one of the city's liveliest nightlife hubs. Recent college grads stagger between bars and clubs on Rush and Division streets, including Mother's, made famous in the 1986 movie *About Last Night*. On Oak Street, it's not cheap drinks but designer names that rule: Prada, Vera Wang, Harry Winston, and Paul Stuart, to name a few. Oak Street Beach tempts with tanned bodies and stellar people-watching.

Riccardo, former football star and Uno's owner Ike Sewell, or Rudy Malnati, Uno's manager and father to Lou, who later opened one of the city's other famous deep-dish dens? Well, really, who cares? The thick, buttery, flaky crust filled with cheese and toppings is a must-try no matter who came up with the recipe.

The Drive—Hugging Lake Michigan on the eastern edge of Chicago is Lake Shore Drive, a little expressway that runs a little less than 16 miles, from Marquette Drive (6600 south) to Hollywood Avenue (5700 north). Its sister "Inner Drive" is a local road that parallels the outer lanes for part of the stretch.

The El—In London it's the Tube, in Boston it's the T. And when you're planning on taking the train around town in Chicago, you'd better be calling it the El. There's some controversy over how to write it, as the CTA itself uses "L," but most locals simply write "El" or even "el," since it's short for "elevated." The El system now encompasses the train lines that run overhead as well as underground throughout downtown and into the neighborhoods, some at street-level.

The Loop—All El lines converge in the Loop, as trains rumble and rattle around a 35-square-block area of elevated tracks. The name dates back to the 1880s and the age of cable cars that turned around in what was and still is Chicago's focal point of finance and government.

Mag Mile—Short for "Magnificent Mile," this moniker identifies the mile-long strip of North Michigan Avenue from Oak Street on the north to the Chicago River on the south. Christened with the name in the 1940s by real estate developer Arthur Rubloff, it lives up to it with 450-plus shops, including three vertical malls.

Pop—Especially if you're from the northeastern US, asking for a "pop" seems a bit strange, even dangerous, but it's OK. Here, you'll get a Diet Coke or Pepsi or Orange Crush or whatever soft drink you'd like. In other words, true-blue Chicagoans don't usually call it "soda."

Hyde Park

Boundaries—East: Lake Shore Drive; west: Cottage Grove Avenue; north: 51st Street/Hyde Park Boulevard; south: 60th Street/Midway Plaisance
Proximity—6 miles south of the Loop
Public Transportation—#6 bus, Metra train: 53rd Street and 57th Street stops

Info—Hyde Park Chamber of Commerce, (773) 288-0124, www.hydeparkchamber chicago.org

A surprising revelation to the uninitiated, Hyde Park exists like a college town within the city. Its esteemed University of Chicago serves to stabilize the neighborhood's economy, with a majority of faculty living in the neighborhood. Independent shops (particularly bookstores) flourish, and housing covers the gamut from elegant old single-family homes to student-friendly rentals. The university's Gothic-style campus is worth touring and includes Frank Lloyd Wright's 1910 Robie House, considered his quintessential Prairie-style structure. Racial integration has taken on practically exemplary status in Hyde Park, boosted by passionate community organizations, and the fact that Barack Obama lived here, and that he and Michelle both worked at the university (their former residence is visible beyond the Secret Service men). Described in detail in Erik Larson's book *Devil in the White City*, Hyde Park's 600-acre Jackson Park was the site of the 1893 World's Columbian Exposition. The mammoth Museum of Science and Industry gave new life to the fair's only remaining building, while Jackson Park now offers a nature escape of woodsy paths, quiet fishing spots, wide open spaces, and a Japanese garden.

Lakeview

Boundaries—East: Lake Michigan; west: Ravenswood Avenue; north: Irving Park Road; south: Diversey Parkway
Proximity—3 miles north of the Loop
Public Transportation—Brown Line El: Diversey, Wellington, Belmont, Southport, Paulina, Addison, Irving Park stops; Red Line El: Belmont, Addison, Sheridan stops; #8, #22, #36, #176, #177, #152 buses
Info—Central Lakeview Merchants Association, (773) 665-2100, www.mylakeview.com; Lakeview Chamber of Commerce, (773) 472-7171, www.lakeviewchamber.com; Lakeview East Chamber of Commerce, (773) 348-8608, www.lakevieweast.com

Making up one of the city's largest neighborhoods, Lakeview consists of several distinct communities: Lakeview East has the actual Lake Michigan views and is just steps from the Lakefront Path, a favorite spot for jogging, cycling, and dog-walking. It also includes the vibrant gay and lesbian area known as Boystown, where the annual Pride Parade brings out all sorts of colorful characters. Lakeview proper lies a bit west, so lakefront vistas are pretty rare (though some posh penthouse condos oblige); instead, it's home runs and fly balls that are common—this is Cubs baseball country. Over the years, the North Side baseball stadium, Wrigley Field, gave rise to its own enclave of a neighborhood that was named, what else, Wrigleyville. Because Lakeview sprawls so far and wide, its hard to pin it down with one description, but it's fair to say that this is sought-after real estate, whether high rises along the Inner Drive, starter rental units in vintage buildings, or spiffy gut-rehab condos along quaint side streets. Scattered throughout are hip shopping strips—Halsted for kitschy and gay-themed gifts; Belmont and Clark for Goth and retro fashions; Southport for trendy women's and kids' clothing; and Broadway for great indie boutiques and bookstores—plus, popular restaurants, local music venues, and small theaters. Slightly west of Lakeview, Roscoe Village is a smaller encompassed community that draws big cheers for its hidden-gem restaurants and shops and family-friendly vibe.

Lincoln Park

Boundaries—East: Lake Michigan; west: Chicago River; north: Diversey Parkway; south: North Avenue
Proximity—2 miles north of the Loop
Public Transportation—Red Line El: North/Clybourn and Fullerton stops; Brown Line El: Armitage, Fullerton, and Diversey stops; #8, #22, #36, #73, #74, #76 buses

Info—Lincoln Park Chamber of Commerce, (773) 880-5200, www.lincolnparkchamber .com

Another expansive neighborhood, Lincoln Park takes its name from the 1,200-acre stretch of uninterrupted green space that parallels the lakefront. Originally named Lake Park, the name was changed to honor Abraham Lincoln after his assassination. It has gone from a community of immigrant farmers to arguably the most famous of Chicago's affluent neighborhoods, minus the DePaul University area, which creates a bubble of young energy and less-expensive housing. Lincoln Park also wins accolades for some of the country's most outstanding restaurants, including Charlie Trotter's and Alinea, both near the popular boutiques lining Armitage and Halsted avenues. The other shopping district is the area around North and Clybourn avenues, sometimes referred to as the Clybourn Corridor. Cultural institutions abound here as well, from the Chicago History Museum to the Peggy Notebaert Nature Museum to the family favorite Lincoln Park Zoo, the oldest free zoo in the country. Rounding out the offerings, Lincoln Park is a bastion of award-winning theaters, including the Gary Sinise–founded Steppenwolf, Victory Gardens (housed at the Biograph Theatre, where John Dillinger was shot), and the Apollo and Royal George theaters. Though not nearly as big as Lincoln Park, the enchanting Oz Park pays tribute to author L. Frank Baum who once lived in the area (there are four Oz-related statues).

Old Town

Boundaries—East: Clark Street; west: Halsted Street; north: Eugenie Street; south: Division Street (including Old Town Triangle Historic District, boundary extends north to Armitage Avenue)

Proximity—1.5 miles north of the Loop

Public Transportation—Brown Line El: Sedgwick stop; #22, #36, #72 buses

Info—Old Town Merchants and Residents Association, (312) 951-6106, www.oldtown chicago.org

A funny thing happened on the way to Old Town's development—it gave rise to one of the most famous improv comedy clubs in the nation. The Second City opened here in 1959 and remains a mainstay of this neighborhood. But Old Town is way more than Second City; it's a community that has witnessed wide economic and demographic swings since its settlement by German-Catholic immigrants in the 1850s. In a funky, wedge-shaped section known as the Old Town Triangle, designated a Chicago Landmark, many homes predate the 1871 Great Chicago Fire and streets buck the city's grid pattern. In the 1930s, Old Town was a popular artists' colony; in the 1960s, a hippie hot spot; and from the 1950s to 1980s, the city's first gay and lesbian haven. Since the closing of Old Town's adjacent, horrendous high-rise housing project, Cabrini Green, rehabbed vintage dwellings and new construction have sprung up, making this a pricey place to live. But you can always come for a laugh, to stroll the boutique shopping along Wells Street, and to check out the city's first sushi bar, Kamehachi of Tokyo, which opened along Wells in 1969.

Ravenswood-Lincoln Square

Boundaries—East: Clark Street; west: Chicago River; north: Foster Avenue; south: Montrose Avenue

Proximity—8 miles north of the Loop

Public Transportation—Brown Line El: Montrose, Damen, Western, and Rockwell stops; Metra commuter train, Ravenswood stop; #22, #92 buses
Info—Lincoln Square Chamber of Commerce, (773) 728-3890, www.lincolnsquare .org; Ravenswood Community Council, (773) 784-0400, www.ravenswoodcommunity.org

The faint sound of oompah-pahs can almost be detected in this historically German area. Today, residents adore Ravenswood for its old-growth trees that shade old brick structures and storefront shops, for its neighborly atmosphere, its expansive public parks, and its walkability, particularly the four-block stretch of Lincoln Avenue—partially cobblestone—that makes up the main drag of lively Lincoln Square. Here, you'll find the Old Town School of Folk Music, a beehive of artistic activity ranging from adult Latin dance classes to kids' concerts to private piano lessons. German heritage is found in sausage shops, a wall-sized mural of a German landscape, a maypole that serves as the focal point for the community's annual Mayfest and German-American Fest, and a section of the Berlin Wall at the Western Brown Line El station.

River North

Boundaries—East: Wabash Street; west: Chicago River; north: Chicago River; south: Division
Proximity—Less than 1 mile north of the Loop
Public Transportation—Brown Line El: Merchandise Mart and Chicago Avenue stops; Red Line El: Grand and Chicago stops; #22, #36, #72, #151 buses
Info—River North Business Association, (312) 645-1047, www.rivernorthassociation

.com; River North Residents Association, (312) 235-2617, www.rnrachicago.org

Abandoned after years as an industrial corridor, then a warehouse district, this neighborhood bordering the Chicago River saw a phenomenal turnaround in the late 20th century when artists snatched up the inexpensive loft space and created one of the country's largest concentrations of art galleries. It grew from there with some of Chicago's chicest restaurants with chefs like Rick Bayless, Jean Joho, and Graham Elliott. It also includes popular tourist destinations including Hard Rock Cafe and Pizzeria Uno, and a thriving nightlife scene. Since the beginning of the 21st century, River North has also gained considerable ground as a place to live, with multiple new high-rise condo buildings—including Trump Tower—adding to the landscape of older structures. The iconic residential Marina City, an innovative forerunner to newer buildings in the 1960s, nicknamed the "corncob towers" for their cylindrical architecture, is also located here. And marking the Chicago River boundary is the world's largest commercial building, the Merchandise Mart, housing furniture showrooms and the LuxeHome interior design boutiques.

Rogers Park (East) (West)

Boundaries—East: Lake Michigan; west: Kedzie Avenue; north: Howard Street; south: Devon Avenue
Proximity—10 miles north of the Loop
Public Transportation—Red Line El: Loyola, Morse, Jarvis, Howard stops (Purple El stop at Howard too); #22, #147, #151, #155 buses; Metra commuter train: Rogers Park stop
Info—Rogers Park Business Alliance, (773) 508-5885, www.rogers-park.com

Part college district, part global melting pot, this far north neighborhood includes both East Rogers Park and West Rogers Park, whose division street is Ridge Road. On the eastern half, it's Loyola University, founded in 1909, and a dozen Lake Michigan beaches that appeal. The west side has grown into a United Nations of cultures, hosting Chicago's largest Orthodox Jewish, Indian, and Pakistani populations—Devon Avenue has been called "Little India"—not to mention strong Russian, Polish, Caribbean, and Mexican communities. Despite shady streets, quiet courtyard apartment houses, and old brick two-flats, it has never reached the sky-high price points of more centrally located neighborhoods, giving it a diverse and dynamic atmosphere, including a bevy of small theaters, ethnic eateries, and live local music venues.

South Loop

Boundaries—East: Lake Michigan; west: Dan Ryan Expressway; north: Roosevelt Road; south: 25th Street
Proximity—Directly south of the Loop
Public Transportation—Red, Orange, Green Line El: Roosevelt stop; Red Line El: Harrison stop; #3, #4, #6, #29, #62, #146 buses
Info—South Loop Neighbors Association, (312) 409-1700, www.southloopneighbors .org

After the 1871 Great Chicago Fire, wealthy Chicago businessmen chose this area to raise their families, creating a row of fancy mansions, some of which still stand along historic Prairie Avenue and 18th Street. But the neighborhood fell out of favor by the 1940s and saw some rough times, until it saw a population surge in the 1990s. Real estate developers and home buyers saw the amazing potential of living adjacent to but outside of the Loop, near the lake and Grant Park, and the recently created Museum Campus (Shedd Aquarium, Field Museum, and Adler Planetarium connected by green space and walking paths)—with views of the city skyline to boot. Though the recession led to a slow-down in construction, the South Loop gained a reputation as a desirable place to live. It's also where you'll find Soldier Field stadium, home to Chicago's NFL Bears; Columbia College; Northerly Island Park, the small airstrip turned park and outdoor music pavilion; and a growing number of music clubs and high-ranked restaurants.

Streeterville

Boundaries—East: Lake Michigan; west: Michigan Avenue; north: Oak Street; south: Chicago River
Proximity—Less than 1 mile north of the Loop
Public Transportation—Red Line El: Grand and Chicago stops; #3, #10, #26, #145, #146, #147, #151 buses
Info—Streeterville Chamber of Commerce, (312) 664-2560, www.streetervillechamber .org; Greater North Michigan Avenue Association, (312) 642-3570, www.themagnificent mile.com

This heavy-hitter 'hood wouldn't have been much at all if it hadn't been for the Great Chicago Fire—and its rubble. Lake Michigan's shoreline once ended basically at Michigan Avenue; east of that is 186 acres of mostly landfill that provided convenient dumping ground after the fire. The neighborhood's name is a nod to a wily guy named Captain George Wellington ("Cap") Streeter who had run his schooner aground here in 1886 and, for a short time and with much conflict with

Vital Statistics

Founded: As a town, 1833; as a city, 1837

Area codes: 312, 773, 872

Population: As of the 2010 census, approximately 2.7 million

County: Cook County

State capital: Springfield

Nearby cities/villages: Oak Park, Lincolnwood, Niles, Skokie, Evanston, Berwyn, Cicero, Evergreen Park, Park Ridge

Elevation: 596 feet

Average temperatures: January: 32 degrees F (high), 18 degrees F (low); July: 84 degrees F (high), 66 degrees F (low)

Annual rainfall: 33 inches

Average days of sunshine: 320

Colleges, universities and vocational schools: Columbia College, DePaul University, DeVry University, Illinois Institute of Art, Illinois Institute of Technology, Kendall College, Le Cordon Bleu College of Culinary Arts, Loyola University, National Louis University, Northeastern Illinois University, Northwestern University, Roosevelt University, School of the Art Institute of Chicago, University of Chicago, University of Illinois at Chicago

Time zone: Central

Major area employers (nongovernmental): Wal-Mart, Inc., Advocate Health Care, J.P. Morgan Chase & Co., Walgreen Co., Abbott Laboratories, United Continental Holdings, AT&T, Motorola

Famous Chicagoans (some honorary): Barack Obama, Oprah Winfrey, Bill Murray, Michael Jordan, Jesse Jackson, David Schwimmer, Hugh Hefner, John and Joan Cusack, Jeremy Piven, Bonnie Hunt, Jim Belushi, Pete Wentz, Scott Turow, Kanye West, Ira Glass

the city, declared himself the governor of the "District of Lake Michigan." After his death, the city quickly gobbled up this prime property. It's now a showplace of luxury hotels and high-rise condos, superlative attractions including the John Hancock Center and Navy Pier, festive city-sponsored events along Michigan Avenue, and more than 450 stores, as well as Northwestern University's downtown campus.

Uptown

Boundaries—East: Lake Michigan; west: Clark Street/Racine Avenue; north: Foster Avenue; south: Montrose Avenue

Proximity—6.5 miles north of the Loop

Public Transportation—Red Line El: Wilson, Lawrence, and Argyle stops; #22, #36, #81, #151 buses

Major airports: O'Hare International Airport, Midway International Airport

Public transportation: CTA, www.transitchicago.com; (312) 836-7000, travel information; (888) YOUR-CTA (968-7282), customer service; Metra commuter train, www.metrarail.com; (312) 322-6900

Driving laws: New Illinois residents have 90 days to obtain a new drivers' license. Driving age is 16 with drivers' education course or 18 without (18 or 21 for a rental car). Front-seat occupants must wear seatbelts; children under 16 must always wear seatbelts. Children under the age of 8 must be in an approved child seat. All vehicles must be covered by minimum liability insurance. Cell-phone conversations must be hands-free; electronic communication while driving is prohibited. Open alcohol containers are prohibited in vehicles. www.cyberdriveillinois.com.

Alcohol laws: State age for purchasing or consuming alcohol is 21. Open alcohol containers are prohibited in vehicles and on streets. Alcohol is not sold before 11 a.m. on Sunday.

Tobacco laws: Legal smoking age is 18. Smoking is prohibited in most enclosed public places and workplaces, including bars, restaurants, shopping malls, government buildings, public restrooms, and public transportation facilities. You must be at least 15 feet away from entrances to these places to smoke outside.

Daily newspapers: *Chicago Tribune, Chicago Sun-Times, Daily Herald, Hoy* (Spanish-language)

City total sales tax: 10.25 percent as of Feb, 2011; hotel taxes are 15.4 percent; car rental tax is 20 percent; an additional 1percent is taxed on all food and beverages bought in the downtown Chicago area; soft drinks are taxed at 13.25 percent; bottled water is taxed an additional 5 cents per bottle.

Important phone numbers: 911, emergency; 311, nonemergency; (800) 222-1222, Illinois Poison Control, www.illinoispoisoncenter.org

City website: www.cityofchicago.org, general information; www.explorechicago.org, tourism information

Chamber of commerce: Chicagoland: 200 E. Randolph St., (312) 494-6700, www.chicago landchamber.org

Info—The Chamber for Uptown, (773) 878-1184, www.uptownbusinesspartners .com; Uptown United, (773) 878-1064, www .uptownunited.org

Before Hollywood's heyday, there was Uptown, where more than 2,000 silent movies were made in the early 20th century, many from the now-defunct Essany Studios. The area's main drag was even named Broadway to evoke New York's theater hub. These days, though the film industry has fled west, a few entertainment relics remain, including the Green Mill jazz club where Al Capone once held court. But the far north neighborhood is probably best known for its close Lake Michigan beaches, its wide range of housing options and prices, and an international community (supposedly more than 60 languages are spoken in this area).

The stretch of Argyle Street from Sheridan Road to Broadway has been dubbed "Little Saigon" for its numerous Southeast Asian restaurants, particularly Vietnamese. A small subset of Uptown, Sheridan Park carves a little space from Lawrence south to Montrose, Clark Street west to Racine Avenue. It's noteworthy for its architectural standouts in styles from Prairie School to Victorian and is designated as a historic district.

Visitor Information Centers

Chicago Water Works Visitor Information Center
163 E. Pearson St.

Chicago Cultural Center Visitors Information Center
77 E. Randolph St.
Both visitor center locations are open daily except Thanksgiving, Christmas Day, and New Year's Day. You can also call 877-CHICAGO (244-2246), 8 a.m. to 7 p.m. daily to talk to a professional tourism official.

West Loop/Greektown

Boundaries—East: I-90/Kennedy Expressway; west: Ashland Avenue; north: Grand Avenue; south: I-290/Eisenhower Expressway
Proximity—Directly west of the Loop

Public Transportation—Blue Line El: UIC-Halsted, Chicago, and Grand stops; Green Line El: Lake stop; #8, #9, #20, #65 buses
Info—West Loop Community Organization, (312) 666-1991, www.westloop.org

The emergence of this neighborhood from warehouse district to urban-chic hot spot could be attributable to Oprah Winfrey. She opened her Harpo Studios here in 1988 in a former armory—and visitors swarmed it every day for taping until her final episode in May 2011. But it also has a lot to do with the fact that the West Loop is a stone's throw from the Loop, and yet still offers amazing skyline views, more spacious living, and less traffic congestion. New and rehabbed condo units went gangbusters in the 1990s; bars worth the trip and a "Restaurant Row" of high-end, high-style restaurants popped up along Randolph Street and the Fulton Market district; and art galleries galore made creative use of old industrial spaces. The boundaries of the West Loop also embrace Greektown, where a large Greek community dwindled after highway construction forced many to move. But their legacy was left in a few bustling blocks' worth of Greek restaurants and their history is told at the National Hellenic Museum. Check out the ironic marker on the Chicago Fire Academy: It was here that the O'Learys' barn once stood, where the Great Chicago Fire of 1871 supposedly began.

GETTING HERE, GETTING AROUND

Chicago has been a major transportation hub practically since day one of its recognition as a destination at all. Jean Baptiste Point DuSable knew this when he set up his trading business along the Chicago River, capitalizing on the Native Americans and Europeans who used it as a thoroughfare. These days, it's much more than boats that make their way into and out of the city. It's easy to get to Chicago in a variety of ways. Fly into one of two international airports, take buses from locations far and wide, chug in by train from suburbs and cities around the country, or drive in from all directions on multilane (and often congested) expressways.

Once you're here, you can easily navigate without wheels on the inexpensive bus and train system that runs 24 hours a day. Cabs are plentiful day and night in most areas, and you could even rent a bike to beat a path through town. If you're attached to your car or need it for convenience sake (we've got kids, we know), it's just as easy to drive around the city. Got a little lost? Don't be shy about stopping someone on the street to ask for help. They'll stop. And they'll happily point you in the right direction. Get the lowdown on how to get around—and then get out there and enjoy.

GETTING HERE

Airports

O'HARE INTERNATIONAL AIRPORT
10000 N. Bessie Coleman Dr.
(773) 686-2200
18 miles northwest of downtown Chicago
www.ohare.com

Whether you love the fact that O'Hare accommodates flights from more than 30 different airlines or whether you loathe its labyrinth of terminals, O'Hare is undeniably a big shot among airports around the world. While it used to claim title as the world's busiest in terms of takeoffs and landings, that statistic has dropped to second busiest (first is in Atlanta), but it is still third busiest when it comes to passengers—more than 76 million in and out each year. Many of those come from overseas, making O'Hare the fourth busiest landing point in the US for international travelers.

Named for World War II naval aviator Lt. Cmdr. Edward H. "Butch" O'Hare, the airport was developed on Orchard Field, the former home of a Douglas aircraft assembly plant—thus, the origins of the airport's three-letter code, ORD. Over the decades, O'Hare has expanded by leaps and bounds, adding terminals, hangars, a connected hotel, parking facilities, rental car agencies, and the first taxiway bridge for planes that spans a public road. It also spurred the construction of the eight-lane Kennedy Expressway in 1960 that specifically linked downtown Chicago to the airport. More multibillion-dollar building projects are under way as the result of ex-Mayor Richard M. Daley's 2005 O'Hare Modernization Program, which will boost the number of runways at O'Hare to eight, six of which will run parallel, an improvement over the current crisscross pattern of runways that ends up delaying planes and frustrating travelers.

O'Hare has four terminals: Terminal 1 is where you'll find gates for United Airlines (and its merged airline, Continental)—one of two airlines with hubs here (American Airlines is the other). Terminal 1 is divided between Concourses B and C, which are connected by an underground tunnel designed in the 1980s and still stuck there with its futuristic neon light tubes that flicker overhead. Terminal 1 also includes all baggage claim areas. Some United gates also fall into Terminal 2, which comprises Concourses E and F, which branch out in a Y shape (make sure you're headed in the right direction, otherwise you'll end up doing a lot of backtracking to get to the other concourse). Terminal 3 contains Concourses G, H, K, and L, all of which take very different paths, so, again, be sure you watch the signs carefully as you make your way to your gate. Separated from the other terminals is Terminal 5, the international terminal. Why no Terminal 4? An old international terminal was designated as number 4, and, while the number isn't used now, there are plans to resurrect it for future use.

> **i** All major car rental agencies can be found at both airports—Alamo, Avis, Hertz, National, etc. Some agency counters are within terminals; others are a short shuttle ride away; all car lots are off-site.

Although it's big and brash and at times unforgiving—as when you've got a flight transfer on the opposite side of the airport—O'Hare has a decent array of traveler amenities. As for food, it ranges from Chicago classics like the Berghoff Cafe (an old German favorite), Billy Goat Tavern (of *Saturday Night Live* fame), several deep-dish pizza parlors, Nuts on Clark for snacks to go, local Goose Island Brewing Company, sweet-treat staple Eli's Cheesecake, and the it-started-here internationally acclaimed Vosges Haut-Chocolat shop, not to mention several joints for Chicago-style hot dogs.

A replica of the fighter plane flown by the airport's namesake in World War II (main hall, Terminal 2) and the Field Museum–loaned Brachiosaurus cast skeleton (Terminal 1, Concourse B) wow kids, while the small aviation-themed offshoot of the Chicago Children's Museum (Terminal 2, departure level) goes even further toward occupying their wait time. Power stations throughout the airport provide passengers with AC outlets and countertop work areas for hooking up computers, cell phones, smart phones, and other devices. The sheer size of O'Hare means that wise travelers get there at least an hour before their flight departure, just to be sure they can make their way through security lines and to their gate on time.

To & From the Airport

DRIVING

The airport is located northwest of downtown Chicago. To get downtown from the airport, follow the sign indicating I-190 to I-90 East, Chicago Loop. This merges with I-94, which takes you to exits to downtown Chicago. Going to the airport, head west on

I-90/94 (the Kennedy Expressway). When the highway divides, stay in the left lanes to follow I-90. Take exit 78 toward I-190 west toward O'Hare and continue to follow the signs into the airport. Each terminal has a separate exit. Rush hour starts at around 3 p.m., so plan accordingly.

PARKING

Once at the airport, there are a few parking options. The short-term Lot A is perfect when you're dropping off or picking up and want to meet your visitors at the baggage claim. It charges $2 for the first hour and $4 for up to 3 hours, but then jumps to a hefty $21 after that, with a $50-a-day max. Near the international terminal is a short-term Lot D, $2 for the first hour, $6 for up to 2 hours. You can also sit in your car at Lot F for free, then wait for your party to call you before you head over to the curbside pickup area—which beats being waved off by nasty airport police and circling the terminals over and over. The close-by long-term lots (upper levels of covered Lot A and open lots B and C) charge $31 per day, while the international long-term lot is $51 a day. The remote economy Lot E reduces costs to $17 per day, while far-off Lot F brings it way down to $9 a day. For those remote lots, a shuttle takes you to the 24-hour Airport Transit System train (ATS) in Lot E, which takes you to the airport within a few minutes. Allow plenty of time to make it to your gate. Call the airport's parking hotline (773-686-7530) to find out if any lots are closed.

i If you drive a hybrid vehicle, look for preferred parking garage spots close to the elevators.

CTA

You can avoid any traffic headaches and parking fees by getting to and from the airport on the El. Via its subway and elevated route—some of which runs directly parallel to the Kennedy Expressway, so you can wave at the drivers stuck in traffic—the Blue Line O'Hare branch transports you literally into the airport. The stop is located in the lower level concourse, which connects easily to Terminals 1, 2, and 3, with Terminal 5 accessible by the airport shuttle tram. Travel time is typically about 45 minutes, but allowing an hour from downtown is safer. The Blue Line runs 24 hours a day every day, making it an option even for the red-eye. The standard El fare is $2.25.

TAXIS & LIMOS

Taking a taxi to the airport from downtown Chicago is a cinch. Any ride you hail from the street or is hailed for you from your hotel will gladly take you to the airport for about $40. To hop a cab from the airport, head to the lower-level curb stand (outside the baggage claim areas), where taxis pick up passengers on a first-come, first-served basis. You should allow at least an hour for a ride either way, more during rush hour. To ride in posher wheels, contact a limousine service from the listing posted across from the lower-level Door C of each terminal.

MIDWAY INTERNATIONAL AIRPORT
5700 S. Cicero Ave.
(773) 838-0600
www.flychicago.com
10 miles southwest of downtown Chicago
Midway opened in 1927 and was originally called Chicago's Municipal Airport. It

changed names in 1949 to honor the World War II turning-point Battle of Midway that took place in 1942. The airport was already being used by the US military and continued to be an important stop-off point for crewmen on their journey across country. There now stands a beautiful Battle of Midway Memorial inside the terminal. Other artwork includes a sculpture of a flying bird that's made from small metal figures of aircraft.

Once an almost charmingly small airport, Midway received a makeover in 2001 that transformed it into a thoroughly modern midsized airport and one of the nation's fastest-growing, serving more than 17 million passengers a year on airlines such as Air Tran, Delta, Frontier, and Southwest, for which Midway is a major hub. There is just one terminal at Midway, but it encompasses three concourses—A, B, and C—and 43 gates. Concourse A sees all international flights; Concourse B is dominated by Southwest; and Concourse C is mostly for Delta.

A triangle-shaped central food and shopping court features a range of options such as local favorites Harry Caray's, Nuts on Clark, Lalo's Mexican Restaurant, Taylor Street Market for Italian specialties, and Manny's Express (a quick-serve version of the city's famous deli). Power stations in Concourses A and B give passengers a place to plug in their electronics.

i One more alternative to flying into Chicago is the small, one-terminal Gary-Chicago International Airport, 25 miles from downtown Chicago. 6001 W. Industrial Hwy., Gary; (219) 949-9722, www.garychicagoairport.com.

To & From the Airport

DRIVING

Midway is located southwest of downtown. To get there, start on Lake Shore Drive traveling south. Exit the Drive for I-55 (the Stevenson Expressway) toward St. Louis (you'll also see a sign that points to I-90/94). Take exit 286 for IL-50/Cicero Avenue. Turn left off the ramp and continue to the airport. Making the reverse trip from the airport to downtown, you have to head out of the airport south on Cicero, then make a U-turn at 59th Street to get back to I-55 heading north back to the city. When the highway splits for Lake Shore Drive north or south, stay left to take it north. The trip takes 20 minutes without traffic, but allow at least 45.

PARKING

If you're picking someone up from Midway, simply pull into the free lot at 61st Street and Cicero Avenue near the main airport entrance; stay there until your party calls for pickup at the curb. There is also a parking garage that offers hourly parking on Level 1, which starts at $4 for the first hour. Daily parking on levels 4, 5, and 6 is $51 for the day. (Level 2 is for rental car pickup and drop-off.) There are several economy parking lots and an economy garage from which free shuttle buses run every 15 minutes 24 hours a day, 7 days a week. The rates for the economy parking max out at $14 for the day. For detailed parking info, call the hotline at (773) 838-0756.

Travel To, From & Between Airports

Shuttles To & From

Go Airport Express (888-284-3826, www.airportexpress.com) shuttle vans are available for shared-ride service between the airport and downtown hotels, homes, and offices, and most suburban communities. From the airport, they pick up outside the baggage claim areas on the lower levels of both the domestic and international terminals, and depart approximately every 10 to 15 minutes. You don't need a reservation to go from either O'Hare or Midway airport to downtown, but reservations are required for the reverse route. The shuttles operate from 4 a.m. for hotels and 5:30 a.m. for suburbs. The fare is $20 to $35 per person. In addition, many downtown hotels offer their own airport shuttle service, so it's worth asking at the front desk, if you're interested.

Shuttles Between

Occasionally a connecting flight splits the departures between Midway and O'Hare airports; figure about an hour for the trip. To get from one to the other, there are a couple of options: **Coach USA** (877-324-7767, www.coach usa.com) buses run from about 8 a.m. to 10 p.m. The one-way fare is $13 and round-trip is $23; kids 11 and under ride free. **Omega Airport Shuttle** (773-734-6688, www.omegashuttle.com) takes passengers by van between airports, operating hourly from 7 a.m. to 11:45 p.m. A one-way fare is $16.

CTA

Getting to Midway by El is quick and easy from downtown. The Orange Line pulls right into a station east of the airport and connected to it by an enclosed walkway (be prepared, though—it's about an 8-minute hike, which feels especially long with bags and children). It takes about 20 to 30 minutes from downtown on the train, which runs 21 hours a day Mon through Sat (it stops from about 1 to 4 a.m.) and on Sunday until 11 p.m. To get to the Orange Line station from the airport, just follow the signs and the orange line painted on the ground. The CTA fare is $2.25 per person.

TAXIS & LIMOS

Taxis pick up on a first-come, first-served basis outside the baggage claim area. The average fare to downtown Chicago is $30, not including tip.

Trains

UNION STATION
225 S. Canal St.
(312) 655-2066
www.amtrak.com, www.metrarail.com
Both Amtrak and Metra trains chug into Chicago's 1925 Daniel Burnham–designed Beaux Arts–style Union Station from points across the state and across the country. Amtrak's Zephyr travels a scenic 51-hour route from

San Francisco, climbing the Rockies and passing through the Sierra Nevada, Colorado canyons, and picturesque rivers and bays. The speedy 90-minute Hiawatha zips you past traffic from Milwaukee's General Mitchell Airport seven times a day (six on Sunday). From New York City on Amtrak's Lake Shore Limited, you'll travel past lovely waterways including the Finger Lakes and the south shore of Lake Michigan. A dozen Amtrak routes in all make their way to Chicago, so no matter where you're coming from, you can make getting here part of the adventure.

Six Metra Rail routes stop at Union Station too: the North Central Service, which travels from far northwest Antioch; the Milwaukee District/North Line, starting at far northwest Fox Lake (just a smidge south of the Wisconsin border); the Milwaukee District/West Line, which begins in far west Elgin; the Burlington Northern Santa Fe (BNSF), starting from way west in Aurora; the Heritage Corridor Line, which originates in far southwest Joliet; and the SouthWest Service route, whose furthest point is Manhattan, Illinois. Food concessions and shops are available at Union Station, with varying hours. The station waiting room is open daily from 5:30 a.m. to 12:40 a.m., with ticket offices open from 6 a.m. to 11 p.m.

i Chicago was one of the first municipalities to include public art funding as a requirement for any renovation or new construction of a municipal building. Look for the results of this at CTA stations, police stations, and other high-profile public buildings.

OGILVIE TRANSPORTATION CENTER
500 W. Madison St.
(312) 496-4777
www.metrarail.com

Locals of a certain age still refer to this train terminal as the North Western Station because of its beginnings as the home of the Chicago and North Western Railway. In 1984, the original 1911 building was razed and replaced with the bulky, glass-and-steel Citigroup Center (said to resemble a locomotive). Chicago and North Western Railway merged with the Union Pacific Railroad in 1995, and two years later, the terminal was renamed the Ogilvie Transportation Center in honor of past Illinois governor Richard B. Ogilvie, who was instrumental in forming the RTA (Regional Transportation Authority), parent of the Metra commuter train lines.

These days more than 40,000 people travel through the Ogilvie Center on three Metra rail lines. The Union Pacific North Line runs from Kenosha, Wisconsin, paralleling Lake Michigan into the city; the Union Pacific West Line rumbles in from far west Elburn; and the Union Pacific Northwest begins in far northwest Harvard, Illinois. The station also includes a food court, shops, and access to the new French Market, a year-round market of local, fresh, gourmet European, and Asian food vendors. The station's upper-level waiting room is open Mon through Sat from 5 a.m. to 12:40 a.m. and on Sun from 7 a.m. to 12:40 a.m., with ticket agents available starting at 5:30 a.m. Mon through Sat and from 7 a.m. on Sun. The lower-level waiting room is open Mon through Sat from 5 a.m. to 6:40 a.m. and closed on Sun, with ticket agents available only Mon through Fri from 6:30 a.m. to 6 p.m.

Buses

CHICAGO DASH
58 Campbell St., Valparaiso, Indiana
(877) 7GO-DASH
www.chicagodash.com
Need a quick and inexpensive ride from Purdue University (or anywhere in Valpo, for that matter) to Chicago or back again? The ChicaGo DASH has got just the ticket. Providing weekday service for just 15 bucks roundtrip or $7.50 one way, this comfy little van does the 90-minute drive for you, with three stops in Chicago: 333 S. Franklin St., LaSalle Boulevard and Wacker Drive, and Michigan Avenue and Randolph Street. Monthly passes are $230 and a 10-ride pass is $70.

GREYHOUND
630 W. Harrison St.
(800) 231-2222, (312) 408-5821
www.greyhound.com
Greyhound operates buses in and out of Chicago every day, an affordable and comfortable option for getting here and back. You can buy tickets online, over the phone, at the Greyhound terminals, or at agents nationwide. Chicago's primary Greyhound station on Harrison Street is located west of the Loop and near the confluence of several highways (I-90, I-94, and I-290) and the University of Illinois at Chicago campus. In addition to this main station, there are three others in the city: at 14 W. 95th St. (312-408-5999); 225 S. Canal St. (312-408-5821); and at the CTA Transit Building, 5800 North Cumberland Ave. (773-693-2474).

MEGABUS
Chicago stop: S. Canal St., adjacent to Union Station
(877) GO2-MEGA (462-6342)
Servicing nearly 50 cities in the Midwest and Northeast (including parts of Canada), Coach USA's super little sister, Megabus, caught on quick with its fares as low as a dollar. Chicago is one of five hub cities (New York, Philadelphia, Washington D.C., and Toronto are the others) and is a popular choice of visitors traveling from places such as Madison, Milwaukee, Cincinnati, and St. Louis. Though the fares are, indeed, generally mega-bargains, they fluctuate depending on how far in advance you book, where you're going, and when. Booking online incurs a 50-cent charge for all tickets, and making a reservation over the phone adds $3. Besides appealing prices, the ride is nice too, aboard a luxury single- or double-decker bus with free Wi-Fi (when service is available). Pack lightly, as Megabus permits just one piece of luggage per person at a total of 62 inches (meaning, the sum of length, width, and height) and a max weight of 50 pounds.

VAN GALDER BUS
(800) 747-0994
www.coachusa.com/vangalder
Van Galder offers a convenient route from (and to) Madison and Janesville in Wisconsin, and South Beloit, Rockford, and O'Hare and Midway airports in Illinois. You can buy tickets online or by phone. If you arrive with the Van Galder bus at either Chicago airport, you can then hop on the El train (Blue from O'Hare and Orange from Midway) to take you into the city. There are also buses that arrive in downtown Chicago at the Amtrak station. A member of the Coach USA family, Van Galder is independently managed and operated. Fares vary depending on destination, from $20 to $29 one way (double these fares for round trip); children are always $10 one way, $20 round trip.

GETTING AROUND

Driving

Navigating the Windy City streets can be relatively simple if you start out with some basic knowledge. Like the fact that Chicago's streets fall mostly into a simple grid pattern. The numbering system starts in the Loop, with State Street as the east-west divider and Madison Street the north-south divider. In other words, go south of Madison, and the numbers increase with the directional "south" beginning their street names; go north, and the numbers get bigger and start with "north." Travel west of State Street and the numbers increase with "west" as their prefix; go east of State Street and the numbers go up with "east" as their beginning. Each block accounts for addresses in increments of about 100. The larger the number, the further away from the State and Madison center line. Each mile is about eight blocks, with every fourth street typically a major intersection. When you're looking for a specific location, it's helpful to know that even-numbered addresses are on the north and west sides of the streets, and odd-numbered are on the south and east sides.

Confusing things slightly are several diagonal thoroughfares that dissect the grid—namely, Lincoln, Clybourn, Milwaukee, Elston, and Clark, all of which radiate out northwest from the city; and Ogden Avenue, which heads southwest out of the city. They can get even homegrown Chicagoans turned around sometimes, but the numbers still follow the system, so, for example, if you're north of downtown and addresses are getting lower in number, you'll know you're heading south into the downtown area. Traveling these diagonals for very long can get a bit tedious, though, because you'll

end up passing through multiple six-way intersections leading to long waits to get through them. If you're turning left at one of these crazy crossroads, be extra-careful as drivers tend to speed through yellow to make it through the light.

Whereas other highway-heavy cities like Los Angeles refer to highways by their numbers, Chicago typically prefers to use their names. Following are some of the major interstates that pass into or around the city, most of which merge at one point or another: The Kennedy (I-90 and I-94) heads west out to O'Hare; the Edens (I-94 and US 41) heads north; the Dan Ryan Expressway (I-90 and I-94) runs south; the Eisenhower (I-290) heads directly into the western suburbs; the Stevenson Expressway (I-55) begins at McCormick Place convention center and heads south and southwest and takes you to Midway Airport; the Veterans Memorial Tollway (I-355), formerly known as the North-South Tollway, goes through the western suburbs, then south; the west-heading Ronald Reagan Memorial Tollway is still more commonly referred to by its old moniker, the East-West Tollway; the Tri-State Tollway (I-294 and I-94) mostly skirts the city, providing a route from some suburbs to O'Hare; the Chicago Skyway (I-90) provides a shortcut into parts of Indiana and southwest Michigan; and, of course, Lake Shore Drive (US 41), which is a mini-highway, follows Lake Michigan from 63rd Street on the south to Hollywood Avenue on the north.

At one time, the commuter rush hour led to increased travel times going into the city in the morning and leaving the city at night. But that is no longer the rule, and congestion can be just as heavy or more so going into the city during rush hour on some of the major highways. When there are sports events at Soldier Field, the United Center, Wrigley Field, or US Cellular Field, highway exits for the stadiums are always busier as well.

Express Lanes

On the Kennedy Expressway, arguably the busiest in Chicago, there is a unique aspect called the Reversible Express Lanes. Created in the 1960s, they comprise two extra lanes in the center of the highway of about 8 miles in length that can switch direction via computer (with a human control as backup), depending on the need. Barriers prevent cars from entering going the wrong direction. Typically, the reversibles are open going south into the city in the morning and north in the evening, but occasionally they are flipped to respond to unexpected congestion. These express lanes only have exits at a few locations, so if you need to get off before an express exit, you should stick to what Chicagoans refer to as the local lanes.

Child Seat Laws

In Illinois, children under 8 years old must sit in a child car seat, the type of which varies depending on age, but always a rear-facing seat for infants. Children between the ages of 8 and 16 must be securely strapped into a seat belt, whether sitting in the back or front of the car. Children weighing more than 40 pounds are permitted to sit in the back seat with only a lap belt if the backseat does not have a lap and shoulder belt combo. If the driver is 16 or 17 years old, then all passengers under 19 must be wearing a seat belt in all positions in the car. A first offense for noncompliance incurs a fine of $50 and thereafter $100. Child safety seats are not required in taxis. For details, visit www.cyber driveillinois.com; and for help with child

car-seat installation, find a Certified Child Passenger Safety Technician through www .buckleupillinois.org.

Cell Phone Laws

While Illinois is one of six states that allow local municipalities to create their own laws about driving and cell phone use, there are several key statewide laws: Wireless phone use is not allowed by anyone driving through a construction or school zone. Composing, reading, or sending a text message or other electronic message at any time while driving is illegal. Drivers under the age of 19 may not use any kind of handheld communication device while driving; and bus drivers are prohibited from using a cell phone while driving children. Under-19 drivers and bus drivers are exempt from that limitation in cases of emergency. For its local law, Chicago bans handheld cell phone use entirely, but allows hands-free or voice-activated.

Drinking & Driving

While it's just common safety sense not to drink alcohol and drive, many people don't realize that laws are actually very stringent on blood-alcohol content levels and, if arrested, fines and penalties are high. In Illinois, while the law states that BAC levels are illegal at .08 (a change in 1997 from .10), a driver may still face conviction with levels between .05 and .08 if other circumstances are present. A first DUI offense in Illinois means up to a year in jail, with potential of an additional 6 months if there was a child under 16 years old in the vehicle. Plus, there are fines of up to $2,500 (higher if children present), license suspension, community service, and the installation of a Breath Alcohol Ignition Interlock Device. In fact, in 2009, Illinois became one of six states to require a BAIID upon first offense.

Parking

Parking in Chicago can be a drag—on the psyche as well as the pocketbook. Downtown, several large parking garages provide convenient access to the Loop, Millennium Park, Loop Theatre District, and other popular places. But they're not cheap. Plan to spend about $20 to $25 for a few hours of garage parking, though some offer early bird rates (typically in before 9 a.m. and out by 6 p.m.) anywhere from $10 to $20.

Parking on Windy City streets practically requires a separate rules and regs book. The important thing is to pay close attention to any signs posted. Certain highly congested neighborhoods have resident-only parking along many of the blocks—sometimes this is enforced 24 hours a day and sometimes only between 6 p.m. and 6 a.m. If you're visiting someone in the neighborhood, they can obtain a visitor permit for you to park in their zoned residential area for the day.

During the spring, summer, and fall, a monthly street-cleaning schedule prohibits parking on certain blocks from 9 a.m. to 3 p.m.; signs are often posted only the day prior, but each aldermanic office does have a schedule of planned street-cleaning days if you'd like to know ahead of time. During the winter, many of the city's main thoroughfares ban parking from 2 to 7 a.m. if there are 2 or more inches of snow. Also, several main drags enforce year-round no parking during rush hour—usually on sides of the street going into the city from 7 to 9 a.m. and traveling out of the city from 4 to 6 p.m.— to essentially open another lane of traffic, allowing it to flow faster and giving buses a place to pull over to pick up passengers, rather than stopping traffic when they stop.

A private company runs Chicago's parking meters now (after a controversial sell-out for quick cash from former mayor Richard M. Daley), and they consist of automated boxes at irregular intervals on each pay-parking block. Wherever you park on one of these metered blocks, you must get a ticket from the meter boxes and return to your car to put it on the dashboard. The box may be right next to your parking spot or it may be halfway down the block (a royal pain for parents with little kids in tow). The parking fees and hours vary depending on where in the city you're parking. In the Loop, meters demand payment 24 hours; the cost is $5 per hour from 8 a.m. to 9 p.m. and $2.50 an hour from 9 p.m. to 8 a.m. General downtown meter spots charge $3 an hour, while outlying neighborhoods are generally $1.50 per hour, with limits of 2 or 3 hours and usually allowing free parking between 8 p.m. and 8 a.m. There are no meter holidays, not even Sunday. Possibly the only good thing about these meter boxes is that they accept credit cards as well as coins (no bills).

Weather

The extreme temperature changes in Chicago can do a number on its streets. Expanding and contracting surfaces often lead to potholes that cause many a bumpy ride— and sometimes a dent or even a flat tire. Long hot, dry spells followed by a summer rain shower can mean oily, slippery roads. And, as the media around the world reported in the winter of 2010–11, a huge and heavy snowstorm can strand drivers on Lake Shore Drive, where blowing winds from Lake Michigan lead to piled mounds of snow. While this scenario was an exceptionally bad one, it's worth noting for its lesson to never underestimate the effects of snow and rain on Chicago traffic.

El Train Lines

Get extra points for remembering the colors of the El train lines:
Brown heads north and a little west; **Red** runs along State Street downtown and branches out beyond that both north and south; **Orange** runs southwest to Midway Airport; **Blue** has two branches, one running to O'Hare Airport and the other west of the Loop to Forest Park; the **Green** line runs west through Oak Park; **Purple** heads straight north from downtown all the way to suburban Wilmette and has an Express from the Belmont station to the Howard station, at the northern city limit in East Rogers Park; the new **Pink** line travels southwest. The **Yellow** line, dubbed the Skokie Swift, is sort of a close cousin of the El, leaving from the Red and Purple Howard station in Chicago to transport riders out to the nearby city of Skokie. The Red Line El travels on tracks both above and below ground, so it's occasionally called the subway, but still grouped under the El umbrella.

CTA

Chicagoans love their public transportation—when they're not cursing it out for being too late, crowded, noisy, dirty, or expensive. Still, as the country's second-largest public transportation system, it's pretty darn good, serving the city and 40 suburbs and taking about 1.6 million people where they need to go each day. The CTA

comprises bus and rail (the El), and works together with sister agencies, the Metra commuter rail and Pace bus system. The El travels underground, at street grade, and above ground (elevated) to 144 stations over eight different lines that cover more than 224 miles including tracks that take passengers to both Midway and O'Hare airports. The bus system includes nearly 12,000 bus stops on 140 routes throughout the city, several of them running 24 hours a day.

A single-ride regular-priced fare aboard a CTA train is $2.25 and aboard a CTA bus is $2. The first transfer within 2 hours of the first ride is at a discount, just 25 cents, and the second transfer within 2 hours of the first ride is free. To get the most bang out of a busy CTA-riding day (or a few days), purchase an unlimited-ride pass that is good for one day at $5.75, 3 days for $14, 7 days for $23, and 30 days for $86. Fare cards can be purchased at every El station, at some major area attractions, and at many retail locations around the city (such as drugstores or grocery stores). The CTA's website provides maps, schedules, trip planners, up-to-date information on delays or construction, online fare-card purchasing, and more: www .transitchicago.com.

Metra Rail

Coming from Union Station, the Metra lines all have several stops within the city of Chicago before heading to their respective suburban destinations. Some people who live in Chicago and near a Metra stop prefer a comfortable and quick trip aboard these commuter trains over the crowded and sometimes standing-room-only rides on the El or bus.

Taxis

A multitude of taxi companies service Chicago, and finding one is usually as simple as standing on a corner for a minute or two in a busy neighborhood like Lakeview or Andersonville, and maybe four or five minutes in less-commercial communities such as Ravenswood or Rogers Park. Most hotels will hail cabs for guests as well. Competition for cabs does heat up in busy areas after a big event, such as a sold-out concert at the Chicago Theatre or opening night of a Broadway in Chicago show, or even when people begin heading home from crowded neighborhoods like Lincoln Park after a must-watch television broadcast of something like the Super Bowl or the Academy Awards. You can always call ahead if you need a ride at a particular time. Some well-known taxicab names in the city include **Checker Taxi** (312-733-4790); **Chicago Carriage Cab** (312-326-2221); **Flash Cab** (773-992-0303); **American-United Taxi** (773-248-7600); and **Yellow Cab** (773-907-0020). Accessible taxis are available by calling (800) 281-4466.

Cab fares begin at $2.25 for the first 1/9 of a mile. The first additional passenger over the age of 12 and under 65 is $1 and then drops to 50 cents for each passenger beyond that. The fare tacks on 20 cents for each additional 1/9 mile and for each additional 36 seconds. These days, all cabs are required to accept credit cards and there is no extra charge to pay that way, but don't be surprised if some of them grumble about it. Tipping 15 percent is typically expected. Due to high gas prices, a surcharge of 50 cents is added when prices are more than $2.70 and $1 when they rise to more than $3.20—a sign in the taxi should alert you to this rule.

Bicycles

For a major metropolitan city, Chicago is surprisingly accommodating to cyclists, and much of that is due to the encouragement and support from former mayor Richard M. Daley. He had grand plans to make Chicago the bike-friendliest big city in the country, enacting his Bike 2000 Plan, which was followed by his Bike 2015 Plan. While there's still work to do, there are now 315 miles of bikeways, consisting mostly of designated bike lanes, signed routes, and off-street trails; the number of bike racks tops 10,000; and bikes are permitted on Chicago Transit Authority trains and buses (except during weekday rush hours of 7 to 9 a.m. and 4 to 6 p.m.).

New in 2010, a bike sharing program was created by Bike and Roll Chicago. It focuses on short rides for commuting or errands and requires a low-cost seasonal membership to participate. Check it out at www.chicago.bcycle.com for more information. And for maps of Chicago trails and bikeways, visit www.dot.il.gov and click on "Bicycling."

HISTORY

It's amazing how clearly Chicago's present character, its claims to fame and, yes, its controversies too have been shaped by its past. You have just to look at some of Chicago's numerous nicknames to discover many of its prominent history-makers and historic happenings.

Perhaps most-used, Chicago's "Windy City" moniker does not, in fact, describe its breezy lakefront location (Chicago doesn't even rank in the top 10 windiest of US cities). Rather, it was popularized when a New York newspaper article derided the civic boosters who argued (with a lot of hot air, evidently) for Chicago's chance to host the 1893 World's Fair—an event that, in turn, left its own description of Chicago as "The White City." Another common city slogan, "The Second City," is never a putdown for Chicagoans, as it most likely stemmed from the city's impressive rebirth after its devastating fire of 1871. And, yes, it also describes Chicago's size, which was the nation's second most populous city behind New York from about 1890 until the late 1980s when Los Angeles topped it, so now we're third.

If you hear Chicago referred to as the "City of the Big Shoulders," you're taken back to the early 20th century and writer Carl Sandburg's ode to the city's hard-earned toughness in his 1916 poem "Chicago." Another of Sandburg's epithets, "Hog Butcher for the World" recalls the city's rough but profitable stockyard heyday. In Frank Sinatra's jaunty "My Kind of Town," Chicago is revered as a "razzmatazz" town that "won't let you down." And indeed, though Chicago is one of the largest cities in the world, its residents regularly describe their hometown as just that: a "town."

Chicago's own chosen motto was "Urbs in Horto," which translates to "City in a Garden," and there was once a prediction that the city would be the "Paris on the Prairie"— a reference to Daniel Burnham and Edward Bennett's 1909 "Plan of Chicago." But alas, Chicago history is not all romance and flowers, but rather a beautifully marred story of sundry scandals, corruption, and prejudice, and a lot of good old-fashioned sweat equity. Chicago wears it all with pride, and this quick shot of Chicago history aims to give you a sense of where that pride stems from.

EARLY HISTORY

Thousands of years before the last great Ice Age, Chicago and much of the Midwest were covered by an enormous expanse of fresh water. As the glaciers retreated, the melting runoff found its way into carved-out basins that eventually formed Lake Michigan and its four sister Great Lakes. It also meant that when Potawatomi and other Native American tribes first entered what is now Chicago in the late 17th century, they found a pretty wet terrain. The name Chicago is thought to be a loose translation of a Native American word meaning "stinking onion," a description of the wild leek plants that were plentiful amid the swampland.

In 1673, Chicago saw the precursor to permanent nonnative settlement with the arrival of the famous French-Canadian duo of Jacques Marquette and Louis Jolliet. Departing from New France, Canada (present-day Quebec), and on orders from France's King Louis XIV, Jesuit missionary Marquette and mapmaker (and gold-seeker) Jolliet were tasked with expanding France's land holdings in the New World. The "Sun King" was out to beat the British at its run for colonial superiority in America. After scouting the area, Jolliet determined that a canal from Lake Michigan to the Mississippi River would ostensibly hand France control of North America. France's plan to gain power in the region failed, though, because it turned out that France was in a bit of financial trouble and couldn't afford to fund a Chicago settlement. Nearly two decades later, the idea of a waterway connecting the Great Lakes to the Great River did actually come to fruition when the Illinois and Michigan Canal opened in 1848.

After Marquette and Jolliet departed, it wasn't until 1779 that the first official nonnative resident of Chicago set up shop. His name was Jean Baptiste Point DuSable, a Haitian-born man of African and French descent who came to Chicago via New Orleans, making his way up the Mississippi to Peoria, Illinois, where he met and married a Potawatomi woman. After moving to Chicago, he established a home and trading post along the north bank of the Chicago River and did a thriving business with Native Americans and European immigrants for almost 20 years before selling his property

and moving to Missouri. At Chicago's 1933 Century of Progress Exposition, a replica of DuSable's home as a rustic 8-by-12-foot cabin didn't quite reflect his success, as his home was actually an impressive nine times larger. In 1961, the DuSable Museum of African American History opened, honoring the heritage of this Midwestern pioneer. The Native American residents weren't so successful, however.

From the late 18th century on, European settlers nudged the Native American people off their tribal lands, including those in the Chicago area. European settlers' fears of Native Americans escalated in 1812 after what's known as the Fort Dearborn Massacre, when British-backed Indians attacked and killed 52 men, women, and children as soldiers and their families were moving out of their federal military fort at Michigan Avenue and Wacker Drive. The fort was burned down, then rebuilt after several years. It later protected nonnative residents during the Black Hawk War of 1832 that effectively dashed any hopes the Native Americans had of maintaining claim to their Chicago lands. And so Chicago gained attention as more European settlers arrived to make this Midwest land their home.

A CITY EMERGES

In 1825, the opening of the Erie Canal created a direct link from New York's Hudson River to Lake Erie, extending shipping potential from the Atlantic Ocean to all the Great Lakes. Chicagoans didn't overlook the opportunity for their own gains. Based on the economic boom in Buffalo, New York— at the eastern point of Lake Erie—optimistic Chicago real estate investors grabbed up prime plots near Lake Michigan. Though

Chicago boasts the first . . .

All-Star baseball game: Comiskey Park, 1933

Black female talk-show host: Oprah Winfrey, 1986

Black Major League baseball coach: Buck O'Neil, Chicago Cubs, 1962

Cracker Jacks forerunner: invented by F.W. and Louis Rueckheim, World's Columbian Exposition, 1893

Deep-dish pizza: Pizzeria Uno, 1943

Ferris wheel: World's Columbian Exposition, 1893

Hospital in America established and controlled by African-Americans: 1891

Mail-order house: Montgomery Ward, 1872

Planetarium in the Western Hemisphere: Adler, 1930

Self-sustained nuclear chain reaction: produced by Enrico Fermi, University of Chicago, 1942

Skyscraper: Home Insurance Building, William LeBaron Jenney, 1885

Softball game: created by George Hancock, 1887

Zipper: debuted at World's Columbian Exposition, 1893

Chicago's population numbered only about 200, it was enough to incorporate as a town by 1833. And then, in 1836 came the big dig that gave Chicago a big population explosion.

The seed of the idea for the Illinois and Michigan Canal had been planted way back when Marquette and Jolliet first visited the area in 1673. Finally, the 96-mile waterway between the Illinois and Mississippi rivers would indeed unite the fledgling town with the already-bustling New Orleans port. The arduous, long-term project required more labor than the city had at the time, and soon thousands of job-seekers descended on the newly formed settlement. The ballooning population quickly pushed Chicago's status beyond "town," and in 1837, the City of Chicago was officially incorporated.

Lucky for the future of Chicago, its first mayor (1837–1838) was William B. Ogden, a businessman and real estate developer who fully believed in the power of transportation. Ogden, who had moved from New York in 1835, had already helped spur the construction of the Erie Canal and helped get the I and M Canal on its way. In his new role, he headed up the charge to construct 100 more miles of streets throughout the city—Ogden Avenue is now named after him. Despite the country's economic woes during the Panic of 1837, Ogden kept Chicago afloat, even encouraging investment from outsiders. After his short one-year term in office, Ogden continued to drum up support for new ways into, out of, and through Chicago, concentrating next on railways.

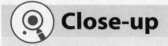 **Close-up**

No Small Plan

If you admire Chicago's expansive lakefront or its easy street-grid system or maybe the gracious green space that comprises Grant Park, you can thank **Daniel Hudson Burnham.** He was the man with **"The Chicago Plan."** Burnham was already an accomplished architect, famous for leading Chicago's 1893 World's Columbian Exposition, when he was hired in 1906 to envision an organized plan for Chicago's future development. Burnham and his right-hand man, Edward Bennett, studied other international cities for inspiration; they assessed the needs of businesspeople and those of consumers; they considered both the aesthetics and logistics of city life; and they understood that getting in and out of the city via an effective highway system was crucial for Chicago's growth.

When it was published in 1909, The Chicago Plan marked the first time a metropolitan city had created such a blueprint, and it laid the groundwork for much of what you see in the city today. Like the lakefront, now a 26-mile stretch of beaches, sports fields, picnic areas, and nature. And the double-decker Wacker Drive that allows trucks to make deliveries to downtown buildings on the lower-level, while cars can skirt the Loop on the upper or lower level. And Navy Pier, one of five recreational piers that Burnham had imagined and that today has been transformed into one of the city's top attractions.

"The Burnham Plan," as it's often called, now serves as the jumping-off point for the new Chicago Metropolitan Agency for Planning's GO TO 2040 strategy that aims to further improve the city and suburbs. Chicago's expecting big things, because, like Burnham famously said, "Make no little plans; they have no magic to stir men's blood."

With several partners, Ogden brought the first steam locomotive to Chicago in 1848 when the aptly named Pioneer chugged in on the nascent Galena & Chicago Union Railroad (at the time, the western town of Galena was experiencing a mining boom, and the railroad smartly tapped into that). Pretty soon, there were 11 train lines running through Chicago. The rail rally helped elevate Chicago to its strategic position as the nucleus of cross-country shipping, moving everything from grain to lumber to meat. Train travel also proved advantageous for Chicago during the Civil War when the Union Army chose Chicago to provide its provisions, seriously snubbing Confederate-siding St. Louis.

All this transportation-expanding activity kept Chicago's population chugging along too, and by 1870, it had reached 300,000. People were lured to the city by its growing economy, as well as its growing meat-packing industry. In 1865, at the opening of the famous (and infamous) 100-acre Union Stock Yard—a clever combination of stockyard and railroad depot that centralized the process from start to finish—Chicago had taken its place as the country's largest meat-packer, a title it kept until the 1920s.

Businesses built up around the meat-packing industry, including manufacturers who used meat by-products to produce everything from soap to glue to violin strings. On the flip side of meat-packing's moneymaking was the acute hardship of the employees who worked in despicable conditions for up to 12 hours at a stretch, sometimes in 100-degree heat. In his 1906 novel *The Jungle,* Upton Sinclair laid bare in graphic detail the plight of these slaughterhouse workers. Eventually, their situation led to the formation of unions and union strikes and, ultimately, some innovative concessions, including the 8-hour workday.

FROM ASHES TO SKYSCRAPERS

Just about the time Chicago was hitting its stride economically, it all went up in smoke—literally. On the evening of October 8, 1871, a fire began in Patrick and Catherine O'Leary's barn on Chicago's west side. Warm, dry weather and mostly wood construction outside the downtown limits caused the fire to spread swiftly, traveling at 65 acres an hour and soon engulfing the entire business district too. After nearly two days, a welcome rainstorm ended the inferno's fury, but not before 300 people died, 100,000 were left homeless, and 18,000 buildings were leveled.

Legend has it that it was the O'Learys' cow that kicked over a lantern that sparked the blaze, but this may not be the "udder" truth. More likely it was a man named "Peg Leg" Sullivan who started the fire when he was at the barn tending to his mother's cow, which also stayed there. Considering the devastation that the Great Chicago Fire left behind, it's no wonder Sullivan came up with the cow version to save his own hide. During and after the fire, two Chicago landmarks took on an important role for residents: Lake Michigan provided safety for many who waded into its waters, and, left standing amid the rubble, the limestone Water Tower

and Pumping Station on Michigan Avenue provided a beacon and gathering place for the homeless (their sandcastle design is a favorite photo op today).

Chicagoans' can-do attitude kicked in fast, though, and the city's intense rebuilding soon began. It was aided by the fact that the lumberyards, stockyards, and railroads survived the fire, so a lot of people could still work, and some infrastructure was still intact. Within two years, the downtown was completely rebuilt, and it only headed up—and up—from there. Seeing a unique opportunity to make a splash on Chicago's newly blank canvas of land, architects arrived from around the world, leading to something of a building frenzy.

In fact, as it turned out, the fire inadvertently led to Chicago's title as the birthplace of the skyscraper. In 1885, construction wrapped on William LeBaron Jenney's 10-story Home Insurance Building at Adams and LaSalle streets (since demolished). Jenney, an engineer by trade, figured out that a structural skeleton of metal columns and beams could offer better support for floors above than the typical weight-bearing stone; plus, metal meant better fireproofing and allowed for more windows. Previously, the taller the building, the thicker the stone walls had to be—the still-standing 16-story Monadnock Building (53 W. Jackson Blvd.) exemplifies this former technique with its incredible 6-foot-thick walls at its base.

Jenney had officially started a trend, and Chicago continued to reach for the sky for decades to come, with masterpieces of engineering and design in styles ranging from Art Deco to Modernism, Post-Modernism to Classic-Revival; from renowned architects and architectural firms such as Louis Sullivan, Daniel Burnham, Burnham and Root,

⊘ Close-up

Notable Chicago Moments—The Good, The Bad, & Otherwise

1779: First Nonnative Settler
Haitian-born Jean Baptiste Point DuSable establishes a trading post along the Chicago River, along with a bake house, dairy, smokehouse, poultry pen, workshop, stable, and barn.

1837: Chicago Incorporates
Chicago earns city status after a population surge of workers who came to build the Illinois and Michigan Canal.

1848: Chicago Board of Trade Founded
To help regulate volatile grain prices, a group of 83 businessmen organize the Board of Trade. In 1930, the CBOT moves into its iconic Art Deco building on LaSalle and Jackson Streets.

1855–1859: Chicago Buildings Raised
Combating drainage problems due to impermeable soil and flat topography, Chicago raises its streets and city buildings 4 to 8 feet.

1886: Haymarket Square Riot
A nationwide climate of labor unrest leaves a stain on Chicago history when a bomb is tossed amid a rally of activists seeking an 8-hour workday; seven police officers and several workers are killed.

1889: Hull House Opens
In the rundown former mansion of real estate developer Charles J. Hull, Jane Addams and Ellen Gates Starr open a settlement house to assist immigrants and other underserved residents. It becomes a model for others across the country.

1892: Opening of first El
The city's famous El train system commences with the Chicago and South Side Rapid Transit Railroad Company, which lays 3.6 miles of track from Congress Street to 39th Street. In 1893, the line extends south to ferry passengers to the World's Columbian Exposition.

1893: World's Columbian Exposition
This grand event attracts more than 27 million people (over half the US population at the time). Glittering, white terra cotta–clad Beaux-Arts buildings give the event its "White City" nickname, and the mile-long Midway Plaisance gives fairgoers an eyeful of entertainment.

1894: Pullman Factory Strike
In 1880, luxury train car magnate George Pullman builds the seemingly utopian Village of Pullman, where his employees work and live. But in 1894, Pullman slashes workers' salaries by 30 percent and refuses to lower rents. Employees strike, and Pullman flees town, faces government investigation, and dies three years later.

1900: Reversal of the Chicago River
In 1885, following heavy rains, massive amounts of sewage drained into the Chicago River and out into the lake, threatening the city's fresh drinking water supply. Rather than figure out a way to keep the river free of garbage, Chicago builds a deep canal that forces the Chicago River to flow backward, sending waste downstream (eventually to St. Louis).

1908: Cubs win the World Series
In a rematch of the 1907 World Series, the Cubs win over the Detroit Tigers. This marks their most recent World Series win, earning them their "Lovable Losers" nickname.

1915: Eastland Disaster

What's meant to be a lovely boat cruise and picnic for 2,500 Western Electric employees and their families turns tragic when the ship, still docked along the Chicago River, sinks, trapping hundreds in its cabins and taking the lives of nearly 845 passengers.

1919: Black Sox Scandal

In 1919, the Chicago White Sox are favored to win the World Series, but a group of eight disgruntled players throw the game. Frustrated with low pay and poor treatment by manager Charles Comiskey, they are accused of fixing the game to earn gambling money. The players, including "Shoeless" Joe Jackson, are later acquitted of gambling charges, but banned from baseball forever and dubbed the "Black Sox."

1933: Century of Progress World's Fair

This fair's 40 million visitors get a peek at a future of washers and dryers, air-conditioning, and other modern amenities. The fair is a huge success, but condemned for ignoring accomplishments of African Americans and women.

1934: John Dillinger Shot

With a pretty face and a penchant for bank-robbing, John Dillinger becomes an FBI target. Agents catch up with him at Chicago's Biograph Theater and shoot him in the adjacent alley.

1955: Richard J. Daley Elected Mayor

Considered the "last of the big-city bosses," the first Mayor Daley serves until his death in 1976. His time in office evokes a mix of attitudes, from condemnation for his failure to desegregate Chicago, to suspicion over possible vote-rigging during the 1960 presidential election, to praise for developing the world's busiest airport (O'Hare).

1968: Democratic Convention Riots

The nation is a pot of boiling emotions in 1968, when it bubbles over in deadly clashes between activists and police during its Democratic Convention.

1969: Chicago Seven Trial

The Chicago Seven, including famed Yippie Abbie Hoffman, is a group of activists indicted by a grand jury for inciting violence during the 1968 Democratic Convention. The trial draws attention to anti–Vietnam War sentiment. Two of the men are acquitted, while five are found guilty on other charges.

1983: Mayor Harold Washington Elected Mayor

Born in 1922 in Chicago, Harold Washington becomes the city's first African-American mayor. He is reelected in 1987, but dies of a heart attack soon after.

1989: Richard M. Daley Elected Mayor

The first Mayor Daley's eldest child of seven is elected in 1989 to complete late Mayor Washington's term. After outdoing his father in years in office, Richard M. Daley retires his mayoral run in 2011. Though city dwellers commend him for some things (Millennium Park, urban renewal, Michigan Avenue greenery), they criticize him for others (selling the parking meters, losing the Olympics, leaving the city with a heavy debt).

2004: Millennium Park Opens

Wildly over budget and delayed by 4 years, Millennium Park nevertheless opens with fanfare and is considered a crowning jewel of Chicago's park system.

2008: President-Elect Barack Obama's Acceptance Speech

Barack Obama wasn't born in Chicago, but the Windy City considers the President an honorary native. When he gives his presidential acceptance speech in Grant Park on November 5, 2008, nearly 240,000 people turn out.

Holabird and Root, Holabird and Roche, Mies van der Rohe, Fazlur Khan, Bertrand Goldberg, and Skidmore, Owens & Merrill. The city traded its claim to the "tallest building in the country" with New York several times, but it maintains it for now with Willis Tower (formerly Sears Tower) built in 1974 and topping out at 108 floors (1,451 feet). That's certainly a far cry from the original skyscraper, but couldn't have existed without Jenney's innovative building technique nearly a century earlier.

THE GANGSTER YEARS

As Chicago settled itself into the 20th century, with its skyline taking shape, its population increasing, and businesses expanding, a shadier side of the city was also gaining ground: its reputation as gangster country. The Chicago Outfit, as it has been termed, started out in prostitution and gambling, but the 18th Amendment (1920–1933) provided an even better vice to exploit. The famously beer-loving German and Irish communities of Chicago were growing, and they were happy to wet their whistles wherever and with whatever they could, even if it was illegal.

While the story of Chicago gangster lore immediately conjures the "Scarface" image of the ruthless Al Capone of *The Untouchables* film fame, he can't take all the credit. It was actually a shrewd man named "Big Jim" Colosimo who originally put Chicago on the mobster map.

Before Prohibition made alcohol the most wanted vice, Colosimo used his potent political connections to stake claim on prostitution, labor racketeering, and gambling. He had recruited his nephew by marriage, John Torrio, who soon took on second in command and likely led to Colosimo's own demise. Torrio, in turn, invited a young New York speakeasy bouncer named Alphonsus Capone to join him in Chicago. Together, Torrio and Capone helped boost business for Colosimo, but when Prohibition arrived, they couldn't convince Colosimo to add bootlegging to his books. So what's a gangster to do? Make the problem disappear, of course. Colosimo was shot and killed in his own cafe, and Torrio and Capone went on to take over the reins, building a bootlegging empire within a few years.

At first, agreements were made between rival gangs to divide up the city into territories, with Torrio and Capone's the biggest, even stretching beyond Chicago. But the gangs got greedy, and pretty soon friction led to fighting and fighting led to killing. Torrio nearly became victim himself, escaping with his life, then retiring from the business in 1925 and leaving the 26-year-old Capone in charge. Capone wasted no time making his mark on organized-crime history. Within a year, he had gained Godfather-like control over the underworld of Chicago, with police shamelessly turning a blind eye with a bribe or two, and political influence gained by the same means.

Gang killings racked up, reaching a peak in 1929 with Capone's most heinous hit on six men (and a doctor) from George "Bugs" Moran's rival gang. Known as the St. Valentine's Day Massacre, it made Capone the indisputable king of gangland. He certainly enjoyed the money that was pouring in from his speakeasies, gambling, and bootlegging. Estimates put his take at $6 million a week. But it turned out Capone did not have a free ride after all. He loved the limelight and the headlines that gave him his larger-than-life persona, and all the living large did him in when the FBI caught drift of his doings and tagged him as Public Enemy Number One in 1930. Though FBI agent Eliot Ness and his colleagues—named the Untouchables for their refusal to take bribes—could never pin him down on murder, they brought him down for tax evasion in 1931.

Capone tried to run the gang from his Atlanta prison, but he was discovered and moved to Alcatraz. After being released in 1939, he lived out his final years on his estate in Florida before dying of a heart attack in 1947.

But the Outfit did not die with Capone. It carried on quite nicely, first led by Frank Nitti and other Capone cronies and then the likes of Tony Accardo, Sam Giancana, and Jimmy Hoffa, raking in even more dough after the end of Prohibition in 1933. And this time the Outfit kept a lower profile, keeping off FBI most-wanted lists while expanding their power into other cities across the country, including Hollywood, where they extorted film studios, and of course eventually into Las Vegas casinos.

But by the 1960s, the nation had a new outlook, and Chicago police had a new guard that wasn't letting the Chicago mobsters get away with their business as usual. Add to that a Civil Rights movement that meant a new crop of leaders was being voted into office, and Chicago's mob mania was starting to fade. Though Chicago gang bosses still have power in some ways, it's not the glamorized life of the Roaring Twenties and Al Capone.

MOVING ON

During the first several decades of the 20th century, Chicago experienced a major influx of immigrants from both Europe and the American South. The diversity of people who came for jobs, new lives, and the pursuit of the American dream—Polish, Italian, Russian, and African-American—added to the city's patchwork quilt of cultures that still exists. But perhaps more than any other, it was black men and women, newly emancipated and escaping Jim Crow laws, who found their way north to the blossoming city.

From 1910 to 1930, Chicago's African-American population exploded from about 44,000 to more than 233,000. Though they came for opportunity, they also met up with discrimination that reared itself in job exploitation and housing discrimination. Most of the black people who came to Chicago were relegated to living in overcrowded and rundown buildings at the outskirts of the city in Chicago's South Side, known as the Black Metropolis. It was part of a national trend later called the Great Migration and is memorialized in Chicago with a bronze statue at Martin Luther King Jr. Drive and 26th Place.

Besides an eager and motivated work force, African-American migrants from the South brought with them a unique musical heritage, which eventually resulted in the sounds of Chicago blues. And though it took a hit with the Great Depression, by the 1950s the blues were beating a path to the mainstream, with Chi-town record labels such as Chess, Vee-Jay, and Cobra signing on legendary musicians including Muddy Waters, Howlin' Wolf, Otis Rush, and Buddy Guy. In 1984, the city of Chicago presented its first annual Blues Festival, now considered the largest free blues festival in the world, attracting more than 500,000 listeners.

Despite their positive impact on Chicago, the growing black population heightened racial tensions in the city, ending up in violence and leading to a historic gathering in Soldier Field held by Martin Luther King Jr. The "Boss" of Chicago at the time, Mayor Richard J. Daley (he reigned from 1955 to 1976) met with King in 1966 to discuss prejudicial housing practices, but unfortunately never achieved any significant change in the atmosphere of discrimination in the city at the time.

By the time Chicago hosted the 1968 Democratic National Convention, civil unrest was at a peak due to anti–Vietnam War sentiments, anger over the assassinations of King and Robert Kennedy, and a general feeling that the Democrats had seriously disappointed constituents on civil rights matters.

While Mayor Daley planned to use the convention as an opportunity to show off Chicago, protesters saw it as a platform to voice their issues. Daley refused to grant permits to protesters and instead amassed 23,000 police and National Guardsmen. It didn't deter the protesters, though. Vivid images on national news revealed clashes between them and the police, resulting in the famous quote, "The whole world is watching." In the end, nearly 600 social activists were arrested, about 220 injured, and, famously, eight indicted by a grand jury on charges of inciting violence—one case was dropped, and the remaining are famously and forever after known as the Chicago Seven.

Though five of the Chicago Seven were convicted, including Abbie Hoffman of the Yippie organization, the charges were later overturned on appeal. Mayor Daley defended his use of the extraordinary number of police and guardsmen and, sadly, much of the nation supported his decision as well.

Richard J. Daley's legacy was marred by these moments, but it's undeniable that he increased Chicago's international prominence in some ways, especially by developing O'Hare Airport. Originally built during World War II as a manufacturing plant for Douglas Aircraft Company near an area called Orchard Field, Orchard Field Airport/ Douglas Field (thus, the ORD initials it has now) was barely used until Daley spearheaded major expansion that was completed in 1962. It quickly assumed its role as the world's busiest airport.

Daley died in office in 1976 after six terms, and two decades later, in 1989, Daley's son Richard M. Daley was elected mayor. The younger Daley took over for Mayor Harold Washington, the city's first African-American mayor, who suffered a heart attack in office. Daley followed in his father's footsteps with a six-term run that ended in 2011. Though he also inherited a knack for controversy (hiring scandals being one of the top contenders) and amassed plenty of detractors, he also attained a kind of clout that no mayor will likely have again, and he gave the city some major improvements: Millennium Park, lots of downtown greenery, a revitalization of Navy Pier as the city's top tourist destination, and a push for eco-friendly strategies throughout the city. There's no doubt that Chicago's newest Mayor Rahm Emanuel has some big shoes to fill.

ACCOMMODATIONS

Are you the type of traveler who drops luggage at the hotel, then zips off to sight-see, returning to the room only to sleep? Or do you luxuriate in the surroundings of a full-service resort that caters to your every desire? In this chapter, you'll find lodging choices for both personalities and plenty in between. What isn't included are a lot of midrange chain hotels. Just know that Chicago does offer those (like Courtyard by Marriott, Residence Inn, and Holiday Inn), and visitors appreciate them for standards that are recognized around the world. Save for several accommodations near O'Hare airport, all other hotels are in the city of Chicago. Suburban hotels, also, are generally of the chain variety and certainly fill needs for travelers who do not intend to stay downtown. But this book is about Chicago, and so Chicago is the focus. With so many options right here—more than 30,000 rooms in dozens of downtown hotels alone—if you're visiting the Windy City, there's no need to stray.

The hotels and inns selected for inclusion up the ante a bit from the norm: Perhaps it's a kick-butt location or super eco-friendliness or simply the clout of longevity. You can search by budget or by general area—Loop, Gold Coast and Old Town, Hyde Park and South of the Loop, Lincoln Park and Lakeview, Magnificent Mile, or River North—or read through and get a feel for what's right for your mood (romance? fun? history?) and your needs (family vacation? quick overnight trip?). Business travelers have their pick of properties, as all types of accommodations offer small meeting rooms or large conference facilities, and most these days provide access to a business center of some kind, whether simply a computer and a printer or a fully staffed room with shipping conveniences.

If you're traveling with kids in tow, you'll be happy to know that hotels are getting darn clever about their cool amenities for little ones, from kid-size bathrobes to coloring books to cookies and milk. Plus, ask about specially priced packages that often include passes to Chicago museums or discounts at family-friendly restaurants. And, finally, if you can't bear to leave Rover behind, let him rove with you. A surprisingly large number of hotels allow dogs too, even fancy schmancy hotels that you might not think would. Though weight limitations on pets and additional fees often apply, Fido can feel right at home with programs that provide bowls, treats, walking services, beds, and more.

OVERVIEW

A couple of warnings on the price of your hotel: What's quoted doesn't usually include garage or valet parking, which can be upwards of $50 a night, though typical in-and-out privileges ease the pain. The total creeps up even more when the city's hotel

ACCOMMODATIONS

tax is tacked on (as of printing, 15.4 percent). A couple of extra notes: If you're a smoker, ask first before booking your room, as many Chicago hotels have gone 100 percent smoke-free. If you'd like a little extra TLC, ask about executive or concierge levels, which add on bonuses like complimentary breakfasts and cocktails and private lounges. Enjoy your stay.

Pricing Code

The following price code reflects the average published double-occupancy rate during peak season. Prices do not include hotel tax, which is 15.4 percent downtown.

$................. **Less than $150**
$$ .... **$150 to $200**
$$$ .... **$200 to $250**
$$$$ .... **More than $250**

TheWit Hotel Chicago,
  Loop, 45
Whitehall Hotel, Magnificent
  Mile, 53
Wyndham Blake Chicago,
  Hyde Park–South of
  Loop, 47

$$–$$$
Sax Chicago, River North, 56
Tremont Hotel, Magnificent
  Mile, 52

$$
The Allerton Hotel,
  Magnificent Mile, 49

Best Western Plus
  Hawthorne Terrace,
  Lincoln Park–Lakeview, 48
Days Inn Chicago, Lincoln
  Park–Lakeview, 48
Flemish House Of Chicago,
  Gold Coast–Old Town, 58
House of Two Urns, Wicker
  Park, 59
Majestic Hotel, Lincoln Park–
  Lakeview, 48
Westin Chicago River North,
  River North, 57

$–$$
Nina's B&B, Andersonville, 59

$
Aloft Chicago O'Hare,
  Rosemont/O'Hare Airport
  Area, 58
Chicago Marriott O'Hare,
  O'Hare Airport Area, 58
Crowne Plaza Chicago
  O'Hare Hotel &
  Conference Center,
  Rosemont/O'Hare Airport
  Area, 58
Holiday Inn Hotel & Suites
  Downtown, Loop, 42

HOTELS

Loop

FAIRMONT CHICAGO, MILLENNIUM PARK $$$$
200 N. Columbus Dr.
(312) 565-8000
www.fairmont.com/chicago

A contemporary look of earthy shades and Asian accents wins high marks for this recently redesigned 687-room high-rise hotel. Close to Millennium Park, Navy Pier, the Art Institute, and the Magnificent Mile, the Fairmont also made it on *Travel + Leisure* magazine's Top 500 Hotels List. It helps that elegant rooms are an above-average 420 square feet with indulgent rain showers in marble bathrooms. The 84 luxury accommodations of the Fairmont Gold upper floors offer complimentary breakfasts and evening nibbles in a private lounge. At the onsite stylish dining spot aria, chef Brad Parsons sources ingredients for his Asian-inspired cuisine right from the rooftop herb garden. Or savor mouthwatering cheeses, an award-winning 500-bottle wine list, and local chocolates at Eno Wine Room. The 11,000-square-foot spa provides a full menu of body and skin services.

HARD ROCK HOTEL CHICAGO $$$
230 N. Michigan Ave.
(312) 345-1000
www.hardrockhotelchicago.com

Why just sleep when you can rock the night away at this offshoot of the world-famous Hard Rock Cafe? One of only seven in the country, Chicago's hotel is located in the pristinely renovated Carbide & Carbon building, a 1929 Art Deco masterpiece designed by the sons of famed architect and urban planner Daniel Burnham. The tall tapered shape and green terra-cotta exterior with glittery gold top was inspired by a champagne bottle, and it suits this place just perfectly—a mix of sparkle and sophistication, partying and pampering. The 381 rooms may vary in size from 350 square feet to a spacious 950-foot penthouse "extreme suite," but all of them come with city views, 40-inch flat-panel LCD TVs, 10 free iTunes downloads, and complimentary Gibson electric or acoustic guitars and headphones so you can jam to your own beat all night long. No strumming experience? No problem. Just tune into the gratis guitar lessons on the hotel TV channel. Spa treatment rooms offer massages, facials, and nail services. Or pop down for some of that champagne at the scene-y Angels & Kings club. At the vibrantly hued China Grill restaurant, designed by Yabu Pushelberg (Trump Hollywood, W Hotel Times Square), it's internationally innovative cuisine that's on the menu.

HOLIDAY INN HOTEL & SUITES
   DOWNTOWN $
506 W. Harrison St.
(312) 957-9100
www.hidowntown.com

This 145-room downtown hotel offers easy access to the Kennedy, Dan Ryan, and Eisenhower Expressways and to the Loop, with its close Blue Line El stop. When you're in a rush or just looking for a quick and convenient spot for a bite, stick around for thin-crust pies at the family-friendly Aurelio's Pizza and Lounge. To experience the best part of this Holiday Inn, stay here during warm weather when you can lounge at the rooftop pool.

HOTEL ALLEGRO $$$
171 W. Randolph St.
(312) 236-0123
www.allegrochicago.com

A three-floor red-carpeted grand staircase begins the star treatment for guests at this Loop Theatre District hotel. Though the 483

rooms are on the small side, they make up for it with bold design splashes like cobalt-colored headboards and trippy patterned carpeting, plus pillow-top mattresses, Aveda bath products, and Jacuzzi tubs (in suites). Traveling with little ones? Ask for in-room child safety kits, a KimptonKids welcome gift, and even stroller rental, as well as "swag bags," create-your-own pizza and ice cream sundae bars, and an animal-print robe to use during their stay. Grown-ups get perks too, like complimentary coffee in the morning and chill-out time at the evening wine reception (including hot chocolate in winter, sangria in the summer). Adjacent 312 Chicago serves Italian-influenced cuisine in a warm, wood-accented setting, and chic Encore offers light meals for lunch or dinner, along with killer martinis. Feel good about your stay here, too, knowing that the Allegro has won awards for its eco-friendliness (like nontoxic cleaning products).

✳HOTEL BURNHAM $$$
1 W. Washington St.
(312) 782-1111
www.burnhamhotel.com

Originally designed as offices in 1895 by Daniel Burnham, John Root, and Charles Atwood (some guestroom doors still feature original mail slots), this National Historic Landmark was a forerunner of steel and glass skyscrapers to come. It was nearly lost to neglect but in 1999 it was lovingly restored and reborn as this beautiful 122-room hotel. Some of the original detailing, such as mosaic floors and marble ceilings, was refurbished, while other features were replicated to bring back the elegance of the original Chicago Style structure. Around the corner from State Street shopping, the hotel now envelops visitors in history and charm. Cozy rooms are plush with custom drapery, rich gold and blue hues, canopied beds, and endlessly appealing views of State Street, Lake Michigan, or the Loop. Feel free to bring your dog, but if you don't, you can borrow a goldfish to keep you company. Kids' packages include building blocks, coloring books, and cookies and milk. The hotel's Atwood Cafe is a standout American restaurant, beloved for its brunch and its scrumptious chicken potpie.

HOTEL MONACO $$$$
225 N. Wabash Ave.
(312) 960-8500
www.monaco-chicago.com

This former hat factory built in 1912 near the Chicago River took on an equally dapper existence when it opened as a Kimpton boutique hotel in 1998. The 192 rooms recently underwent a total facelift, giving them an ornate look, complete with chocolate brown hues and lipstick red carpeting, mahogany tables, European-style chaise longues, and mirrored headboards. You don't even have to leave for pampering: Spa professionals can come right to your room. Taller-than-average guests can request a fitting room—i.e. 9-foot-long king-size beds, longer bathrobes, and higher showerheads. On the lower level, the Prairie Style–inspired South Water Kitchen stands on its own for exceptional creative takes on American favorites like macaroni and cheese and boneless beef short ribs.

HYATT REGENCY CHICAGO $$$
151 E. Wacker Dr.
(312) 565-1234
www.chicagohyatt.com

A major renovation completed in 2011 gave this two-towered hotel a well-deserved makeover, with sleek lines, artsy photography, and inviting cocoa and pumpkin hues. Popular with convention crowds, thanks to its 2,019 guestrooms and more than 228,000 square feet of meeting space, the Hyatt Regency also boasts super-size drinking and eating. Like steaks at Stetson's Chop House that top out at 48 ounces, and the famous BIG Bar's 1,400-plus-item beverage menu including draft beer in sizes "big," "bigger" and "biggest." Guestrooms range from standard to the 1,045-square-foot Presidential Suite that lives up to the name with views of downtown, the river, Lake Michigan, and Navy Pier. Allergies get you down? Opt for a Respire by Hyatt room, which adheres to a six-step allergen-reducing process. Cut down on hassles of traveling with tots with the Hyatt's Babies Travel Lite program: Order all your baby necessities online and pick them up at check-in.

HOTEL 71 $$$
71 E. Wacker Dr.
(312) 346-7100
www.hotel71.com

A prime location along the Chicago River means that many of the 307 rooms in this 39-story contemporary boutique hotel look down onto the busy waterway. The penthouse ballroom goes even further, boasting floor-to-ceiling windows, while the first floor Hoyt's restaurant serves up American comfort food along with great street-scene people-watching. Head down to the Riverwalk for summer dining, stroll south to the Art Institute or cross over the river for Mag Mile shopping. Standard amenities like 300-thread-count sheets, windows that open, and in-room Keurig coffeemakers kick up the comfort level.

*PALMER HOUSE HILTON $$$$
17 E. Monroe St.
(800) 445-8667, (312) 726-7500
www.palmerhousehiltonhotel.com

At more than 140 years old, this stunning historic hotel in the heart of the Loop is the oldest continuously operating hotel in the US. Bestowed as a wedding gift from Potter Palmer (founding partner of Marshall Field's department store) to his wife Bertha in 1871, the hotel tragically burned down in the Chicago Fire of the same year. Not to be deterred, Palmer rebuilt and reopened in 1873 as the first fully fireproof hotel. Since then, it has hosted international celebrities and society elites, but remains welcoming to all, attaining accolades as one of the most luxurious hotels in the world. Recently renewed to its original grandeur, its vast lobby awes with fresco-graced cathedral-like ceilings, Tiffany statues, plush seating, and dazzling chandeliers. Most of the 1,639 rooms were remodeled with tasteful and unique decor. Added were a new 10,000-square-foot health club, 54 suites, a lobby bar, the casually elegant Lockwood restaurant, a million-dollar penthouse suite, and an Executive Level for the most discerning of guests. Another Palmer House claim to fame: Its chefs purportedly created a recipe that inspired the first brownie.

RENAISSANCE CHICAGO
DOWNTOWN HOTEL $$$$
1 W. Wacker Dr.
(312) 372-7200
www.renaissancechicagodowntown.com

This upscale, 27-floor hotel has a riverfront location within a stone's throw of the Loop and just across from River North art galleries and dining. Done up in sophisticated modern style, the 513 rooms and 40 suites make snuggling in easy with their comfy duvet covers. Plus, all rooms have windows that open onto the city below, many with views up and down the river. In the Concierge Lounge, rooms come with upgrades such as breakfast and afternoon hors d'oeuvres. For a little playtime, the skylit indoor pool, whirlpool, and steam room are open to all guests, and Sony Playstations are available for an hourly charge.

THE SILVERSMITH HOTEL & SUITES $$$
10 S. Wabash Ave.
(312) 372-7696
www.silversmithchicagohotel.com

Urban on the outside, classy on the inside, this 1896 National Landmark hotel sits right along the El tracks and in the middle of what's known as Jeweler's Row. Its composite façade shows signs of Moorish and Romanesque Revival on top, hints of Arts and Crafts on the lower half, and a decidedly Chicago Style in its flat roof and consistently sized windows. The soft lobby with its thick blocky columns and restored marble takes on the Arts and Crafts feel, as do the 143 rooms and 63 suites. The connected Ada's Restaurant brings in a 1950s-era atmosphere, with orders of New York–style deli plates, kishke, matzo-ball soup, and more.

SWISSÔTEL $$$
323 E. Wacker Dr.
(312) 565-0565
www.swissotelchicago.com

A triangular triumph of glittering architecture designed by Harry Weese, the European-tinged Swissôtel boasts an amazing location at the meeting point of the Chicago River and Lake Michigan. Which means extraordinary views from many of the 661 rooms, some of which come equipped with telescopes. Refined luxury is typified in the 2,000-square-foot Presidential Suite, which impresses with high-end artwork, a fireplace, private gym, and access to the Executive Club Lounge. All guests can enjoy the breathtaking panoramas from the 7,500-square-foot 42nd-floor health club and pool. Kids get V.I.K. status here with free meals at the Geneva Restaurant, and themed, 2-room Kids' Suites, replete with kid-size tables and chairs, coloring books, DVDs, video games, stuffed animals, and, if you choose to purchase a museum package, decorations that match the museum.

W CHICAGO CITY CENTER $$$$
172 W. Adams St.
(888) 627-9034, (312) 332-1200
www.whotels.com/citycenter
Marked by a giant crimson W on its exterior canopy, this financial district hotel can get nearly as high-energy as an open-call trading floor. The glam lobby—a merging of the building's original 1928 Beaux-Arts decor, contemporary furnishings, and bold neon accents—doubles as a nightclub, pulsing with DJ-spun music and dressed-to-be-noticed young professionals. The 369 rooms provide a retreat of modern comforts, including the signature W Hotel beds (choose from the W Pillow Menu, if you'd like), and offer in-room massages from Bliss Spa. Pets are equally pampered with toys, special beds, and even turndown treats. The W's Whatever/Whenever service grants requests both simple and outrageous. Nibble on small bites in the lobby or the second-level balcony that overlooks it, or try the eclectic small-plates menu at aptly named IPO. Ready to hit the town? Call down for a complimentary chauffeured ride; if you'd like, direct your driver to the equally hip

and happening W Chicago Lakeshore (644 N. Lake Shore Dr., 312-943-9200) to take advantage of the pool, restaurants, and bar there too.

THEWIT HOTEL CHICAGO $$$
201 N. State St.
(312) 467-0200
www.thewithotel.com
With a prime location like theWit's—walkable to the Loop Theatre District, Michigan Avenue, the Chicago Riverwalk, and Loop El stations (double-glazed windows keep train rumbles at bay)—you'd expect something extraordinary. And that's exactly what you get. From Jackie Koo's striking white and glass façade with its startling yellow streak to the seriously modern 2-story glass lobby lit by custom-designed angel-wing chandeliers, theWit succeeds in both style and substance. The 298 rooms and 42 suites blend artistry and geometry with their neat lines and flashes of color. Suites feature fully equipped kitchens, while theSpa rooms indulge with large soaking tubs. Or take advantage of the high-end spa for massages and more. Then head up to 27th-floor all-weather ROOF, named one of the 10 best rooftop bars in the country by USAToday.com. The hotel expresses its own wit in wake-up calls recorded by The Second City actors mimicking famous Chicagoans such as Al Capone. Critically acclaimed Italian hot spot Cibo Matto gives guests a reason to stay in for dinner.

Gold Coast–Old Town

ELYSIAN HOTEL $$$$
11 E. Walton St.
(800) 500-8511, (312) 646-1300
www.elysianhotels.com

ACCOMMODATIONS

From the moment you pull up to its quiet, French-style entranceway set back from the street, you know this is no ordinary city stay. A class act all the way, the elegant 60-story hotel-slash-private residence houses just 10 guestrooms on each of floors 7 through 26 (188 total), ensuring intimacy and a welcoming sense that you're definitely a VIP here. The smallest room is more than 600 square feet, the largest, the 26th-floor, 3,160-square-foot Presidential Suite. Decor mixes cool, contemporary furnishings like white Carrera marble bathrooms and mirrors that double as TVs with the warm comforts of a fireplace (in most rooms), furnished terrace, 460-thread-count Italian linens, and terry bathrobes. Tailor a health club session just for your needs or simply relax in the whirlpool, sauna, or steam room, available in both the men's and women's relaxation lounges. The Michelin two-star-rated RIA is a fine-dining destination all its own, and if you've left your car at home, a chauffer-driven luxury Lexus is at your disposal.

HOTEL INDIGO CHICAGO $$$
1244 N. Dearborn Pkwy.
(866) 521-6950, (312) 787-4980
www.hotelindigo.com
This mid-priced boutique hotel is tucked into the tree-lined streets of the Gold Coast. The 165 rooms and 2-room suites create a kind of Cape Cod beach-house ambience, with bright cheerful colors (think periwinkle blue and carroty orange), hardwood floors, whitewashed furnishings, and photo murals of objects like sea glass on sand or a delicious-looking bunch of blueberries. Even the accessories go beyond the norm, including blue phones, shell-shaped lights, and Krups single-brew coffeemakers.

✳SOFITEL CHICAGO WATER TOWER $$$$
20 E. Chestnut St.
(312) 324-4000
www.sofitelchicagowatertower.com
Slicing through the sky with grace and beauty, this 32-floor prism of glass was designed by renowned French architect Jean-Paul Viguier. Well situated near Gold Coast restaurants and nightlife, as well as steps from Oak Street and Mag Mile shopping, it offers modern luxury accommodations and top-notch service. From the sleek, spacious, couch-filled lobby scented with dramatically displayed fresh flowers to its grand glass staircase and its multilingual concierge staff, the Sofitel aims to impress. Sink into a velvety club chair with a martini at Le Bar or dine at fine-dining Cafe Des Architectes.

THE SUTTON PLACE HOTEL $$$$
21 E. Bellevue Place
(866) 378-8866, (312) 266-2100
www.suttonplace.com
Upscale without being uptight, this independent hotel has received high marks from travelers who appreciate the friendly service. Though they offer complimentary Cadillac rides (by appointment), you probably won't need one with a location within walking distance to some of the Gold Coast's best restaurants and shops. In fact, if you intend to drop some cash at close-by Michigan Avenue or Oak Street shops, ask about the hotel's retail discount program. The 246 rooms, done up in homey neutrals, feature deep soaking tubs, plush robes, and Gilchrist & Soames bath products. On the ground floor, the Whiskey Bar & Grill is a mainstay hot spot from club mogul Rande Gerber (a.k.a. Cindy Crawford's hubby).

THE TALBOTT HOTEL $$$$
20 E. Delaware Place
(800) 825-2688, (312) 944-4970
www.talbotthotel.com

Done up in hunter-green velvet armchairs, fireplace, Oriental rugs, and mahogany-paneled walls, the lobby of this 149-room hotel welcomes with an air of old-fashioned hospitality. Built in 1927, the AAA Four Diamond hotel has also been named by *National Geographic Traveler* magazine as one of its favorite US hotels (just two in Chicago were listed). In the rooms expect classic simplicity, with bonuses like free Wi-Fi, turn-down service, and umbrellas in the closet (how civilized). Belly up to the bar at cozy Basil's, named for Basil Kromelow, the hotel's owner since the early 1960s.

Hyde Park–South of Loop

*ESSEX INN $$$
800 S. Michigan Ave.
(312) 939-2800
www.essexinn.com

Considering the amenities here—free shuttle to the Magnificent Mile and Navy Pier, huge glassed-in 4th-floor indoor pool, free Wi-Fi—this South Loop hotel gives you big bang for your buck. It's also just a block from the famous Buddy Guy's Legends blues club and one of the closest off-site hotels to McCormick Place. All of the 254 brightly decorated rooms and suites include refrigerators (perfect for those dining leftovers), and many have views of downtown Chicago, the lakefront, or Grant Park.

*HILTON CHICAGO HOTEL $$$$
720 S. Michigan Ave.
(312) 922-4400
www.hiltonchicagohotel.com

When this AAA Four Diamond historic hotel across from Grant Park was built in 1927, it ranked as the largest in the world, containing 3,000 rooms, a bowling alley, rooftop miniature golf course, and movie theater. But the Depression took its toll, and in 1942, the US Army bought it for use as barracks. Conrad Hilton purchased it in 1945, then in 1984 closed it for a year to transform it into the grand dame it is today. Spanning an entire city block, it now boasts 1,544 larger rooms (including Executive Floor rooms on floors 23 through 25), a magnificent marble lobby, and classic appointments like cherry furnishings and brass fixtures. The 18,000-square-foot health club boasts Chicago's only indoor hotel running track, plus indoor pool and sundeck. Irish bar Kitty O'Shea's pours pints of Guinness and gets even greener and wilder on St. Patrick's Day. Besides being featured in a slew of movies (notably *The Fugitive* and *My Best Friend's Wedding*), the Hilton also claims to have hosted every US President since opening.

WYNDHAM BLAKE CHICAGO $$$
500 S. Dearborn St.
(312) 986-1234
www.hotelblake.com

The 19th-century former offices of Morton Salt make up part of the home to this historic Printers Row hotel (it was merged with the adjacent Duplicator building in 1987). The classy stay puts you close to the Art Institute, Millennium Park, and State Street shopping and just a few minutes' stroll from the Red Line El. In the 162 guestrooms, chocolate browns and deep reds create a warm feel, while 12-foot ceilings and large windows make it airy and light. Take advantage of complimentary continental breakfast, in-room spa services, and the Zagat-rated

Custom House Tavern for contemporary American cuisine.

Lincoln Park–Lakeview

*BEST WESTERN PLUS HAWTHORNE TERRACE $$
3434 N. Broadway Ave.
(888) 675-2378, (773) 244-3434
www.hawthorneterrace.com

Set back from the street behind a quaint, brick-paved patio, this 83-room Lakeview hotel certainly bests your average Best Western. Meticulously neat rooms come with complimentary bottled water and continental breakfast, free Wi-Fi, and fitness room with therapeutic whirlpool and dry sauna. Its location doesn't hurt either, in the middle of the bustling Boystown hub.

DAYS INN CHICAGO $$
644 W. Diversey Pkwy.
(888) 576-3297, (773) 525-7010
www.daysinnchicago.net

Guests often describe this Lincoln Park hotel as "boutique," and not surprisingly so. Though the 133 rooms (including 45 business class) are simple, they come with plushly covered beds, free Wi-Fi, free access to the around-the-corner Bally's Total Fitness, and complimentary deluxe breakfast (think fresh-squeezed juice, bagels, and waffles). Once known as the "rock and roll Days Inn" for its many pre-fame musical guests—everyone from Radiohead to Alanis Morissette to Gregg Allman—it still rocks. Case in point: awards like Days Inn Hotel of the Year, general manager of the year, and several awards for quality. Plus, check out the fun photo-op with a Chicago "Cows on Parade" cow in the entrance hallway.

MAJESTIC HOTEL $$
528 W. Brompton St.
(800) 727-5108, (773) 404-3499
www.majestic-chicago.com

You're part of the neighborhood at this 1920s-built hotel along a quiet Lakeview street, and just a short walk to Lake Michigan. The lobby, complete with gas fireplace, gives you a sense of the upscale, old-English charm you'll also find in the 52 rooms. If you can, it's worth splurging for a larger room with sunny sitting area. Not all is old-fashioned, though: Roomlinx Interactive TV is offered, as well as passes to the nearby Fitness Formula health club. Complimentary continental breakfast, coffee and tea service, and afternoon cookies too. The Majestic's nearby sister hotels are similar in style: the City Suites (933 W. Belmont Ave., 800-248-9108) and Willows (555 W. Surf St., 800-787-3108).

Magnificent Mile

AFFINIA CHICAGO $$$
166 E. Superior St.
(866) 246-2203, (312) 787-6000
www.affinia.com

Feather and down? Built-in speakers? Or magnetic therapy? They're three of the six pillow options you can select from at this hip, custom-happy 215-room hotel. Other personalizations include your choice of complimentary care package such as the "Walking Tour Kit" with music-loaded iPod Shuffle, pedometer, towel, and more; the "BYOB Kit," stocked with a wine carrier, coupon for a local wine shop, and picnic blanket; and one that's family-focused including board games and a kids' digital camera. Pet-friendly packages include a visit from a pet psychic, travel bowl, pet taxi, and treats. Treat yourself at *Top Chef Masters* winner Marcus Samuelsson's

C-House restaurant or make your way up to the 29th-floor C-View lounge where the modish outdoor terrace and indoor lounge may just outdo the views of the surrounding cityscape.

THE ALLERTON HOTEL $$
701 N. Michigan Ave.
(877) 701-8111, (312) 440-1500
www.theallertonhotel.com
You can't miss the iconic "Tip Top Tap" sign on the upper stories of this 443-room national landmark hotel built in 1924 in Northern Italian Renaissance architecture. The sign harkens back to the 1940s and '50s when the hotel housed a fashionable lounge of the same name. Now, since a recent multimillion-dollar renovation, the Tip Top Tap offers ballroom space, and the hotel's updated rooms feature a comfortably sophisticated look.

THE AVENUE CROWNE PLAZA CHICAGO $$$
160 E. Huron St.
(877) 283-5110, (312) 787-2900
www.avenuehotelchicago.com
Just a half a block from Michigan Avenue shopping and plenty of public transportation, this high-rise hotel stresses geniality among its staff. Of the 350 rooms, 150 are suites, making this a practical option for families and business travelers. Kid-friendly rooms feature Wii video games, adorable bedding, children's books and bath products, bean bag chairs, stuffed animals, and games. For work on the go: free in-room Wi-Fi, and kitted-out Tech Rooms with iMacs. Signature zebra-print chairs add a playful flair to otherwise standard rooms (higher-priced rooms pair matching zebra robes), while rain showerheads, organic toiletries, and optional

in-room spa treatments make chilling easier. Views come easy at the outdoor pool or at the 40th-floor indoor Sky Lounge that's open for buffet breakfast. On the street level, the adjoining Elephant & Castle bar and restaurant pours 26 beers on tap in a heavy-on-the-wood English pub-style ambience.

i Most Chicago hotels provide concierge services. They can often help you get same-day reservations for popular restaurants or VIP status at no-reservations eateries; they can secure theater tickets, arrange tours, provide you with information, maps, discounts to shops, and more. Just ask.

CHICAGO MARRIOTT DOWNTOWN MAGNIFICENT MILE $$$$
540 N. Michigan Ave.
(800) 228-9290, (312) 836-0100
www.chicagomarriottdowntown.com
An attention-grabbing vertical cone of color rocketing out of a circular bar is the focal point of this hotel's vast, glittering lobby. It's also a sign of the re-energizing of this conveniently located, convention-friendly hotel. Some of the 1,173 stylish rooms offer windows that open, others spectacular views of the Mag Mile below.

CONRAD CHICAGO $$$
521 N. Rush St.
(312) 645-1500
www.conradchicago.com
This swanky, modern hotel features enclosed access to the upscale Shops at North Bridge, whose chi-chi retail names include Nordstrom, Hugo Boss, Louis Vuitton, and Stuart Weitzman. Plus, each of the 311 rooms and suites provides little luxuries like a bathrobe and slippers, 42-inch flat screen TV, Bose

sound system, and choice of pillows. Take over the Presidential Suite and bask in 2,000 square feet with a secluded terrace overlooking the Magnificent Mile. The original 1928 building that stood here was the Midwest headquarters for McGraw-Hill Publishing Company; it was torn down in the 1990s, but the historic façade was dismantled and rebuilt for the new structure, earning it Chicago landmark status for its Art Deco style and its fascinating exterior sculpture by late Chicago artist Gwen Lux.

THE DRAKE HOTEL $$$$
140 E. Walton Place
(800) 553-7253, (312) 787-2200
www.thedrakehotel.com

Old-fashioned elegance doesn't get any better than at this storied landmark hotel. Just a step inside is like a step back in time. After all, its guest list has included Queen Elizabeth, Princess Diana, and Queen Beatrix of the Netherlands. Some of its 535 rooms run on the small side, so we suggest reviewing square-footage online and requesting the roomiest room you can, or one with such a stunning Lake Michigan view that you won't mind the tight quarters. Presented in 1920 by brothers John and Tracy Drake, the hotel was always meant to be a star, the first so-called "urban resort"—and it remains as such. Its nautical-themed fine-dining Cape Cod Room still ranks high among seafood lovers (see if you can make out Marilyn Monroe's initials etched into the wood bar), while the Coq d'Or, which opened a day after the repeal of Prohibition, is world-famous for its Bookbinder soup. The lovely, tropical Palm Court, with its live harp music, is the perfect setting for finger sandwiches and scones during its afternoon tea. What a bonus that this Hilton hotel happens to also be at the northern tip of Mag Mile shopping and across from Oak Street beach.

*FOUR SEASONS HOTEL CHICAGO $$$$
120 E. Delaware Place
(312) 280-8800
www.fourseasons.com/chicagofs

This graciously appointed hotel is the cream of the crop, banking on sophisticated hospitality, but steering far clear of stuffy. Staff members smile as they open doors for you, the sun-filled Roman-themed pool stocks swim noodles and kickboards for kids, there are Radio Flyer wagons for taking kids around town, and guests can ring up the Ice Cream Man for in-room sundaes (for romance-seekers, there's a Martini Man and Butler of Bubbly too). The 345 rooms and suites practically glimmer with polished marble, bright-white linens, and huge picture windows looking from its guestroom floors 30 through 46 (it's in the seventh-tallest building in Chicago) down onto the city, the lake, and the Mag Mile. For an elegant yet approachable meal, don't leave—taste award-winning local chef Kevin Hickey's take on American cuisine with an eye for locally sourced ingredients, including herbs from the hotel's own garden.

INTERCONTINENTAL CHICAGO $$$$
505 N. Michigan Ave.
(800) 628-2112
www.icchicagohotel.com

Worth a peek even if you don't stay here, this historic 792-room hotel was built in 1929 for the Shriners men's association as their luxury Medinah Athletic Club, but closed in 1934 due to the stock-market crash. After a major renovation effort that involved the restoration consultant for the Sistine Chapel, the hotel opened in 1990 and then, in

2001, debuted its ornate mosaic tile–floored, 4-story lobby—the only hotel with a front entrance directly opening to the Magnificent Mile. Recalling the opulence of its initial life are spaces like the themed banquet rooms—King Arthur Foyer and Court, the decadent Louis XVI–style Renaissance Room, the Grand Ballroom (boasting North America's largest Baccarat crystal chandelier)—as well as the Spanish Tea Court with its Majolica tile–lined fountain, and the original junior Olympic-size pool where late *Tarzan* movie star Johnny Weissmuller once trained. Recently redone rooms sometimes reveal their age in their odd sizes and shapes, but they convey a welcoming, classic charm and include free access to that pool (though there's a fee for use of the accompanying fitness center).

THE JAMES HOTEL $$$$
55 E. Ontario St.
(877) 526-3755, (312) 337-1000
www.jameshotels.com

Sleek and artsy meet warm and welcoming at this 297-room hotel (106 suites) just off North Michigan Avenue shopping. A sense of urban chic describes the guestrooms, with ambient lighting, slate tile in the bathrooms, and understated decor. Guests are privy to complimentary Wi-Fi, complimentary luxury car service, pampering at the onsite Spa by Asha, and even a guided city running tour that highlights architecture and public art. Take time as you check in to browse the eclectic modern art, including a rotating gallery of local artists' works in the business lounge. Popular with an after-work crowd, the JBar gets creative with its cocktails, while dry-aged meats are the focus at award-winning chef David Burke's Primehouse.

MILLENNIUM KNICKERBOCKER
   HOTEL $$$$
163 E. Walton Place
(312) 751-8100
www.knickerbockerhotel.com

Some history and intrigue come with a stay here. Opened in 1927 as the Davis Hotel, its rumored gangster connections gained credence during a 1980s renovation that uncovered a secret door and staircase. Its grand Crystal Ballroom is still a knockout with a 25-foot-high domed ceiling and original built-in illuminated dance floor. Guests enter through a lofty 2-story lobby and are just a block from Lake Michigan and down the street from Mag Mile shops and the John Hancock Center. Petite rooms include 40-inch flat-screen TVs and posh bedding.

OMNI CHICAGO HOTEL $$$$
676 N. Michigan Ave.
(800) 843-6664, (312) 944-6664
www.omnihotels.com

All 347 rooms in this Magnificent Mile hotel are suites, making family stays particularly comfortable. Plus, kids get treated to games and books, a backpack, a list of local family attractions, and a safety and first-aid kit. Sign up for the free guest loyalty program to take advantage of perks like free in-room Wi-Fi, newspaper delivery, and complimentary morning beverage. The 676 Restaurant & Bar serves breakfast, lunch, and dinner with built-in views of the bustle below. While not all rooms offer such spectacular views, you can request one or, when weather permits, just take it all in on the 5th-floor outdoor deck, right off the indoor pool.

PARK HYATT CHICAGO $$$$
800 N. Michigan Ave.
(800) 778-7477, (312) 335-1234
www.parkchicago.hyatt.com

Soaring above the Historic Water Tower, this haute hotel's slim, 68-story building houses guestrooms on 18 of its floors and private luxury residences on the others. The hotel impresses with unpretentious yet spot-on service, 198 handsomely outfitted rooms (13 suites), and museum-quality artwork throughout (think fossil specimens, framed art photography, and glass ceiling sculptures by Dale Chihuly). The award-winning and recently revamped NoMI restaurant stuns with its Mag Mile panorama and its artfully presented American contemporary cuisine. Most rooms reward guests with magnificent views, many with balconies or window seats. Allergy-prone? Opt for a hypo-allergenic room. Smokers are welcome in the new continuously air-filtered rooms. In warm weather, grab a complimentary bike (replete with helmet, lock, bottled water, and bike map) and hit the town on two wheels.

✳PENINSULA CHICAGO $$$$
108 E. Superior St.
(312) 337-2888
www.peninsula.com/chicago

Celebrating its 10th anniversary of making a fuss over every guest, this award-winning, crème de la crème hotel features 339 rooms (83 suites) with superior furnishings and a classy feel. At the highest level, the Peninsula Suite boosts the brilliance with a wrap-around terrace and outdoor whirlpool. Dining is also of the highest caliber. The Lobby restaurant, with its awesome 20-foot-high windows, offers iPads for single diners, as well as a 3-course prix-fixe lunch, perfect for busy VIPs. Its stunning spa treats mind and body and was a key factor to the Peninsula's ranking by *Health* magazine as America's Healthiest Hotel.

RITZ-CARLTON CHICAGO $$$$
160 E. Pearson St.
(312) 266-1000
www.fourseasons.com/chicagorc

Consider yourself royalty at this exquisite Four Seasons–owned Ritz-Carlton located on the upper floors of Michigan Avenue's prime shopping destination, Water Tower Place. A 2010 extreme makeover gave the spacious, 12th-floor lobby a luxe look and an airy new raved-about restaurant, deca. Of the 434 rooms (91 suites) on floors 15 to 30, even the most economical have city or Lake Michigan vistas that wow, and shiny marble bathrooms. Cool blues and warm browns complement a mix of contemporary and classic furnishings. When only top-shelf will do, it has to be the Presidential Suite, a 2-story wonder separated by spiral staircase and lit by soaring windows; 24-hour personal assistant, Rolls-Royce transportation, and daily 90-minute massage all included. No matter your means, you can take advantage of the state-of-the-art fitness facilities and bright indoor pool. Pint-sized travelers get wide-eyed when they see their in-room cookies and juice, coloring books, and kiddie bath products. Free cookie-making in the kitchen is also available, and the new roving Candy Man gets grown-ups giddy too, selling candy by the pound right at your hotel door.

TREMONT HOTEL $$-$$$
100 E. Chestnut St.
(312) 751-1900
www.tremontchicago.com

Personalized attention makes up for a lack of flashy amenities (except for free Wi-Fi) at this charming hotel just off the hustle and bustle of North Michigan Avenue and near Rush Street nightlife. Of the 130 rooms and suites, corner rooms tend to be larger, so snatch one if you can; for long-term stays, the next-door Tremont House equips you with full kitchens. Let the chefs do the cooking at Mike Ditka's, a manly man's restaurant with requisite giant steaks and chops in a sports-themed setting.

WHITEHALL HOTEL $$$
105 E. Delaware Place
(800) 948-4255, (312) 944-6300
www.thewhitehallhotel.com

Like its nearby neighbor, the Tremont Hotel, this vintage boutique hotel stays true to its old-fashioned roots. Built in the 1920s as elegant apartments, it was converted to a hotel in the 1950s and has been restored and updated several times since. Guests over the years included Katharine Hepburn, Robert Redford, and the Beatles. It now comprises 222 rooms that embody a slower-paced grace and sensibility than many modern hotels (check out the mosaic tile in the bathrooms—it's all hand-laid). Higher-end rooms and suites are decked out with restored antique mahogany and offer turndown service.

River North

AMALFI HOTEL $$$
20 W. Kinzie St.
(312) 395-9000
www.amalfihotelchicago.com

Consistently rated high by guests for its friendliness and proximity to shopping, dining, and the Merchandise Mart, the recently redecorated Amalfi brings the feel of the eponymous Italian coast to its spaces with rich sunset-y hues of gold, scarlet, and orange. Check-in is first-class, as you're seated at an individual desk with your "Experience Designer," who helps you plan your stay. Show up for the evening reception with Italian hors d'oeuvres and open premium bar (the signature Amalfitini is a doozy with vodka, limoncello, peach schnapps, and triple sec). The 215 rooms and suites all include free Wi-Fi, bathrooms with dual showerheads and Aveda products, and complimentary continental breakfast. Corner suites impress with curved glass windows. Head down to the adjacent Keefer's for dinner or get it delivered by local favorite Harry Caray's Italian Steakhouse.

DANA HOTEL & SPA $$$$
660 N. State St.
(888) 301-3262, (312) 202-6000
www.danahotelandspa.com

Urban-chic. Ultramodern. Super-cool. Just a few phrases that begin to describe this 26-story, 216-room boutique hotel in River North, within walking distance to nightclubs, art galleries, and restaurants. The dazzling façade of glass and aluminum has its modest side too—a lean footprint that allows for only about 5,700 square feet per floor. It's rare to see hardwood floors in a hotel room, but that's what you get here—natural, sustainable woods to be sure—accompanied by exposed concrete ceilings and floor-to-ceiling windows with phenomenally urban bird's-eye views. Rain-shower bath fixtures, bathrobes and slippers, free Wi-Fi, and, in many rooms, private balconies, round out the upscale offerings. Feeling the energy from the 26th floor? Head up to mingle with Chicago's high-heeled set at the indoor-outdoor Vertigo Sky Lounge, which keeps things hot year-round with its ice bar (in cold months, feel free to use the provided blankets or snuggle by the fireplace). Dining

(◉) Close-up

Q&A with a Concierge

Concierges in Chicago comprise a fairly tight-knit group of professionals. Some of them have served at the same hotel for decades, including Jon Winke, who started working at the Ritz-Carlton in 1975 at the age of 20.

Insiders' Guide: What drew you to the career of concierge?

Jon Winke: I started as a bellman, working under the supervision of a concierge. I saw how he was able to make a difference in our guests' stay and thought I could also be an ambassador to our hotel and the city of Chicago. The experience I received from my honeymoon stay at our hotel in San Francisco convinced me that this is what I wanted to do for my career. . . . This Ritz-Carlton is owned and managed by Four Seasons Hotels, which just celebrated its 50th birthday in March 2011. I am the longest-termed employee at The Ritz, having worked here for over 35 years. The hotel celebrated my 35th anniversary with a Jon Winke Day.

IG: What keeps you at the job?

Winke: I can help make our guests' dreams come true. I enjoy the daily challenges it brings; it gets my adrenaline going when a guest says, "I know you probably won't be able to do this . . ." The concierge motto is: "As long as it is legal and moral, we can do it." My motto is: "If you have an impossible request, give me a few minutes. If you need a miracle, it may take a little longer."

IG: What is one of your best memories from working at the Ritz-Carlton?

Winke: I will never forget being able to throw a first pitch from the mound at Wrigley Field before a Cubs game when I was president of the Chicago Hotel Concierge Association. I have been lucky enough to have the hotel's support in furthering my career as a Les Clefs d'Or member (www.lcdusa.org) by attending concierge meetings as far away as Spain and Rio de Janeiro.

IG: What have been some of the most unusual requests you have gotten over the years?

Winke: Before competing against the Chicago Bulls, the New York Knicks decided one Saturday that they needed a pre-game practice before they played the Bulls Sunday afternoon. They asked me if they could use the hotel's ballroom as their practice court. With the help of the Ritz-Carlton's banquet staff, I worked overnight to break down a wedding that had been held in the ballroom, and then gave the Knicks masking tape to create a makeshift court on the ballroom carpet. The Bulls

is stylish too at aja, serving Asian-influenced seasonal cuisine.

**EMBASSY SUITES CHICAGO–
DOWNTOWN/LAKEFRONT** $$$
511 N. Columbus Dr.
(312) 836-5900
www.chicagoembassy.com

One of the greatest appeals of this 455-room all-suite hotel is its complimentary cooked-to-order hot breakfast. But that doesn't diminish its other pros: close to Navy Pier, onsite 21-screen movie theater, indoor pool, and convenient parking garage. Each 2-room suite overlooks the 11-story, skylit atrium and offers lake or city views.

beat them anyway. Another time, a guest wanted to see the premiere of a movie, but he didn't want anyone sitting within three rows of him. I rallied hotel staff members to go to the theater and buy enough tickets to block off several rows. Then, after the movie the guest asked for two of every item on the McDonald's menu to be delivered to his suite.

IG: What are some of your favorite places to go in the city?

Winke: a) Wrigley Field or a Rooftop across from Wrigley; b) Navy Pier (IMAX Theater, Harry Caray's Tavern, Riva, fireworks in summer on Wednesday and Saturday, boat rides, Chicago Children's Museum); c) The Second City is always good for an evening of laughs; d) Millennium Park for free concerts and reflecting on life at "The Bean"; e) Bike riding on the lakefront path; f) The architectural boat cruise is my favorite summer recommendation for guests; and g) Segway tours are a fun way to learn about the city.

IG: What do you love about Chicago?

Winke: Being born and raised in Chicagoland, I echo Sammy Cahn's song made famous by Frank Sinatra "My Kind of Town (Chicago Is)." I love the easy access in getting around Chicago, whether using public transportation or walking. The lakefront is my favorite place, from the biking and jogging paths up north to Oak Street Beach, Navy Pier, Museum Campus, Soldier Field, McCormick Place, and the Museum of Science & Industry. The neighborhoods, culture, theater, restaurants, shopping, nightlife, and sports teams make Chicago a city of epic proportions. It is virtually impossible to get to know the whole Chicago experience in one trip, so it's easy to see why so many visitors keep coming back for more.

IG: Do you have any tips for visitors on how to get the most out of their Chicago trip?

Winke: Plan ahead: Call your hotel concierge in advance to help plan out your itinerary and do research on the Internet. Your concierge can assist in the one thing you might not have enough of: Time! For instance, we have pre-purchased tickets to the major museums and sights in Chicago, so our guests are able to bypass long lines and get immediate access with our VIP tickets. We also have priority seating passes to some restaurants that do not take reservations, and we have contacts we can call to get guests into restaurants that say they're booked. The show or sports event that you want to see might be sold out, but concierges have connections to get premium tickets in most cases.

HOLIDAY INN CHICAGO MART PLAZA   **$$$**
350 W. Mart Center Dr.
(800) 465-4329, (312) 836-5000
www.martplaza.com
Certainly the closest beds when you've got business at the adjacent Merchandise Mart, this 521-room chain is far from just convenient. Wi-Fi is free and so are the surprisingly stunning city panoramas. The 15th-floor atrium lobby is an inviting space to lounge, with its earthy tones, plenty of comfy seating, and a soothing water wall. The trendy Cityscape bar takes full advantage of the views, while the pleasant ItaliAsia restaurant goes above typical hotel dining. A variety of room and suite sizes are available, culminating in the duplex suite, with full living room

and dining room. Families will appreciate the 16th-floor indoor, skylit pool.

HOTEL FELIX $$$
111 W. Huron St.
(877) 848-4040, (312) 447-3440
www.hotelfelixchicago.com

Reduce your carbon travel-print at this eco-friendly, 12-story boutique hotel, a sleek, modern contrast to its preserved 1926 façade. Things like recycled flooring in the fitness room, bamboo floors in the full-service spa, florescent lighting throughout, organic coffee served in the lobby, and motion-sensored heating, ventilation and air conditioning in the 225 guestrooms. Though the sepia-toned rooms are small, they offer welcome amenities like free Wi-Fi, bathrobes, and luxurious bedding. Upscale American restaurant Elate features seasonal and local produce.

PALOMAR CHICAGO $$$$
505 N. State St.
(877) 731-0505, (312) 755-9703
www.hotelpalomar-chicago.com

Don't call it a lobby; the Palomar, like other Kimpton boutique properties, has a "living room." And this one is all whites and golds and decidedly warm and inviting. Here, guests gather in the evening to sip on complimentary organic wines by the fireplace, grab a cup of fair-trade coffee in the morning, or simply settle into one of many comfy-chic couches. In the 261 guestrooms (23 suites), the style is comfortably modern, with framed original artwork depicting Chicago's 1893 World's Columbian Exposition, expansive windows, deep soaking tubs, animal-print bathrobes (for kids too), and a smart economy of space that includes sliding bathroom doors (a little cumbersome

for kids, so watch out). The "Forgot it? We've got it!" program sends up necessities you left behind, while the workout channel offers personalized yoga and Pilates (yoga kits available). Head to the 17th-floor indoor pool to splash around or take in some sunshine and city views on the outdoor deck. A green roof exemplifies the hotel's commitment to earth-friendliness, and guests arriving in hybrid vehicles receive 25 percent off parking. The River North location means a multitude of restaurants are within walking distance, but you could also stay for chef Heather Terhune's New American cuisine at the Palomar's lovely Sable Kitchen & Bar.

SAX CHICAGO $$–$$$
333 N. Dearborn St.
(312) 245-0333
www.thompsonhotels.com

In a hotel whose corporate "manifesto" states that it's inspired by the likes of Julie Christie, Steve McQueen, and Pablo Picasso, it's no surprise that your stay includes a little sexy drama, a little defiance, and plenty of creativity. Located in the Marina City complex—across from the House of Blues music venue—this eclectic 353-room hotel might offer typical boons like bathrobes and 300-thread-count linens, but it also features damask prints, gourmet goodies in the minibar, and a hot social scene in the lobby's Crimson Lounge. And no matter that there's no in-house restaurant: The adjacent Bin 36 Restaurant and Wine Cellar and across-the-parking-lot Smith & Wollensky Steak House do just fine, thank you. Plus, the House of Blues also serves Southern cooking that's pretty good, along with a don't-miss Gospel Brunch.

SHERATON CHICAGO HOTEL & TOWERS $$$

301 E. North Water St.
(877) 866-9214, (312) 464-1000
www.sheratonchicago.com

Although this flagship hotel along the Chicago River often hosts conventions that can easily fill every one of its 1,209 guestrooms (40 suites) and its 120,000 square feet of meeting space (including the largest hotel ballroom in the Midwest), it doesn't feel impersonal. In fact, the blissful beds alone make it a welcome retreat. Lake Michigan, Chicago River, or city sights compensate for otherwise vanilla rooms, and walkability to Navy Pier, the Mag Mile, and Millennium Park are a bonus. For business travelers, the enormous Presidential Suites include a conference table and iMac with printer. All guests have free use of the indoor heated pool, though the fitness center requires a fee. Dine at Shula's Steak House, whose namesake Don Shula coached the 1972 Miami Dolphins' undefeated season (menus are hand-painted on official NFL footballs). For fancy cocktails in a swanky setting, head over to Chi Bar, designed by Jeffrey Beers, whose other projects include the Cove Atlantis in Paradise Island and Fontainebleau in Miami Beach.

TRUMP INTERNATIONAL HOTEL & TOWER $$$$

401 N. Wabash Ave.
(877) 458-7867, (312) 588-8000
www.trumpchicagohotel.com

Eschewing the blinding glow of gold that Donald Trump has embraced in the past, his Chicago River–front hotel and residential tower goes for a more sleek, modern, and mature design. That's not to say there isn't some flash here—after all, it's a shimmering 92-story glass and steel building, the third-tallest in Chicago. Plus, it recently received AAA Five-Diamond status (less than 1 percent of hotels in the world meet these top-notch standards). Its 354 guestrooms, suites, and signature Spa Rooms fill floors 14 through 27 and start at a nearly unheard-of 600 square feet. Amid subtle grays, tans, and muted purples, rooms feature 10-foot-high windows that look out to the river, city skyline, Wrigley Building, and Lake Michigan. All rooms have full kitchens or kitchenettes, and suites add fireplaces. Let executive chef Frank Brunacci do the cooking at the impeccable Sixteen restaurant. Come summer, get those 16th-floor views alfresco with a cocktail at the spacious Terrace at Trump. Or sip like a star in the chicest of settings at Rebar. Though upscale, Trump caters equally to little ones, with its free Trump Kids program, offering kiddie cocktails, PlayStation games, chocolate chip cookies, and personalized business cards for your Trumps-in-training.

WESTIN CHICAGO RIVER NORTH $$

320 N. Dearborn St.
(312) 744-1900
www.westinchicago.com

A decidedly '80s exterior belies the thoroughly modern interior and resoundingly friendly guest service of this 424-room hotel close to the Loop and a hop, skip, and jump from Michigan Avenue shopping. Suites, on levels 18 through 20, offer access to the Executive Lounge, garnering complimentary extras like iMac computers and continental breakfast. Three in-house restaurants include a branch of Chicago's beloved Kamehachi Sushi Bar, surrounded by the Japanese-inspired Hana Lounge.

ACCOMMODATIONS

O'Hare Airport Area

ALOFT CHICAGO O'HARE   **$**
9700 Balmoral Ave., Rosemont
(847) 671-4444
www.aloftchicagoohare.com
Way more than just an airport hotel, this affordable stay punches things up with vibrant colors and alternative soundtrack, as well as 9-foot ceilings and huge windows in the 251 uncluttered, urban-inspired rooms. A quick shuttle ride from O'Hare and within walking distance of the Stephens Convention Center, it also offers free Wi-Fi, 42-inch TVs, and Bliss Spa products. The airy lobby encompasses Re:mix lounge with its hipster vibe and pool table; Re:fuel where you can grab from the "snack-attack" menu; and the W xyz bar for signature drinks like the Razzle Dazzle and the Rock & Republic. The natural light–filled indoor pool area connects to the 24-hour fitness facility (you can download a portable workout program before you get there).

CHICAGO MARRIOTT O'HARE   **$**
8535 W. Higgins Rd.
(773) 693-4444
www.marriott.com
Expect upstanding Marriott service at this no-frills business- and event-friendly hotel just a block from the Blue Line El station. Sound-resistant, floor-to-ceiling windows in the 681 guestrooms keep airport noise at a minimum, while bonus features include an indoor-outdoor pool, free O'Hare shuttle, modern fitness room, and inexpensive breakfasts.

**CROWNE PLAZA CHICAGO O'HARE
   HOTEL & CONFERENCE CENTER**   **$**
5440 N. River Rd., Rosemont
(866) 242-1055, (847) 671-6350
www.crowneplazaohare.com
The 503 rooms of this airport hotel, complete with sunlit indoor pool, were recently updated to be more stylish (a little gold, a little teal), more comfortable (7 layers of bedding), and more eco-friendly (CFL light bulbs, high-efficiency plumbing). Light sleeper? Put away the pills and pick up the provided sleep mask, lavender spray, and sleepytime CD. Or check into the 10th floor, an ultimate quiet zone—don't worry, you'll get a guaranteed wake-up call. Roomlinx rooms are totally teched-out, and for a small upcharge, you can also take advantage of the Executive Club Lounge with complimentary continental breakfast, evening snacks and beverages, and free Wi-Fi.

INNS & BED-AND-BREAKFASTS

FLEMISH HOUSE OF CHICAGO   **$$**
68 E. Cedar St.
(312) 664-9981
www.innchicago.com
Live like the old-money rich in this historic Gold Coast greystone. Built in 1892 as a single-family row house—the name comes from its Flemish Revival–style design—it was divided into apartments in the mid-20th century. In 1997, it was lovingly transformed into this charming 7-room inn by hosts Mike Maczka and Tom Warnke, who also happen to live in the 4-story building, close to Oak Street and Michigan Avenue shopping, and Rush and Division Streets nightlife. Unlike typical bed and breakfasts, the Flemish house doesn't have a common eating area. Instead, Maczka and Warnke stock guests' refrigerators with all the fixings needed for a lovely breakfast in your own apartment-style suite, each with complete kitchen setup and full bathroom. Personal touches from the hosts—like handwritten notes, candles in

your room, and a binder full of suggested area activities—make you feel right at home. Children must be school age and older.

Hostelling International

The only Hostelling International facility in Chicago is the **J. Ira and Nicki Harris Family Hostel,** a budget-friendly option for travelers who don't mind bunk beds and communal living. The 500-guest, all-ages facility (under 18 must be accompanied by an adult) is a popular choice for foreign visitors, though half the guests come from around the country. In a safe area of downtown, within walking distance to Millennium Park and easily accessed by El, its single-sex rooms accommodate 6 to 10 people and most have showers and restrooms. Your rate also includes free continental breakfasts, free Wi-Fi in the spacious family room-like lobby, access to the community kitchen and dining area, billiards, videos, and table tennis. 24 E. Congress Pkwy., (312) 360-0300, www.hichicago.org.

HOUSE OF TWO URNS   **$$**
1239 N. Greenview Ave.
(773) 235-1408
www.twourns.com
Claiming status as the longest-running bed and breakfast in Chicago (open since 1991), this Wicker Park spot offers a range of accommodations in its 9 units, from the room large enough for a family to the petite-sized Alice's

Room, perfect for a solo traveler. Some rooms have Jacuzzi tubs, four include fireplaces, and all are sweetly furnished with antiques. The building itself is a vintage relic, a 1912 brownstone that was once a Polish bakery. Owner-artist Kapra Fleming took the name from the twin concrete urns that adorn the rooftop, as well as original stained glass urns in the windows. Fleming and her artist husband Miguel now operate the inn, which showcases Miguel's own works for sale in the gift shop. Rates include a full breakfast with options such as fresh-baked muffins, raisin bread French toast, and homemade jam made from berries picked in the Two Urns garden. Free Wi-Fi and access to a seasonal rooftop patio too. Also free parking.

NINA'S B&B   **$–$$**
1303 W. Winona St.
(773) 878-1252
www.ninasbedndbreakfast.com
The white picket fence around this Victorian house clues you in to the homey hospitality you'll get at this 2-room inn, tucked away along a tree-lined block in the vibrant Andersonville neighborhood. Specializing in accommodations for women, particularly lesbian visitors, Nina's motto is "For Women by Women." Brightly lit rooms lean toward the chic-modern side, both with private bathrooms, off-street parking, and private entrance.

ROSCOE VILLAGE GUESTHOUSE   **$$$**
2104 W. Roscoe
(773) 633-3567
www.roscoevillageguesthouse.com
These beautifully decorated condo-type suites located close to El stops in Roscoe Village (as well as Lincoln Park and Old Town) create a comfortable home base to explore

the city. The units can typically accommodate up to 8 guests and feature showplace-
like furnishings including cherry cabinets,
stainless steel kitchen appliances, granite
countertops, hardwood floors, fireplaces,
hot tubs, and high-end bathroom fixtures.
Renting all the Roscoe Village Guesthouses
means a gathering of up to 80 people can
stay.

WHEELER MANSION   **$$$$**
2020 S. Calumet Ave.
(312) 945-2020
www.wheelermansion.com
Gold-framed paintings, silk curtains, and
antique vanities and nightstands. These are
perfectly fitting for the Italianate architecture
of this elegant National Landmark treasure, a
survivor of the 1871 Chicago Fire named a
top restoration on HGTV. After various uses,
including as a distribution warehouse for the
Murphy Butter and Egg Company, the mansion was narrowly saved from the wrecking
ball. It opened in 1999 as this unique lodging option, just two blocks from McCormick Place. All 11 rooms (including 4 suites)
include private bathrooms (suites have gas
fireplaces) and come with buffet breakfast in
the traditional dining room.

RESTAURANTS

Chicago's famed food classics always score high with diners: deep-dish pizza, big juicy steaks, drippy Italian beef, and topping-heaped Chicago-style hot dogs (some estimates put the number of hot dog stands alone at around 3,000). But there is oh so much more gastronomic goodness to this City of Big Shoulders. In fact, there are so many restaurants here—more than 7,300—that Chicago could just as fittingly be called the City of Big Appetites.

And it's been that way pretty much since the city started taking shape in the early 19th century. As the city swelled with both residents and visitors, so did a natural need for eating establishments. The Loop business district became a melting pot of cuisines and the place where quick-serve lunches and cafeterias first became popular, while menus throughout the neighborhoods reflected the home countries of the immigrant populations who landed there. Fortunately for adventurous diners, communities in every area of the city continue to be hidden gems chock-full of interesting restaurants, from Indian in West Rogers Park to Vietnamese in Uptown and inventive American in Bucktown.

One thing has changed over the years, and that is the sophistication level of Chicago chefs and their restaurants—their light has continued to shine brighter and has earned attention of food aficionados across the globe. We can now happily crow about two chefs in particular who have received the Outstanding Chef Award from the James Beard Foundation (a.k.a. the Oscars of the dining world)—Rick Bayless of Topolobampo, Frontera Grill, and XOCO; and Grant Achatz of Alinea, a destination that has also achieved a rare AAA Five-Diamond status. Adding to the award-winning roster: Richard Melman, head of the hugely successful (and amazingly delicious) Lettuce Entertain You Enterprises restaurant conglomerate, who won the 2011 James Beard award for Outstanding Restaurateur, a category only in existence since 2005. In another newish category, the Best Chef: Great Lakes, a Chicago chef has won 3 out of its 5 years; and of the James Beard Best Chef: Midwest title, 11 of the 21 awards have been claimed by Chicago chefs.

The accolades don't mean much, though, unless these chefs have got the chow to back it up—and they undeniably do. While our list doesn't come close to covering it all (let us know if your favorite isn't included here), we've tried to choose restaurants that span the spectrum of food types, location, and price. You'll find some of the city's tried-and-true taste sensations, as well as its more eclectic and ethnic offerings, and we encourage you to try a little of both.

OVERVIEW

The chapter organizes restaurants by type of cuisine, with neighborhoods typically mentioned within the text. All restaurants accept major credit cards, unless noted otherwise. As is the law in Chicago, all restaurants prohibit smoking inside and within 15 feet of any entrance, exit, or window that opens.

Price Code

The following price code represents the average price of two dinner entrees, not including drinks, appetizers, dessert, tax, or tip. For restaurants that serve meals other than dinner, figure on prices being up to 20 percent less, although some restaurants do not change their prices at all for lunch. Also, note that restaurant tax in Chicago is 10 percent or 11 percent, depending on whether the restaurant is considered downtown or just in the city. It's customary to tip 15 percent to 20 percent on the pre-tax total of your bill.

$.................. **Less than $30**
$$ .... **$30 to $50**
$$$ .... **$50 to $70**
$$$$ .... **More than $70**

Del Seoul, Lincoln Park, Korean, $, 101

DMK Burger, Lincoln Park, Burgers, Hot Dogs & Sandwiches, $, 70

Edwardo's, Gold Coast, Deep Dish Pizza, $, 85

Epic Burger, South Loop/ Lincoln Park, Burgers, Hot Dogs & Sandwiches, $, 70

Fat Willy's Rib Shack, Logan Square, Classic American & Southern, $$, 73

Fritz Pastry, Lincoln Park, Bakeries & Dessert, $, 65

Frontera Grill, River North, Mexican, $$–$$$, 105

The Gage, Loop, Contemporary American, $$$, 78

Gemini Bistro, Lincoln Park, Contemporary American, $$, 78

Gene & Georgetti, River North, Steakhouses, $$$, 109

Gibsons Bar & Steakhouse, Gold Coast, Steakhouses, $$$$, 109

Gilt Bar, River North, Contemporary American, $$, 79

Gino's East, Streeterville, Deep Dish Pizza, $, 85

Giordano's, River North, Deep Dish Pizza, $, 85

The Girl & The Goat, West Loop, Contemporary American, $$$, 79

Goose Island Brew Pub, Lincoln Park, Gastropubs & Brewpubs, $–$$, 89

Graham Elliot, River North, Contemporary American, $$$$, 79

Grahamwich, River North, Burgers, Hot Dogs & Sandwiches, $, 70

Great Lake, Andersonville, Italian & Pizza, $, 95

Greek Islands, Greektown, Greek, $, 93

GT Fish & Oyster, River North, Seafood, $, 107

Hae Woon Dae, West Rogers Park, Korean, $, 102

Hai Yen, Uptown, Vietnamese, $, 111

Harry Caray's Italian Steakhouse, River North, Steakhouses, $$$, 110

Haymarket Pub & Brewery, West Loop, Gastropubs & Brewpubs, $, 89

Heaven On Seven, Loop, Classic American & Southern, $, 74

Hema's Kitchen, West Rogers Park & Lincoln Park, Indian, $, 94

Henri, South Loop, French, $$$$, 88

Hoosier Mama Pie, West Town, Bakeries & Dessert, $, 65

Hopleaf, Andersonville, Gastropubs & Brewpubs, $$, 90

Hot Chocolate, Bucktown, Contemporary American, $$, 80

Hot Doug's, Avondale, Burgers, Hot Dogs & Sandwiches, $, 71

Hub 51, River North, Contemporary American, $$, 80

Hubbard Inn, River North, Gastropubs & Brewpubs, $$, 90

Ina's, West Loop, Breakfast & Brunch, $, 67

India House, River North, Indian, $–$$, 94

Jam, Ukrainian Village, Breakfast & Brunch, $$, 67

Kamehachi, Old Town, Japanese, $$, 100

Kuma's Corner, Avondale, Burgers, Hot Dogs & Sandwiches, $, 71

L2O, Lincoln Park, Seafood, $$$$, 107

Lao Sze Chuan, Chinatown, Chinese, $, 72

Leopold, West Town, Belgian, $$, 66

Lillie's Q, Bucktown, Classic American & Southern, $, 74

Longman & Eagle, Logan Square, Gastropubs & Brewpubs, $$, 90

Lou Malnati's, River North, Deep Dish Pizza, $, 86

Lou Mitchell's Restaurant, West Loop, Breakfast & Brunch, $, 69

Lula Cafe, Logan Square, Contemporary American, $$, 80

Manny's Coffee Shop & Deli, South Side, Classic American & Southern, $, 74

Mastro's Steakhouse, River North, Steakhouses, $$$$, 110

Maude's Liquor Bar, West Loop, French, $$, 88

Mercat A La Planxa, South Loop, Spanish, $$$, 108

Mexique, West Town, Mexican, $$–$$$, 105

Mia Francesca, Lakeview, Italian & Pizza, $$, 96

Mixteco Grill, Lakeview, Mexican, $$, 105

Moto, West Loop, Contemporary American, $$$$, 80

Mr. Beef, River North, Burgers, Hot Dogs & Sandwiches, $, 71

My Pie, Bucktown & Northbrook, Deep Dish Pizza, $, 86

Nacional 27, River North, Latin American & Cuban, $$, 103

Naha, River North, Contemporary American, $$$$, 81

Next, West Loop, Contemporary American, $$$$, 81

Nightwood, Pilsen, Contemporary American, $$, 81

North Pond, Lincoln Park, Contemporary American, $$$$, 82

Old Town Social, Old Town, Gastropubs & Brewpubs, $, 91

One Sixtyblue, West Loop, Contemporary American, $$$, 82

Orange, River North/Lincoln Park/River West/Roscoe Village, Breakfast & Brunch, $, 69

Osteria Via Stato-Pizzeria Via Stato, River North, Italian & Pizza, $$, 96

Owen & Engine, Logan Square, Gastropubs & Brewpubs, $$, 91

Paris Club, River North, French, $$, 88

Parthenon, Greektown, Greek, $, 93

Phoenix, Chinatown, Chinese, $, 72

Piccolo Sogno, West Loop, Italian & Pizza, $$, 97

Piece, Wicker Park, Italian & Pizza, $, 96

Pizano's, Magnificent Mile/Loop/Glenview, Deep Dish Pizza, $, 87

Pizzeria Uno, River North, Deep Dish Pizza, $, 87

Prairie Fire, West Loop, Contemporary American, $$, 82

Province, West Loop, Contemporary American, $$, 83

The Publican, West Loop, Contemporary American, $$, 83

The Purple Pig, Magnificent Mile, Mediterranean, $$, 103

Revolution Brewing, Logan Square, Gastropubs & Brewpubs, $$, 91

Riccardo Trattoria, Lincoln Park, Italian & Pizza, $$, 97

Rockitbar & Grill, River North & Wrigleyville, Burgers, Hot Dogs & Sandwiches, $$, 71

Saigon Sisters, West Loop, Vietnamese, $$, 112

Schwa, West Town, Contemporary American, $$$$, 83

Sepia, West Loop, Contemporary American, $$$, 84

Shaw's Crab House, River North, Seafood, $$$$, 107

Sixteen, River North, Contemporary American, $$$$, 84

Smith & Wollensky, Marina City, Steakhouses, $$$$, 110

Smoque BBQ, Irving Park, Classic American & Southern, $, 74

The Southern, Bucktown, Classic American & Southern, $$, 75

Spacca Napoli, Ravenswood, Italian & Pizza, $, 97

Spiaggia/Cafe Spiaggia, Magnificent Mile, Italian & Pizza, $$$$, 97

Sun Wah Bar-B-Q Restaurant, Uptown, Chinese, $, 73

Sunda, River North, Pan Asian, $$, 106

Superdawg Drive-In, Jefferson Park, Burgers, Hot Dogs & Sandwiches, $, 72

Sushisamba, River North, Japanese, $$$, 100

Sushi Wabi, West Loop, Japanese, $$, 100

Table Fifty-Two, Gold Coast, Classic American & Southern, $$$, 75

Tac Quick Thai Kitchen, Wrigleyville, Thai, $, 110

Takashi Restaurant, Bucktown, Japanese, $$$, 101

Tango Sur, Lakeview, Latin American & Cuban, $–$$, 103

Taxim, Wicker Park, Greek, $$$, 93

Terzo Piano, Loop, Italian & Pizza, $$–$$$, 98

Thai Lagoon, Bucktown, Thai, $, 111

Three Aces, Little Italy, Gastropubs & Brewpubs, $, 92

Topolobampo, River North, Mexican, $$$$, 105

Tru, Streeterville, Contemporary American, $$$$, 84

Urban Belly, Logan Square, Pan Asian, $, 106

Vincent, Andersonville, Belgian, $$, 66

XOCO, River North, Mexican, $, 106

Yolk, South Loop, Breakfast & Brunch, $, 69

Zealous, River North, Contemporary American, $$$, 85

BAKERIES & DESSERT

✳BLEEDING HEART BAKERY $
1955 W. Belmont Ave.
(773) 327-6934
www.thebleedingheartbakery.com
With her brightly dyed hair and plethora of tattoos, owner Michelle Garcia is easy to spot. But this punk rock pastry princess is more than just a colorful character. Garcia is passionate about using local, organic, and sustainable ingredients in the creative—and delicious—treats displayed in glass cases at her Roscoe Village bakery. Garcia, along with husband, Vinny, have won numerous awards and have been featured on several local TV shows. Her Take a Hike scone has a loyal following, while the intricate wedding cakes are an art to behold. Other not-to-be-missed items include a rotating selection of cupcakes, brownies, bars, and teacakes. Open Tues through Sun; closed Mon.

FRITZ PASTRY $
1408 W. Diversey Pkwy.
(773) 857-2989
www.fritzpastry.com

At this Lincoln Park shop, pastry chef–partner Nate Meads drops the fancy-pants desserts he used to make at some of the city's top restaurants (Tru, Everest, Blue Water Grill), and instead focuses on classic European-inspired pastries—think croissants, macarons, danishes, and brioches. And locals couldn't be happier. You can taste them all here, as well as at downtown's Grahamwich (Graham Elliot Bowles' sandwich haven) and at Intelligentsia coffee shops. The quaint brown-and-blue space also offers coffee drinks and teas and, in keeping with its local-is-better mantra, artwork from area artists. Open daily from breakfast through early evening.

HOOSIER MAMA PIE $
1618-½ Chicago Ave.
(312) 243-4846
www.hoosiermamapie.com
She's worked at some of the city's top restaurants, but often what Paula Haney found herself craving after a day of whipping up super-creative desserts was a piece of pie. Finding it was another story. And so Hoosier Mama Pie Company was born. Haney started

with made-from-scratch seasonal pies that showed up at coffeehouses and farmers' markets all over town. They were such a delectable hit that this self-taught pastry chef and Indiana native now makes it much easier to get a slice of her scrumptious creations at her West Town shop. Decide among a daily rotating selection of sweet and savory pies—think classic apple, peanut butter, lemon chess, and chicken potpie—along with muffins and scones and coffee from local roaster Metropolis. If you want a little of everything (who can blame you?), visit on a Friday and opt for a flight of three small slices. Open Tues through Sun; closed Mon.

BELGIAN

LEOPOLD   **$$**
1450 W. Chicago Ave.
(312) 348-1028
www.leopoldchicago.com
Chicago Avenue is quickly becoming a hot destination for dining, including this Belgium-inspired restaurant with influences from France and Germany. It's a tasty combination for the hearty and flavorful food of chef Jeffrey Hedin—who features an ever-changing menu of dishes including smoked rabbit with mustard spaetzle, housemade pierogi, and seared diver scallops with caramelized endive. Look for a Euro-heavy wine and beer list, including eight on tap, plus cocktails featuring spirits from Leopold Brothers, a small-batch distillery in Colorado. Now taking reservations, Leopold's seating options include cozy banquette seats, an extra-long bar, and for those looking for more of a lounge experience, the sofas up front. Open for dinner Tues through Sun; closed Mon.

VINCENT   **$$**
1475 W. Balmoral Ave.
(773) 334-7168
www.vincentchicago.com
At this quaint Andersonville restaurant, chef Joncarl Lachman taps into his Dutch heritage with a nod to that famous "Starry"-eyed painter, Vincent van Gogh. Lachman also shows off his dedication to ingredients from local and sustainable farms and purveyors (he owns the Boystown favorite HB as well). The end result includes items like Dutch mustard soup with crab salad, housemade pâtés, and roasted seasonal vegetables on quinoa. Mussels, a house specialty, come with a choice of 5 different preparations, all served with perfectly crispy French fries. A nightly 3-course dinner ($25) is available as well. Keep the Dutch vibe going with a cocktail made with genever, the classic Dutch gin. Open for dinner Tues through Sun, and brunch on Sun.

BREAKFAST & BRUNCH

✳ANN SATHER   **$**
909 W. Belmont Ave.
(773) 348-2378
www.annsather.com
It's not the fanciest, nor the hippest, but it's definitely one of Chicago's favorite breakfast destinations. More than 60 years ago, the real-life Ann Sather bought a Swedish-owned diner and put her own magic into it. Beginning in 1981, Sather had prepared Tom Tunney (now a Chicago alderman too) to take over for her, and he has done a bang-up job, debuting several small cafes and opening the Andersonville location in 1987, a perfect complement to the neighborhood's Swedish roots. Though Sather passed away in 1996, the restaurants continue to live

by Ann's original philosophy of wholesome food at low prices—and they're famous for her warm, gooey, icing-laden cinnamon buns that you can get as a side to your main dish or just get them to go and devour at home. Besides the buns, Ann Sather serves up some of the best Swedish pancakes with lingonberries you'll find anywhere, along with three-egg omelets, and a soup, salad, and sandwich menu at lunch. Open for breakfast and lunch daily. A second location is at 5207 N. Clark St. (773-271-6677).

THE BONGO ROOM $
1470 N. Milwaukee Ave.
(773) 489-0690
www.thebongoroom.com
A welcoming mainstay in Wicker Park since 1993, a few years before the neighborhood hit its hipster stride, the Bongo Room continues to rake in praise for its attention to detail—for its servers and staff who keep tables cleared of clutter and water glasses and coffee mugs filled (mmm . . . Intelligentsia coffee), and for the creative twists on a.m. favorites that come out of the kitchen lickety-split. Good thing they're quick, too, because you're probably hungry if you've timed your arrival wrong. Get here before the doors even open, and you're good to go; show up 10 minutes too late, and you're doomed to drool awhile. Check out the menu to bide the time. Savory stars include the breakfast burrito and croissant sandwich, along with omelets cooked to perfection and blanketing fresh ingredients of your choosing. Orange-ricotta pancakes with gingersnap brown-sugar butter; and white chocolate and four-berry cheesecake flapjacks prove that starting out the day sweet can be just as heavenly. Portions are generous, but leftovers like that never go to waste.

There's also a newer South Loop location at 1152 S. Wabash Ave. (312-291-0100). Open for breakfast and lunch daily (brunch on the weekends too).

INA'S $
1235 W. Randolph St.
(312) 226-8227
www.breakfastqueen.com
They don't call Ina Pinkney the "Breakfast Queen" for nothing. At her West Loop diner she's well known for signature dishes such as her scrapple, a version of a mid-Atlantic dish with cornmeal, cheddar cheese, black beans, and corn, with a side choice of meat and eggs "your way"; and Heavenly Hots (thin pancakes topped with a fresh fruit compote). Besides the food, customers are smitten with her extensive collection of salt and pepper shakers, many brought in by loyal fans. Lunch, offered every day except Sunday, features a selection of soups, salads, and sandwiches. The atmosphere may be nothing special, but the friendly and attentive service make up for it. Open daily for breakfast and lunch (on Sun, only breakfast is served until 2 p.m.)

JAM $$
937 N. Damen Ave.
(773) 489-0302
www.jamrestaurant.com
At this quaint Ukrainian Village spot, your morning meal gets the culinary love it deserves. With a Charlie Trotters' alum in charge of the open kitchen, you'll find an artisanal approach to ingredients with inventive dishes such as malted custard French toast, buckwheat crepes with lamb and, of course, house-made jams. The first tip-off that this place isn't breakfast as usual comes in the changing amuse-bouche. The

🔍 Close-up

Windy City Wake-Ups: Top Coffee Spots

When it's that perfect perk you're looking for, you could settle for the chain standard or you could try one of Chicago's favorite indie spots (we vote for the latter).

Intelligentsia (3123 N. Broadway St.; 773-348-8058; www.intelligentsiacoffee .com) tops the list, not only for its early domination—begun in 1995 and now with shops in New York and several in California—but also for its care toward growers and customers, its homey atmosphere, and the stunning coffee that's roasted daily and lovingly filtered directly into your cup. Call about monthly tours of its West Loop Roasting Works.

For the three friends behind Bridgeport **Coffee House** (3101 S. Morgan St.; 773-247-9950; www.bridgeportcoffeecompany.com), it's all about being part of the community, hosting events like jazz on Sunday and kids' play groups; plus, they roast and blend their own beans.

Get back to the future at Wicker Park's 1980s-geeked-out **The Wormhole** (1462 N. Milwaukee Ave.; 773-661-2468; www.thewormholecoffee.com), replete with a DeLorean for decor, Gremlin dolls, movie posters from *Ghostbusters, The Blues Brothers* and *Top Gun,* and a rather carefree happy attitude, not to mention the Metropolis coffee, some of it made into crazy-delicious concoctions.

Go to the source itself at the **Metropolis Coffee Company** (1039 W. Granville Ave.; 773-764-0400; www.metropoliscoffee.com), a local art-filled space near the Red Line El in Edgewater. Another close-to-the-El stop is **The Perfect Cup** (4700 N. Damen Ave.; 773-989-4177; www.perfectcupchicago.com), a friendly neighborhood favorite—you'll feel like they know you—that was recently expanded and is just steps from the Damen Brown Line El stop; try owner Anne Nuqui Merritt's special blend of espresso, coffee, chocolate, and steamed half-and-half (mmmm).

Cafeneo (4655 N. Lincoln Ave.; 773-878-2233) sits under the Brown Line tracks in Lincoln Square and serves decent crepes too. Over at **Darkcloud** (2122 N. Halsted St.; 773-857-2449; www.darkcloudcoffee.com), the contemporary decor counters the old-fashioned approach to making and serving coffee. It doesn't focus on one particular bean, but rather rotates the selection and shares the love with you—happily recommending the right brew for your mood and holding classes and workshops (many free) to educate customers about coffee culture. Bleeding Heart Bakery goodies sweeten the deal.

Pretty murals of trees and a bright, airy space brings people to Uptown's **Ch'Ava** (4656 N. Clark St.; 773-942-6763; www.chavacafe.com); the excellent coffee and equally good seasonally focused menu of real food keeps them coming back.

hip factor is high—concrete-topped tables, Lucite chairs, sleek flower arrangements—but so is the comfort level with a big front window, warm white-and-gray walls, and super-friendly service. Non-breakfast lovers can opt for the Butterkasse cheese–topped burger. But no matter what you order, be sure to bring cash because credit cards aren't accepted, and get there before the 3 p.m. closing time. During winter months, it's open Mon, and Wed through Sun (closed Tues) for breakfast and lunch; then spring and summer, it's open daily for breakfast and lunch.

Most coffeeshops offer free Wi-Fi these days (some with purchase), so feel free to bring your laptop and hang for awhile.

LOU MITCHELL'S RESTAURANT $
565 W. Jackson Blvd.
(312) 939-3111
www.loumitchellsrestaurant.com
When it comes to classic Chicago experiences, a meal at this West Loop restaurant is definitely on the list. Open since 1923, this institution has had more than its fair share of big-name celebrities enter under its iconic red neon sign. It's easy to tell why. For instance, any restaurant that doles out gratis doughnut holes and mini boxes of Milk Duds rates high in our book. You get those when you wait in line (which you probably will) for the terrific baked-in-house pastries and moderately priced breakfast and lunch items, including fluffy pancakes, waffles, and omelets. Also worth noting ahead of time: it's cash-only here. Open for breakfast and lunch every day.

ORANGE $
738 N. Clark St.
(312) 202-0600
www.orangerestaurantchicago.com
With four locations in the city and one in the northwest suburb of Glenview, this chainlet proves that breakfast really is the most important meal of the day. Taking a creative approach, signature items include the "fruishi," which is fresh fruit sushi-style with fruit juice–infused rice, pancake flights, French toast kabobs, and the Green Eggs & Ham (scrambled eggs with basil pesto and diced ham). But traditionalists have plenty to choose from too, including eggs Benedict, build-your-own scrambles, and hearty omelets. Organic seasonal produce and ingredients from local farms add to this family-friendly restaurant's appeal. For kids, the Fruity Pebble Baby Cakes are a slam dunk. For lunch, a varied selection of sandwiches and salads dominate the menu. Open daily for breakfast and lunch. Additional city locations are at 2413 N. Clark St. (773-549-7833), 730 W. Grand Ave. (312-942-0300), and 2011 W. Roscoe St. (773-284-0999).

Want to hit all the cool coffeehouses in town? New to Chicago is the Tour de Cafe, a punch card that gets you 20 drip coffees at 20 different independently owned java shops for just 20 bucks. No expiration date. Purchase online at www.tourdecafe.com, or call (773) 348-1227 for more info.

YOLK $
747 N. Wells St.
(312) 787-2277
www.yolk-online.com
Not surprisingly, you'll find plenty of egg dishes at all three locations of this popular breakfast and lunch spot. In addition to the usual egg suspects, you'll also find more inventive dishes such as pot roast Benedict, Tuscan frittata, and smoked salmon scrambler. Bonus: No extra charge for egg whites or Egg Beaters. That playful mentality of the menu applies to the decor as well, with its vivid splashes of blue and yellow and its fun egg artwork. Not an egg enthusiast? Opt for dishes that think outside the carton: four varieties of oatmeal, crepes, waffles, and pancakes. French toast gets a makeover as well, with the resounding favorite being the

banana nut bread version. Lunch includes an equally creative selection of soups, salads, and sandwiches. Open daily for breakfast and lunch. Two additional locations are at 355 E. Ohio St. (312-822-9655), and 1120 S. Michigan Ave. (312-789-9655).

BURGERS, HOT DOGS & SANDWICHES

∗DMK BURGER $
2954 N. Sheffield Ave.
(773) 360-8686
www.dmkburgerbar.com

There's something to be said for a burger you can actually sink your teeth into—not just stare at wondering how you'll get your mouth around it. You see, these patties don't need size to prove their merit. Made from grass-fed beef (and, as the menu says, "love"), they're perfectly sized for polishing off without feeling piggish. That's not to say you won't need that extra napkin (or three), because with toppings like New York pastrami, French gruyère, sauerkraut, and remoulade (that's the #3), or roasted Hatch green chile, fried farm egg, Sonoma Jack cheese, and smoked bacon (the #4), these patties pile on the messy goodness. No surprise, considering the duo behind DMK (notice the initials)—David Morton of Morton's steakhouse fame and Michael Kornick who established himself with fine-dining restaurant MK. Non-beef options: lamb, turkey, salmon, and portobello. Be prepared to wait for a table; the bar is just as crowded, but the music is loud, so being shoved together is a good thing. Service is literally with a smile, and burgers are all $11 or under. The must-try side: Parmesan and truffle-cream fries. Open for lunch and dinner daily.

EPIC BURGER $
517 S. State St.
(312) 913-1373
www.epicburger.com

The casual attitude of this counter-service spot might just project the wrong impression—in fact, a whole lot of affection and preparation goes into making their burgers, fries, and shakes. After all, they use 100-percent natural, nonfrozen beef; baked-daily buns from a local bakery; fresh-cut fries; and real, unprocessed ingredients such as Wisconsin cheese, cage-free organic eggs, and nitrate-free bacon. The effort pays off, with burgers that are juicy, flavorful, and definitely worth the calories. Plus the atmosphere makes it perfectly fine for families. Open for lunch and dinner daily. A second location is at 1000 W. North Ave. (312-440-9700).

GRAHAMWICH $
615 N. State St.
(312) 624-9188
www.grahamwich.com

Celeb chef Graham Elliot likes to have fun, and his lighthearted attitude carries through to this River North quick-serve spot where newsboy-clad staffers create made-to-order sandwiches, such as a barbecue pork belly on corn bread, and a grilled cheese with prosciutto and tomato marmalade. For sides, choose from housemade chips, flavored popcorn, green salad, or pickles made from seasonal vegetables. Beat the crowds and stop by for breakfast with a selection of croissants, panini, and pastries from local Fritz Pastry. Open daily for breakfast and lunch, dinner Mon through Sat.

HOT DOUG'S $
3324 N. California Ave.
(773) 279-9550
www.hotdougs.com

Even though this small "encased meat empo-
rium" has been featured in everything from
Anthony Bourdain's travel show to the *New
York Times,* owner/chef Doug Sohn hasn't let
it go to this head. You'll still find him behind
the counter smiling away as he takes your
order. It's nearly inevitable there'll be a line
down the block (this place is tiny and popular), but that will give you time to decide
which of the cleverly named—and thoughtfully prepared—hot dogs to try. Perhaps The
Salma Hayek (which has, in the past, been
called the Madonna and the Ann-Margret),
an andouille sausage described as "mighty,
mighty, mighty hot!" Or maybe The Elvis, a
Polish sausage "smoked and savory—just
like the King." The daily specials always offer
something unusual, including a recent Catalonian pork sausage with saffron rouille, but
the regular menu doesn't disappoint either
and includes a sure-thing Chicago-style hot
dog with all the proper toppings. Add some
delish duck-fat fries to your order if you
come on Friday and Saturday, the only days
it's offered. Cash only. Open for lunch Mon
through Sat.

KUMA'S CORNER $
2900 W. Belmont Ave.
(773) 604-8769
www.kumascorner.com

What Hot Doug's is to encased meat, Kuma's
Corner is to burgers—only louder and with a
bigger, brashier attitude. More bar than restaurant actually, this Avondale corner spot
has become as famous for its hearty, half-
pound Angus beef burgers served on puffy
pretzel rolls as it has for the wait it takes to

get one. A heavy metal mentality permeates,
from the burger names (the Black Sabbath
includes chili, pepper jack cheese, and red
onion) to the tattooed servers to the music
itself. An extensive craft beer menu makes
the inevitable long wait seem less so, if you
can even find a spot to stand inside. Open
for lunch and dinner daily.

MR. BEEF $
666 N. Orleans St.
(312) 337-8500

In Chicago, Italian beef sandwiches are just
as much a part of the gastronomic landscape as deep-dish pizza. And one of the
best places to get one is at this small River
North spot, which is reportedly a favorite of
Jay Leno's. But be warned: The slow-roasted
beef sandwich dripping in natural juices isn't
easy to eat. That's part of the fun, though,
along with the proper way to order one,
which to any true Chicagoan means asking
for the entire sandwich, roll and all, to be
"dipped" into the sauce for even more juici-
ness. For an extra spicy kick, get it "hot." Cash
only. Open Mon through Thurs from 8 a.m.
to 7 p.m., Fri from 8 a.m. to 5 p.m. and 10:30
p.m. to 5 a.m. (perfect for a post-last-call
stop); Sat from 7 a.m. to 3 p.m. and 10:30 p.m.
to 5 a.m.; closed Sun.

ROCKITBAR & GRILL $$
22 W. Hubbard St.
(312) 645-6000
www.rockitbarandgrill.com

The trio behind these River North and Wrigleyville (3700 N. Clark St., 773-645-4400)
sports-centric hot spots (also the team
behind Sunda and Underground) know
what it takes to put together a buzz-worthy
restaurant that not only draws locals but
visiting celebs as well. Even its comfy-stylish

design hails from Nate Berkus of *Oprah* fame. But there's more going on than just a see-and-be-seen vibe. The well-prepared food goes beyond basic pub grub, with dishes such as barbecue glazed salmon and half roasted chicken. And the biggest draw happens to be the burgers, including the namesake Rockit Burger made with Kobe beef and topped with melted brie, fried shallots, and a medjool date aioli. For Cubs game-goers, the Wrigleyville location is a great alternative to the typically boisterous bars in the area. The weekend brunch with its Bloody Mary bar ($5) and malted Belgium waffles is worth waking up for. The locations have different hours. River North: Open daily for lunch, dinner, and late-night (brunch on Sat and Sun); Wrigleyville: Open Mon through Wed only during home Cubs games, Thurs and Fri for dinner only (except on game days), open for Saturday brunch and dinner and Sunday brunch only.

SUPERDAWG DRIVE-IN $
6363 N. Milwaukee Ave.
(773) 763-0660
www.superdawg.com
This Jefferson Park spot has gotten plenty of hype over its long life, but there's a reason people still line up here—besides simply getting a peek at the goofy boy and girl hot dog figurines on its roof ("Maurie" and "Flaurie") and indulging in some kitschy carhop service. Open since 1948, this family-owned slice of history serves a terrific all-beef hot dog with all the right Chicago-style trimmings, along with some crispy fries in a cute red box. (They also serve burgers, fried shrimp, and grilled cheese sandwiches, but that's not why people flock here.) Up the nostalgia factor and get a thick and creamy milkshake. You can get your dogs every day from lunch till the wee hours.

CHINESE

LAO SZE CHUAN $
2172 S. Archer Ave.
(312) 326-5040
www.tonygourmetgroup.com
If you're looking for authentic Chinese food, look for the name most mentioned around Chicago: Tony Hu. He also owns nearby Lao Beijing, Lao Shanghai, and Lao You Ju, which are also in Chinatown. And while the typical dishes get plenty of nods at Lao Sze Chuan, it's the fiery dishes of this Szechuan restaurant that draw the biggest crowds. Popular picks include spicy ma po tofu, salt and pepper prawns, and double-cooked pork. Those with less heat-seeking palates will also find plenty of options on this huge menu, from won ton soup and crab Rangoon to the signature hot pot that's sort of like a Chinese-style fondue. Open daily for lunch and dinner.

PHOENIX $
2131 S. Archer Ave.
(312) 328-0848
www.chinatownphoenix.com
At this Chinatown favorite, it's the extensive selection of dim sum that attracts hordes of hungry regulars from the area and beyond. Tip: Get in by 10 a.m. on the weekends to avoid a long wait. Don't look to the rather cool staff to tell you what to order—even asking about what's what on the illustrated menu gets a rattling-off of nearly unintelligible—to non-Chinese-speakers—descriptions. But if you aren't a picky eater, the adventure of not knowing what you're getting is really what makes this fun. Expect

tasty dumplings, sticky rice with chicken and lotus root, and barbecued pork rolls. Got a hankering for something specific? Signal to one of the headwaiters who will try and track it down for you. If you'd rather play it safe, the restaurant also features an extensive classical Chinese menu. Open for breakfast, lunch, and dinner daily.

✳SUN WAH BAR-B-Q RESTAURANT $
5041 N. Broadway
(773) 769-1254
www.sunwahbbq.com
Eric Cheng began his Sun Wah restaurant story in New York, where he honed his Hong Kong–style barbecue skills for happy customers. When he moved to Chicago, he opened his restaurant in Uptown's Argyle Street enclave. It remained there until he and his now-grown children—all with a talented hand in the business—swung around the corner into this loftlike space. It seats more than 240 people and features some 200 dishes, including the famous crispy smoked Beijing duck "feast" for two that most diners come for. This off-menu item is presented and carved tableside, then the carcass is returned to the kitchen to create duck-infused soup. Sun Wah also earns high marks from local food lovers for its other barbecue dishes, including pork and spareribs (check out the front window warming cases for an eyeful). The large room can get loud, and service can sometimes be spotty, but one bite of that super-crispy duck skin, and you'll forgive any faults. Just be sure to call ahead to order it. Open for lunch and dinner Sun through Wed, Fri and Sat (closed Thurs).

CLASSIC AMERICAN & SOUTHERN

BIG JONES $$
5347 N. Clark St.
(773) 275-5725
www.bigjoneschicago.com
A longtime supporter of the farm-to-table movement, chef-owner Paul Fehribach combines his commitment to local ingredients with creative cuisine based on traditions of Lowcountry, Cajun, Creole, and Carolina cooking to create this Andersonville labor of love. The narrow, cozy space with its cheerfully colored walls is a perfect backdrop for fun, hearty dishes such as shrimp and grits, gumbo ya-ya, and fried green tomatoes or fried cauliflower. Save room for the baked-to-order red velvet cake with house-made ice cream and toffee brittle. The weekend brunch menu also features a wide selection of area purveyors whose ingredients can be found in dishes like eggs New Orleans, crispy oatmeal cakes, and andouille with poached eggs. The local love comes in liquid form too, as the cocktail menu highlights spirits from Wisconsin's Death Door and North Shore distillery in north suburban Lake Bluff. Open daily for lunch and dinner, and for brunch on Sat and Sun.

FAT WILLY'S RIB SHACK $$
2416 W. Schubert Ave.
(773) 782-1800
www.fatwillys.com
Rather than serve barbecue from only one region, the owners of this Logan Square hideaway did their homework and gathered up all the favorites, including baby back ribs, brisket, and pulled pork, all under one roof and all made from scratch. Sauce lovers appreciate the five options available, and making everyone happy are the top-notch

ingredients that go into side dishes such as collard greens, bacon-studded baked beans, and green onion–cheddar cornbread. A popular spot for cops, Fat Willy's is nothing fancy, but frankly we're suspicious of a barbecue joint that is. Open for lunch and dinner daily.

HEAVEN ON SEVEN $
111 N. Wabash Ave.
(312) 263-6443
www.heavenonseven.com
Third-generation chef Jimmy Bannos has been serving up his take on New Orleans–style food at this Loop restaurant for more than 31 years. His efforts (successful, of course) earned him a place in the Chicago Chef's Hall of Fame. Located in the historic Garland Building, the original location is a favorite for downtown office workers who devour dishes such as oyster po'boys, Louisiana crab cakes, and jambalaya, and who chill out with the super-friendly atmosphere and service. The wall of hot sauces at both restaurants is a sign of good—and spicy—things to come. It does get a serious lunch rush, so stop by for breakfast if you'd rather not fight for attention. Cash only at the Wabash location. There's also a location in west suburban Naperville (224 S. Main St.). Wabash Avenue is open for breakfast and lunch Mon through Sat; Michigan Avenue location (600 N. Michigan Ave., 312-280-7774) open for lunch and dinner daily, brunch on Sat and Sun.

LILLIE'S Q $
1856 W. North Ave.
(773) 772-5500
www.lilliesq.com
Don't let chef Charlie McKenna's fine dining restaurant-filled résumé deter you—this guy knows his barbecue. Need convincing? His numerous wins on the tough barbecue circuit over the years should do the trick. Or, better yet, test it out for yourself at this Bucktown restaurant where you'll find his signature 15-ingredient "Carolina Dirt" rub (wonderful on his slow-cooked pork shoulder), baby back ribs, baked beans with house-smoked bacon, and plenty of other finger-lickin'-good treats. In between sips of craft beer, take time to admire the meat-hook light fixtures, reclaimed farmhouse wood tabletops, and rustic-chic silver chairs. Open every day for lunch, dinner, and drinks.

MANNY'S COFFEE SHOP & DELI $
1141 South Jefferson St.
(312) 939-2855
www.mannysdeli.com
Since 1946 some member of the Raskin family has been running the show at this South Side institution (the signage and interior look just as old), a home-style cafeteria that attracts patrons from all walks of life, including President Obama. Grab a tray and line up with the rest of them as you eye the options behind the long glass counter and choose from signature stuff like towering corned beef sandwiches, meat loaf like mama used to make, and matzo ball soup that would make grandma jealous. Early risers will appreciate the 6 a.m. opening and the fluffy three-egg omelets and thick challah French toast. Open daily for breakfast, lunch and dinner.

SMOQUE BBQ $
3800 N. Pulaski Rd.
(773) 545-7427
www.smoquebbq.com
There's your everyday brisket and then there's dry-rubbed brisket that's spent 15

hours in the smoker. That should answer any questions about whether this Irving Park joint is serious about their 'cue. If you're still unsure, you could also scan the four-page "manifesto" on their website that states, "If the world made any sense, Chicago would be known as a great BBQ town," and continues on to describe philosophies and opinions regarding sauces, baby backs vs. spares, ribs, pulled pork, brisket, and even sides. But you could just forget all that and head over to the 50-seat, quick-serve BYOB spot where you'll find a wide variety of smoking styles from around the country. The menu is pretty much limited to barbecue, but you won't mind once you've tried the pulled pork smoked over apple and oak wood, and baby back and St. Louis ribs. Plus that pink smoke ring around the meats tells you this is the real deal. Sides feel the love too, including their cornbread, macaroni and cheese, and brisket-studded baked beans, a top pick by Guy Fieri when he stopped in with his *Diners, Drive-ins and Drives* crew. For dessert? Peach cobbler, of course. Open Tues through Sun for lunch and dinner.

THE SOUTHERN $$
1840 W. North Ave.
(773) 342-1840
www.thesouthernchicago.com
Chef Cary Taylor has worked at some of Chicago's top restaurants (Avenues, Blackbird), but he's really a good ol' Southern boy at heart. That's fine with us because he brought the best of it from Georgia to the comforting dishes at this hip Bucktown restaurant and lounge: Standouts are his shrimp and grits, johnnycakes, and a Southern-style poutine with cheese curds. A sit-back-and-relax attitude is evident in the decor, a mix of rich, dark woods and steel-accented stools at numerous high-top tables. There are also two outdoor patios, including a casual rooftop space. Liquids to suit the Southern leanings include small-batch bourbons, more than 70 whiskeys, Southern (and local) beer, sarsaparillas, Georgia julep cocktails, and punch-bowl libations for groups of 10 to 15. Open Tues through Fri for dinner and, on the weekend, lunch too. Closed Mon.

TABLE FIFTY-TWO $$$
52 W. Elm St.
(312) 573-4000
www.tablefifty-two.com
The Windy City is a long way away from Mississippi, the Carolinas, and Georgia, but that doesn't stop chef Art Smith from channeling them here at his Gold Coast restaurant. Well known for being the personal chef to Oprah Winfrey, a local favorite of President Obama, and for authoring numerous cookbooks, Smith keeps it low-key at this petite restaurant that looks and feels like a cozy bed-and-breakfast with its glowing tin ceiling and butter-yellow walls. Pre-meal freebies of buttermilk–goat cheese biscuits and deviled eggs start things off on the right foot. Keep that howdy y'all feeling going with fried green tomatoes, cornmeal-crusted catfish, and pecan pie. If reservations are hard to come by, opt for one of the five seats at the bar. Open daily for dinner and a new Sunday Southern brunch.

CONTEMPORARY AMERICAN

✳ALINEA $$$$
1723 N. Halsted St.
(312) 867-0110
www.alinea-restaurant.com
Even before it opened its doors in 2005, Alinea and its chef Grant Achatz (rhymes

with "jackets") had the food world buzzing. These days everyone who has experienced it talks about food that defies labels. Call it what you like—molecular gastronomy, sci-fi food, or just plain wacky—but odds are once you've tried it (that is, if you can get in) you'll never look at restaurant dining in the same way again. Case in point: Achatz's butterscotch-glazed bacon draped over a wire on a metal stand. Anything but simple. And that goes for everything on the 16- or 18-course menu. The minimalist decor and subdued ambiance only hint at the mysteries that await. Come with an open mind and a full wallet. Open for dinner Wed through Sun.

BIN 36 $$$
339 N. Dearborn St.
(312) 755-9463
www.bin36.com

For descriptions that demystify wine, Bin 36 could have written the book. Part wine store, part tavern, but mostly restaurant, this next-to-the-river spot in the Marina City enclave takes the whole daunting grape experience and makes it fun. Try a variety of wine flights, 48 wines by the glass, numerous classes and events, and chat up Brian Duncan, a James Beard award nominee who has been known to refer to himself as the "wine chef." He oversees the wine program and blends the Bin 36 brand wines himself. He's particularly beloved around town for his passion for vino and the down-to-earth way he expresses it. Pair your wine pick with delectable artisan cheeses at the oval-shape bar or opt for a full meal from chef John Caputo's menu of creative contemporary American dishes such as steamed mussels, cheese fondue, and black pepper–crusted swordfish. Open daily for breakfast, lunch, and dinner.

*BLACKBIRD $$$
619 W. Randolph St.
(312) 715-0708
www.blackbirdrestaurant.com

This is the restaurant that started it all for executive chef Paul Kahan, who now has four restaurants under his well-used toque (look for a butcher shop to open soon too). He's also racked up plenty of awards, including a James Beard for Best Chef of the Midwest. But perhaps his best dining contribution is as a pioneer of the farm-to-table movement, which comes across in menus that reflect the seasons and showcase local purveyors. Fascinating combinations like roasted farm chicken and sausage with cauliflower, maitake mushrooms, kaffir limes, and applewood broth are a perfect foil for the chic, minimalist decor. Opened more than 13 years ago, Blackbird is still a Chicago dining powerhouse. Open for lunch Mon through Fri, dinner Mon through Sat; closed Sun.

BOKA $$$$
1729 N. Halsted St.
(312) 337-6070
www.bokachicago.com

Following the ingredient-first mantra he picked up as a chef at fine dining restaurant Charlie Trotter's, Giuseppe Tentori creates dishes that are a feast for both eyes and palate. While calling his cuisine "clean and simple," the Italian native admits he's a fan of innovative pairings for his Mediterranean-influenced dishes. To wit: beautiful stuffed squid with baby spinach, spicy pineapple, and black tapioca, a signature dish. This chic Halsted Street restaurant offers a convenient spot to dine before heading to the Steppenwolf Theatre across the street (ask about a specially priced pretheater menu).

The restaurant's fabric-draped ceiling and romantic garden are rather theatrical as well. Open nightly for dinner.

THE BRISTOL $$$
2152 N. Damen Ave.
(773) 862-5555
www.thebristolchicago.com
Wondering how fresh the food is at this Bucktown restaurant? Just check out the chalkboard on the back wall that lists the daily-changing offerings. Owned by a trio of industry vets, including chef Chris Pandel, this intimate neighborhood bistro of sorts keeps it uncomplicated. From its decor—recycled-wood communal tables, cement-topped bar—to the food, which focuses on seasonal dishes with Mediterranean roots, like handmade ravioli, roasted bone marrow, and seared swordfish with fried kale. Offal fans get treated to a selection of unusual meat cuts made possible by the butchering of animals in-house. Handcrafted cocktails are a specialty here or opt for one of their craft beers. The same attention to farm-fresh ingredients applies to their Sunday brunch. Open every day for dinner and for Sunday brunch.

Food Guide

We've given you lots of choices, but we understand that decisions are hard, particularly when you're hungry. Waiting to help is the **Culinary Concierge,** accepting Chicago food-related questions every day from 10 a.m. to 6 p.m. at the Chicago Cultural Center. Reservations are up to you, but at least you'll have figured out where to make them. 77 E. Randolph St., (773) 744-6630.

CHARLIE TROTTER'S $$$$
816 W. Armitage Ave.
(773) 248-6228
www.charlietrotters.com
There may be plenty of newer kids on the block (Alinea, for starters), but there's a reason this Lincoln Park restaurant has been a destination for food enthusiasts from around the world for more than 20 years. The elegantly decorated 2-story 1900 brownstone presents the perfect backdrop for the sophisticated food of chef Charlie Trotter, a self-taught chef who's worked in some 40 restaurants and has pretty much won every food award possible. With an emphasis on ingredients—Trotter was an advocate for local farmers long before it became chic and now works with some 95 of them—the daily-changing tasting menus (the only option) highlight the best each season has to offer with dishes such as whole roasted squab with Alaskan licorice, toasted pistachios, and heirloom beets. Though tastes push the envelope, the traditional jacket-recommended policy still remains. The per-person price hovers right around the $250 mark. Open for dinner Tues through Sat; closed Sun and Mon.

THE GAGE $$$
24 S. Michigan Ave.
(312) 372-4243
www.thegagechicago.com
This Loop restaurant has a split personality and that's a good thing. In the front is a traditional pub with one of the city's best Guinness pours and a beautiful 50-foot oak bar. Toward the back of this late 19th-century Louis Sullivan–designed building is a more serious restaurant, with big brown leather booths and plenty of tablecloth-covered tables. No matter where you sit, you'll win

with the creative, globally influenced food of chef Dirk Flanigan, a semifinalist for the title of Best Chef Great Lakes Region in the 2011 James Beard Awards (check out what this local culinary star does with French cuisine at next-door Henri). The menu's four different sections, plus sides, are arranged in order of size, making a personalized—and shareable—meal easy. Start with the fried chicken livers and smoked haddock brandade before moving on to heartier plates such as roast saddle of elk or seared bigeye tuna. Adding to the overall impression are stunning views of Millennium Park right across the street. Open daily for lunch and dinner.

GEMINI BISTRO   **$$**
2075 N. Lincoln Ave.
(773) 525-2522
www.geminibistrochicago.com
The stars aligned when executive chef–owner Jason Paskewitz teamed up with Ryan and Anna O'Donnell to open this Lincoln Park corner restaurant. The space, divided neatly in half into bar area and dining room, welcomes with warm dark woods, hanging exposed lightbulbs of the 19th-century kind, and an approachable, elevated-comfort-food menu that changes every couple of months. Three sections offer plates small, medium, and large. The smalls lean toward salads and soups—the tomato tastes fresh from the garden, paired with a light little grilled-cheese triangle. Mediums are apps big enough for two to share, though you might want to keep the beef carpaccio for yourself. Entrees fall into the large category, with top sellers including a buttery-soft braised short rib with a cute terrine of rich baked beans; and a pair of grilled lamb chops atop a square of spinach and feta

pie. Cocktail accompaniments can kick hard like the Velvet Old Fashioned with Maker's Mark, Cointreau, and bitters; or run cool and refreshing like the Cucumber Northside, a blend of gin, muddled cucumber, lemon, mint, and soda. Dessert doesn't get any sweeter than the skillet sundae, a hot, thin, gooey chocolate chip cookie à la mode sprinkled with candied walnuts. The crew's new and equally tempting venture in Lincoln Park is **Rustic House** (1967 N. Halsted St.). Open Tues through Sun for dinner; closed Mon.

GILT BAR   **$$**
230 W. Kinzie St.
(312) 464-9544
www.giltbarchicago.com
Contrary to what its name may imply, Gilt Bar isn't a fancy-schmancy spot with frou-frou food. Although with an owner who's done stints at some of the world's top dining establishments, including The French Laundry, that wouldn't be a stretch. Instead, you'll find a tavern-style restaurant whose emphasis is on rustic shared plates like ricotta gnocchi and oven-roasted pork meatballs, classic handcrafted cocktails—and a good dose of not taking itself too seriously. It's a vibe felt throughout the River North restaurant, from the front seating area filled with mismatched reclaimed-wood tables and chairs to the cozy bar with its brass countertop. In the main dining area, a starburst chandelier dominates the room. Grab a spot on either of the two cushy leather sofas for appetizers and a craft beer or head to the lounge where the tufted black leather banquette makes a perfect spot to take it all in. Downstairs is the cash-only cocktail haven Curio. Open Tues through Sat, happy hour to late night.

*THE GIRL & THE GOAT $$$
809 W. Randolph St.
(312) 492-6262
www.girlandthegoat.com

When Chicagoan Stephanie Izard won Bravo's *Top Chef* season four, local viewers and food enthusiasts alike were ecstatic. When she announced she'd be opening a new restaurant with co-owners Rob Catz and Kevin Boehm, they were salivating for months. Judging from the constant mob scene at her West Loop spot, it seems the wait was worth it. Once you make it into the 7,400-square-foot space featuring a "rustic decor with a bit of badass," as Izard describes it (translation: antique fireboxes, reclaimed-jar lights, chunky butcher-block tables), you'll find food inspired by Spain, Italy, and Southeast Asia. Dishes have included lamb-stuffed calamari; ham frites with smoked tomato aioli; and wood-oven roasted pig face that's less intense than it sounds. Not surprisingly, there are goat dishes too. The baked-in-house bread costs extra, but no one complains, with rotating offerings such as the Stecca, featuring roasted garlic and white anchovy butter. Couldn't score a reservation? Grab a spot at the long bar instead. Open for dinner nightly.

GRAHAM ELLIOT $$$$
217 W. Huron St.
(312) 624-9975
www.grahamelliot.com

There's never a dull moment with chef Graham Elliot. From his appearances on *MasterChef* to wrangling some of the city's best toques into arranging food booths at the annual music festival Lollapalooza, to engaging in Twitter spats. And there's nothing dull when it comes to the food at his eponymous restaurant, either. Here the award-winning chef has created a concept that is, in his words, "fine dining redefined." That means, in addition to doing away with dress codes, white tablecloths, and elaborate floral displays, you'll find contemporary American food that's big on breaking rules and even bigger on flavor. Take his signature deconstructed Caesar salad with stuffed brioche Twinkies and Pop Rock–studded foie gras lollipops, for example—radical, but delicious. Open for dinner Mon through Sat; closed Sun (except during the summer).

HOT CHOCOLATE $$
1747 N. Damen Ave.
(773) 489-1747
www.hotchocolatechicago.com

How'd owner and pastry chef Mindy Segal land recognition in *GQ, O: The Oprah Magazine,* and on *The Martha Stewart Show*? That's easy; they've all caught wind of her to-die-for sweet creations. Before opening her always-busy Bucktown restaurant, Segal baked up deliciousness at some of Chicago's best restaurants, including Spago, Charlie Trotter's, and MK. We could easily dine here solely for the dessert or one of the seven different kinds of hot chocolate that's more lusciously rich and creamy than we could ever dream possible (try the half and half—half espresso and half dark hot chocolate), served with homemade marshmallows. But the dinners of artful comfort food, much of it made with locally produced sustainable ingredients, rank equally impressive. Like roasted Gunthorp Farms half-chicken; grilled bone-in pork chop; housemade fettuccine with Laughing Bird Caribbean white shrimp; and a terrine of macaroni and cheese too good to serve just to kids. Open for dinner only on Tues, and for lunch and dinner Wed through Fri; open for brunch, lunch, and dinner Sat and Sun; closed Mon.

HUB 51 $$
51 W. Hubbard St.
(312) 828-0051
www.hub51chicago.com

This River North restaurant from brothers R.J. and Jerrod Melman might come off a bit slick, but when your father, James Beard–winner Rich Melman, is head of an über-successful restaurant empire—Lettuce Entertain You Enterprises—that eager-to-please mentality goes with the territory. It also means that any time of the day or night, Hub 51 is packed with locals and visitors chowing down on juicy burgers, tacos with housemade tortillas, and even some worthy sushi. The bar area gets an equally lively crowd with its varied selection of draft beers, wines by the glass, sake, and a daily cocktail on draft. Open daily for lunch, dinner, and late-night dining; open for brunch Sat and Sun.

LULA CAFE $$
2537 N. Kedzie Blvd.
(773) 489-9554
www.lulacafe.com

Long before Logan Square became the trendy neighborhood it is today, Lula Cafe was dishing out organic and artisanal fare for which it has since become well known. Husband-and-wife team Jason Hammel and Amalea Tshilds looks locally for the ingredients on their daily changing menu—their Monday night 3-course farm dinner is a real treat. Past dishes have included cherrywood-smoked quail with pickled watermelon rind; poached line-caught cod with white asparagus; and roasted leg of lamb with Puy lentils. Brunch here is a ritual for Chicago's artsy types, hence the crowds, or stop by for breakfast or lunch during the week and skip the wait. Open Mon, Wed through Sun for lunch and dinner; closed Tues.

MOTO $$$$
945 W. Fulton Market
(312) 491-0058
www.motorestaurant.com

As for that whole molecular gastronomy movement? It doesn't get much crazier—and we mean that in the nicest way—than chef Homaro Cantu and his restaurant, Moto. An alum of Charlie Trotter's, Cantu constantly goes way beyond the expected—like food cooked with lasers, edible menus, and multicourse meals that are a multisensory science experiment. But at the root of his cooking are seasonal, artisanal ingredients; just don't expect to see them presented in a typical way. The prix-fixe menus are $135 per person for 10 courses, $195 for 20 (prepare to roll happily home). For a more down-to-earth experience, Cantu's neighboring iNG (951 W. Fulton Market, 855-834-6464) focuses on Asian-inspired dishes in a chic setting that's fitting of this former art gallery, but still made with plenty of scientific flair. Dinner and cocktails served Tues through Sat.

NAHA $$$$
500 N. Clark St.
(312) 321-6242
www.naha-chicago.com

Combining her Armenian roots with cooking experience at the Four Seasons Hotels, Carrie Nahabedian produces food that is both classic and contemporary in a sophisticated atmosphere that's never pretentious. Her loyalty to local and sustainable purveyors can be seen all over the menu in dishes such as Great Lakes whitefish with beech mushrooms and wheat berries, and organic Carnaroli risotto with braised oxtails and golden chanterelles. Lunch diners should definitely opt for the Angus beef burger on a housemade brioche bun (we get ours topped with flavorful Spanish cabrales blue cheese), while in the lounge it's the glazed chicken wings that are irresistible. Open for lunch Mon through Fri and dinner Mon through Sat; closed Sun.

NEXT $$$$
953 W. Fulton Market
(312) 226-0858
www.nextrestaurant.com
First the good news: The newest restaurant from award-winning chef Grant Achatz—whose restaurant Alinea is often touted as the best in the US—and his very talented staff are totally worth all the hype. The bad news? It's kind of a tricky matter to get in the doors to try it. Asking diners to use a never-before-used reservations system via all-inclusive tickets sold online, the waiting list already far exceeds the demand. But if you're feeling lucky, head over to the West Town restaurant for one of the few unreserved tables. (Another option is to head next door to Aviary, Achatz's ultimate in creative cocktail lounges.) Just as innovative as the reservation system is the menu, which features a different time period and country every few months. Opening menu featured Paris 1906 and "next" is anybody's guess. Let us know what you experienced. Open for dinner Wed through Sun; closed Mon and Tues.

NIGHTWOOD $$
2119 S. Halsted St.
(312) 526-3385
www.nightwoodrestaurant.com
This off-the-beaten-path Pilsen restaurant is worth the trek. From the same ingredient-savvy couple as Logan Square's popular Lula Cafe, Nightwood also features a get-it-before-it's-gone seasonal menu. Which doesn't bother its loyal followers who appreciate the pared-down yet bold flavors of dishes that have appeared, such as buttermilk-fried Wisconsin sweetbreads, spit-roasted chicken from Slagel Farm and foie gras agnolotti with white truffle and almonds. Come for Sunday brunch and be sure to start with one of their made-in-house doughnuts—if the bacon-butterscotch is available, try it, seriously. The atmosphere is laid back–classy with zig-zag wood floors, brick walls, and large windows. Our favorite spot is right in front of the open kitchen. Open for dinner Mon through Sat and brunch on Sunday.

✳NORTH POND $$$$
2610 N. Cannon Dr.
(773) 477-5845
www.northpondrestaurant.com
If you're wondering whether chef Bruce Sherman is truly dedicated to using local and seasonal products at his restaurant, his neat vegetable and herb garden right outside his Lincoln Park restaurant should help clear up any confusion. Or check out Sherman's credentials, which include a "Most Sustainable Chef" recognition by Share Our Strength, a nonprofit organization helping to end hunger in America. But the best way to find out is to dine at this lovely spot whose dishes include soft-boiled farm egg with a potato-mushroom terrine and veal sweetbreads, and slow-roasted halibut with

chive butter, poached Gulf shrimp, lentils, and cherries. Built in 1912 and originally used as a warming shelter for ice skaters, North Pond was redesigned to reflect a warm Arts and Crafts style and offers romantic views of the surrounding park, the serene pond it was named after, and the Chicago skyline. Open for dinner Wed through Sun from Jan through Apr and also on Tues from May through Dec; open for brunch on Sun; from June through Sept, open for lunch Tues through Fri; closed throughout the year on Mon.

ONE SIXTYBLUE $$$
1400 W. Randolph St.
(312) 850-0303
www.onesixtyblue.com

With its airy, white-tablecloth setting, including an expansive open kitchen, you'd never know that this West Loop restaurant used to be a pickle factory. Then there are the surprises on the plate from chef Michael McDonald, a Charlie Trotter's alum, who uses market-fresh ingredients to inspire his contemporary American cuisine in dishes such as house-cured salmon with a pumpkin pancake and Slagel Farm pork shank with an apple-balsamic reduction. Located near the United Center, this sophisticated yet cozy restaurant co-owned by basketball legend Michael Jordan is a great pre-event spot. Looking for something more casual? Settle in at the contemporary lounge, which features nightly specials and an extensive bar menu, and attracts a loyal following both after work and later in the evening. Open for dinner Mon through Sat; closed Sun.

PRAIRIE FIRE $$
215 N. Clinton St.
(312) 382-8300
www.prairiefirechicago.com

Fans of Sarah Stegner and George Bumbaris' off-the-beaten path Prairie Grass Cafe in Northbrook will find a closer friend in this West Loop restaurant. Here, the former Ritz-Carlton Chicago chefs continue to spread their love for local ingredients (Stegner, after all, is one of the founders of the city's famed Green City Market). She incorporates them into dishes like spicy goat sausage, sautéed Lake Superior whitefish, and Niman ranch bacon–topped pizza. Fortunately, their signature blue-cheese burger and stellar eggs Benedict appear on both location's menus. Settle into a booth in the main dining room of the former Beaux-Arts railroad generator station or at the bar, often packed with after-work locals. Either way, save room for a slice of a scrumptious seasonal pie, made from recipes from Stegner's mom. Open for lunch Mon through Fri, dinner daily, and brunch on Sat and Sun.

PROVINCE $$
161 N. Jefferson St.
(312) 669-9900
www.provincerestaurant.com

After 10 years as chef at Nacional 27, Randy Zweiban thought he'd go with an easier-to-pronounce English name for his first solo project. But ironically, everyone tries to pronounce Province with a French accent (as in the region in southern France), when the American way is just fine. But Zweiban's not worried too much; his creative American cuisine, influenced by Spain and South America, is easy to love no matter what. The menu is cleverly categorized by size (small, big, bigger)—think tapas, but more customized—with dishes such as beer-steamed mussels with house-made chorizo, and farm-raised shrimp and organic grits with manchego cheese. Don't miss the ceviche, a signature Zweiban dish. Bonus: The restaurant received a Gold Level LEED certification, the first full-service Chi-town restaurant to do so. Its look is all about blending natural style—a 16-foot-high petrified tree sculpture, cork and recycled wood tabletops—with modern aesthetics, like a bright pink wall and ambient recessed lighting. Open Mon through Fri for lunch and dinner, Sat for dinner; closed Sun.

THE PUBLICAN $$
837 W. Fulton Market
(312) 733-9555
www.thepublicanrestaurant.com
To find inspiration for their third restaurant, the crew behind Blackbird, Avec and more recently, Big Star, tapped into their personal passions for beer, pork, and oysters. Or, as executive chef Paul Kahan calls it, "the holy trinity." And it is mighty heavenly, to be sure. The daily changing menu from chef Brian Huston features dishes like house-made charcuterie (sausages, terrines, pâtés), wood-roasted fish, and more animal parts than you can shake a knife at. The tasty Farm Chicken is a favorite, served atop a bed of crispy fries. The 100-plus craft beers have diners rethinking this whole wine-pairing thing, and then there's the upscale beer hall-esque decor—huge communal tables, booths enclosed with swinging doors—that has fans and a few foes. For the record: The James Beard Association awarded The Publican with Outstanding Restaurant Design a few years back, so see for yourself what you think. Open daily for early afternoon snacks, dinner, and brunch on Sun.

SCHWA $$$$
1466 N. Ashland Ave.
(773) 252-1466
www.schwarestaurant.com
West Town's Schwa has gotten plenty of press. Some not-so-good, like the fact that actually getting someone on the phone to make a reservation—the only way in—is a patience-challenging endeavor. But then there was the 2009 9-page feature in *GQ* magazine about chef-owner and Chicago native Michael Carlson, describing his place as "the most revolutionary restaurant in America." And once you do actually get a table at this 26-seat storefront spot (we'll cross our fingers for you) Carlson's avant-garde 9-course tasting menu definitely warrants the wait. Just a few fair warnings: The alt rock and hip-hop music can get loud, no cell-phone conversations are allowed, and the restaurant is BYOB. Open for dinner Tues through Sat.

SEPIA $$$
123 N. Jefferson St.
(312) 441-1920
www.sepiachicago.com
This West Loop restaurant didn't miss a beat when its much-lauded opening chef left. Rather it seems to have gotten even better with Andrew Zimmerman (previously at NoMI) in charge. Housed in a former 1890s print shop in the West Loop, this "modern speakeasy" exudes easy elegance, with custom-made tile floor, brick walls, stunningly modern chandeliers, and antique mirrors. Zimmerman's ingredient-driven, seasonal cuisine shines with dishes like monkfish with chorizo, judion beans, Serrano ham and piperade; and pork porterhouse, buttermilk mashed potatoes, collards, and ham hocks. The front bar is perfect

for lingering with a cocktail before or after dinner. Serving lunch Mon through Fri and dinner every day.

SIXTEEN $$$$
Trump International Hotel & Tower
401 N. Wabash Ave.
(312) 588-8030
www.trumpchicagohotel.com

It's not every day you dine under a quadruple-tiered, 14-foot Swarovski crystal chandelier floating elegantly from a 30-foot-high ceiling. But nothing less would do for The Donald—or for you when you pull out the stops to experience this classy white-tablecloth restaurant on the 16th floor (thus the name) of Chicago's soaring Trump tower. Giant curved windows look out to the Wrigley Building, the Tribune Tower, and the pedestrian life below. The menu of modern American cuisine from acclaimed chef Frank Brunacci is equally impressive, earning one star in Chicago's first-ever Michelin Guide. Trust the chef to do you right with his blind tasting menu, or choose from entrees such as farm-raised venison, served with parsnip ravioli, brussels sprouts, and juniper; or smoked lamb loin and lamb shank, accompanied by a "purple potato tower," curry, roasted beet, and horseradish. Desserts are as fancy as they are delicious. Open daily from 6:30 a.m. for breakfast, Sunday brunch, lunch Mon through Sat, and dinner Mon through Sat.

TRU $$$$
676 N. St. Clair St.
(312) 202-0001
www.trurestaurant.com

When Tru opened its doors back in 1999 with award-winning chefs Rick Tramonto and partner Gale Gand in charge, along with Lettuce Entertain You's Rich Melman, it marked a new era in Chicago haute cuisine. Now many years—and chefs—later it continues to woo diners with its progressive French cuisine, fine dining service, and luxe surroundings (yes, that is an Andy Warhol hanging on the wall). Young chef Anthony Martin has quickly gained a following for dishes such as duck consommé with foie gras ravioli and Wagyu beef short ribs braised with aromatics; his white sturgeon "caviar" is a playful twist on a sometimes straitlaced ingredient. Be prepared to spend some money for the 3-course spectacle, and, gentlemen, don't forget your jackets. Open for dinner Mon through Sat.

ZEALOUS $$$
419 W. Superior St.
(312) 475-9112
www.zealousrestaurant.com

There are plenty of rousing reasons why this chic River North restaurant has lasted some 17 years—and they all point to the passion of chef-owner Michael Taus. Housed inside a converted warehouse, the contemporary loftlike space is a perfect match for the modern American cuisine of this Culinary Institute of America grad. Global inspiration can be found in dishes such as Szechuan blue crab cakes and a short stack of mango pancakes with foie gras. But Taus also sticks closer to home as his bone-in pork chop with Illinois corn spoon bread shows. Be sure to get a glimpse of the impressive, 15-foot glass-enclosed wine cellar in the private dining room. Open for dinner Tues through Sat; closed Sun and Mon.

DEEP DISH PIZZA

EDWARDO'S $
1212 N. Dearborn St.
(312) 337-4490
www.edwardos.com

This local chain (there are nine in Illinois, Indiana, and Wisconsin; the one listed is in the Gold Coast) doesn't serve strict deep-dish; this stuff's stuffed, meaning there's a layer of sweet crust, then the toppings and cheese, then another layer of crust, and then the herb-y sauce. It's another take on fork-and-knife pizza, and the most craved variety here is the Fresh Spinach.

GINO'S EAST $
162 E. Superior St.
(312) 266-3337
www.ginoseast.com

Once coaxed out of their deep-dish pan, these thick babies ooze hot mozzarella, barely contained by the flaky golden crust. They've been a hit since Gino's East opened in 1966. Nearly as celebrated as the pizza itself are the graffiti-covered walls, scribbled up by patrons throughout the years; if you can find an empty spot, add your own "Kilroy was here." Get a little extra pizzazz with your pizza at the 633 N. Wells St. outpost, a former Planet Hollywood.

GIORDANO'S $
730 N. Rush St.
(312) 951-0747
www.giordanos.com

"In good we crust," reads a sign at this pizza place, opened in 1974 by two Italian brothers looking to bring their mother's Old World recipe to America. Another stuffed version, it gets pretty unanimous thumbs-up by diners who visit from around the world. Gooey cheese; fresh toppings between a buttery, mile-high crust; and a thin layer of chunky tomato sauce. There are now 55 Giordano's in Illinois and Florida; the Mag Mile locale gets particularly packed.

> **i** Many of these pizza spots now offer gluten-free options and some deliver around the country; if you are sane, a small pie usually suffices for two people; if you're a monster, by all means, get more.

LOU MALNATI'S $
439 N. Wells St.
(312) 828-9800
www.loumalnatis.com

Does the name Malnati ring a bell? That's because Lou is the older son of Rudy Malnati Sr., Uno's numero-uno manager (and possibly deep-dish designer). Lou introduced his first restaurant in near-suburban Lincolnwood in 1971. Now, with more than 30 locations, Lou's (as locals call it) sees hordes of workday lunchers and post-work diners at this primo River North spot. The newest at 1120 N. State St. is also the largest and sports a chic design in contrast to the others' traditional brick walls, wood booths, Chicago memorabilia, and red-and-white-checked tablecloths. But the incredible crispy-flaky crust with just a touch of breadiness, perfectly sweet sauce, and generous toppings are the same all around. Uno's may have the history, but Lou's has plenty of locals on its side.

MY PIE $
2010 N. Damen Ave.
(773) 394-6900
www.mypiepizza.com

A fourth-generation baker from Bialystock, Belarus, put this pi (written with

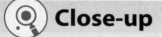 # Close-up

Go Deep

Deep-dish pizza. It's a rite and a right of being a Chicago visitor or newbie resident. But before digging in, we've got a slice of deep-dish history for ya: According to records, the delicacy originated at a pizza joint near North Michigan Avenue named simply **The Pizzeria.** It was opened in 1943 by former University of Texas football star Ike Sewell and his restaurateur buddy Ric Riccardo, who already owned a successful Italian eatery nearby. Though Riccardo died in 1954, Sewell charged ahead and, in 1955, debuted a twin-sister spot just a block away. The first one became the legendary **Pizzeria Uno,** and the new location, **Pizzeria Due.** But who concocted the famed deep-dish recipe? Well, it depends on whom you ask. Riccardo seems to have brought the pizza idea to the table, but Sewell balked at pizza as an entree. They compromised on a heartier pie—a casserole-type version whose dough is baked into a super-deep pie pan for a super-thick crust; cheese comes next, then toppings, then sauce. You would rarely dare eat this with your hands, making it the meal that Sewell had desired. Sewell always labeled himself the deep-dish inventor, but Riccardo's wife insisted it was her hubby's creation. And then again, it might very well have been manager Rudy Malnati Sr. Nowadays, we don't argue, we just eat.

the mathematical symbol) on Chicago's deep-dish map about 30 years ago. It continues to get high marks at this petite Bucktown site for its soft-in-the-middle style and fresh tomato chunks. Plus, they do a matzo pizza during Passover and send chocoholics to heaven with its Chocolate Insanity dessert. There's more space at its suburban Northbrook site (1361 Shermer Rd.; 847-715-9009).

PIZANO'S $
864 N. State St.
(312) 751-1766
www.pizanoschicago.com
An offering from Rudy Malnati Jr., the Sr.'s younger son from a second marriage, this lively joint just off the Magnificent Mile boasts a solid deep-dish with a buttery crust that's a little less bulky than others. Carry the concept into dessert with the

baked-in-a-pizza-pan chocolate chip cookie, topped with ice cream, chocolate syrup, and whipped cream. Find Pizano's in the Loop too at 61 E. Madison St. (312-236-1777) and in Glenview at 1808 N. Waukegan Rd. (847-486-1777).

PIZZERIA UNO $
29 E. Ohio St.
(312) 321-1000
www.unos.com
The original. The most famous. The busiest. No matter the time of day, stomachs of hungry folks can be heard grumbling as they wait for a table. The saving grace: Servers take orders before you're seated, so that when you are, it's just another 15 minutes or so before your dish of deliciousness arrives. We recommend the Chicago Classic with crumbled sausage, chunky tomato sauce, and mozzarella and Romano

cheeses. If you don't mind sacrificing the big-shot Uno name, you'll get the same pies much quicker at **Pizzeria Due** (619 N. Wabash Ave.; 312-943-2400). Though under the international corporate umbrella of Uno Chicago Grill, Chicago's two locations have a distinctly deep-dish-focused menu (the others include all kinds of other mass-appeal items) and, of course, authentic atmosphere.

FRENCH

*BISTRO 110 $$
110 E. Pearson St.
(312) 266-3110
www.bistro110restaurant.com

Yes, this Mag Mile restaurant is just steps from one of the city's busiest shopping districts, but Bistro 110 is much more than just a convenience. Headed up by French-born chef Dominique Tougne, who once worked with renowned chef Joël Robuchon (he has more than 25 Michelin stars for his restaurants around the world), this charming spot has been serving up traditional French fare, such as escargots en croute, artichoke baked with brie, steak frites, and cassoulet, for 20 years. The wood-burning oven gets put to good use for dishes like wood-roasted organic salmon and the warm roasted whole cloves of garlic that arrive at every table to be eaten with crusty French bread. Head to the lounge area for a more casual setting, lighter meals, and an excellent selection of craft beers from Chicago-based company Goose Island. You can get back to the shops now, or just kick back with another glass and enjoy the pleasant change of pace. A gluten-free menu is available on request. Open Mon through Sat for lunch and dinner, brunch and dinner on Sun.

BISTRONOMIC $$
840 N. Wabash Ave.
(312) 944-8400
www.bistronomic.net

Well-respected chef-about-town Martial Noguier, whose cooking chops includes stints at Chicago's one sixtyblue and Cafe des Architectes, now has a restaurant to call his own. And we're thrilled. Here in this softly lit bistro with rich red walls, cozy dark wood, and fancy crown molding, you'll find all the classics done right from the French-born chef—housemade country pâté, *salade niçoise*, pan-roasted duck *magret*—along with plenty of seasonally inspired dishes. Noguier is also a big fan of local artisanal cheeses, which he offers by the ounce, in flights, and also in a delicious daily grilled cheese of the day. The menu of small, medium, and large plates, as well as "cans" and "jars" (Picholine green olives and sardines, for example) means you can design a meal to suit your mood. A spot at the U-shaped bar in the back means your meal comes accompanied with great views of the restaurant's casually chic crowd and the white-jacketed Noguier as he greets customers throughout the night. Open daily for dinner.

HENRI $$$$
18 S. Michigan Ave.
(312) 578-0763
www.henrichicago.com

Architect Louis Henri Sullivan's claim to fame may be for ornately crafted steel-frame skyscrapers. But at the South Loop restaurant bearing his name (the terra-cotta façade on the historic building is his) the focus of your attention will be slightly more down to earth with mergings such as fig-glazed duck breast, Dover sole meunière, and foie gras and lobster Wellington. From the same partners as neighboring The Gage, including executive chef Dirk Flanigan, Henri borrows from the building's turn-of-the-19th-century vibe with velvet-covered walls, ornate chandeliers, and mohair-covered settees. Look for an equally enticing cocktail list as well, including drinks made with grape-based spirits, as well as an all-organic and biodynamic wine selection. Lunch Mon through Fri offers an impressive menu with lower prices. Open for dinner every day.

MAUDE'S LIQUOR BAR $$
840 W. Randolph St.
(312) 243-9712
www.maudesliquorbar.com

Restaurateur Brendan Sodikoff has already earned a name for himself with Chicago's Gilt Bar (its neighboring Doughnut Vault, with its get-'em-while-they're-hot artisanal treats, is equally buzz-worthy). So it comes as no surprise that his newest French-inspired venture is packing them in on a nightly basis. A former Alinea chef turns out spot-on renditions of foie gras pâté, short rib bourguignon, and roasted bone marrow. The atmosphere is reminiscent of a 1920s Parisian dive bar with vintage chairs, mismatched chandeliers, and lots of flickering candles. Drinks range from champagne cocktails and Sazeracs to the more creative "smashes." For a quieter evening, reserve a table in the upstairs lounge area. Open Tues through Sat, dinner served until midnight, bar open until 2 a.m. For more information on Maude's, flip to the Nightlife chapter.

PARIS CLUB $$
59 W. Hubbard St.
(312) 595-0800
www.parisclubchicago.com

Hardcore French-food traditionalists may quibble with the liberties this restaurant takes with its small and large plates of French food—croque monsieur fingers?—but that doesn't seem to bother the crowds that gather here on a nightly basis. Helmed by multi-award-winning chef J. Joho (who was also behind Brasserie JO, the previous long-time restaurant at this address), Paris Club has other big names behind it too: It's run by RJ and Jerrod Melman, sons of restaurateur extraordinaire Rich Melman and owners of nearby HUB51 and SUB51, which makes it no surprise that this River North spot aims to make French food more user-friendly for a new generation of diners. Dishes include chicken drumettes, individual puff pastry–topped escargots, ahi tuna steak frites, and paper bag snapper. A bit further afield are the duck cracklings with spicy vinaigrette, pig's feet bonbons, and sautéed foie gras with braised pineapple. The bustling bar with its reasonably priced wine on tap and fun cocktails (the "limonade" has lavender soda) makes for a great place to take in the scene over a few small plates. As the night progresses, be prepared for a loud, clublike atmosphere to take over. Just open: Studio Paris, its rooftop lounge. Open nightly for dinner, late-night dining Mon through Sat.

GASTROPUBS & BREWPUBS

BANGERS & LACE $
1670 W. Division St.
(773) 252-6499
htpp://bangersandlacechicago.com

The name says it all, but if you're not up on your culinary slang, we'll fill you in: This warm Wicker Park spot focuses on housemade sausage (bangers) and craft beers (lace)—and both get equal attention. Overseen by a certified cicerone (that's a beer pro in regular-speak), the beer selection features some 32 on draft as well as an extensive bottle selection, including some rare vintages. Pairing perfectly is the variety of sausages, including Sheboygan veal brats, lamb merguez, and Irish bangers, available as plates and sandwiches. Or just nibble on onion rings, crispy corn nuts, and Bavarian-style pretzels. The neighborhood bar vibe sneaks in some stylish upgrades, including a hand-built mahogany communal table, vintage light fixtures, and a wood-burning stove in the back room. Open Mon through Fri for lunch, dinner, and late-night; Sat and Sun for brunch, lunch, and dinner.

GOOSE ISLAND BREW PUB $–$$
1800 N. Clybourn Ave.
(312) 915-0071
www.gooseisland.com

The granddaddy of Chicago breweries, Goose Island was creating handcrafted ales and lagers before it was cool—their jump-start on the trend means flavorful Goose Island beers can now be found across the country. And we're proud to say, it all started back in 1988 at this Lincoln Park brewery, which is a perfect spot to try any one of the 25 or more seasonal drafts available on a daily basis, whether in the main dining room or at the square-shaped bar. The menu features easy-to-love, mostly beer-friendly items, including spicy sriracha wings, hearty burgers, mussels, and fish-and-chips. If you're interested to know more about the story behind the suds, ask about the tours that are typically offered on Saturday and Sunday. Open daily for lunch and dinner from 11 a.m.

HAYMARKET PUB & BREWERY $
737 W. Randolph St.
(312) 638-0700
www.haymarketbrewing.com

Mention craft brewing in the Midwest and it's inevitable the name Pete Crowley will pop up. A veteran brewer for some time, including 10 years at River North's popular Rock Bottom Brewery, the award-winning Crowley puts his own money where his mug is at this West Loop beer hall. Here, 16 beers are brewed on-site and you can see the shiny stainless steel brew tanks from the main dining room. The best way to enjoy the brews? Order a few in the 4-ounce size until you find one you like. This casual spot nods to the 100-year history of its building with mosaic tile floors and exposed brick, but it certainly caters to the sports-loving crowd with numerous TVs tuned to the latest game. Head to the back bar for a more low-key ambience, as well as the Drinking & Writing Theater, which hosts regular shows. The menu sticks with the laidback vibe, with dishes like smoked chicken legs buffalo style, juicy bratwurst, pizzas, and crispy sweet potato tater tots. Open daily for lunch and dinner from 11 a.m.

HOPLEAF $$
5148 N. Clark St.
(773) 334-9851
www.hopleaf.com

Belgian and Belgian-style beers are the focus at this Andersonville neighborhood gastropub, which features a mind-blowing 325 craft beers and about 45 on tap (nice selection of wines and ciders too). The beer list can be understandably daunting, as can the inevitable crowds (an upcoming expansion should help), but the friendly vibe and upscale pub grub make it all OK. Beer geeks will appreciate the pairing of proper glassware with the various beer styles. Just as much attention has been paid to the food too, with raves for signature dishes such as mussels with frites, organic Montreal-style brisket, and a duck Reuben sandwich. The front room can get noisy, but that's part of its charm. Head to the back dining room for a more conversation-friendly experience. Bar open from 3 p.m. daily; kitchen open Mon through Fri from 5 p.m., Sat and Sun from 4 p.m. Only 21 and up.

HUBBARD INN $$
110 W. Hubbard St.
(312) 222-1331
www.hubbardinn.com
A visit to this hopping River North spot—which bills itself as "Chicago's first continental tavern"—is worth it just to check out the eclectic interior design, with its Moroccan tiles, glowing orblike light fixtures, mahogany and marble bars, and off-kilter paintings (monkeys in old-fashioned portraits, for example). The downstairs main bar area with its communal-style tables attracts a lively, chic crowd, while upstairs it's more sedate. Like the carefully concocted decor, the beverage menu gets its fair shake of attention too: a varied selection of about 15 wines by the glass, a worldly beer list—Victoria lager from Mexico, Hitachino ale from Japan, Coopers sparkling ale from Australia—as well as whiskies and scotch. Inspired by the travels of writer Ernest Hemingway, the continental European small plates menu also goes for a global approach, with dishes ranging from

bacon-wrapped dates to a hearty lamb burger, pan-seared scallops in brown butter pumpkin puree to house-made ravioli with truffled sheep's milk ricotta. Open Mon through Sat from 11 a.m. to late night, closed Sun.

LONGMAN & EAGLE $$
2657 N. Kedzie Ave.
(773) 276-7110
www.longmanandeagle.com
The guys behind Chicago's indie music club Empty Bottle partnered with a cutting-edge local graphic designer-slash-artist and carpenter-slash-builder to create Logan Square's Longman & Eagle, another multiple-hyphenated spot (bar-restaurant-inn) that quickly became the city's next big thing and shows no signs of letting up. Join the hipster set over wild boar sloppy joes, smoked pork rillettes, and roasted marrow bones with red onion jam from chef Jared Wentworth. Toast your good fortune at snagging a seat at the bar with a seasonal craft beer or painstakingly made whiskey cocktail. The no-reservations policy means there's inevitably a wait, but the lovingly prepared farm-to-table food is your reward. Extend the experience by booking one of the six artsy-chic overnight guestrooms located upstairs. Open daily for brunch-lunch (starts at 10 a.m.) and dinner, closing 2 a.m. or later. During the week, Mon through Fri, it's also open for light breakfasts of coffee and pastries, perfect for grabbing to go before hopping on the adjacent Blue Line El stop.

OLD TOWN SOCIAL $
455 W. North Ave.
(312) 266-2277
www.oldtownsocial.com

With its abundance of flat screens, high-top tables, and young baseball-hat-wearing diners, you might think this is just a typical sports bar—but this one stuns with cool touches like handblown glass fixtures, a carved-wood fireplace, Oriental rugs, and antique furnishings. And chef Jared Van Camp puts his fine dining experience to good use with a varied selection of charcuterie and smoked meats. They're great on their own, but even better when they find their way into other menu items, including the wonderful side dish of roasted brussels sprouts with pancetta. The casually styled space lends itself well to made-to-be-shared plates. Favorites? The lamb sausage and tomato flatbread, spicy duck wings, and trio of mini corn dogs made with house-made sausages. There's a creative cocktail menu, as well as an impressive craft beer list. Open Mon through Fri for dinner and late-night, and Sat and Sun for lunch too.

✳**OWEN & ENGINE**   **$$**
2700 N. Western Ave.
(773) 235-2930
www.owenengine.com
The boring new-construction building across from a movie multiplex (you can park there for $2) belies an interior that you'd swear was a renovation of an old house. Husband-and-wife team Arden and Bo Fowler—they also own adjacent Fat Willy's Rib Shack, popular with Chicago police—did this place up right. Right down to the black-and-white mosaic tile under the barstools, overstuffed leather couch and chairs (in the quieter upstairs space), the ever-so-slightly tattered Oriental rugs, and the best fish-and-chips you'll find this side of the pond, which is just one of many bright spots on its

everything-made-from-scratch British comfort food menu. House-made bangers and mash, rack of lamb, and ribeye served with Yorkshire pudding are others. The outrageous beer menu guides you to a perfect sip with its crafty three- or four-word flavor descriptions. Or order up from the cocktail menu, offering drinks like the Limey, a blend of gin, lime, sugar, and spices; or the O&E Pimm's Cup, a blend of Pimm's No. 1 Cup, wild strawberry liqueur, lemon, cucumber, mint, and ginger beer. Open Mon through Fri for dinner and late-night dining; and for brunch (11 a.m. to 3 p.m.) and dinner on Sat and Sun.

REVOLUTION BREWING   **$$**
2323 N. Milwaukee Ave.
(773) 227-2739
www.revbrew.com
Judging by the diverse crowd, everyone from local hipsters to stroller-toting moms, this Logan Square brewpub is just what the up-and-coming neighborhood needed. You can't miss the exterior logo with its clenched fist (the motif continues inside where four wooden fists anchor the bar and draft handles are shaped like fists). Inside the rustic-chic space with its high restored-tin ceiling from the original 100-plus-year-old building, light fixtures crafted from beer-aging barrels, and beautiful wood rectangle bar, you'll find 14 taps pouring beer that's all developed in-house. Belly up to the bar—if there's room—and nosh on appetizers like decadent bacon-fat popcorn and applewood smoked wings before moving on to heartier plates including burgers, sandwiches, wood oven–fired pizzas topped with seasonal ingredients, and other beer-friendly pub fare. Adventurous beer-lovers should definitely taste the

sudsy desserts, like the chocolate chunk bread pudding made with mild ale. Power to the people. Open Mon through Fri from 11 a.m., Sat and Sun from 10 a.m. for brunch.

THREE ACES $
1321 W. Taylor St.
(312) 243-1577
www.threeaceschicago.com

The Little Italy neighborhood on Chicago's South Side has undergone a restaurant resurgence, and this Italian small-plates, farm-to-table spot is one of the highlights. Plus, with DJs spinning everything from hard rock to rockabilly, garage rock to hard country, this neighborhood joint is definitely a far cry from the expected. Its rock and roll soul attracts a cool crowd that not only appreciates the high-volume soundtrack, pool table, Elvis pinball machine, and photo booth, but also the food from chef Matt Troost. Divided into "farm," "mill," "sea," and "barn," menu options includes arancini on a bed of oxtail ragu, beer-steamed mussels, pizzettas, and two-hands-required burgers. There's a terrific selection of craft beers and creative cocktails (like Flight of the Living Dead, a risky mix of Wild Turkey, Lillet, Cointreau, fresh lemon juice, and an anise rinse), as well as fun bar snacks like pork-fried nuts and butterscotch doughnuts with bacon brittle. Open Mon through Fri from 5 p.m., Sat and Sun from 11:30 a.m.

GREEK

ATHENIAN ROOM $
807 W. Webster St.
(773) 348-5155

Even before *30 Rock*'s Tina Fey proclaimed her love for this Lincoln Park restaurant,

specifically its "unbelievable" roasted chicken, the reasonably priced Greek food had earned it plenty of fans. Set on a tree-lined street just steps away from the chic shopping enclave along Halsted Street and Armitage Avenue, regulars swear by the flavorful gyros, pork tenderloin shish kebab, and, yes Tina, the kalamata-style chicken with its bounty of crisp fries. Don't expect much in the way of decor, but with these low prices we don't mind a bit. Tip: If you want to hang out at just-around-the-corner Glascott's Saloon (2158 N. Halsted St.), you can get food to go from Athenian Room; just stop by here first to order and carry it over, or if the Athenian Room guys aren't too busy, they'll bring it right to you. Great, inexpensive Greek food combined with a little Irish pub action? Not a bad arrangement, thanks. Open for lunch and dinner daily.

*GREEK ISLANDS $
200 S. Halsted St.
(312) 782-9855
www.greekislands.net

Open since 1971, this restaurant prides itself on treating customers like family. Which, in the case of a Greek family, means a crowd-pleasing menu of made-from-scratch food and imported-from-Greece ingredients like extra virgin olive oil, cheeses, herbs, spices, and more. And by crowd-pleasing, we mean that it's always packed in here, but the wait is never too terrible, as experienced servers are quick to turn tables. Signature dishes include Greek-style pasta with cheese, baked lamb with artichoke hearts, and house-made lamb and beef gyros. But don't shy away from more unexpected items like hot lima beans in a tomato sauce or their flown-in-fresh seafood (it is the Greek Islands, after all). Large groups in particular will feel welcome, and the $19.95 family-style menu makes ordering easier. Bonus: There's a reasonably priced wine list, including 20 or so from Greece and most available by the glass. Free valet parking. Open for lunch and dinner daily.

PARTHENON $
314 S. Halsted St.
(312) 726-2407
www.theparthenon.com
Even if this family-owned and family-friendly restaurant didn't invent saganaki as they claim they did, we'd still be fans of the flaming cheese dish that always comes served with an enthusiastic "Opaa!" A Greektown anchor for more than 40 years, the spacious, 300-plus-seat restaurant also boasts a big, fat, Greek menu: With more than 140 items to choose from, not including the daily specials, there truly is something for everyone. Sharing is encouraged for the generous servings of dishes like panfried zucchini, moussaka, stuffed grape leaves, and shish kebabs. Lamb lovers will appreciate the abundance of offerings, including braised, roasted, and baked varieties. Not sure what to get? The family-style dinner for two or more people ($19.95 each) serves up a Greek smorgasbord of specialties. Open daily for lunch, dinner, and late-night dining.

TAXIM $$$
1558 N. Milwaukee Ave.
(773) 252-1558
www.taximchicago.com
Odds are that nothing on the menu at Taxim (pronounced Tax-SEEM) will look familiar. In other words, there's no flaming cheese and no moussaka here. But what this Wicker Park spot does have is flavorful regional foods you'd find all over Greece and Asia Minor. In fact, to find inspiration for his menu, executive chef–owner David Schneider taps into his own Greek heritage and the taste discoveries he's made on many trips to his family homeland. Here, he turns them into dishes like *tsipoúra me radíkia* (oven-roasted whole Cretan sea bass, lemon and olive oil, and sautéed dandelions) and *bamies laderes* (baby okra with sun-dried tomatoes and semolina bread). The easier-to-pronounce duck gyro with a pomegranate reduction is equally delicious, as is the house-made Greek yogurt. With its distinctively Mediterranean ceiling arcs, an all-Greek wine list, copper-topped tables, Byzantine-style decor, and boisterous crowd, you'll be ready to clink glasses of ouzo in no time. Open for dinner Wed through Mon; closed Tues. Open for lunch on Sat and Sun as well.

INDIAN

CUMIN $
1414 N. Milwaukee Ave.
(773) 342-1414
www.cumin-chicago.com
One of the newer Indian restaurants in town, Cumin focuses on modern Nepalese and Indian cuisine, which has earned the Wicker Park spot a Michelin Guide Bib Gourmand nod (its casually chic vibe probably didn't hurt either). Though similar in cooking and taste to Indian cuisine, Nepalese food doesn't use any dairy products and tends toward milder flavors. While you'll see some typical Indian dishes, including chicken tikka masala and samosas, it's the more exotic Nepalese specialties that get foodies talking. Signature items include chicken *momo* (steamed dumplings), *chhoela* (marinated chicken cooked in a tandoor), and *gorkhali*

khasi (bone-in goat meat cooked with Nepalese spices). A selection of Indian beers are available, as well as lassi, a non-alcoholic yogurt drink. Stop by during lunch for its buffet to get a little taste of a lot of different dishes; then come back for dinner. Open for lunch and dinner Tues through Sun, dinner only on Mon.

✳**HEMA'S KITCHEN** $
2439 W. Devon Ave.
(773) 338-1627
www.hemaskitchen.com
This casual, family-run restaurant always tops the list of Indian-food lovers in Chicago. It won raves long ago at its first location along the heavily Indian Devon Avenue and then carried that over to its Lincoln Park location at 2411 N. Clark St. (773-529-1705). While some aficionados might argue that the original locale is more authentic, both have all the popular dishes, including chicken vindaloo, lamb curry, shrimp biryani, and 10 assorted breads. Vegetarians are in luck with 20-plus dishes to choose from, and the BYOB no-corkage-fee policy is much appreciated. Open daily for lunch and dinner.

INDIA HOUSE $–$$
59 W. Grand Ave.
(312) 645-9500
www.indiahousechicago.com
A bit fancier than your standard Indian spot (and with slightly higher prices to match), this downtown restaurant offers some 250 different menu items ranging from upscale dishes of Bombay and Delhi to scrumptious Indian street food. Insiders know that the best value is the all-you-can-eat lunchtime buffet (get there early, especially on Friday, to beat the crowds of hungry office workers), which offers an extensive selection of frequently refreshed items. Head to the back of the restaurant if you want to catch a peek as the chefs prepare your tandoor-oven dishes in the glass-enclosed kitchen. Desserts are better than average, including a fragrant rice pudding. For beverages, there's Indian beer, plus a variety of wines and drink specials. Suburban locations in Buffalo Grove, Schaumburg, Oak Brook, and Hoffman Estates too. Open daily for lunch and dinner.

ITALIAN & PIZZA

✳**CERES' TABLE** $$
4882 N. Clark St.
(773) 878-4882
www.cerestable.com
Despite an odd location across from a cemetery, this quaint Italian restaurant has plenty of positive attributes. First and foremost, chef Giuseppe Scurato, who has worked at some of the city's best restaurants including BOKA and Landmark. Here, Scurato taps into his native Sicilian background and takes advantage of seasonal and local ingredients to create dishes such as baby artichoke salad with black truffle vinaigrette, Dietzler Farm calf's liver with brown butter sauce, and bacon-wrapped Sicilian meat loaf. Desserts like blueberry pie with merlot sauce and vanilla gelato are equally comfort-inducing, as is the decor, with dark woods and cozy booths. Plus, the sound-absorbing ceiling tiles mean you can actually hear your fellow tablemates. *Grazie.* Open for dinner Mon through Sat.

COALFIRE $
1321 W. Grand Ave.
(312) 226-2625
www.coalfirechicago.com

There's nothing fancy about this West Town eatery—14-or-so tables, exposed brick walls, and extra-large cans of tomatoes that serve as pizza platforms. But the 800-degree coal-fired oven is the true star, anyway, baking up piping hot pizzas with a crunchy yet chewy crust and just the right amount of charring. Order one of nine signature Coalfire creations—favorites include the prosciutto with mozzarella and tomato sauce; and the white pizza with mozzarella, ricotta and romano cheeses, fresh basil, garlic-infused oil, oregano, and fresh ground pepper—or create your own from 13 gourmet toppers. Skip the only-okay salads and go for that extra slice. Open Tues through Sun for lunch and dinner, closed Mon.

DAVANTI ENOTECA $$$
1359 W. Taylor St.
(312) 226-5550
www.davantichicago.com

We've got to hand it to restaurateur Scott Harris (who also owns Mia Francesca, and is a partner at Purple Pig)—he sure knows how to give diners exactly what they want. With this Little Italy find, Harris once again has a hit on his hands. The rustic-chic decor—repurposed wood, exposed beams, wall shelves filled with wine bottles (pick one and enjoy with your dinner for a $7 corkage fee)—is complemented by reasonably priced Italian small plates. His extensive menu includes plenty of cured meats and artisan cheeses, as well as antipasti, salads, bruschettas of the day, pizzas, and heartier entree-sized plates. Bold flavors include white anchovies with leccini olives and linguine with sea urchin. Only downside? The no-reservations policy. Use the wait time to narrow down your menu choices. You'll need it. Open daily for lunch and dinner.

GREAT LAKE $
1477 W. Balmoral Ave.
(773) 334-9270

It's not easy being named the best pizza in America by GQ magazine, especially when you're just a minuscule spot where each of the pies is painstakingly made by hand by the owner. But so it goes at this Andersonville restaurant, which has probably earned way more attention than the passionate couple that owns it ever asked for, or possibly even imagined. Three to five pizzas change regularly depending on what seasonal, organic, and local ingredients are available. The restaurant's seasonal salads even received mention in Chicago's first Michelin guide in 2011, touting them as "beaming fresh." Decide for yourself if the inevitable wait is worth it. We sure think so. And you can easily kill some time walking around window-shopping through Andersonville or scouting for a bottle of vino to take back to the BYOB spot. It's important to note that they don't take substitutions on pizzas—get them "as is" or not at all—but you won't be disappointed. Open for dinner Wed through Sat.

MIA FRANCESCA $$
3311 N. Clark St.
(773) 281-3310
www.miafrancesca.com

While this Lakeview restaurant not too far from Wrigley Field isn't new or cutting edge, that's just fine with the happy diners who have flocked here since it opened in 1992. The approachable Northern Italian food set in a casually chic ambience has spawned a ton of siblings in Chicago and surrounding suburbs (19 in the Chicago area alone, plus some in Wisconsin, North Carolina, California, and Arizona, all equally successful). On crowded weekend nights, head to the back coach house to wait or, if there's room, simply pull up at the bar to dine. The menu, while not lengthy, is filled with tempting seasonal appetizers, pastas, pizzas, and entrees. Tip: Ask for half orders of the pasta to try more items, to save yourself from over-stuffing, or just to save room for tasty tiramisu. Our faves? Fried calamari, prosciutto, artichoke, and mushroom pizza topped with a runny egg, and the linguine with mussels. Those with gluten allergies feel the love too with their own entree and dessert menus; plus, the kids' menu is one of the few that make us wish we were under 12 again. Then again, with its affordably priced wine list, we're glad we're not. Open for dinner Mon through Fri, lunch and dinner Sat and Sun.

OSTERIA VIA STATO & PIZZERIA VIA STATO $$
620 N. State St.
(312) 642-8450
www.osteriaviastato.com

This casual River North restaurant has a split personality, and that's a good thing. On one side is the casual Pizzeria Via Stato, where you'll find tasty small plates (definitely try the house-marinated olives), a handful of fresh salads, and extra-crispy Roman-style pizzas with classic toppings, including an always interesting pizza-of-the-month. On the other side is swankier Osteria Via Stato (a great date spot), featuring heartier Italian fare with a seasonal bent. Larger parties or super-hungry diners can dive into the Dinner Party menu ($38.95), which features an extensive selection of antipasti, pasta, and main course options. Or go a la carte with dishes such as slow-cooked pork shank, seafood stew, and hand-rolled cavatelli with wild

mushrooms. The Pizzeria is open for dinner nightly, and for lunch and dinner Mon through Sat; the Osteria is only open for dinner.

PIECE $
1927 W. North Ave.
(773) 772-4422
www.piecechicago.com

Forget deep-dish or trendy Neapolitan-style. At this lively Wicker Park joint, the name of the game is oblong-shaped New Haven pizza. That means you choose from red, plain, or white pizza, then top it with any of the usual suspects or with fancier options like goat cheese, fresh basil, bacon, and clams. In addition to those tasty pies, Piece also has earned plenty of loyal fans for its award-winning, hand-crafted beer, whose pun-heavy names—a Dysfunctionale, anyone?—are only part of the fun, which also includes lively DJ karaoke every Thurs night and live band karaoke on Sat at 11 p.m., so you can live out your rock star fantasy and have great pizza and beer too. The plethora of TVs means sports fans can have it all, just better. Open daily for lunch and dinner.

PICCOLO SOGNO $$
464 N. Halsted St.
(312) 421-0077
www.piccolosognorestaurant.com

Depending on the season, Piccolo Sogno presents two different experiences. Colder temps finds diners inside, sitting at the long, Italian marble-topped bar with its Art Deco back wall, or in the intimate main dining room, with its Murano glass light fixtures and cornflower-blue walls. They nibble on pizzas from the wood-burning oven or devour plates of hearty house-made pastas, Roman-style roasted pork, and whole roasted fish. Once things start to warm up, the coveted tables are in the lush tree-filled patio, considered to be the best in the city. Fair-weather friends, indeed. Open for lunch Mon through Fri, dinner every day.

RICCARDO TRATTORIA $$
2119 North Clark St.
(773) 549-0038
www.riccardotrattoria.com
This cozy Lincoln Park restaurant consistently earns praise from some of the city's top critics for its authentic, regional Italian food. Credit goes to chef Riccardo Michi, who started his culinary career in Italy before moving on to the US where he opened the popular Bice restaurants. Now, his family-run operation (wife Veronica is sous chef) serves up favorite Italian classics, including beef carpaccio, porcini mushroom risotto, and spaghetti carbonara. Regulars know to skip those for the more creative entrees, such as tripe Florentine, orecchiette with wild boar sausage, and roasted Cornish hen. Open for dinner nightly.

SPACCA NAPOLI $
1769 W. Sunnyside Ave.
(773) 878-2420
www.spaccanapolipizzeria.com
Long before Great Lake began churning out its handcrafted pizzas, this Ravenswood spot had Chicago 'za lovers abuzz. A labor of love for owners Jonathan Goldsmith and Ginny Sykes, their passion for Italy is evident in everything from the pizza oven hand-built by artisans direct from Napoli to the made-in-Italy dough mixer and the imported ingredients. And then there's the proof that's in the pies—simple margherita

with its *fior di latte* mozzarella, and fresh basil; the Diavola with bufala mozzarella, spicy salami, and basil; and a white pizza topped with smoked mozzarella, prosciutto di parma, arugula, and parmesan. Even the salads are worth checking out, dressed simply with extra virgin olive oil and aged balsamic vinegar from Italy. The all-Italian wine and beer list pairs deliciously. Open for lunch and dinner Wed through Sun, dinner only on Tues; closed Mon.

SPIAGGIA/CAFE SPIAGGIA $$$$
980 N. Michigan Ave., 2nd Fl.
(312) 280-2750
www.spiaggiarestaurant.com
While we didn't need a presidential seal of approval to whet our appetites at this exquisite jacket-required winner, we definitely can appreciate the Obamas' affection for it—rumor has it that President Obama is a huge fan of the wood-roasted scallops. Since opening in 1984, chef-partner Tony Mantuano has never wavered from his vision of serving authentic Italian cuisine—even when some of the city's big-name restaurateurs told him he'd never survive without a meatball on his menu. Instead, there are dishes like hand-rolled gnocchi with Umbrian black truffles, and wood-roasted rabbit wrapped in pancetta. The softly lit dining room features tiers that afford stunning views of Lake Michigan just beyond the 40-foot-high windows that overlook the Magnificent Mile. It sets a perfect scene for the many marriage proposals that happen here. Looking for something a little more casual? Head next door to Cafe Spiaggia for terrific wood-oven pizzas, flavorful pastas, and Italian beers on tap. Open daily for dinner.

TERZO PIANO $$–$$$
159 E. Monroe St.
(312) 443-8650
www.terzopianochicago.com

When you set out to design a museum restaurant, there are two general options: Let the art take center stage; or use all that creativity lining the walls as your muse. One step inside the Art Institute's new Modern Wing restaurant and it's obvious they went for the latter. With a focus on sustainable, local ingredients from family-run farms, this Italian-Mediterranean restaurant from chef Tony Mantuano (Spiaggia) is full of artistic touches. The strikingly white third-floor space (even the cheese cart is white) evokes a nearly futuristic vibe with white oak floors, translucent resin tables, floor-to-ceiling windows, and Eames and Herman Miller furniture. There's just as much visual appeal in the cuisine at this elegant lunch spot (open for dinner on Thurs only), including the farro salad with Wisconsin Parmesan, the lamb burger with house-made onion jam, and seasonal flatbreads. And when you're done, spend some time admiring the Kandinskys, Kellys, de Koonings, and Picassos that hang in the Modern Wing exhibits. Open daily for lunch.

JAPANESE

ARAMI $$$
1829 W. Chicago Ave.
(312) 243-1535
www.aramichicago.com

They're partners in some of Chicago's most popular bars—Small Bar, which has three locations, and The Exchange—but what brothers Ty and Troy Fujimura really wanted to do was open a restaurant that paid homage to their Japanese heritage and grandparents' old general store in Hawaii. That dream's a reality with West Town's chic-urban Arami, a space they designed themselves and opened with well-known local sushi chef B.K. Park. Look for authentic Japanese dishes like ramen with a rich, earthy broth, and *donburi* (rice bowls), as well as pristine sushi, special rolls, and an extensive sake list. This restaurant has quickly earned a loyal following, so reservations are highly recommended. Open for lunch and dinner Tues through Sat, dinner on Sun. Closed Mon.

CHIZAKAYA $
3056 N. Lincoln Ave.
(773) 697-4725
www.chizakaya.com

Don't expect to find sushi at this Lakeview Japanese restaurant. Rather, Chicago native and Charlie Trotter vet chef Harold Jurado puts his own seasonal and sustainable spin on dishes typically found in a Japanese pub. That means mini skewers of baby octopus, chicken skins, duck hearts, or shishito peppers, creative hot and cold starters, and noodle dishes, including a tasty house ramen with braised pork and a slow-poached egg. Creativity applies to the cocktail list as well, and definitely take a sip from the selection of shochu (a vodkalike spirit similar to sake, but distilled instead of brewed), or the reasonably priced sake and wines. The restaurant's somewhat imposing blocky black exterior gives way to a cozy and intimate front room and a neighorhoody feel in the back room with communal tables and open kitchen. Open for lunch and dinner Tues through Sat; closed Sun and Mon.

Five Worth the Drive

Chicago's restaurants can keep your plate endlessly full, but there are also some top-rated restaurants in the suburbs. Here are five we crave.

Courtright's. Tucked in among 2 acres of woods, Courtright's exudes romance and sophistication. William and Rebecca Courtright have gone to great lengths to achieve a sense of history in the restaurant's Arts and Crafts style and to give people a reason to return for the seasonally focused cuisine and 11,000-bottle wine cellar. 8989 S. Archer Ave., Willow Springs; (708) 839-8000; www.courtrights.com.

Inovasi. Have you ever seen a menu organized by inspiration—music, family, dreams, "someone else"? It's how chef John des Rosiers creates his, and the results are a global fusion of ingredients (French, Italian, South American) that do more than just sound interesting on paper. The quirky concept makes sense in this casually warm space, all woods and soothing blues. 28 E. Center Ave., Lake Bluff; (847) 295-1000; www.inovasi.us.

Nieto's. After 30 award-winning years, Debbie and Carlos Nieto closed their venerated French gem Carlos'. Sad faces vanished at word of the couple's brand-new concept, Nieto's, which dusts off some of the former fancy-pants feel and replaces it with a casual elegance and lower price points. Rest assured, the Nietos' impeccable attention to detail, warm hospitality, and love of French cuisine remains. 429 Temple, Highland Park; (847) 432-0770; www.carlos-restaurant.com.

Vie. Chef Paul Virant, who also helms Perennial Virant in Chicago (1800 N. Lincoln Ave., 312-981-7070), gives serious thought to his seasonally changing and mostly locally sourced menu of American cuisine at this Michelin-star restaurant. But he keeps it all deceptively simple, spotlighting fresh ingredients and providing stellar service. The sleek, chic decor is a fitting backdrop. 4471 Lawn Ave., Western Springs; (708) 246-2082; www.vierestaurant.com

Wholly Frijoles. Chef J. Carmen Villegas began his career with Lettuce Entertain You restaurants and made his own splash with this family-owned hidden gem. Don't mind its strip-mall setting; the cozy-cute interior and Mexican specialties with a gourmet twist more than compensate. 3908 W. Touhy Ave., Lincolnwood; (847) 329-9810; www.whollyfrijoles.net.

COAST   **$–$$**
2045 N. Damen Ave.
(773) 235-5775
www.coastsushibar.com

With its BYOB policy and wallet-friendly sushi, this Bucktown spot has been packing 'em in for nearly a decade. While there's a small selection of entrees, such as tamarind duck and various teriyakis, it's the extensive menu of modern rolls that are the main draw here. Sushi purists might make fun of the unconventional maki like the Sunrise roll of seared ginger tuna with mint wrapped in mango or the White Dragon, with shrimp tempura, cream cheese, and wasabi mayo, but that just means there's more for the rest of us to enjoy. The handcrafted furniture and dimly lit dining room add to the hip factor. Open nightly for dinner and lunch as well on Sat and Sun.

KAMEHACHI $$
1400 N. Wells St.
(312) 664-3663
www.kamehachi.com
Considered Chicago's first sushi bar, the third-generation-owned Kamehachi first opened across from The Second City in 1967, when sushi was exotic and largely unheard of by non-Japanese people; some of its first regulars were actors from the famous theater like John Belushi. The restaurant moved two blocks south in 1994 and has remained a go-to sushi favorite for locals and visitors alike—its long list of celebrity diners these days includes Alec Baldwin, Jessica Simpson, Teri Hatcher, and Kevin Spacey. Kamehachi translates to "eight turtles" in Japanese—the turtle and the number 8 symbolize good luck and long life—and it's clear that the restaurant has some of that mojo, with now two additional downtown locations, one in suburban Northbrook, and a Loop cafe. Open daily for lunch and dinner.

SUSHISAMBA $$$
504 N. Wells St.
(312) 595-2300
www.sushisamba.com
It might get attention (and a predominantly pretty, young crowd) for its scene-y vibe and

splashy decor of glowing blues, oranges, and reds, but this spacious, split-level River North hot spot—there are equally vibrant sister spots in New York, Miami Beach, and Vegas—also delivers on the food, which merges the flavors of Brazil, Japan, and Peru with super-fresh sushi (and an environmentally prudent ban on bluefin tuna). Grab a spot in the fashionably loud, rounded front bar or head upstairs to the rooftop lounge for potent fruity cocktails, playful small plates, and sashimi. The main dining room serves up a more traditional meal, where we love anything that comes off the robata grill, including short ribs, sea bass, and various seasonal vegetables. Japanese-style Kobe beef is also available when you've got a little extra cash to spend. Brunch takes a twist with menu items like *feijoada* (Brazilian stew) and toasted spice cake with yuzu pickled berries. Got little diners with you? There's something fun for them too, like baby bento boxes, mini sliders, and fizzy kiddie cocktails. FYI: You'll either love or hate the bathroom decor, but do remember to bring a couple of singles for the attendant. Open daily for lunch and dinner, brunch on Sun.

SUSHI WABI $$
842 W. Randolph St.
(312) 563-1224
www.sushiwabi.com
The understated, Zen-like decor of this West Loop fave puts the focus on the artfully arranged sushi and other Japanese specials; the word *wabi* itself translates to a kind of stark artistic serenity, with an emphasis on what's described as "refined simplicity." Sushi traditionalists are rewarded with top-notch nigiri and maki, as well as a lengthy list of special rolls. Non-raw-fish eaters and vegetarians have options here too, ranging from

grilled salmon with house-made plum sauce and peppercorn-crusted tuna to grilled Japanese eggplant and seaweed salad. One of the early players on Chicago's sexy sushi scene, Sushi Wabi still draws a chic crowd that doesn't mind the tight space and high-volume music. Open for lunch and dinner Mon through Fri, dinner only on Sat and Sun.

TAKASHI RESTAURANT $$$
1952 N. Damen Ave.
(773) 772-6170
www.takashichicago.com
What do you do after you've won a James Beard award, served as chef de cuisine at multi-starred restaurants (Ambria, Tribute), and opened a 250-seat stunner at the Wynn Las Vegas? Well, if you're chef Takashi Yagihashi, you create an eponymous intimate restaurant in Bucktown. Earning itself a commendable one star from Michelin, Takashi is an earth-toned space, with hardwood floors and graceful bonsai. The menu does away with the traditional 3-course meal and instead presents a mouthwatering selection of shareable small plates that merge all the best of Japanese cooking with contemporary French-American fare. Translation: chilled house-made tofu with an umami-ginger soy sauce, sake-steamed Mediterranean mussels, and Amish chicken with shimeji mushrooms and eggplant cooked in a clay pot. Looking for something more low-key? Hit the restaurant on Sunday evenings for its special menu featuring various styles of Japanese noodles, including ramen, soba, and buckwheat. Beverages include an international wine list as well as hard-to-find bottles of sake. Open for dinner Tues through Sun, as well as brunch on Sun (the noodle menu's served then too); closed Mon.

KOREAN

CRISP $
2940 N. Broadway
(877) 693-8653
www.crisponline.com
What this tiny Lincoln Park counter-service restaurant lacks in decor, it more than makes up for in tasty food. If the name doesn't clue you in, perhaps the roll of paper towels on each of the communal tables will. Crisp specializes in delicious, Korean-inspired fried chicken (incidentally, voted the best fried chicken in America by *Travel + Leisure*, if you doubt it) and isn't for those who are afraid to get their hands dirty. There are three sauces to choose from and the Funke chicken is available in whole or half orders as well as wings only. The Seoul Sassy, from a family recipe, has a subtle sweetness to it in its ginger, soy, and garlic blend, while the barbecue sauce is deliciously spicy and sweet. You'll also find other Korean-inspired fare to try, such as an adaptation of the classic *bi bim bop* (Buddha bowls) and burritos filled with rice and beef *bulgogi*. Open Tues through Sun for lunch and dinner (closes at 9 p.m.); closed Mon.

DEL SEOUL $
2568 N. Clark St.
(773) 248-4227
www.delseoul.com
The trend may have started in L.A. with the Kogi food trucks, but this casual, cute Lincoln Park eatery (an expansion is in the works) does its own take on modern Korean barbecue, with winning results. Must-try items include the *kalbi* tacos (grilled beef short rib), sesame-chile shrimp *banh mi* sandwiches, and fries topped with spicy kimchi, pork belly, melted cheese, and sour cream. For these prices (nearly everything's under $10),

you can over-order if you'd like. Open daily for lunch and dinner.

HAE WOON DAE $
6420 N. California Ave.
(773) 764-8018
A little off the beaten track and stuck amid a strip mall, this no-frills West Rogers Park spot manages to draw a loyal late-night crowd of diners (it's open until 5 a.m. nightly) for its raved-about Korean barbecue that brings sizzling coals right to your table, along with an ample selection of customary side dishes. Larger groups can opt for a private room, but the main area is livelier. Word to the wise: No matter where you sit, expect to leave with the aroma of sweet smoke infused into your clothes. It's a small price to pay for delicious cook-your-own *kalbi* barbecue ribs, pork belly, and more adventurous tripe and tongue. Open for dinner nightly and lunch on Sat and Sun.

LATIN AMERICAN & CUBAN

CAFECITO $
26 E. Congress Pkwy.
(312) 922-2233
www.cafecitochicago.com
This small South Loop Cuban sandwich shop is basically counter service with a smidgen of tables and a couch, but it's a huge hit for its flavorful and reasonably priced food. Come early and you'll be rewarded with a half-dozen breakfast sandwiches as well as potent coffee drinks. But it's the lunch menu that really shines, with 20 different pressed sandwiches to choose from. The Cubano (roast pork, ham, swiss cheese, pickles, and mustard) is a top choice, while non-meat lovers can indulge in the Provoletta, filled with grilled provolone cheese, roasted red peppers, and chimichurri sauce. Platters get you more food, with a choice of five proteins, and sides of rice, beans, and plantains. Know before you go: The under-6-bucks price tag for most of the sandwiches has quickly lured students from nearby colleges, so it's bustling all day. Open for breakfast, lunch, and dinner Mon through Fri; open for breakfast and lunch only on Sat and Sun.

CARNIVALE $$
702 W. Fulton St.
(312) 850-5005
www.carnivalechicago.com
It's big and bold and it fully lives up to its name with spirited music and colorful over-the-top decor, including a checkerboard jewel-toned skylight and oversize light fixtures. The playful, 35,000-square-foot space serves as the fitting backdrop to the equally lively food: a spicy mix of dishes from Cuba, Puerto Rico, Mexico, Spain, and South America that incorporate an abundance of local ingredients, some of which come right from the restaurant's rooftop gardens. Definitely start with a tasting of ceviches before moving on to chunky guacamole and empanadas made with beef from local purveyor Dietzler Farm. Main courses include a selection of wood-grilled dishes, including the Churrasco, a Nicaraguan-style beef tenderloin, as well as seafood and fish, and a mouthwatering vegetarian dish of seasonal veggies, mushrooms, wheat berries, roasted squash, cresenza cheese, and Peruvian red pepper. To go with that party atmosphere, there are plenty of festive specialty cocktails, plus rum flights and a long list of tequilas. Party on, people! Open for lunch Mon through Fri and dinner nightly.

NACIONAL 27 $$
325 W. Huron St.
(312) 664-2727
www.n27chicago.com
When it opened in 1998, Nacional 27 was one of the first downtown Chicago restaurants to offer seriously good south-of-the-border cuisine—and we don't mean just Mexico. It's still riding high on its tropical Miami Beach vibe and a mean menu of cuisine from an impressive 27 different Latin American countries (hence, the name). It also happens to be a rocking nightlife spot and serves up spectacular handcrafted cocktails. On the weekends, the music gets pumping and salsa dancing kicks into high gear. Make a meal out of the extensive small plates menu of ceviche, mini tacos, skewers, and empanadas; or go all out with entrees such as chimichurri-crusted filet and farm-raised chicken mole verde. Open for dinner and late-night dining at the bar Mon through Sat; closed Sun.

TANGO SUR $-$$
3763 N. Southport Ave.
(773) 477-5466
With soft lighting, flickering candles, exposed brick walls, and seductive Latin music, this Argentinean eatery qualifies as romantic. Unless you're a vegetarian, actually, and then the large portions of meat might rather turn you off. But back to carnivorous couples: In-house butchers straight from *carne*-loving Argentina carve on a daily basis, turning out dishes like *bife vesuvio* (grilled steak filled with spinach), *lomo* (filet mignon), and *parrillada,* a mixed tableside grill topped with all kinds of meaty goodness. The generous portions make splitting a totally fair option, and the BYOB policy means more dinero to spend wooing your date. Open for dinner

nightly, Sat open late afternoon and on Sun at noon.

MEDITERRANEAN

AVEC $
615 W. Randolph St.
(312) 377-2002
www.avecrestaurant.com
This West Loop wine bar and restaurant has been a staple for eight-plus years on the local dining scene, and it was a local forerunner in the ingredient-based small-plates style of eating. James Beard Award–winning chef Koren Grieveson turns out delectable Mediterranean-inspired dishes such as burrata with charred leeks, whipped brandade with house-made garlic bread, and chorizo-stuffed dates, a signature item. Expect to get to know your dining neighbors at this small restaurant, with its communal tables and tightly packed bar. And expect a wait for a table. Open daily from late afternoon to late night.

✳THE PURPLE PIG $$
500 N. Michigan Ave.
(312) 464-1744
www.thepurplepigchicago.com
As the name indicates, there is a ton of terrific swine-centric items at this cute Michigan Avenue wine bar: pork-fat-fried almonds (we dare you to eat just one), pork liver pâté, pork blade steak with *nduja* (spicy, spreadable sausage) and honey, and pig's ear with crispy kale. But this intimate restaurant tucked inside an office building is more than just a pig heaven. Non-pork lovers get in on the flavorful action too, with seasonal dishes such as the shaved brussels sprouts with pecorino and Parmigiano reggiano or house-cured bacala brandade from

local chef Jimmy Bannos Jr. No matter what you choose off the Mediterranean-inspired menu, there are plenty of wallet-friendly wines to pair with the totally sharable small plates. Grab a spot at the U-shaped bar or one of the three communal tables and prepare to settle in. Open daily for lunch, dinner, and late-night dining.

MEXICAN

BIG STAR $$
1531 N. Damen Ave.
(773) 235-4039
www.bigstarchicago.com
To hear the owners tell it, Big Star is simply a honky-tonk bar with a tacqueria. But don't let that description fool you. Long before the doors even opened at this Wicker Park spot, Chicago foodies and scenesters were buzzing about it. And for good reason: The group behind the project also has their names attached to some of the city's hottest restaurants and lounges, including Blackbird, Avec, The Publican, and The Violet Hour. Thankfully, Big Star has more than lived up to its hype. With the 1950s bars of Bakersfield, California, as its muse, the decor takes on an almost unfinished look, with concrete floors, exposed light bulbs, and painted brick walls. Dominating the room is a square wood bar with six wooden booths lining one wall. To drink, there are under-the-radar whiskies, bourbons, and tequilas, as well as craft beers from around the country. Or opt for one of their creative cocktails. To eat, award-winning chef Paul Kahan has created a small selection of tacos (the *al pastor* has already earned signature status), plus sides and snacks, like house-made chips and salsas. Added bonus: The star power behind Big Star doesn't translate to astronomical prices.

Though cash only, there's an ATM conveniently located by the front door. Open daily for lunch, dinner, and late-night dining. For more about Big Star, check out the Nightlife chapter.

CHILAM BALAM $$
3023 N. Broadway
(773) 296-6901
www.chilambalamchicago.com
While its name comes from an ancient Mayan text filled with mysterious foreboding, there's nothing ominous going on at Chilam Balam. Rather it's a happy tale of farm-focused Mexican food at this Lakeview restaurant. Combining the skills he learned while at famed Frontera Grill and Topolobampo with a love for local ingredients, chef Chuy Valencia keeps the shareable food frill-free at the intimate subterranean spot. But that certainly doesn't mean boring—try Oaxacan-glazed pork ribs, shiitake mushroom empanadas, and brussels sprouts with a cinnamon cream. The ambience is equally laid back, with pillow-topped wood benches, brightly colored walls, and chillax music. Save some dinero with Chilam's BYOB status, and know that it's cash only. Open for dinner Tues through Sat; closed Sun and Mon.

FRONTERA GRILL, TOPOLOBAMPO $$–$$$$
445 N. Clark St.
(312) 661-1434
www.rickbayless.com
For authentic Mexican food in Chicago (and really the entire country), the chef most often mentioned is Rick Bayless, winner of Bravo TV's *Top Chef Masters* Season 1. He has devoted his life to studying traditional styles of Mexican cooking and has graciously

brought them back to his wildly popular Chicago trio of restaurants: Topolobampo, Frontera Grill, and the newest addition on his block—they're all literally in a line down Clark Street—XOCO (aptly taken from Mexican slang meaning "little sister"). Well known for his love of sustainable ingredients and the people who produce them, Bayless's nonprofit Frontera Farmer Foundation grants help support local agriculture. Bayless himself uses the ingredients to create authentic dishes with his personal twist. For elegant Mexican cuisine, Topolobampo is the place to go, while for a more casual meal, Frontera Grill's tacos al carbon, crispy taquitos, and flavorful salsas can't be beat. Stop at quick-service XOCO for to-go tortas, caldos, and churros. Be prepared for large crowds at each one—at Frontera and Topo, sip on amazing margaritas to bide your time. Topolobampo and Frontera are open for lunch Tues to Fri, dinner Tues through Sat, and brunch at Frontera on Sat; XOCO is open for breakfast, lunch, and early dinner Tues through Sat; brunch on Sun. All are closed Mon.

MEXIQUE $$–$$$
1529 W. Chicago Ave.
(312) 850-0288
www.mexiquechicago.com
At first, locals wondered about the Mexican-French fusion going on at this West Town restaurant. But then chef Carlos Gaytan set them straight, explaining that merging these two isn't so crazy after all when you consider that they have a history dating back to the French invasion of Mexico in the 1860s. Plus, Gaytan himself is a native of Mexico with extensive French culinary training. And then there's the ultimate test, found in delicious dishes like *achiote* and tequila-braised pork rillettes, escargots with chimichurri butter,

and a raved-about trio of shrimp, avocado mousse, and mole with plantains. To keep the emphasis on the food, Gaytan, along with wife-designer Ilimar Isaac, kept the interior of the 80-seat restaurant simple with earth tones and a glass-enclosed kitchen. Visit on Tues for half off bottles of wine. Open for lunch Tues through Fri, dinner Tues through Sat, and brunch on Sat and Sun.

MIXTECO GRILL $$
1601 W. Montrose Ave.
(773) 868-1601
While the chef's name at Mixteco might not ring a bell—we predict it won't stay that way for long—the places he's worked at will. That's because Rodolfo Neri has spent time in some of the city's most famous Mexican-inspired kitchens including Frontera Grill-Topolobampo, Chilpancingo, and Fonda del Mar. Now, at this far-north Lakeview spot, he taps into all that experience to create Mexican food that's flavorful, fresh, and authentic. We're big fans of his Ensenada-style fish tacos and rack of lamb in black mole, not to mention the low prices and BYOB policy. Tip: Beat the inevitable dinnertime crowds and go for their weekend brunch. Open for dinner Tues through Sun and brunch Sat and Sun; closed Mon.

XOCO $
449 N. Clark St.
(312) 334-3688
www.rickbayless.com
As chef-partner of Frontera Grill and Topolobampo, Rick Bayless is no stranger to authentic Mexican cuisine. But at XOCO, he's taking it to the streets—literally. Next door to his other River North restaurants, you'll find all the rustic Mexican street food Bayless himself adores in one quick-service,

environmentally friendly spot (it boasts LEED Gold Certification). In the morning, people line up for made-to-order churros and hot chocolate from cacao beans roasted and ground in-house. At lunchtime, tortas (Mexican sandwiches) take center stage in the wood-burning oven, like one stuffed with pork braised overnight and topped with pickled red onions. In the evening, people clamor for the caldos, richly flavored meal-in-a-bowl soups. The open kitchen, with its street-facing window, means you get an insider's peek at the whole process too, and it gives you something to do during long waits. Try your luck any Tues through Sat for breakfast, lunch or dinner. Closed Sun and Mon.

PAN ASIAN

BELLY SHACK $–$$
1912 N. Western Ave.
(773) 252-1414
www.bellyshack.com
Chef Bill Kim had already amassed a posse of fans for his authentic noodle soups at Urban Belly in the Logan Square neighborhood. At Belly Shack, he taps into his Korean roots and his wife's Puerto Rican background to create flavorful fusion dishes such as hot and sour hominy soup, crispy plaintain chips with chimichurri sauce, and a barbecued tofu jibarito sandwich. As at Urban Belly, the ambience here is totally casual. Order your food at the counter, then grab a spot in the 44-seat dining room, which blends reclaimed materials with graffiti-inspired art, to wait for its delivery. For dessert, it's gourmet soft-serve ice cream with toppings like bacon-chocolate-chip cookie crumbles and mint brownie. Open Tues through Sun for lunch and dinner; closed Mon.

SUNDA $$
110 W. Illinois St.
(312) 644-0500
www.sundachicago.com
It doesn't get much hipper than Sunda, the River North Asian hot spot from the same owners as Rockit Bar & Grill and sexy nightlife spot The Underground (see the Nightlife chapter). But in addition to its scenester status and chic decor—don your trendiest threads—200-seat Sunda serves up some seriously original dishes, including crispy sushi rice topped with Kobe beef tartare, lemongrass beef lollipops, red curry–bronzed black cod, and Indonesian corn fritters. To match the exotic food, restaurant and hotel designer Tony Chi, who worked on Chicago's NoMi as well as Alain Ducasse's Spoon in Hong Kong, has created a suitably thought-provoking and feng shui–inspired space full of red travertine marble and black bamboo. Open for lunch Mon through Fri; restaurant and lounge open daily for dinner and late-night; brunch on Sun.

URBAN BELLY $
3053 N. California Ave.
(773) 583-0500
www.urbanbellychicago.com
Who would have thought that one of Chicago's favorite chefs would be found in a BYOB self-service, communal table–only, out-of-the-way spot in a mini mall next door to a Laundromat? But that's exactly where you'll find Urban Belly, Bill Kim's ode to noodles, rice, and dumplings. Kim is no stranger to fine dining, having worked at Charlie Trotter's, Trio, and Le Lan, and it shows in dishes like his beautifully flavored pork belly ramen in a pho broth, and juicy lamb and brandy dumplings. As his first solo venture (he also owns Logan Square's

Belly Shack, both Michelin Bib Gourmand winners), he keeps it simple, doing away with fine dining niceties—and you won't miss them a bit. Open Tues through Sun for lunch and dinner.

SEAFOOD

⁕GT FISH & OYSTER **$**
531 N. Wells St.
(312) 929-3501
www.gtfishandoyster.wordpress.com
The crew behind Girl & the Goat, Perennial Virant, BOKA, and Landmark have succeeded again with this recently opened River North hot spot. Chef Giuseppe Tentori (the G and the T in the name) worked for more than 10 years at fine dining restaurant Charlie Trotter's before joining up with restaurateurs Kevin Boehm and Rob Katz at BOKA, where his Mediterranean-influenced cuisine earned high marks, including a *Food & Wine* Best New Chef nod. At GT Fish & Oyster he turns his attention to the sea with winning results: pristine oysters served with creative accompaniments, seafood plates such as whole chorizo-stuffed squid atop saffron-infused rice that are big enough for two. Equally stunning is the space itself, including a boomerang-shaped table perfect for walk-ins. Open nightly for dinner.

L2O **$$$$**
2300 N. Lincoln Park West
(773) 868-0002
www.L2Orestaurant.com
This serene, almost spa-like space, filled with Macassar ebony columns, plush couches, and white leather chairs quickly caught the attention of food lovers when it opened in 2008. But there's been an equally noteworthy change recently: the exit of chef

Laurent Gras, whose first name was part of the inspiration for the restaurant's moniker (along with a reference to the seafood-heavy menu). But not to worry. The Lincoln Park destination still boasts a coveted three stars awarded in Chicago's first Michelin Guide, backing by James Beard Award–winning mega-restaurateur Rich Melman of Lettuce Entertain You (Outstanding Restaurateur, 2011), and talented chef Francis Brennan in charge. Expect signature items, such as the made-in-house breads, pristine sashimi platter, and fluffy soufflés. Tip: If you're not willing to commit to an entire meal (and its lofty price tag), snag a spot in the small lounge for creative cocktails and inventive small plates. Open for dinner Wed through Mon; closed Tues.

i Chicago's food reporter for ABC 7 Chicago, Steve Dolinsky has won 12 James Beard Foundation Awards for his TV and radio work; that's practically the most JBF awards anyone has won for anything. Check out his always taste-tempting blog at www.wbez.org/blogs/steve-dolinsky.

SHAW'S CRAB HOUSE **$$$$**
21 E. Hubbard St.
(312) 527-2722
www.shawscrabhouse.com
There may be flashier and newer seafood joints in town, but locals have long had a soft spot for this River North old-timer (here for more than 25 years). Whether sitting in the New Orleans-themed Oyster Bar slurping on fresh oysters and delicious lobster bisque or enjoying a meal in the main dining room decked out in rich woods and white tablecloths, you'll feel right at home. With seasonal seafood flown in daily—photos of

the restaurant's seafood purveyors line the walls—Shaw's has earned a loyal following for everything from its Alaskan King crab legs and Copper River salmon to Florida black grouper. The Sunday all-you-can-eat brunch ($43), featuring oysters, shrimp cocktail, roasted beef tenderloin, omelet and waffle stations, and an abundance of sweets, is worth fasting for. Open for lunch and dinner daily, brunch on Sun.

SPANISH

CAFE BA-BA-REEBA! $$
2024 N. Halsted St.
(773) 935-5000
www.cafebabareeba.com

With its reasonably priced tapas, pitchers of fruity sangria, and festive atmosphere, this Lincoln Park restaurant always draws a fun-loving crowd (especially during warmer months when the covered patio is open). Featuring all the usual Spanish suspects— chorizo-wrapped dates, house-marinated Spanish olives, beef skewers, shrimp with garlic and olive oil—it's easy to make a flavorful meal out of the small plates. But be sure to try the paella, a well-known favorite among Chicago's Spanish residents. Gluten-free diners can take advantage of their special menu. Open for dinner nightly, and brunch on Sat and Sun as well.

*CAFE IBERICO $$
737 N. LaSalle Blvd.
(312) 573-1510
www.cafeiberico.com

Long before tapas became a well-known dining style, this River North restaurant was educating diners about the shareable small plates and about Spanish food, in general. Years later, Cafe Iberico's Spanish chef-owner still keeps it authentic with dishes such as *salpicon de mariscos* (seafood salad), *queso de cabra* (baked goat cheese) and jamon Iberico. That España vibe carries over to the wine list, delectable sangria, and to what's on the TV—instead of local sports, you'll be watching soccer, the occasional bullfight, and quirky Spanish television shows. Upstairs, sister restaurant Pintxos serves up Basque-style tapas on the weekends focusing on skewered meats, seafood, and vegetables, and for dessert, adorable tasting portions of flans, bread pudding, and crepes. Open daily for lunch and dinner.

MERCAT A LA PLANXA $$$
638 S. Michigan Ave.
(312) 765-0524
www.mercatchicago.com

The bright and colorful decor, along with stunning views of Millennium Park just outside the towering windows, may be the first elements that catch your eye at this South Loop restaurant in the Blackstone Hotel. And then, the creative Spanish cuisine, overseen by celeb-chef José Garces, will impress you even more. Taking inspiration from the Catalonian region of Spain, chef de cuisine Cory Morris creates dishes that are both straightforward like perfectly grilled meats and seafood, and a bit more inventive, such as butter-poached lobster with roasted garlic flan. We recommend trying some of both. An extensive selection of mostly Spanish wines complement dishes such as flatbread topped with clams and smoked bacon, tender pork belly with truffles, and grilled house-made sausages. Open for breakfast, lunch, and dinner daily.

STEAKHOUSES

DAVID BURKE'S PRIMEHOUSE $$$$
616 N. Rush St.
(312) 660-6000
www.davidburkesprimehouse.com
Chicago is clearly no stranger to great steak-houses, but New York import David Burke's Primehouse in the James Hotel manages to hold its own and then some. The classic genre gets reinvented here, creating a restaurant that is a blend of hip, traditional, and upbeat. There are plenty of must-try appetizers, including the surf and turf dumplings filled with barbecued short ribs and lobster, the pretzel-crusted crab cake, and a Caesar salad prepared tableside. But it's the meat, dry-aged in their in-house Himalayan salt–tiled room, that's the main draw. Executive chef Rick Gresh is known for his commitment to using locally grown produce and for his creative limited specials (if the lobster tater tots are available, get them). Don't be a stranger. Open daily for breakfast, lunch, and dinner; brunch on Sat and Sun.

GIBSONS BAR & STEAKHOUSE $$$$
1028 N. Rush St.
(312) 266-8999
www.gibsonssteakhouse.com
Everything is big at this Gold Coast restaurant, from the oversized martinis to football-sized baked potatoes to Flintstone-esque steaks. Complete with wood-paneled walls, white-jacketed waiters, and cushy red-leather booths, Gibsons does it up the classic way. And the regulars who have been drawn here for more than 20 years, including plenty of celebs and sports stars (their photos line the walls), wouldn't have it any other way. Though the menu has a few non-meat options, with 14 prime-rated steaks to choose from—we're partial to the porterhouse—beef reigns supreme at this Gold Coast legend. Open for lunch and dinner daily.

GENE & GEORGETTI $$$
500 N. Franklin St.
(312) 527-3718
www.geneandgeorgetti.com
There are certainly flashier and hipper steak joints around (this is a meat-loving town, after all), but for old-school Chicago experiences, Gene & Georgetti is one of the best. Founded in 1941 by Gene Michelotti and partner Alfredo Federighi (his nickname was Georgetti), this River North restaurant right under the El tracks may not look like much—low ceilings in a dark, leather-laden space—but that hasn't stopped the slew of celebrity regulars, dating back to Frank Sinatra and Bob Hope up to Vince Vaughn and present-day politicians. The waiters can be a little tough, but not the steaks, which are well-seasoned, expertly done, and delicious. The time-honored appeal also applies to the lengthy menu, which features throwback dishes such as calf's liver, creamed spinach, and spaghetti with meatballs. Chicago adores this place so much, it bestowed Michelotti with a nearby honorary street name. Open Mon through Sat for lunch and dinner.

HARRY CARAY'S ITALIAN STEAKHOUSE $$$
33 W. Kinzie St.
(312) 828-0966
www.harrycarays.com
This River North restaurant is named for the late, legendary Chicago Cubs announcer, so it's no surprise that it's decked out with practically a museum's worth of baseball memorabilia, estimated at some 1,500 pieces. But

there's much more to this place than just a sports fantasy. Inside the 100-year-old historic landmark building, you'll find a white tablecloth restaurant, attentive service, and some amazing food, focusing on an excellent selection of prime steaks and chops, fresh fish, and Italian dishes. One of Harry's favorites—and now a legend in itself—is the chicken Vesuvio. Not looking for a full meal? Order something from the sandwich cart (open until 4 p.m.) at the lively bar—which measures in at 60 feet, 6 inches to replicate the distance from pitcher's mound to home plate. The bar is also where you'll be privy to complimentary helpings of Harry's famous homemade potato chips that leave you greasy-fingered and wanting more. There's also a Harry Caray's Tavern at Navy Pier, and a Harry Caray's Italian Steakhouse in Rosemont near O'Hare Airport and in Lombard. Open daily for lunch and dinner.

MASTRO'S STEAKHOUSE $$$$
520 N. Dearborn St.
(312) 521-5100
www.mastrosrestaurants.com
Not for the budget-minded—but, really, how many steak joints are?—this River North newcomer is winning over diners for its impeccable service, ritzy decor, and top-notch steaks. The dimly lit, two-level space, at one time the revered Spago, draws a well-dressed crowd who come for the wet-aged steaks, ranging from an 8-ounce petite filet to a massive 48-ounce double-cut porterhouse (we dare you). There are scrumptious accompaniments too, like Caesar salad and sides such as scalloped potatoes, gorgonzola mac and cheese, and roasted brussels sprouts with pancetta (opt for half portions to try more). Take in the classy milieu minus

the food at the piano bar. Open for dinner nightly.

SMITH & WOLLENSKY $$$$
318 N. State St.
(312) 670-9900
www.smithandwollensky.com
Even without its prime views of downtown and the river—reserve an outdoor table during the warmer months to make the most of them—this two-level New York import in the Marina City complex is worth a visit for its dry-aged beef and flown-in-daily lobster. Choose from classics such as prime rib, bone-in rib eye, and Kansas City–cut sirloin, as well as filet mignons served six different ways (gorgonzola-crusted is our pick) and offered in 10- and 14-ounce portions. Lighter options mean fresh salads like the signature Wollensky or asparagus and crab meat. Not just for expense-account dining, the destination also caters to smaller budgets and appetites with its bar menu, which includes a selection of tasty flatbreads, a hearty tenderloin and spinach salad, and buffalo fried oysters. Finish off with hand-made pastries. Open daily for lunch and dinner.

THAI

TAC QUICK THAI KITCHEN $
3930 N. Sheridan Rd.
(773) 327-5253
www.tacquick.net
You could order off the regular menu at this Wrigleyville area BYOB spot, but clued-in diners know that the restaurant's best dishes are to be found on the translated Thai-language menu and the weekly specials. Not for the timid, these dishes pack some powerful flavors and spice levels, such as the *sai krog isaan* (fermented pork and rice sausage)

and *pa lo* (star anise–braised tofu with pork). Even if you're not up for the more daring dishes, you'll still be pleased with standard soups, noodles, and curries, all of which rank better than the average local Thai restaurant. Though the menu doesn't list them, there are usually a couple of desserts available if you ask. Open for lunch and dinner every day.

THAI LAGOON $
2322 W. North Ave.
(773) 489-5747
www.thai-lagoon.com
Surprisingly modern compared to the ambience of many of Chicago's Thai restaurants (check out the artwork from local artists), this Bucktown spot balances it out with some winning traditional Thai dishes. The extensive menu features flavorful chicken coconut soup, shrimp glass-noodle salad, and fragrant tamarind curry with fresh spinach—plus come on Friday and Saturday evenings and nearly 20 different sushi rolls get thrown into the mix. Save some dough at lunchtime with the $5.95 special that includes a vegetarian soup, choice among four entrees, and a cucumber salad. BYOB. Open for dinner nightly, and for both lunch and dinner Fri through Sun.

VIETNAMESE

BA LE SANDWICH & BAKERY $
5014 N. Broadway
(773) 561-4424
www.balesandwich.com
There are plenty of other *banh mi* sandwich spots and bakeries in this Uptown 'hood, but the cheerfully casual, counter-service Ba Le stands out for its house-made French baguettes and the goodies that get stuffed into them—this family-run favorite has been doing it for more than 20 years, and they've got it right. Start with a light Vietnamese spring roll before moving onto the crispy sandwiches. The barbecued pork with its lemongrass marinade is a top seller, as is the Ba Le Special filled with pâté, ham, headcheese, pork roll, and house-pickled daikon and carrots. Its in-house bakery means dessert is a must, particularly the chocolate croissants. We're happy to report that a recent expansion added more seats, and there is also a new location in Chinatown (2141 S. Archer Ave.). Open for breakfast, lunch, and dinner daily.

HAI YEN $
1055 W. Argyle St.
(773) 561-4077
www.haiyenrestaurant.com
The original Argyle Street location was the first and less fancy, while the newer Clark Street spot (2723 N. Clark St., 773-868-4888) gets more points on atmosphere. But both serve excellent Vietnamese cuisine. In fact, as far as favorites go, Hai Yen has some of the best *pho* (beef noodle soups) you'll find in town. Signature appetizers include *bo la lot* (marinated beef and pork wrapped in a Hawaiian leaf), and *goi du du* (green papaya salad with shrimp and pork). Those looking for an immersion experience can opt for the 5- or 7-course dinner of traditional Vietnamese beef dishes, available at the Argyle location. The list of drinks will get you out of a rut, offering options like limeade with seltzer or the adventurous Soda *Sua Hot Ga* (club soda, condensed milk, and egg yolk). Argyle Street is open Thurs through Tues for breakfast, lunch, and dinner (closed Wed); the Clark Street location is open for dinner nightly, as well as lunch Fri through Sun.

SAIGON SISTERS $$
567 W. Lake St.
(312) 496-0090
www.saigonsisters.com

You won't find traditional Vietnamese cuisine at this cozy West Loop spot in the Fulton River District. Instead, sisters Mary Nguyen Aregoni and Therese Nguyen (along with mom Suu) playfully combine Vietnamese flavors and ingredients to create dishes that are truly their own. That means for lunch there are riffs on *banh mi,* like the Sun Tanned Cow, a sandwich filled with coconut milk–braised Wagyu beef with kaffir lime leaf, and steamed buns. And at dinner, the menu really gets wild, with a mixture of small and large plates whose standouts include hoisin-glazed quail with red rice fritter, citrus-cured arctic char with green papaya remoulade, and caramel prawns with duck egg over fried rice. A minimalist decor with works by local contemporary artists provides a hip backdrop. Also find more traditional Vietnamese sandwiches at the Saigon Sisters booth in the French Market (131 N. Clinton St., 312-496-0094), where a business-y crowd stops by for lunch to go. Open for lunch and dinner Mon through Sat (closed Sun).

NIGHTLIFE

Save for a few designated dry wards (usually determined by vote), nearly every neighborhood in Chicago boasts at least a couple of bars. When tallied up across the city, according to a writer with the Chicago Bar Project (www.chibarproject.com), there are about 1,800. They vary from old-timey kinds of places to red-velvet-rope hot spots. They fit every style, mood, personality, and budget. They have live bands and DJs or loads of flat-screen TVs; they let you come as you are or require some fancier duds; they have long wine lists and handcrafted martinis, or just cheap beer and spicy wings. Some focus on entertainment, while others complement cocktails with gourmet dining menus. A few are practically brand-new, and others are long-established institutions. With so many options to choose from, you could try a different place every night. Or hop around to several in one night—and into the wee hours of the morning, as some are open until 5 a.m.

OVERVIEW

While some nightlife destinations have split personalities depending on the day or the hour, we've listed them under the category that makes the most sense. So, for example, even if some people (or you—we're not judging) might spontaneously rock out to music at a bar, it wouldn't be considered a dance club unless that was the main draw.

Some bars tout happy hours, but that's not actually permitted in Chicago. If they advertise a "happy hour," it probably has to do with food—free or discounted apps, all-you-can-eat buffet, something like that. In order to offer a drink deal, it has to be happy "all day," because the law states that offering a discount on liquor or all-you-can-drink kind of thing during only limited hours is prohibited. That's why you'll see daily drink deals more commonly than happy-hour specials. Most bars close at 2 a.m. during the week and 3 a.m. on Saturday—in addition to about a hundred 4 a.m. bars (that close

at 5 a.m. on Saturday)—so, you can take advantage of those daily deals right up into the next day too.

Another no-no in Chicago bars is smoking. Banned a few years ago in public places, including all bars and restaurants, smoking is now only permitted outdoors and at least 15 feet away from entrances, exits, and windows that open. There was some uproar from bar owners, but it didn't take locals long to figure out how to deal with the change—and the fact that going home after a late night without smelling like an ashtray wasn't so bad after all.

Before you head out to paint the town red, it's important to know that Chicago bouncers do their jobs pretty well. If you don't have a valid ID with you—if you're from outside the country, bring your passport in addition to your foreign ID—you might not get in, no matter how much gray you have in your hair. The drinking age is 21, and that's what you'd better be.

Lucky for us, Chicago's roving taxis and mostly 24-hour CTA train (and some bus) travel make it easy to get out and about without driving, so designating a driver for the night isn't necessarily required. On New Year's Eve, Chicago has even been so generous as to offer 1-cent rides on the CTA to discourage drinking and driving. But if you do ever choose to drive, be aware that, like all other states, Illinois hands down pretty stiff penalties if you're found to be at or above the legal blood alcohol limit of .08 percent; and also like every other state, Illinois has an implied consent law that means that drivers automatically give their consent to take a breath or blood test. Oh, and one more thing on the serious stuff: It's illegal in Chicago for anyone in a vehicle, not just the driver, to drink alcohol or possess an open bottle, unless it's a chartered bus or van of some kind; open bottles of liquor are required to be in the trunk. But it's more fun to drink at the bar anyway. So get out and enjoy yourself—responsibly!

BARS

BIG STAR
1531 N. Damen Ave.
(773) 235-4039
www.bigstarchicago.com
Expect a wait for service and a stool at this tequila-happy hangout; tables are few, though warm months open up the spacious front patio. The vibe is low-key hipster (this is Wicker Park, after all), sporting simple concrete floors and honky-tonk tunes. With co-partner Paul Kahan of Blackbird fame behind the scenes, you won't be disappointed by the Tex-Mex menu, either, including a mouthwatering pork belly taco and amazingly inexpensive homemade guac and chips. Cocktails with fitting names like

the Stockyard Pony and Sarsaparilla Springs accompany an intriguing list of mostly 5-buck bottled and on-tap brews; an extensive list of true Kentucky-made whiskeys, and a couple dozen tequilas and mezcals. Open daily for lunch, dinner and late-night. For more information about Big Star, check out the Restaurants chapter.

BOILER ROOM
2210 N. California Ave.
(773) 276-5625
www.boilerroomlogansquare.com
Opened by two of the team members behind Simone's (they both feature similar seatbelts-turned-seats), this Logan Square stop is, well, sizzling hot. Doubling as a pizza place with New York–style slices (there's even a vegan option), it's popular during warm months when the picnic tables come out, and the patio opens. Prices are friendly, as are the bartenders who pour a rotating selection of suds that has included Founders, Young Two Brothers, and Lion Stout from Sri Lanka, cans of Half Acre and Anderson Valley, and potent blends in drinks like their Toy Gun with white pepper and peach schnapps. The cash-only policy can be a drag, but if you draw from the ATM there, they'll compensate you with a shot of Jameson. So, cash out and bottoms up. Open Mon through Fri from 4 p.m. to late night, Sat and Sun from noon.

BONNY'S
2417 N. Milwaukee Ave.
(773) 486-8480
Walls covered in wood paneling (exterior and interior), red lights, stiff drinks, a chalkboard of inexpensive craft beer options—plus, the requisite PBR on draft, if you must—guys in baseball caps shooting the breeze on simple black swivel stools. It's all part of the

laid-back charm of this casual beyond-the-fray Logan Square hang. What people love is that it's open till 4 a.m. (Sat till 5 a.m.), has a photo booth to capture those inebriated poses with your posse, and conversation-level danceable DJ-spun '80s and '90s mixes. What isn't as great: the cash-only policy (there's an ATM by the bathrooms), but that's the way it is at this neighborhood bar. Open Sun through Thurs from 10 p.m., Fri and Sat starting at 9 p.m.

Designated Drivers

Drink and drive? Definitely not. Designate a driver? Hard to decide who. Unless it's a trustworthy tee-totaler from **BeMyDD.** The company has branches in nearly 50 cities around the country, including Chicago. Just give them a call for the pick-up service or plan ahead for their Reserve a Driver program, which sets you up with a well-dressed driver who picks you up, takes you there, waits till you're done, and drives you back to your starting point. If you drove somewhere and realized after-the-fact that you drank one margarita too many, the pick-up service sends out two drivers—one to take you home and the other who drives your vehicle back. The reservation service charges $12.50 to $15 an hour, while the pick-up price is $25 an hour plus a few additional fees. All much cheaper and safer than an accident or a fine. (877) U-BE-MYDD (823-6933); www.bemydd.com.

CALIFORNIA CLIPPER
1002 N. California Ave.
(773) 384-2547
www.californiaclipper.com
The neon sign above this Humboldt Park bar touts that it's "air-conditioned," a holdover from back in the day. Established by brothers Gus and Joe Caporusso and their sister Toni in 1937, the homey atmosphere has remained much the same, and even a renovation maintains the retro feel with red lighting, linoleum floor tiles, and red vinyl booths. Friday and Saturday nights feature live bands of the country-folk-bluesy kind, and there's the occasional spoken word event. But what people do most here is drink, and the drinks are worth the trip—good, old-timey concoctions like Mai Tais, Brandy Alexanders, Singapore Slings, and their famous Purple Martins (they claim to be the only bar to have grape soda in their soda gun). Beware the no-frills ladies' room, and be prepared with a designated driver: Few cabs venture to this sometimes sketchy neighborhood. Open nightly from 8 p.m.

FOUNTAINHEAD
1970 W. Montrose Ave.
(773) 697-8204
www.fountainheadchicago.com
This trendy corner tavern had its Ravenswood neighbors practically knocking down the door before it opened—they needed something like this (there's not much bar action around), and it delivers for them happily. The Ayn Rand novel of the same name doesn't have much to do with this place, say the owners, except the "craftsmanship" that they aim for in their food (mussels, burgers, mac and cheese) and drink. A mahogany bar, fireplace, hardwood floors, and ambient lighting attract young couples and groups

of friends. Sample from the impressive and ever-evolving list of small-batch and craft brews on tap and in bottles, or the wicked-good whiskey menu. Open from 4 p.m. Mon through Fri, plus lunch on Sat and brunch and late lunch on Sun.

LATE BAR
3534 W. Belmont Ave.
(773) 267-5283
www.latebarchicago.com
Considering this Avondale bar doesn't even open until 10 p.m. and serves practically till dawn, its name fits just right. Whether you fit in here is up to you: Goth reigns, along with a little punk, ska, and even 1980s flashback. For instance, you'll feel right at home with hot pink hair, a mohawk perhaps, ripped stockings, and thigh-high black leather boots. Such attire would be especially suitable for Saturday's Planet Earth night, a beloved New Wave club night spawned by veteran DJs Kristine Hengl and Dave Roberts nearly two decades ago for other clubs until they opened Late Bar together a few years back. Cash only. Open Tues through Sat; closed Sun and Mon.

✳MARIA'S PACKAGED GOODS & COMMUNITY BAR
960 W. 31st St.
(773) 890-0588
communitybar.wordpress.com
It's not fancy, but this Bridgeport bar and liquor store has an artsy grass-roots feel—overhead lights made from beer bottles, a tin ceiling, local artwork along the walls, and an easy merging of old-timers and young. There are 18 taps, literally hundreds in bottles and most sold in their store coolers too, from Ace Pear Cider to Three Floyds Zombie Dust. Plus, fun reasonably priced cocktails like the

Marszewski Mule (Smirnoff vodka, lime juice, and Goslings ginger beer), named for brothers Ed and Mike and mom Maria who own the place. Look for drink specials like dollar-off deals. The liquor store is open from 11 a.m. daily; the bar is open from 4 p.m. daily.

MATCHBOX
770 N. Milwaukee Ave.
(312) 666-9292
www.facebook.com/thematchbox
Plan to get up close and personal with the people around you at this long and skinny—just a few feet wide at its narrowest—River West favorite. Bartenders banter, strangers become friends, and the drinks are top-notch. They've been mixing classic gimlets and old-fashioneds, and fruit-infusing their alcohol since before it was trendy again; be sure to request a brandy-soaked cherry (or two). Open nightly.

MOE'S CANTINA
155 W. Kinzie St.
(312) 245-2000
www.moescantina.com
Lots of space, lots of flat-screen TVs for sports-watching, made-from-scratch caipirinhas, margaritas, and mojitos, plates full of shareable Latin-influenced nibbles, and gaggles of pretty young things dressed to party. Located in River North, this Moe's (the original is in Lakeview, 3518 N. Clark St., 773-248-0002) is perfectly placed for letting loose after work and then hopping on the nearby El for the ride home. Huge retractable doors open up for an indoor-outdoor experience when it's warm. Be patient: When it's packed, as it often is after 10 p.m. on the weekends, it might mean waiting a bit for that drink. Open from lunch through late night.

✳SHEFFIELD'S
3258 N. Sheffield Ave.
(773) 281-4989
www.sheffieldschicago.com

Close but not crazy-close to Wrigley Field, this handsome bar in the Lakeview 'hood has been in business since 1980 and was one of the first bars to offer craft brews. It still has a rock-solid list of bottles like Lagunitas IPA, Left Hand Milk Stout, and Half Acre Daisy Cutter Pale Ale, as well as an equally interesting selection of nearly 20 beers on tap. The menu gives great descriptions, so go ahead and experiment. Order some of their mouth-watering barbecue (the sauce was created right here) and grab a seat out back during summer for a perfect combo. Or sing for your supper at the bimonthly open mic night. Open daily for lunch, dinner, and late-night (kitchen closes a few hours before the bar).

SIMONE'S BAR
960 W. 18th St.
(312) 666-8601
www.simonesbar.com

Brought to you by an impressive team—veteran bar owners Michael Noone (Danny's bar and Francesca Restaurants), Russ and Desiree Grant (Streetside, Northside), and design duo Alter Ego—this super-cool Pilsen joint attracts a diverse crowd. And it's no surprise why. Despite some gripes about the music volume set a bit high, it's got such a wild and crazy atmosphere that it just works. Tripped out with a bar top that once served as a bowling lane, a DJ station made from old pinball machines, a strip of wall painted by local graffiti artists, and booth seats fashioned from former seat belts, it's almost overstimulating. But no worries: Just belly up for a bottle of Rogue Dead Guy, Anderson Valley Oatmeal Stout, or Three Floyds, and

you'll be fine. Hit them up on a Sunday, and the seasonally rotating 16-ounce draughts are just 4 bucks. Or try one of the souped-up cocktails like a Quickie with Maker's Mark, Koval ginger, Hum liqueur, and ginger beer. The reused decor, plus a rooftop garden and solar panels have earned Simone's a Green Restaurant Association certification. Oh, yes, they also serve a menu of soups, salads, sandwiches, and pizzas. And there's a gallery and performance space to boot. Open daily for lunch, dinner, and late night.

SWEETWATER
225 N. Michigan Ave.
(312) 698-7111
sweetwatertavernandgrille.com

A solidly work-friendly Loop location at South Water Street and Michigan Avenue attracts hungry crowds at lunch and happy hour to this stylish sports bar. Huge street-level picture windows (i.e., good for people-watching), curved booths, long communal high tables, finished cement floors, stone-brick columns and walls, and the glow of 23 flat-panel TVs draw them in. The 70 beers are conveniently categorized by type—like white and wheat, lambics, fruit-infused, seasonal—and comfort-bar-food menu runs from entree-size salads to juicy burgers, chicken potpie to lamb chops. Gluten-free options too. Open Mon through Sat for lunch, dinner, and late night; Sat and Sun open for brunch through dinner.

BLUES CLUBS

B.L.U.E.S.
2519 N. Halsted St.
(773) 528-1012
www.chicagobluesbar.com

Go ahead and get the blues at this DePaul University area club, whose claim is as "the oldest blues bar in the world with live blues 365 days a year." Sure enough, musicians like Otis Clay, Eddie Clearwater, Big Time Sarah, and Pistol Pete pack 'em in early at this cozy spot for honest-to-goodness goodtime blues. And if you're not a blues aficionado, there are enough regulars to get you up to speed. On Sunday, get more blues for your buck with reciprocal admission to Kingston Mines. Cover $5 to $10. Open nightly at 8 p.m.; music starts at 9:30 p.m.

BLUE CHICAGO
536 N. Clark St.
(312) 661-0100
www.bluechicago.com
Its River North locale makes Blue Chicago a lively treat for tourists. Try to save a table at the far end of the bar to get a closer vantage point for the totally local, often female singers who belt it out from the intimate stage. But the excellent acoustics make any seat a good seat. There's no food here, so eat before or after. Cover $8 on weeknights, $10 weekends. Open nightly.

✳BUDDY GUY'S LEGENDS
700 S. Wabash Ave.
(312) 427-1190
www.buddyguys.com
Guy's legend started in Louisiana as a teenager when he acquired his first guitar (it's now displayed at the Rock and Roll Hall of Fame), but it flourished when he arrived in Chicago in 1957. In the 1990s, Guy got his due, with three Grammy Awards including one for *Damn Right, I've Got the Blues*. These days he travels the country, but comes back every January to his honorary hometown for a monthlong series of sell-out concerts

at his 20-plus-year-old club. Though Guy was a session guitarist at the famed Chess Records studio, his style was for the wilder side—and he still cranks it with a smile and a hearty laugh as if he's the luckiest singer in the world. If you don't catch him, you're sure to hear any number of other fantastic blues artists. A full dinner menu brings a taste of Guy's Southern roots with fried okra, Cajun popcorn crawfish tails, catfish, jambalaya, gumbo, and a Peanut Buddy Pie for dessert. It's first-come, first-served seating, so get here early. After 8 p.m., it's 21 and over only. Bring your own instrument on Monday night for open blues jam at 9:30 p.m. Cover is $10 to $20, higher for Buddy Guy performances. Sunday through Thursday music starts at 9:30 p.m.; Friday features an acoustic set from 5 to 8 p.m., then opening bands at 9 p.m., headliners at 10:30 p.m.; Saturday acoustic sets from 6 to 8:30 p.m., opening bands at 9:30 p.m., headliners at 11 p.m.

KINGSTON MINES
2548 N. Halsted St.
(773) 477-4646
www.kingstonmines.com
Low-key and a bit gritty, it doesn't much matter. It's the high-quality nonstop blues seven nights a week on two stages that brings the masses to this Lincoln Park standard that's been hitting the right note since it opened more than 40 years ago. Look for the long orange awnings that span the block, and feel free to make this your dinner destination too, because the wings and rib tips or any other Cajun specialties from in-house Doc's Rib Joint (order at the window and take it back to your table) do just fine. Cover $5 to 15; free for college students and faculty Sun through Thurs with ID and $10

for them on weekends. Sun two-for-one admission deal with B.L.U.E.S. Open nightly.

NEW CHECKERBOARD LOUNGE FOR BLUES 'N' JAZZ
5201 S. Harper Ave.
(773) 684-1472

Originally a Bronzeville institution, this got new digs when the club's building began falling apart and the city forced it to close. Happily for fans, it found a new home in Hyde Park, in a large space that's convenient for University of Chicago locals too. Cover charge $3 to $10. Open nightly.

ROSA'S LOUNGE
3420 W. Armitage Ave.
(773) 342-0452
www.rosaslounge.com

It's not very easy to get to, but that's why people love Rosa's, a dark, dive-y bar with killer drinks (read: strong) and even better bands. Regular performers include soul-blues singer Vance Kelly and Mississippi transplant Melvin Taylor. Italian immigrant owners Tony Mangiullo and his mom Rosa add a personal touch to the place, earning them their self-described subtitle as "Chicago's friendliest blues lounge." Cover $5 to $15. Open Tues, Thurs, Fri, and Sat; closed Sun, Mon, and Wed.

COMEDY

THE ANNOYANCE THEATRE
4830 N. Broadway
(773) 561-4665
www.annoyanceproductions.com

When a theater's staple show is called "Co-Ed Prison Sluts," you know you're in for something a bit off-kilter. Since the Uptown theater's first show in 1987—a Halloween horror flick parody called "Splatter Theater"—founder Mick Napier and hundreds of performers have presented more than 100 shows in genres from full-length plays to cabaret to improvisation including "Skiing is Believing," "That Darned Antichrist," and the improv-night "Messing with a Friend," featuring local comedian Susan Messing. Annoyance is uncensored, so parents thinking of bringing kids should proceed with caution. The adjacent Annoyance Bar gets theatergoers revved with reasonably priced drinks and board games. Feel like you've got some funny in you? Annoyance also offers classes. Ticket prices vary.

COMEDYSPORTZ
929 W. Belmont Ave.
(773) 549-8080
www.comedysportzchicago.com

This improv competition outfit has outlets in more than 20 cities and the UK, and that's because it's a formula that works. Set up like a sports event, two teams rumble for the win by playing short-form improv games and racking up the biggest audience laughs. Buy a few beers and laugh a little harder. A referee calls out to the audience for suggestions, meaning every show is different. The ref also keeps order between teams and calls a "brown bag foul" if a cast or audience member curses. The clean mouths end with ComedySportz's anything-goes Late Night Series including its popular "The Hot Karl," Saturday at midnight. But bring the kids along to the 10-and-under shows, like the recent adaptation of "Cinderella." Ticket prices vary. Showtimes most Thursdays, Fridays, and Saturdays. Check website for full schedule.

IO THEATER
3541 N. Clark St.
(773) 880-0199
www.chicago.ioimprov.com
Formerly ImprovOlympic, iO was founded in 1981 by Charna Halpern and the late Del Close, a legendary duo who made a lasting mark on comedy by inventing "the Harold" long-form improv, and expounding the notion of improv as an artform and philosophy. These days, the iO features two stages, two bars, and more than 30 improv and sketch-comedy shows a week. Not to mention an acclaimed comedy school (students get in free to most shows) and an iO branch in Los Angeles. Though at times hit-or-miss, some of the more guaranteed guffaws are from acts including Cook County Social Club, the Deltones, the Cupid Players' show "Cupid Has a Heart On," and The Armando Diaz Experience. After all, alums include celebs like Tina Fey, Rachel Dratch, Mike Myers, Tim Meadows, and Andy Dick. Tickets $5 to $20. Open nightly.

✳THE SECOND CITY
1616 N. Wells St.
(312) 337-3992
www.secondcity.com
As the launching pad for an incredible number of today's comedy stars, The Second City's roster of household names is astonishing: Alan Alda, Dan Aykroyd, Tina Fey, John and Jim Belushi, Bonnie Hunt, Stephen Colbert, Bill Murray, Gilda Radner, Joan Rivers. And many of their faces can be found in the framed photos that line the walls of this famous sketch comedy theater. At more than 50 years and running, it's as funny and fearless as ever—the actors throw punches and punch lines at politics, science, society, and anything else they can think of. Since its debut in 1959 by a determined group of former University of Chicago students, The Second City has spawned a second Chicago revue, the E.T.C. (right around the corner), as well as 11 touring companies, three training centers, corporate communications, and a TV and film operation. Shows are generally considered OK for kids 16 or over, but remember this is a nightclub atmosphere with drinks and depictions of adult situations. Seating is based on arrival and can land you craning your neck if you're late—and an easy target if you're right under the stage. For a few extra bucks, premium seats are much more comfortable. Order a few drinks and nibble from the apps and dessert menu in the cabaret-style theater, or ask about dinner packages with area restaurants. Tickets $16 to $27 (plus processing fees). Shows run nightly.

ZANIES
1548 N. Wells St.
(312) 337-4027
www.zanies.com
Don't blame us if your sides hurt when you leave a show at this standup comedy club. Why? Performers like Chelsea Peretti (writer for *Parks and Recreation*), Kyle Kinane, Dwayne Kennedy, Karen Rontowski, and Gilbert Gottfried, that's why. Tickets from $10. Two-item (food or drink) minimum per person. Get $5 off your ticket and a discounted meal with a dinner and a show deal. Performances nightly.

CLUBS & DANCE CLUBS

8 FIFTY 8
858 W. Lake St.
(312) 455-2776
www.8fifty8.com

Alongside the El tracks in the West Loop runs a velvet rope with tight-skirted women and shiny-shoed guys making their way into this hopping nightclub. With a modern-gilded look—thick, swirly gold frames around liquor shelves, glittery chandeliers—its DJ range includes Top 40s, dance, rock, house. With more-than-average seating options, you're welcome to sit pretty with your cocktail or do your thing on the dance floor. Everyone's considered a VIP here, and you can check in online to thwart the cover charge. No cover before 11 p.m.; $5 to $20 after that. Open Fri and Sat.

EXCALIBUR
632 N. Dearborn St.
(312) 266-1944
www.excaliburchicago.com
Multiple levels and multiple scenes make this nightlife institution tick. Dance like crazy, lounge on a velvet couch, play some pool or table hockey, or just stand back and get in some great people-watching. Housed in an imposing Henry Ives Cobb structure built in 1892 for the Chicago Architecture Society, this fortress of fun opened in 1989 and is still one of the first city clubs that suburban area kids rush to when they hit drinking age. While some of its own age is beginning to show, and some of its style can tip a bit cheesy, its sheer size—60,000 square feet—makes it great for groups and general grooving. Thursday gets raves for Latin night, while Friday features the offbeat one-man show "Supernatural Chicago." On Saturday, the "Bad Boys of Live Late Night" get the crowd jumping with silly dance contests. Beware the steep climb to the bathrooms. Cover $10 and up, $25 for the Friday night show (includes two beverages). Open Wed through Sat from 7 p.m.; kitchen open Fri and Sat from 8 p.m.

They're big on private parties too, accommodating from 50 to 3,000.

LASALLE POWER CO.
500 N. LaSalle St.
(312) 661-1122
www.lasallepowerco.com
Depending on when you go, this cavernous club could be a cool happy-hour hang, a fancied-up bar-food dinner spot or a crazy dance party palace. Three levels dole out different scenes, the first two pump it up with a diet of danceable DJ-spun house, rock, pop, and Top 40 tunes; the third floor gets wild with live local (and occasional national) alt-rock bands on a professional stage. Besides music, LPC takes its decor seriously with framed rock concert photos and plastered concert bills, faux-vintage wallpaper, long buttoned-leather banquettes, and various chandeliers and globe lighting. No cover. Open Thurs through Sat nights.

THE MID
306 N. Halsted St.
(312) 265-3990
www.themidchicago.com
Get ready to mash at this 4 a.m. West Loop electronica den that's "somewhere in the middle of a live music venue and an upscale nightclub." With music foremost in its soul—featuring live bands and some of the nation's most innovative DJs—The Mid wins over ravers with its state-of-the-art sound system that pumps that deep bass loud and clear. A raised stage, large dance floor with bars on either side, and a third bar on the wraparound balcony make it convenient to keep glasses filled. Plus, women will appreciate the clean and attended bathrooms. Past acts have included Ice Cube, Steve Angello, Rae Kwon of Wu Tang, and Steve Aoki. Though

some complain of high drink prices, it comes with the high-energy territory. Monday is industry night. Cover price usually $20. Open Mon, Fri, and Sat.

NEO
2350 N. Clark St.
(773) 528-2622
www.neo-chicago.com

In Lincoln Park, the norm is sports bars, chic lounges, and neighborhood bars, but Neo is a world unto its own. Letting your hair down here means dying it blue or shaving it off entirely. The norm here is multiple piercings and tattoos, combat boots, black makeup, black clothing. Makes sense too: The tagline states that this punk-disco-goth-anything-goes gem has been "serving Chicago's underground since 1979." And then there's Thursday night, when the scene goes all '80s-new-wave, and a crazy, eclectic crowd comes out to party like it's 1999. So head down the dark alley to the hideaway door if you feel like bucking the trendy. And don't worry if you don't get there until midnight—it's when the vampires come out to play too; plus, they're open till 4 a.m. (5 a.m. on Sat). Cash only. Cover ranges from zero to $5. Open nightly.

✳SPYBAR
646 N. Franklin St.
(312) 337-2191
www.spybarchicago.com

No need to fly to Miami—the partying is just as hot right here at this below-street-level River North dance club. Globally and locally renowned DJs spin house on Friday and Saturday, Latin on Sunday, and the "I Heart Thursdays" mainstream mix on Thursday, while a young crowd swarms the dance floor (the later it is, the more packed it gets). Bottle service is a smart option for groups to secure a seat (and for guys who like to impress the girls), and there are two VIP booths, one near the main floor and one tucked off to the side for more intimate mingling. Hey slouchers, there is a dress code, so leave your gym shoes, flip-flops, and baggy clothes behind. Cover $20. Open Mon, and Wed through Sun from 10 p.m. to 4 a.m.; closed Tues.

GAY BARS & CLUBS

✳BERLIN
954 W. Belmont Ave.
(773) 348-4975
www.berlinchicago.com

Pasties, black eyeliner, feather boas, glitter—and that's just the guys at this raucous Lakeview favorite. It's a hot, sweaty memorable mashup of gay, straight, transsexual, black, white, and those who just like to experiment. The throngs come out for top-notch DJ-ing of avant-garde and alternative music and for theme nights like Madonna-Rama every first Sunday, '80s night the second Sunday, and Disco Obsession the last Wednesday. Cover $3 to $7 and higher for special events. Open till 4 a.m. (5 a.m. on Sat), it just gets crazier as the night goes on. Open Tues through Sun; closed Mon.

BIG CHICKS
5024 N. Sheridan Rd.
(773) 728-5511
www.bigchicks.com

Often assumed to be a lesbian bar because of its name, this cheerful Uptown favorite is truly a friendly, come-one-come-all type place, which happens to tilt toward a gay crowd. Part neighborhood bar, part casual eatery, part dance club, Big Chicks swings easily all ways. The moniker is a nod to the nickname of owner and so-called den mother, Michelle Fire—check out her image depicted among other artistic renditions of lovely large ladies by national, local, and international artists. On Monday, the buck burger deal brings in hordes who sit, drink, eat, and chat. It's a similar feel on Sunday afternoon with the free buffet (with drink purchase) and specials on vodka lemonades. And pulling from all over town on the first Thursday of the month are FKA (formerly known as) nights, a bawdy, rowdy trip into transgender territory. Beware the cash-only policy. No cover. Open Mon through Fri at 4 p.m., Sat at 3 p.m., Sun for brunch at 10 a.m. (food is also served nightly).

*CREW
4804 N. Broadway
(773) 784-2739
www.worldsgreatestbar.com

Gay sports bar, an oxymoron you say? Not at this Uptown hot spot, one of the first of its kind in the country, in fact. An all-around friendly feel includes a worthy bar menu of flatbread pizzas, nachos, tacos, and wraps. The beer menu rocks (about a dozen on tap), and daily specials rank high like Wednesday half-price martinis, Friday PBR cans for 2 bucks, and their famous beergarita pitchers on Sunday for just $12.50. For $5, you can aim to become a Crew Beer God—just drink all the beers at Crew in under a year and you get your picture pinned up on their wall (plus discounts on tap beer). You're fine in jeans and a college sweatshirt here, but you'll also see more (or less) dressed-up clientele. You'll get the typical Cubs, White Sox, Bulls, and Bears on 20-plus HDTVs, and don't be surprised if a group of guys express their enthusiasm with a four-part harmony of "Take Me Out to the Ballgame." Open for lunch, dinner, and late-night (open till 2 a.m. Thurs through Sat).

DOWNTOWN BAR & LOUNGE
440 N. State St.
(312) 464-1400
www.downtownbarandlounge.com

Filling a void and far from the cluster of Boystown bars, Downtown puts gay-friendly (though certainly not exclusively so) smack-dab in the middle of River North. Reviving the space that was once the popular gay bar Gentry, this classy joint provides spacious room for sipping signature martinis or a glass of wine after work, or before or after a show at nearby House of Blues or a Loop theater—there's even a drink called The Goodman (as in, the theater) with Bulleit bourbon, brandied cherries, and sweet vermouth. Open nightly (Mon through Fri from 3 p.m., Sat and Sun from 2 p.m.).

JACKHAMMER
6406 N. Clark St.
(773) 743-5772
www.jackhammer-chicago.com

Up at the north end of Andersonville, this 5 a.m. bar is known for its basement-level leather-and-fetish-only space called The Hole (on Friday and Saturday the leather dress code is enforced), where chaps and harnesses, toned muscles, and monthly underwear nights appeal. But it's an equally deserving destination as a dance club (there's a disco ball, after all) and neighborhood bar with pool, darts, and Wii and arcade games. DJs spin Wednesday through Monday, while Tuesday is karaoke, and Sunday is open mic night. Never a cover unless it's a special event, and in that case it's $5, but includes a drink coupon. Open nightly.

ROSCOE'S TAVERN
3356 N. Halsted St.
(773) 281-3355
www.roscoes.com

Daily drink specials, DJs spinning danceable beats, friendly bartenders at six bars whirling out drinks at breakneck speed, and shirtless gay men for the ogling make this one of Boystown's most popular late-night spots. Monday and Wednesday are karaoke nights, Tuesday features drag contests, and the last Thursday of every month brings a twist on the wet T-shirt with the wet boxer contest. Can't handle the heat? Head out back to the patio. During warm weather, a sidewalk cafe is also open for light meals. Generally no cover. Open daily.

SIDETRACK
3349 N. Halsted St.
(773) 477-9189
www.sidetrackchicago.com

With its sleek hardwood floors, exposed brick, and sunny multilevel rooftop space, this could be any average club. But it's in the heart of Boystown, and it's anything but average. Since opening in 1982 without even a sign outside, it has expanded into more than eight neighboring storefronts, added bars, and become a mainstay of gay-man meet-ups. Where else can you find three nights devoted to show tunes? Fruity liquor-laden slushes fit right in. No cover. Open nightly from 3 p.m. (during the summer from 1 p.m. on Sat and Sun).

LIVE MUSIC CLUBS

EMPTY BOTTLE
1035 N. Western Ave.
(773) 276-3600
www.emptybottle.com

This Ukrainian Village dive may be dark, sometimes deafening, a bit on the dingy side (yard-sale couches provide seating, bathrooms are graffiti-filled), and sometimes slightly smelly, but music-lovers love it. They come for the friendly atmosphere, the cheap beer—there are exactly two wines by the glass—and music seven nights a week, which changes nightly and ranges from the noise-rock of Jucifer to Cacaw's minimalist punk to local fun garage-punk-R&B band The Yolks. Wednesday features jazz of all shapes and forms. Cover can be nothing or up to $15. Cash only. Open nightly.

HIDEOUT
1354 W. Wabansia Ave.
(773) 227-4433
www.hideoutchicago.com

A musical love shack off the beaten path and one of a kind. That's the Hideout. No signage, no frills, and practically hidden along the industrial North Branch of the Chicago River. It's home to a friendly hipster crowd who come to hear any and all types of music: soul, acid jazz, punk, funk, ethnic, blues. Well-known performers like Neko Case, the Swell Season, the Waco Brothers, Ken Vandermark, Billy Corgan, and others rocked the small crowds here before they hit the big-time—and they've been known to stroll back in from time to time. The Hideout also has a history of giving, like their recent participation in Tom's Shoes' One Day Without Shoes campaign to raise awareness about childhood poverty. Cover varies, generally $5 to $10. Open Mon through Sat, and for special events on Sun.

LINCOLN HALL
2424 N. Lincoln Ave.
(773) 525-2501
www.lincolnhallchicago.com

The team behind 20-year-old-plus music venue Schubas gets it right again with its younger but bigger sister. Devoted music fans appreciate the open sightlines and loyalty to strong, clear sound. But with decent prices on drinks (about $5 for tap beers, $8 or so for cocktails) and a bona-fide dinner menu—tempura chicken salad, arugula pesto baguette, wild mushroom flatbread— it goes above and beyond. The diverse range of acts has included dance-indie fusion band Delorean, hot new Reggae master Collie Budz, England's pop-folk star John Wesley Harding, and Danish band the Raveonettes. Reserve a dinner table through their website and you'll get rock star seating on the balcony an hour before the show. Ticket prices vary, around $10 to $20. Open nightly.

METRO & SMART BAR
3730 N. Clark St.
(773) 549-0203
www.metrochicago.com
Since 1982, this adjacent pair of clubs has grown up with the Chicago music scene. Smart Bar focuses on raging DJ sets from national acts and local up-and-comers (and a disco night on Sunday), while Metro is the live band venue, which from its start has promoted emerging musical talent. The wow-really? before-they-were-famous list includes R.E.M., Soul Asylum, Depeche Mode, Veruca Salt, Moby, and Jane's Addiction. Testament to Metro's influence on the national stage: Bob Dylan played at its 15th anniversary celebration. These days, catch DJ Nocturna, the Dodos, Femi Kuti, Man Man, and Death Cab for Cutie. Get there early to get upfront or a coveted balcony spot. Early all-ages shows start at 6:30 p.m. or 7 p.m. Other shows are 18 and over. Tickets can be purchased online or at the box office, but day-of purchases

are cash only and only sold after doors have opened. Tickets $5 to $40. Hours vary.

✳SCHUBAS TAVERN
3159 N. Southport Ave.
(773) 525-2508
www.schubas.com
You may wonder about the two Schlitz globe logos decorating the exterior here in terra-cotta bas relief. They hint back to the history of this building, built by the Milwaukee-based brewery in 1903 as one of its many "tied" houses, which funneled its products through saloons it built throughout the Midwest. Opened in 1988, Schubas still serves Schlitz on tap along with an approachable list of a dozen other beers, 20 in bottles and a can or two. You can down them at the original refurbished mahogany bar or take them with you into the intimate back room where nightly live music shows range from rock to folk, funk to country. Some concerts offer reserved seating, but most are sold out and standing room only, so be prepared. The adjacent Harmony Grill is a solid dinner (and brunch) option for down-home American cooking—mac and cheese is a specialty, and it's half price on Wednesday. Admission for concerts (purchase online or at the door). Open Mon through Fri lunch through late night, Sat and Sun breakfast through late night.

UNDERGROUND WONDER BAR
650 N. Dearborn St.
(312) 266-7761
www.undergroundwonderbar.com
Down in a low-ceilinged, low-maintenance, but decidedly high-energy garden level space, owner Lonie Walker showcases eclectic musical stylings of all varieties. Three nights a week—and nights go on until the

early morning here—Walker and her Big Bad Ass Company Band grace the tiny stage too. She has created such a welcoming atmosphere that some of her most enthusiastic regulars are themselves musicians and other club owners. But anyone can join the party. Just take note of the quirky tradition of raising your arms in the air and shouting "Wonder Bar!" whenever prompted. A light menu is offered (call ahead to double-check). Cover $8 to $15. Open from 7 p.m.

JAZZ CLUBS & PIANO BARS

ANDY'S JAZZ CLUB
11 E. Hubbard St.
(312) 642-6805
www.andysjazzclub.com

Andy's roots date back to 1951 when it was opened by entrepreneur Andy Rizzuto as a newspaperman's shot-and-a-beer bar. It changed hands a couple of times and, in 1977, Andy's hosted a weekly jazz concert. It didn't take long for jazz to define this River North club. Now Andy's presents two sessions seven days a week, including a jam session Sunday at 9 p.m. In addition to all styles, from traditional to Afro-pop, Andy's serves up a decent menu of sandwiches, pizzas, pastas, steak, ribs, and seafood. Cover $5 to $15. Open nightly from 4 p.m. to 1 a.m. Sun through Thurs, and until 1:30 a.m. on Fri and Sat; music starts an hour after opening; kitchen is open from 4:30 p.m.

DAVENPORT'S PIANO BAR & CABARET
1383 N. Milwaukee Ave.
(773) 278-1830
www.davenportspianobar.com

A snazzy atmosphere, baby grand, potent and pricey cocktails, and servers and bartenders who belt out show tunes and lounge favorites. Got an itch to perform? Feel free to request the mic and share your song too—a lot of regulars do just that. The small backroom professional cabaret theater features acts that are often flamboyant, sometimes hysterical, frequently moving, and always top-notch. No cover for the bar except $2 Fri and Sat after 10 p.m. Cabaret prices vary, generally $10 to $20 with two-drink minimum. Open Mon, Wed through Sun; closed Tues.

GREEN MILL
4802 N. Broadway
(773) 878-5552
www.greenmilljazz.com

Opened in 1907 and during the Roaring Twenties a Prohibition-era speakeasy frequented by Al Capone, the Green Mill is now a standard for jazz sets by local and touring acts. Don't expect to chit-chat during the show, though, as you'll likely get shushed by other audience members or the staff. Just sip your drink (no food here), sit back, and have a listen. On Sunday, it's the popular Uptown Poetry Slam, started here by Marc Smith back in 1985 and the forerunner of the national poetry slam movement. Cover $6 to $12 for all shows. Open nightly.

HOWL AT THE MOON
26 W. Hubbard St.
(312) 863-7427
www.howlatthemoon.com

Round up your pack and head to the Chicago location of this small national chain to howl the night away with the wild and crazy dueling piano players. On weekend nights, expect the place to be wall-to-wall (it's popular with birthdays and bachelorette parties); weekday shows are a little less dense, but no less rowdy, as conventioneers and business travelers often make this their post-work release. Buckets, bombs, and the shareable 24-ounce Wailin' Bones mixed drinks loosen up even the most modest. Thursday features full bands all night. Cover $5 to $10. Open nightly.

＊JAZZ SHOWCASE
806 S. Plymouth Ct.
(312) 360-0234
www.jazzshowcase.com
Quintets, quartets, trumpeters, vocalists, saxophonists, pianists, mainstream and making their way. You'll hear them all at this intimate South Loop club, a local gem that's jumped around since opening in the Gold Coast in 1947 and landed most recently in the historic Dearborn Station building. Framed photos and posters of jazz musicians line the walls, flickering candles create a sultry setting at small tables in front of the stage, and red velvet curtains frame the windows. Original owner Joe Segal, now in his mid-80s and considered the forefather of Chicago jazz, still introduces the acts, while his son Wayne runs the operations. A Sunday matinee is geared toward kids. Get there early for a spot on one of the comfy couches. It's cash only for the $5 to $20 cover charge, but credit cards are accepted at the bar. Open daily; sets at 8 p.m. and 10 p.m. (Sunday's matinee is at 4 p.m.).

THE REDHEAD PIANO BAR
16 W. Ontario St.
(312) 640-1000
www.redheadpianobar.com
A sassy redhead winks from her neon sign, beckoning you to take your clubbing to this sexy, sophisticated, subterranean piano bar. For more than 18 years, the Redhead has presented charismatic performers like native Chicagoan Stan Karcz, likened to Billy Joel;

David Scott Crawford, a regular at the Redhead since 2001 who once toured with Otis Clay; and John Zamojcin whose repertoire swings from Frank Sinatra to John Mayer. Get up close and cozy at the piano or sit back for a listen with a premium bourbon in hand—or a glass of wine or champagne, a single-malt scotch, some cognac, or one of the 40 cocktail blends like a Wildberry Explosion (Stoli blueberry vodka, pomegranate mix, and a splash of Cointreau) and a Flirtini (Yes vodka, Chambord, and pineapple juice with a float of sparkling wine and garnished with a lemon twist). Note: This is a kinda classy place, so business casual attire is required. There's no cover charge, but know that during the cold months, there is a required complimentary coat-check. Open nightly from 7 p.m.

LOUNGES, WINE & COCKTAIL BARS

CUVEE
308 W. Erie St.
(312) 202-9221
www.cuveechicago.com
A bit of L.A. pretension reigns supreme at this posh nightclub with its private alley entrance and beautiful people (in other words, dress right and your chances of getting in are higher). Ladies who look the part often skip the line, while guys usually pay a price to get in, though table reservations for bottle service carry some clout. If you're aiming for VIP status, plan to drop a thousand bucks or more for bottles of high-end champagne, vodka, rum, whiskey, or other such liquids; in other words, beer does not rank here. Cover varies (not cheap either). Doors open at 11:30 p.m. on Wed and Thurs, 11 p.m. on Fri and 10 p.m. on Sat. Be fashionably late.

ENO
505 N. Michigan Ave.
(312) 321-8738
www.enowinerooms.com

Don't let the limited menu of wine, cheese, and chocolate at this Michigan Avenue spot deter you—while it's spare on diversity, it's high on quality. A cozy dark-wood sliver of a wine bar, Eno draws in a mix of after-work locals and visitors staying in the attached InterContinental hotel. Not an oenophile? The knowledgeable and friendly staff makes the whole choosing process easy, as does the variety of wine flights available. Pair with cheeses hailing from as close as the farmlands of Wisconsin to the far reaches of Spain. The mouthwatering selection of chocolates and truffles is ever-changing, but if the menu features anything from Madison's Gail Ambrosius, it's a sure thing. Open Sun through Thurs early evening to late night, Fri and Sat from 1 p.m.

IN FINE SPIRITS
5418 N. Clark St.
Shop: (773) 506-9463; bar: (773) 334-9463
www.infinespirits.com

Creative cocktails that include made-in-house ingredients, hard-to-find wines and beer, and an inventive small plates menu attract a loyal clientele to this cute Andersonville wine bar and lounge. Reasonable prices and friendly staff don't hurt either. Grab a spot at the long bar or, if weather permits, head to the back for a table in the "secret" patio. Favorites from the seasonal food menu include duck confit rillettes, za'atar-spiced marcona almonds, and the signature cowboy sandwich with pulled pork, Gouda, and sweet pickled onions. Weekday specials sweeten the deal, and the neighboring wine shop means if you like what you've been drinking, you can take it home too. Open for dinner nightly.

MAUDE'S LIQUOR BAR
840 W. Randolph St.
(312) 243-9712
www.maudesliquorbar.com

Like a heady French perfume, Maude's woos you in with the promise of romance and rendezvous, Paris-style. Its dimly lit space, eclectic lighting, deliberately rustic furnishings, and limited French-inspired menu (foie gras and raw oysters included) appeals to a hip, young crowd looking for that *je ne sais quoi*. Reservations are highly recommended to sit upstairs at the communal tables, but you are welcome to embrace the vibe in the downstairs bar too. Be sure to try the Smokey Violet cocktail. No cover. Open Tues through Sat evening. For more information on Maude's, read its listing in the Restaurants chapter.

POPS FOR CHAMPAGNE & WATERSHED
601 N. State St.
Pops (312) 266-7677; WaterShed (312) 266-4932
www.popsforchampagne.com

For nearly 30 years, Pops has been tops. The extensive 100-plus-bottle menu of bubbly ranges from a vintage $650 bottle of 1996 Dom Pérignon down to a nonvintage Delamotte Brut for $92. Plus there are half-bottles and magnums, and a cold and hot small-plates menu of caviar, raw oysters, mussels, cheese, and charcuterie. The River North club's swank setting makes a perfect backdrop to date nights, but the upbeat atmosphere is equally suited for a girls' night out. Three nights a week (Sun to Tues) feature live jazz with no cover charge. Downstairs, the

Hotel Bars

You don't need to get a room to get into the action at these hotel hot spots.

Bernard's Bar. This small, hushed space in the Elysian Hotel breathes class with chocolate-brown velvet couches and a cocktail list that includes the Brown Derby (bourbon, grapefruit, and honey) and the Trompe l'Oeil (tequila, grapefruit, and pomegranate bitters). Perfect to wind down your day. Open nightly. 11 E. Walton St.; (312) 646-1300; www.elysianhotels.com.

Crimson Lounge. Victorian-style couches, mirrored walls, fancy-framed oil paintings of Victorian-ish-looking people, and even a signature scent involving sandalwood and patchouli. It sets the sensual scene at this clubby Sax Chicago bar. 333 N. Dearborn St.; (312) 923-2473; www.crimsonchicago.com.

J-Bar. Chic and modern-artsy (think video installations), this James Hotel lounge has a scenester feel with trendy cocktails (like the mojito Diego with rum, lime, and mint foam), DJs spinning Wednesday through Saturday and a third-Thursday comedy show. Open Wed through Sat; closed Sun through Tues. 610 N. Rush St.; (312) 660-7200; www.jameshotels.com/chicago.

Potter's Lounge. In the historic Palmer House hotel, this sophisticated enclave is decorated with large photos of some of the legendary list of performers with connections to Chicago and the Palmer House, including Nancy Wilson, Hugh Hefner, Carol Channing—who played the hotel's now-gone Empire Room more than any other person—and Phyllis Diller, the last person to entertain at the Empire Room in 1976. Retro cocktails and a small plates menu too. Open Wed through Sat. 17 E. Monroe St.; (312) 917-4933; www.potterschicago.com

ROOF. Voted one of the 10 best rooftop bars in the country by *USA Today,* there's good reason. Up on the 27th floor of theWit Hotel, the sexy year-round space attracts a beautiful crowd that warm toes during winter at built-in fire pits, gaze out at the city lights from floor-to-ceiling windows, and jam to live bands during ROOF Live every Tuesday. Cover $10 Fri and Sat after 9 p.m. Open Mon through Sat; open Sun during warm weather. 201 N. State St.; (312) 239-9501; www.roofonthewit.com.

Whiskey Bar and Grill. Popular in warm weather for its outdoor seating along scenester-heavy Rush Street, this is a long-standing favorite for looking good and sipping fine whiskeys and bourbons. Sutton Place Hotel, 1015 N. Rush St.; (312) 475-0300; www.gerberbars.com.

comfy windowless WaterShed scales things down with a laid-back vibe and regional beer and cocktail menu, plus a light-bite menu. No cover. Pops is open daily from 3 p.m. (1 p.m. on Sat); WaterShed is open Mon through Sat from 5 p.m.; closed Sun.

ROOTSTOCK WINE & BEER BAR
954 N. California Ave.
(773) 292-1616
www.rootstockbar.com

With a staff that reads like a who's-who from some of Chicago's favorite drinking and dining spots, it's no wonder this Humboldt Park spot has become a favorite hangout for chefs and other restaurant industry vets. The cozy, lived-in vibe—an eclectic mix of vintage furniture and local artwork—makes it a perfect spot to kick back while sipping wines and beers from small producers. For the food, chef Duncan Biddulph chooses local and seasonal ingredients when possible for small and large plates, such as Belgian-style mussels, organic burgers, and house-made chicken liver pâté. Rootstock is a bit off the beaten path, but worth the trek. Open Mon through Sat for dinner and late-night dining. Sunday brunch is served from 11 a.m. to 4 p.m. during spring and summer.

THE UNDERGROUND
56 W. Illinois St.
(312) 644-7600
www.theundergroundchicago.com

Evoking a secret military hideaway, complete with hidden alley entrance, this offering from nightclub mogul Billy Dec crosses the line into dance club with its pounding DJ sets. But its many seating options—paired with artillery cases for cocktail tables—impressive cocktail and bubbly list, and a menu of upscale, late-night light bites elevate the atmosphere. Clever cocktails include the "seductively fruity, skinny with a bit of danger" Bond Girl. Expect a wait after midnight; once you're in, you're at ease, soldier. Cover generally $20. Open Thurs, Fri, and Sun till 4 a.m., Sat till 5 a.m.

*THE VIOLET HOUR
1520 N. Damen Ave.
(773) 252-1500
www.theviolethour.com

When a fancy framed note at the entrance explains that there is no cell phone use allowed, no Budweisers or Cosmopolitans served, no reservations, proper attire required, and a request to "not bring anyone to the Violet Hour that you wouldn't bring to your mother's house for Sunday dinner," you think, "Man, this better be good." And it is. Voted one of the best bars in America by *Esquire* magazine, this Wicker Park gem gets its elegantly dramatic scene from 19th-century English Georgian and French Directory design. It gets its kudos mostly for its custom-made cocktails from serious mixologists (there are even varying kinds of ice to appropriately coordinate). Intensely high-backed blue leather chairs, periwinkle drapes, and flickering candles on delicate, tall white tables provide the perfect sipping space. While complaints of long lines are warranted (get there before 7 p.m. to avoid them), the flip side is that only enough people are allowed in to fill the seats. No cover. Open nightly.

*WEBSTER'S WINE BAR
1480 W. Webster Ave.
(773) 868-0608
www.websterwinebar.com

In 1994, this Lincoln Park favorite jump-started the wine bar trend in Chicago—and it shows no signs of slowing down. Artisanal and family-owned wineries are the focus of the more than 40 wines by the glass and 500 reserve wines from around the world; learn more about them at regular wine tastings and classes. Matching the impressive grape selection is an equally flavorful and wine-friendly selection of internationally influenced small plates, including grilled shrimp skewers, Alsatian-style *tarte flambée,* and a selection of cheeses and cured meats. The neighboring movieplex makes this a great pre- or post-flick stop. Or simply settle in for an evening of intimate conversation at a cozy table. Open nightly.

✳**THE WHISTLER**
2421 N. Milwaukee Ave.
(773) 227-3530
www.whistlerchicago.com
Amazing cocktails, amazing prices (most $8). You ask for more? You get a friendly, hipster crowd, live music with no cover charge, and an ever-changing storefront gallery designed by local artists—by the way, don't let that display window throw you off, you're in the right place. Finding a seat at this spot in increasingly cool Logan Square might require your own creativity; it's small and often jammed. The homey outdoor patio expands capacity by a handful (open year-round, as long as there isn't ice on the ground). Live music most nights and a last-Friday soul and funk music party. No cover. Open nightly.

SPORTS BARS

BENCHMARK
1510 N. Wells St.
(312) 649-9640
www.benchmarkchicago.com

This spacious, 2-story addition to Old Town from the Four Corners Tavern Group (Brownstone, Sidebar, Schoolyard) begs the question: Why didn't anyone think of this before? We're talking about the retractable roof that means they can boast a year-round beer garden. And that's just one of the appeals: There are also 46 TVs for watching a multitude of sports, 12 tap beers and 34 bottles (not only Bud and Miller Lite, but also Pyramid Haywire Hefeweizen and Dogfish), and a menu to satisfy munchies like mozzarella coins and hot soft pretzels, and bigger appetites like cheeseburgers, Asian salads, and fish tacos. The famous Four Corners' skillet cookie hits the sweet spot. Open daily (Sat and Sun from 11 a.m.).

BULL & BEAR
431 N. Wells St.
(312) 527-5973
www.bullbearbar.com
As the name suggests, this 5,300-square-foot River North spot references the stock market with its financial industry characterizations—the menu is called the "Wells Street Journal." But the top draws here are the tabletop taps at five premium booths. Book ahead of time if you want to take advantage of these trendy, pay-as-you-pour seats. Or just pull up a barstool for a regular or tall-sized draught and upscale bar food like bison burgers, crab cakes, and truffle mac and cheese. The Pajama Jam brunch serves up everything from turkey chili to chicken quesadillas to homemade pop tarts. Open daily from lunch through late night.

THE CUBBY BEAR
1059 W. Addison St.
(773) 327-1662
www.cubbybear.com

You don't have to be a Chicago Cubs groupie to have a good time at this old favorite across from Wrigley Field, but it doesn't hurt. On game days, expect some craziness, drunken debauchery, and potentially a wait to get in. Don't expect fancy drinks (or even glasses) or upscale food. Do expect to give in to the fun. There's also a lively lineup of live music acts, many of them cover bands like Rock Candy and Sixteen Candles, and popular live salsa on Sunday. Winter hours: Mon through Thurs for dinner and late night; Fri through Sun for lunch through late night; summer hours: non-game days open daily lunch through late night; game days open earlier (10 a.m., and on Sat at 9 a.m.).

*THE FIFTY/50
2047 W. Division St.
(773) 489-5050
www.thefifty50.com
Having met as managers at Joe's Seafood, Prime Steak, and Stone Crab in Chicago, Fifty/50 co-owners Greg Mohr and Scott Weiner scored big with their own sporty, friendly, three-level Ukrainian Village bar and restaurant. Top menu options include their "triple secret" Heaven Burger with double-cream brie, pears, and smoked-berry jam; raved-about mac and cheese; wings with smoked-in-house and aged sauce; and sweet potato fries. Of course, there's a hefty drink menu too. Beer cocktail, perhaps? Open daily for lunch and dinner, and Saturday and Sunday brunch.

GAMEKEEPERS
345 W. Armitage Ave.
(773) 549-0400
www.gamekeeperschicago.com
Neon beer signs? Check. College sports banners? Yep. Dozens of TVs with sports all the time? That too. Baskets of wings and platters of nachos? Of course. This corner tap is a college sports bar through and through. It gets packed on weekend nights because it's a 4 a.m. bar (5 a.m. on Saturday). And though it definitely attracts a recently graduated co-ed crowd (wear your college sweatshirt, and you'll fit right in), it's also a tradition for alumni who have drunk at this Lincoln Park bar since they were legal—and it opened in 1984, so that's a long time. The beer flows fast here, though some gripe it's overpriced. To help it go down easy, check out the daily specials like $7 Bud pitchers on Monday, $4 imports on Wednesday, and $5 Bloody Marys on Saturday and football Sundays. An occasional live band too. Open Mon through Fri from 4 p.m., Sat from 10 a.m., Sun from 11 a.m.

HARRY CARAY'S TAVERN
Navy Pier
600 E. Grand Ave.
(312) 527-9700
www.harrycaraystavern.com
This Navy Pier watering hole debuted in 2010 and is one of several offshoots of the original Harry Caray's Italian Steakhouse (named for the late, great Chicago Cubs announcer; see the Restaurants chapter for more information). It's popular with families, groups, and out-of-towners, and boasts a host of celebrity owners, from actors Jeremy Piven and James Denton to sports heroes like former Chicago Cubs Hall of Famer Ernie Banks and Chicago Blackhawk Patrick Kane. Besides a full menu of burgers, steak, seafood, and pizzas, the fun-loving liquids list features Tiki Bar Cocktails such as the Wrigley Rita, and signature cocktails created in honor of each of Harry's famous investors—including one for his wife called Dutchie's Splash

with Finlandia vodka, cranberry, OJ, and a lime. Don't worry, there are plenty of beer options too. And don't miss the museum of sports memorabilia. Open daily from lunch through late dinner.

MURPHY'S BLEACHERS
3655 N. Sheffield Ave.
(773) 281-5356
www.murphysbleachers.com
If you don't have seats at the ballgame, at least you can have the crowd at this historic bar across from Wrigley Field. Since the 1930s, Murphy's has evolved from hot dog stand to bar and finally to legend, when Jim Murphy bought it in 1980. Murphy opened the first rooftop overlooking the ballpark in 1984, spawning many more nearby and establishing Murphy as an icon himself. Murphy's now serves regular Joes and celebs alike (spotted: Billy Corgan, Bill Murray, Denise Richards, Kenny Chesney) who come for the atmosphere and for more than 70 beers and a long list of whiskeys, from an 80-proof Black Bush to 94-proof Old Forester Birthday Bourbon. Sling back an extra in honor of Murphy, who passed away too young in 2003. Plus, there's a menu of mozzarella sticks, pizza, Reuben sandwiches, hot dogs, and—a nod to Murphy's roots—fish-and-chips. Daily specials like $3 Half Acre or Goose Island beers or $4 Jack Daniel's cocktails are great on non-game days. Open daily from 11 a.m., 9 a.m. on game days.

THEORY
9 W. Hubbard St.
(312) 644-0004
www.theorychicago.com
Take a step up from banners and baseball caps at this comfortably-chic sports lounge. The first offering from local former DJ and

sports nut Joel Sorinsky is a respectable one that tries hard to please, and where serious service misses are made up for with attention from the manager and maybe a complimentary drink or two. Its River North location means it's a hit for happy hour. The upscale, though not outrageously priced, bar menu scores with items like fajita lettuce wraps, pesto panini, chips and homemade guac, nacho bites, and jicama salad. If you come for specials including $2 sliders on Saturday and $5 Absolut cocktails on Thursday, you'll save some cash for an extra drink (try the refreshing cucumber martini). Get on Sorinsky's good side when you cheer for his alma-mater University of Iowa Hawkeyes. Open daily from 11 a.m.

TIMOTHY O'TOOLE'S PUB
622 N. Fairbanks Ct.
(312) 642-0700
www.timothyotooles.com
Combine the trappings of an Irish pub—a Guinness "black list," for example—with a sports bar—tons of TVs (we're talking 60-plus)—and you get this rowdy Streeterville spot. There's also a full menu of burgers, ribs, chicken sandwiches, baskets of finger-licking fried apps, and award-winning wings (tip: of the seven sauces, the extra spicy clinched it). The Sunday brunch features a $20 bottomless Bloody Mary bar and $16 bottomless Mimosa bar. Any team jersey will get you in the spirit, but be forewarned that this is Bears football land. Open from 11 a.m. Mon through Fri and from 9 a.m. Sat and Sun.

WESTEND BAR & GRILL
1326 W. Madison St.
(312) 981-7100
www.westendwestloop.com

Over near the United Center, there aren't as many downtown drinking spots, but the founders of Four Corners Tavern Group opened this one a few years ago. Though some complain of too-loud music, it gets points for friendly service; plenty of space at the U-shaped bar and leather booths; a creative menu that includes surprises like chopped smoked turkey wraps, barbecue chicken nachos, and bacon cheddar pizza (along with standards and a kids' menu too); and its free shuttle to Chicago Blackhawks and Bulls games. It fills up fast with pre-game drinkers, so get there early or right before the game starts when ticketholders file out. Open Mon through Fri from 5 p.m. (4 p.m. on game days), Sat and Sun 11 a.m. (9 a.m. on game days).

PUBS & TAVERNS

BLOKES & BIRDS
3343 N. Clark St.
(773) 472-5252
www.blokesandbirdschicago.com
You can still slosh around at Wrigleyville's standard sports-centric bars, but when you're in the mood for a change of pace, head over to Blokes & Birds. Slang for guys and girls, this classy bi-level gastropub highlights great British imports, like European "football," punk rock, and a scene-stealing menu of spot-on lobster potpie, Scottish salmon, vegetarian curry, and bacon-wrapped medjool dates. That's not to take away from the outstanding craft beer selection: Abbot Ale, Wells Bombardier, and J.K. Scrumpy Hard Cider. Don't know your porter from your stout? Ask for a sample. If you're planning to drop in for a nip, hang in the downstairs bar and shoot some pool; for a full-on dinner experience, the upstairs bar obliges with communal wooden

tables and a fireplace. Open daily from 5 p.m. (earlier for morning soccer kick-offs); brunch served Sat and Sun.

*CELTIC CROSSINGS
751 N. Clark St.
(312) 337-1005
www.celticcrossingschicago.com
Though it gave in and added a few TVs recently, this Irish pub in River North is still one of the most charming, conversation-friendly in town. You can't miss the rich red exterior; follow it in and you'll be warmly welcomed by its traditional old-fashioned bar, wood-burning fireplace, live music most nights—including Irish sessions on Sunday—and a perfect Guinness pour. Irish coffees come with hand-whipped cream, and Thursday features $5 Irish Car Bombs. Open Mon through Fri from 3 p.m., Sat and Sun from noon.

ENGLISH
444 N. LaSalle Blvd.
(312) 222-6200
www.englishchicago.com
Wide, rounded Art Deco–inspired overhead lights, vintage photos, ornamented columns, and unique ironwork take their cue from the exterior of the historic terra cotta–glazed Veseman Building that now houses this River North pub-slash-club. The eating part takes the spotlight, actually, and praise is high for the sliders and the English crisps: waffle fries topped with Guinness-braised pork belly, sharp cheddar, sweet cabbage, scallions, and sour cream. But drinks definitely offer a fine mix of imported and domestic beer, a few wines, and the signature cocktails—the Pimm's Cup brings a bit of English tradition to the place. Lunch is laid-back, while Thursday, Friday, and Saturday late night attract a

young partying crowd and a loud, DJ-spun soundtrack of British rock mixed with everything from '80s to contemporary. Open Mon through Sat at 11 a.m.; closed Sun except during NFL season.

FADÓ IRISH PUB
100 W. Grand Ave.
(312) 836-0066
www.fadoirishpub.com
You wouldn't know it, but this multilevel River North establishment is actually a small national chain. That's because Fadó (pronounced f'doe) goes to great lengths to ensure authenticity, including its decor direct from "the island" itself, its mostly Irish waitstaff, its live Irish music, and, of course, its skillfully poured (you'll wait a couple of minutes for it) Guinness. The spirited atmosphere makes friends out of strangers, gives out-of-towners a welcoming spot to wind down, and provides for gatherings to watch rugby or soccer matches. Get a taste of Ireland with Fadó's worthy fish-and-chips, a boxty, or some corned beef and cabbage. Get a real, raucous feel for it during the St. Patrick's Day celebration! Open Mon through Fri from 11:30 a.m., earlier on Sat and Sun for sports games.

✳GUTHRIES TAVERN
1300 W. Addison St.
(773) 477-2900
All your favorite childhood board games (think Clue, Scrabble, Jenga, Boggle, and Battleship), plus a stellar beer selection including weekly craft specials make for a cozy, good time in Wrigleyville and a far throw from the usual Cubs-crazed bars (in fact, you won't even find any Cubs decor here). On

the outside, the ivy-covered exterior could pass as a private home, save for the sign and the bright red door. Inside, plain drop-ceiling tiles get a lift from local artwork and photography, and one odd panel crammed with doll heads. Guthries is a neighborhood bar of the friendliest type, attracting a mostly young crowd and perfect for a second date when a game of Connect 4 can make a personal connection even stronger. Not much in the way of food, but they don't mind if you bring in some snacks of your own. Open nightly until 2 a.m. (Sat until 3 a.m.).

THE KERRYMAN
661 N. Clark St.
(312) 335-8121
www.thekerrymanchicago.com
Some call the layout strange, others appreciate the separated spaces and atmospheres of the trilevel River North pub that's heavy on wood and stone. Named for an Irishman who is said to have landed in America before Columbus, the Kerryman is a product of brothers Mick and Trevor O'Donoghue, themselves hailing from County Kerry, Ireland, and established club and hotel owners back home and in Britain and Spain. Here, they've created a modern take on the Irish pub, featuring local DJs, dancing, and a late-night trendy pickup place. The Irish-influenced menu stands on its own and includes Claddagh wings, an Irishman's quesadilla (with Irish cheddar and Irish bacon), Galway seafood chowder, a club sandwich with hard-boiled egg, and Gaelic chicken. During warm months, snag an alfresco sidewalk table where drapes are actually beautiful hanging plants. Open daily from 11 a.m.

ATTRACTIONS & MUSEUMS

There had been no attraction like it before and arguably none like it since: Chicago's 1893 World's Columbian Exposition. And it led to the formation of several of the city's top attractions and museums that we enjoy today. The Field Museum began its existence in the only structure left standing on the fairgrounds, the Palace of Fine Arts building. Originally named the Columbian Museum of Chicago, its first exhibits comprised the anthropological specimens, gems, taxidermy, and other items from fair collections. After the Field Museum moved in 1921 to new digs closer to downtown, the Museum of Science and Industry moved in and now attracts more than 2 million visitors each year. To stay in business during a downturn, the MSI pioneered the idea of corporate-sponsored exhibits.

The Navy Pier Ferris wheel is also a direct descendant of the World's Fair, where the very first Ferris wheel debuted, a marvel even taller than the Eiffel Tower.

Also with links to the Columbian Exposition is the Art Institute of Chicago, owing a large part of its highly acclaimed Impressionist collection to Bertha Honore Palmer, the fair's chairman of the Board of Lady Managers. People once sought invitations to the Palmer home just to get a glimpse of her collection of paintings, and now, thanks to her posthumous donation, any visitor can see her Monets, Renoirs, Degas, and more.

The Peggy Notebaert Nature Museum doesn't have World's Fair ties, because it can actually trace its founding back to 1857 (long before the 1893 event and named something different back then), earning it the title of the city's very first museum. Its new building in Lincoln Park is a mainstay of school and camp groups, mom-and-tot meet-ups, and family outings.

The Field Museum now ranks up there with the Smithsonian, and has been joined in Chicago by a host of other historic, artistic, cultural, and just plain entertaining museums. The Adler Planetarium was the country's first planetarium; the Brookfield Zoo established the first barless animal habitats in the US; the DuSable Museum of African American History was the first of its kind in America; and the National Museum of Mexican Art is considered a model for other ethnic museums in the city and beyond.

The chapter includes family-friendly attractions and others that skew to more mature audiences. They range from the spiritual to the frivolous, from emotionally moving museums to attractions that encourage you to get out and move.

ATTRACTIONS

ADLER PLANETARIUM
Museum Campus
1300 S. Lake Shore Dr.
(312) 922-7827
www.adlerplanetarium.org

A trek into this star-studded institution—the first modern planetarium opened in the Western Hemisphere—is quite simply out of this world. Founded in 1930 by Chicago businessman Max Adler, the landmark granite building's unique look comes from its 12-sided polygon design; each corner represents a sign of the zodiac. But it's astronomy that shines inside. The highlight is the newly transformed Grainger Sky Theater, featuring the latest in cinematic special effects. Two other theaters provide equally compelling entertainment: The 3D Universe Theater and the all-digital, Definiti Space Theater run shows including "Journey to the Stars," narrated by Whoopi Goldberg, and "One World, One Sky: Big Bird's Adventure" aimed at younger audiences. Bringing the galaxy down to earth are interactive exhibits like "Telescopes: Through the Looking Glass," displaying some of the world's most amazing galaxy-gazers; and "Shoot for the Moon," whose centerpiece is the fully-restored Gemini 12 spacecraft, along with fascinating stories of space travel. The recently opened "Planet Explorers" is a hands-on discovery zone for kids with stars in their eyes. Discount days offer free general admission and occur periodically through the year, though they tend to get very crowded. General admission $10; seniors $8; children 3 to 11 $6; shows are extra. Hours vary throughout the year, so be sure to check the website before you head out.

i The third Thursday of each month at the Adler Planetarium features Adler After Dark, a 21-and-over clubby night with music, cash bar, and entry to the shows as well as a chance to peer through the Doane Observatory telescope. $10 in advance; $15 at the door.

BAHA'I HOUSE OF WORSHIP
100 Linden Ave., Wilmette
(847) 853-2300
www.bahai.us/bahai-temple

One of just seven temples of the Baha'i religion in the world, this stunning wedding cake-like, multitiered circular structure north of the city welcomes visitors to marvel at its meticulously landscaped grounds and its serene prayer hall (no photos inside), showcasing a 135-foot-high dome. The requisite nine sides of the building symbolize several things in the Baha'i faith including completeness. The gardens and auditorium are open every day from 6 a.m. to 10 p.m. Wander in any time or join a devotion Mon through Fri at 9:15 a.m. and 12:30 p.m. or to hear the choir sing on Sunday at 12:30 p.m. Free admission (surprisingly, donations are not accepted). Open daily.

✳BROOKFIELD ZOO
3300 Golf Rd., Brookfield
(800) 201-0784; (708) 688-8000
www.brookfieldzoo.org

Chicagoans do adore their local free zoo, but when they want to see even more wild animals of the world, they head about 14 miles west of downtown to this sprawling park that opened in 1934. There's a lot to see, so pace yourself and then put your roaming on pause to watch a dolphin presentation (there are at least two every day). Or jump aboard the narrated Motor Safari (available early spring through late fall for an extra fee) for an on-and-off trip that rolls you to four prime stops throughout the zoo (great for tired feet). At the Great Bear Wilderness, there are plenty of big bears, but also bison and bald eagles. Jump over to the Australia House for a chance to see creatures from Down Under—a Southern hairy-nosed wombat, an emerald tree boa, emu, and kangaroos of course. There's also a Hoofed Animals exhibit with Bactrian camels, Grevy's zebras, and antelope; a seasonal butterfly exhibit; a play zoo; an African savanna; and a children's zoo where you can watch milking and wool-spinning demonstrations. General admission $13.50; seniors and children 3 to 11 $9.50 (some activities have extra fees). Open most of the year from 10 a.m. to 5 p.m. From Memorial Day weekend through Labor Day, zoo hours are 9:30 a.m. to 6 p.m.; and on Sun from Memorial Day to Labor Day, the zoo stays open until 7:30 p.m.

BUCKINGHAM FOUNTAIN
Lake Shore Drive between Balbo Drive and Jackson Boulevard
(312) 742-PLAY (7529)
More than 14,000 gallons of water per minute are pumped through 134 jets; 820 lights create a brilliant and ever-changing effect each warm-weather night; and every hour for 20 minutes from mid-April to mid-October (if the weather cooperates), a center jet shoots water 150 feet into the air. It's these impressive numbers that add up to one beautiful Grant Park icon. Dedicated in 1927 and donated to the city by Kate Buckingham in honor of her late brother, the ornate marble and granite structure was designed by Edward H. Bennett (co-author of the Chicago Plan of 1909) who took his inspiration from the Latona Basin at Versailles. The four seahorse sculptures decorating its perimeter symbolize the states

that border Lake Michigan (Illinois, Wisconsin, Michigan, and Indiana). During winter, the fountain is turned off, but draped in dramatic white lights. Free. When in season, it's in operation from 8 a.m. to 11 p.m. daily.

CHICAGO ARCHITECTURE FOUNDATION
224 S. Michigan Ave.
(312) 922-3432
www.caf.architecture.org
Founded in 1966 when a group of passionate locals banded together to save Chicago's historic Glessner House, the Chicago Architecture Foundation has since evolved into one of the most important advocates for architecture and design in the city. Its 480 fully trained volunteers lead nearly 90 different tours, and present exhibits, lecture series, workshops, and special events throughout the year. Its home base in the Santa Fe Building across from Grant Park features the permanent exhibit "Chicago Model City," which includes a large scale model of Chicago and gives you an intro to the city before embarking on a tour or setting out for exploring on your own. Also hosted here, every third Sunday of the month from Sept through May is CAFamily Studio, free programming geared toward kids ages 3 to 12. Be sure to stop at the top-notch gift shop where you'll find a creative selection of architecture- and Chicago-centric housewares, games, gifts, cards, jewelry, and more. Free admission to exhibits; tour fees vary. Open daily. For more details about the tours, check out its listing in the Tours chapter.

CHICAGO BOTANIC GARDEN
1000 Lake Cook Rd., Glencoe
(847) 835-5440
www.chicagobotanic.org

Do More, Save More

If you're planning to visit multiple attractions and museums during your travels through the Windy City, then you might want to take advantage of one of the two major commercial discount booklets that can save you some serious dough. Here's a breakdown:

Go Chicago Card: (866) 628-9031, www.smartdestinations.com/chicago
Price: Depends on number of days of use. For example, a 1-day pass for an adult is $66.99, $44.99 for a child; a 7-day pass is $169.99/$129.99
Savings: Up to 55 percent off single-ticket prices
What's included: Admission to 28 attractions including a boat tour, John Hancock Observatory, Adler Planetarium, Art Institute, Field Museum, Shedd Aquarium, Chicago History Museum, Brookfield Zoo.
Time limitation: You can purchase a pass for 1, 2, 3, 5, or 7 days
What to know: The first attraction visited activates your pass and begins your first day. You can visit any attraction once per day. You must activate your pass within 1 year following the end of the calendar in which you purchase your pass (e.g. purchase Feb 2012, and it will expire Dec 31, 2013).
Where to buy: Online, or at the locations
Bonuses: Also get special savings such as 10 percent to 20 percent off in some attraction gift shops, as well as other retail and dining locations.
Additional info: You can also buy a customized Custom Pass, only filled with the attractions you choose and good for up to 30 days from first use. Savings on these build as you add more attractions.

Chicago CityPASS: (888) 330-5008, www.citypass.com
Price: Adults $76; children 3 to 11 $59
Savings: 50 percent
What it includes: VIP access to five Chicago attractions (choose from seven): Shedd Aquarium, Field Museum, Skydeck Chicago, Adler Planetarium or Art Institute of Chicago, John Hancock Observatory or Museum of Science and Industry
Time limitation: Passes are valid for 9 days from first use.
What to know: The first attraction you visit activates your card for the first day. The passes included are for one-time admission to each attraction. You have at least a year to activate your pass before it expires. Tickets must be purchased within 6 months of first use in order to obtain the actual book of tickets.
Where to buy: Online, or at any of the locations (same price either way)
Bonuses: The passes included in a CityPASS booklet generally include VIP admission, meaning no waiting in lines, admission to many special exhibits, and often theater shows.

A quick drive up north and right off the highway takes you to this picturesque bounty of blooms. The history of these gardens dates back to 1890 and includes records of a chrysanthemum show hosted at the 1893 World's Columbian Exposition. The official gardens didn't take root until 1972, but they have since been nurtured into 24 diverse display gardens and four natural areas that extend across 385 acres that encompass fruit and vegetable gardens, greenhouses, nine islands, and several lakes. Spring and summer are obviously the busiest seasons with a seemingly endless array of color and texture. From early May through Oct, the 7,500-square-foot Model Railroad Garden is an added attraction; the intricately designed, all-natural miniature railroad pays homage to the great landmarks of America like the White House and Statue of Liberty, and some right here at home like Wrigley Field. You might think winter would deter visitors, but it's actually a surprisingly beautiful time to visit, as the gardens become an amazing celebration of the season with 750,000 lights twinkling amid the hushed quiet. From Thanksgiving through the beginning of the New Year, winter also brings indoor holiday displays, including the festive and spectacular Wonderland Express, an indoor model railroad where garden-size trains traverse a magical scene of more than 80 Chicago landmarks, created from natural materials (a short film shows the incredible work that goes into making it). Admission is technically free, but there is a parking fee (members receive parking included in their dues) of $20 for cars and $25 for vans; on Tuesday, senior citizens may park for $7. On Sunday, from spring through early fall, a trolley runs from the nearby Glencoe Metra station and is $2 roundtrip per person. There are also bicycle trails through the gardens and plenty of racks to lock up and then linger among the greenery. Open daily 8 a.m. to sunset. See the listing in the chapter on Parks & Recreation as well.

✳**CHICAGO CULTURAL CENTER**
78 E. Washington St.
(312) 744-6630
www.chicagoculturalcenter.org
Having lived out a long life as the city's first central public library and Civil War memorial, this impressively ornamented 1897 structure took on a second vital city service as its hub of cultural activities. Pop in here to experience everything from theater events to art exhibitions, lectures to film series, and music and dance performances nearly every day—almost all of it free. The building is a Neo-Classical architectural gem in its own right. When it was built, it was called the People's Palace because it was funded with a 1 percent tax instead of with private donations. With updates throughout the years, the building—whose 2,357 wooden piles were driven 75 feet down into solid earth—is as sturdy as it was when it was built. A stroll reveals its extensive use of marble, polished brass, and intricate mosaics of glass, stone, and mother-of-pearl. Not to mention the world's largest stained-glass Tiffany dome, measuring in at 38 feet in diameter, plus another even larger glass dome on the other side of the building. Oohs and aahs are free, as is admission to the center; some events have nominal fees, so check the calendar. Open daily.

i Free tours of the Chicago Cultural Center are offered Wed, Fri, and Sat at 1:15 p.m.; they leave from the Randolph Street lobby.

✳GARFIELD PARK CONSERVATORY
300 N. Central Park Ave.
(773) 638-1766
www.garfieldconservatory.org
No matter the month, tropical plants, flowering desert cacti, lush ferns, delicate orchids, and other gorgeous greenery flourish under the grand glass domes of this historic conservatory just a short skip west of downtown. Completed in 1908, the Jens Jensen–designed structure is now listed on the National Register of Historic Places and run by the Chicago Park District (along with its sister Lincoln Park Conservatory). Encompassing an Aroid House, Palm House, the playful and interactive Children's Garden, a Desert House, the Fern Room—boasting one of the oldest plants on earth—a seasonal display house, and a show space (a spectacular setting for a wedding), the indoor splendor stretches approximately 2 acres. Adding in the stunning outdoor gardens, including a Demonstration Garden and a take on Monet's garden in Giverny, France, the total bumps to more than 14 acres, landing Garfield Park in the top five largest conservatories in the country. But it's more than just a pretty face. A full slate of activities and programs includes flower shows, a craft beer tasting, a sweets festival, art exhibits, seedling sales, an active beehive, and more. A severe storm in summer 2011 shattered dozens of the dome's oldest windows, and efforts are underway to replace them; you might want to donate a few extra bucks to the cause. Free (free parking lot too); some fees apply for special events and exhibits. Open daily 9 a.m. to 5 p.m., with extended hours on Wed until 8 p.m.

i Need some green thumb tips? Ask a master gardener at the Garfield Park Conservatory's Plant Information Clinic located in the lobby of the Palm House every Sat from noon to 4 p.m.

GRACELAND CEMETERY
4001 N. Clark St.
(773) 525-1105
www.gracelandcemetery.org
The names you'll find at this 119-acre Northside cemetery read like a who's who of Windy City movers and shakers, making it as much a stroll back through Chicago history as it is a final resting place. Amid the parklike setting of old-growth trees, a pond, subtle hills, and lush, landscaped lawns, are buried the likes of architects Louis Sullivan, Daniel Burnham, and Ludwig Mies van der Rohe—his minimalist style carried right through to his simple black granite marker designed by his grandson, architect Dirk Lohan. You'll also spot the tombs of famous Chicago business moguls such as Potter Palmer, whose ostentatiously large Greek temple is unmissable. A giant stone baseball marks the grave of William Hubert, who founded the National League of Professional Baseball. Of all the markers, the must-see here is the understated Louis Sullivan–designed Getty Tomb, built for the wife of lumber merchant Henry Harrison Getty. You're free to roam the grounds on your own—pick up a map at the office or download it from the website—or join one of the tours led by either the Chicago Architecture Foundation or the Chicago History Museum (check their respective calendars for dates). Tours charge a fee. Open daily until 4:30 p.m.; office closed on Sun.

HANCOCK OBSERVATORY
John Hancock Center
875 N. Michigan Ave., 94th Floor
(888) 875-VIEW
www.hancockobservatory.com
You're above it all when you zoom up to the 94th floor of the John Hancock building. To help guide your gaze around the spectacular, 360-degree views (you can see up to 80 miles and four states), just plug into the free hand-held multimedia Sky Tour, narrated by former *Friends* star and founder of local Lookingglass Theatre David Schwimmer (it comes in seven languages and a kids' version too). Feel the breeze 1,000 feet up when you step across the screened-in walkway called the SkyWalk; take advantage of the sky-high concierge; and settle in for more stunning views while enjoying fancy coffees, Italian light bites, and beer, wine, and cocktails at the Lavazza Espression Cafe. General admission $15; ages 3 to 11 $10; under 3 free; a fast-pass is available for an additional fee; the Sun & Stars ticket (an additional $4) allows you entrance during the day and then again at night for a different look. Open daily 9 a.m. to 11 p.m. (last admission is 10:30 p.m.). Read more about the John Hancock Center's architectural significance in the chapter on Architecture.

i One of the best times to visit the Hancock Observatory is when Navy Pier presents its summertime fireworks displays every Wednesday and Saturday nights. Check the Navy Pier schedule for times; www.navypier.com.

LINCOLN PARK CONSERVATORY
2391 N. Stockton Dr.
(312) 742-7736
www.chicagoparkdistrict.com

You'll leave the daily grind behind as you enter this balmy paradise of palms, ponds, ferns, and orchids. Built between 1890 and 1895 as both a showplace for exotic plants and flowers and as the nursery for city gardens, this petite conservatory sits adjacent to the Lincoln Park Zoo and is a low-key and pleasant space, particularly on chilly days. Free. Open daily 9 a.m. to 5 p.m.

LINCOLN PARK ZOO
Cannon Dr. at Fullerton Pkwy.
(312) 742-2000
www.lpzoo.org
What began in 1868 with a pair of swans from New York has grown into a 49-acre home to more than 1,200 animal species, from aardvarks and alpacas to leopards, flamingos, bears, and zebras—and it's one of the few remaining free zoos in the nation. Stroller-pushing moms and dads appreciate the manageable size of the zoo and flock here during the summer. Be sure to visit the family of endangered African gorillas and chimpanzees—wave hello to Sai, the most recent addition to the white-cheeked gibbon family—watch the monkeys playfully swing from vine to vine, feed the cows at the Farm-in-the-Zoo, cheer the seals on as they show off their sleek moves, and take a ride on the hand-crafted carousel. The new half-mile Nature Boardwalk, made of entirely recycled materials, skirts the fully restored ecosystem of the zoo's manmade pond where you might spot native fish, frogs, turtles, birds, and insects. In winter, the annual ZooLights celebration brings a festive sparkle to the zoo. Free; extra fee for some activities; parking on the east side of the zoo starts at $17 for up to 3 hours, but there's free (hard-to-find sometimes) street parking, as well as several nearby CTA

bus stops. Open 365 days a year. A listing in the Kidstuff chapter presents additional information.

MILLENNIUM PARK
201 E. Randolph St.
Between Michigan and Columbus
Avenues
(312) 742-1168
www.millenniumpark.org

It might have opened four years and many thousands of dollars beyond its original 2000 goal, but Millennium Park was still an instant hit. Who knew that a silver, 110-ton object now known as "The Bean" would become one of Chicago's most recognizable icons? Officially titled *Cloud Gate,* artist Anish Kapoor's sculpture spans 33 feet high and 66 feet across and is a favorite photo-op among the many architectural and artistic elements in this 24.5-acre downtown green space. No less impressive is star-chitect Frank Gehry's ribbons of brushed stainless steel that curl in and out of each other to create the Jay Pritzker Pavilion—branching out overhead is a complex trellis of steel pipes that carry the sound system to the expansive area of lawn seating. Free concerts and other events take place here throughout the warm-enough months. And perhaps the most fun of the public art pieces is Jaume Plensa's *Crown Fountain,* a pair of 50-foot-high glass block towers that face each other across a very shallow reflecting pool. The towers are embedded with video images of people's faces that represent a cross-section of Chicago's communities. From spring through fall, the towers stream and spout water, providing giddy city splashing for kids and grown-ups too. For quieter times, stroll the lovely Lurie Garden, bring a bag lunch to sit at the Wrigley Square and peristyle;

browse the changing public art installations; or cross over Lake Shore Drive on the Gehry-designed pedestrian bridge. Indoor concerts, dance, music, and family programs are scheduled throughout the year at the Harris Theater. There's also a bike rental facility, daily kids activities during the summer, and ice skating during the winter. A second bridge designed by Renzo Piano connects the park to the Art Institute's Modern Wing across the southern end of the park. Free (Harris Theater ticket prices vary). Open daily 6 a.m. to 11 p.m. Also see the listing in the Parks and Recreation chapter, as well as in the sidebar focused on Public Art in this chapter.

✳MORTON ARBORETUM
4100 SR 53, Lisle
(630) 968-0074
www.mortonarb.org

When an arboretum can list more than 4,000 types of trees, shrubs, and other plants from 40 different countries within its midst, you know this is no paltry park. In fact, this 1,700-acre Eden of all things green and growing is the fourth most-visited public garden or arboretum in the country. And lucky us, it's only about 25 miles west of Chicago. Established in 1922 by the founder of the Morton Salt Company, Joy Morton (the son of J. Sterling Morton, who founded Arbor Day), it features 16 miles of trails through woodland, wetland, and prairie; a 1-acre maze garden; herb garden; fragrance garden; a 4-acre children's garden that encompasses 10 themed spaces; and other specially designed gardens. Drawing visitors throughout the year are events including the Yule Log Hunt, theater performances, art shows, and sled-dog demonstrations. Admission $11; seniors $10; children ages 2 to 17 $8; under 2 free; discount Wed admission is $7; seniors $6;

children $5. Free parking daily. Open 365 days a year; grounds open 7 a.m. to sunset; visitor center opens at 9 a.m. (closes 4 p.m. or 5 p.m. depending on the month); children's garden opens at 9:30 p.m. (closes at 4 p.m. or 5 p.m.)

i The Children's Garden at the Morton Arboretum scores big with little ones, and parents should come prepared with an extra set of clothes for getting dirty and wet, as well as water shoes for the Secret Stream and Wonder Pond.

NAVY PIER
600 E. Grand Ave.
(312) 595-PIER
www.navypier.com

More than 8.6 million visitors a year can't be wrong, right? Right. Built in 1916, the historic pier was first a shipping and recreational facility, and later served time as a military training facility as well as an early University of Illinois at Chicago campus. Since undergoing a major revitalization effort in July 1995, Navy Pier is considered one of the Midwest's top visitor destinations. You can easily spend the entire day at Navy Pier with 50 acres of rides, restaurants, gardens, museums, shops, street performances, live theater, and more. The biggest attraction? In literal terms, that would be the 15-story-tall Ferris wheel, which takes a slow 7-minute revolution around as you snap stellar city shots. The 50,000-square-foot Children's Museum is a huge hit with families, while the Chicago Shakespeare Theater has a lineup of shows for all ages. Set sail aboard one of the many cruises that push off from the docks here, or operate your own remote-control boat (yep, they're here too); catch an IMAX movie;

play a round of mini golf; hop a ride on the musical carousel; stroll the galleries of the free Smith Museum of Stained Glass; and get lost in Amazing Chicago's Funhouse Maze. No need to leave when it's time to eat; just grab a quick bite in the food court or settle in at any one of the full-service restaurants including Bubba Gump, Harry Caray's, the new Jimmy Buffet's Margaritaville Tavern and Grill, and the more upscale seafood spot, Riva. Special events include summertime twice-weekly free fireworks displays, and a massive indoor winter festival. Prices for attractions vary. Parking fees are rather high, so be prepared. Open daily.

i From Memorial Day through Labor Day you can avoid the frustratingly steep parking fees at Navy Pier by arriving by free trolley from several downtown locations. Visit www.navypier.com (click on FAQs) for a trolley route map and schedule.

*SHEDD AQUARIUM
Museum Campus
1200 S. Lake Shore Dr.
(312) 939-2438
www.sheddaquarium.org

Chicagoans may love their lake, but it's the creatures of the seas that get the attention at this historic and world-renowned aquatic museum. With the vision and major funding from Marshall Field & Company chairman John G. Shedd, this awe-inspiring institution opened in 1930 and, through changes, improvements, and additions that nearly doubled its size, it still logs approximately 2 million visitors a year. They come to see attractions such as one of the world's largest indoor marine mammal exhibits—in the 3-million-gallon saltwater Oceanarium, where belugas, dolphins, sea otters, and sea lions frolic. And then there's the 360-degree, 90,000-gallon Caribbean Reef tank, teeming with 70 species of animals, including sharks, eels, a sea turtle, and a rainbow of beautiful fish—feeding time in here is a kick to watch. In the Amazon Rising exhibit, you'll spot piranhas, spiders, anacondas, and crocodiles. Explore a lagoon, mangrove forest, and fishing village, and safely check out the sharks in the Wild Reef habitat. Kids go wild in the interactive Polar Play Zone, while it's the dolphins and belugas that play it up in the daily aquatic show. Ticket prices start at $28.95 for adults, and $19.95 for children 3 to 11; certain exhibits and aquatic shows incur additional fees. Several scheduled days throughout the year offer free general admission (tip: Get there early as these days get super-crowded). Open Mon through Fri 9 a.m. to 5 p.m., Sat and Sun 9 a.m. to 6 p.m.

SKYDECK CHICAGO
Willis (formerly Sears) Tower
233 S. Wacker Dr.
(312) 875-9447
www.theskydeck.com
It feels like you're on top of the world when you venture up the 1,353 feet to the near-top of the tallest building in the western hemisphere (at 1,451 tall and 110 stories, 1,730 feet if you count the antennae). With expansive views as far as 50 miles and four states, this 103rd-floor lookout now also allows you to see straight down—if you dare. Just step into the glass-box Ledge that juts out 4.3 feet from the side of the building, and look down right through the glass floor to the street below. Arguably the most stunning time to go is just before sunset when the city twinkles with pinks and yellows as the sun goes down to the west. Got children in your group? Before you head out, check out the Skydeck's website for Kids' Club games, quizzes, scavenger hunt lists, and coloring pages. Note: The entrance to the Skydeck is on Jackson Boulevard. Admission $17; children ages 3 to 11 $11. Open Apr through Sept 9 a.m. to 10 p.m., Oct through Mar 10 a.m. to 8 p.m. See the Architecture chapter for more information about the Willis Tower itself.

WRIGLEY FIELD
1060 W. Addison St.
(773) 404-CUBS
www.chicagocubs.com
It may not be the biggest, the cleanest, or the most convenient, but as Major League Baseball stadiums go, Wrigley remains one of the most beloved. The affectionately named Friendly Confines is the second-oldest stadium next to Boston's Fenway, and its ivy-covered walls practically whisper with history. Built in 1914, it's named for the Wrigley family who bought the Chicago Cubs in 1920. The original 1937 scoreboard is still used and still changed by hand. Controversy surrounded the introduction of lights in 1988, but night games have since merged with other Wrigley traditions, like braving the blazing sun in the bleacher seats; singing "Take Me Out to the Ball Game" during the 7th-inning stretch; and, for fans without tickets, waiting along the streets surrounding the stadium to snag a ball that's hit out of the park. Daily tours of Wrigley take you behind the scenes (some sections closed on game days) and often include a chance to walk onto the field. Individual tour tickets $25; children under 2 free (group discounts). For more information about the Chicago Cubs and getting tickets to a game, see the Spectator Sports chapter.

MUSEUMS

*ART INSTITUTE OF CHICAGO
111 S. Michigan Ave.
(312) 443-3600
www.artinstituteofchicago.org

Names like Picasso, Monet, de Kooning, Degas, Chagall, Seurat, and Van Gogh fill this world-class art museum. Founded in 1879, it moved into its current Beaux-Arts building in 1893, just in time to impress visitors to the World's Columbian Exposition here the same year. One of the museum's most famous collections began with the bequest in 1924 of 52 Impressionist and post-Impressionist paintings from the collection of Bertha Honoré Palmer (wife of retail and hotel tycoon Potter Palmer); a year later, the museum received the donation of its pièce de résistance, George Seurat's large-scale pointillist masterpiece, *A Sunday on La Grande Jatte*. Within its 11 curatorial departments, the museum boasts more than 300,000 works of art that span 5,000 years and nearly every continent and style, from armor to sculptures, photography to textiles. The distinctive Thorne Miniature Rooms are also a longtime favorite and feature 68 meticulously scaled-down versions of home interiors in designs ranging from late 13th century to the 1930s. Major temporary exhibits have showcased the works of Henri Matisse, Winslow Homer, Edward Hopper, and Jasper Johns. The 2009 addition of the glittering Renzo Piano–designed Modern Wing brought the Art Institute renewed international acclaim, and made room for an extensive modern exhibit drawn from the museum's permanent collection, as well as rotating exhibits from well-known contemporary artists. General admission $18; children, students, and seniors $14; children under 14 are free. Open Mon through Wed and Sat and Sun from 10:30 a.m. to 5 p.m., open until 8 p.m. on Thurs and Fri. For information about the Modern Wing's restaurant Renzo Piano, see the Restaurants chapter.

CHICAGO HISTORY MUSEUM
1601 N. Clark St.
(312) 642-4600
www.chicagohistory.org

If you need proof that history can be totally entertaining, this museum provides it in spades. Like the "Treasures" exhibit that includes a 1978 Chevy low-rider car; and an exhibit called "Sensing Chicago" that gives kids a history lesson through the senses— they can smell the wild onions that gave the city its name, hear the roar of the Great Chicago Fire of 1871, and taste (sort of) a Chicago-style hot dog by being the hot dog in a pillow bun. Founded in 1856 and first called the Chicago Historical Society, its holdings have grown to more than 22 million artifacts and documents and include the world's second-largest costume collection. In 2006, the name got an update, along with 75 percent of its public space. The focal exhibit, "Chicago: Crossroads of America," introduces visitors to some of Chicago's most influential moments, memories, and industries. It features the first El car (walk aboard if you'd like), a replica jazz club, a doll saved from the Great Chicago Fire, local innovations of all types, and sports memorabilia. Free guided and audio tours are available for "Crossroads." A series of semi-animated dioramas tells the story of the city's rise, its burning, and its rebirth. On the first Friday of each month, see what the curators have brought up from storage to be the chosen artifact in "Unexpected Chicago." Admission $14; seniors and students 13 to 22 with ID

10 Art Institute Must-See Paintings

You could spend days wandering the many absorbing and thought-provoking galleries of the Art Institute, but if you're short on time, we say these heavy-hitter paintings should be tops on your viewing schedule (they're listed alphabetically by artist).

Paris Street; Rainy Day, Gustave Caillebotte, 1877; Medieval to Modern European Painting and Sculpture, Gallery 201

The Child's Bath, Mary Cassatt, 1893; American Art, Gallery 273

Nighthawks, Edward Hopper, 1942; American Art, Gallery 262

Time Transfixed, René Magritte, 1938; Medieval to Modern European Painting and Sculpture, Gallery 396A

Bathers by a River, Henri Matisse, 1909-1917; Medieval to Modern European Painting and Sculpture, Gallery 391A

Stacks of Wheat, Claude Monet, 1890/91; Medieval to Modern European Painting and Sculpture, Gallery 243

Blue and Green Music, Georgia O'Keeffe, 1921; American Art, Gallery 271

A Sunday on La Grande Jatte, Georges Seurat, 1884; Medieval to Modern European Painting and Sculpture, Gallery 240

The Assumption of the Virgin, Domenikos Theotokopoulos (El Greco), 1577-79; Medieval to Modern European Painting and Sculpture, Gallery 211

American Gothic, Grant Wood, 1930; American Art, Gallery 263

$12; children 12 and under are free. Open Mon through Sat 9:30 a.m. to 4:30 p.m.; Sun noon to 5 p.m.

DRIEHAUS MUSEUM
40 E. Erie St.
(312) 482-8933, ext. 21
www.driehausmuseum.org

A passion for the past prompted Chicago businessman and philanthropist Richard H. Driehaus to acquire the 1879 mansion built for banker Samuel Mayo Nickerson—and then turn it into an elegant museum. After 5 years of careful restoration, it opened in 2008 as both a showcase for Driehaus' own impressive 19th- and early 20th-century art and design collection, as well as a glimpse back to the splendid lifestyle of Chicago's Gilded Age elite. The Italian palazzo-style home reaches 3 stories and includes elements of Egyptian, Chinese, Japanese, Moorish, Renaissance Revival style, and more. The dining room, one of the most majestic of the spaces, features walls of quarter-sewn white oak and a massive oak table with claw feet—in its center lies a silver punch bowl designed by Louis Comfort Tiffany that was displayed at the 1893 World's Columbian Exposition. Each room of the home is like this, with ornate wood detailing, period furnishings, and significant works of art. For more information about visiting the museum, its admission, and hours, call or check the website.

DUSABLE MUSEUM OF AFRICAN AMERICAN HISTORY

740 E. 56th Place
Washington Park, corner of 57th Street and Cottage Grove
(773) 947-0600
www.dusablemuseum.org

Named for Jean Baptiste Point DuSable, a Haitian with African and French roots who established Chicago's first nonnative settlement, this South Side museum was founded in 1961 by teacher and art historian Dr. Margaret Burroughs. One of the few cultural institutions of its kind, the DuSable presents intriguing history, politics, art, culture, and memorabilia of Africans and African Americans. The museum is small enough to see it all, but if you're looking for highlights, check out uniforms of African Americans who have served in the military; artifacts of the Civil Rights movement; the bas-relief wooden "Freedom Now Mural" depicting Africans' journey to North America beginning in 1619; and the interactive "A Slow Walk to Greatness: The Harold Washington Story," which delves into the life of the late Chicago mayor. *Note:* If you take public transportation to the museum, you should know that you do need to walk about a block through a slightly dodgy part of town. Admission $10; students and seniors $7; children ages 6 to 11 $3; under 5 free; free to all every Sun. Open Tues through Sat 10 a.m. to 5 p.m., Sun noon to 5 p.m.; closed Mon.

i On select Fridays from January through June, the Field Museum hosts Dozin' with the Dinos, featuring fun family activities, self-guided tours, workshops, and the chance to unroll your sleeping bag for a real-live night at the museum.

✳FIELD MUSEUM

Museum Campus
1400 S. Lake Shore Dr.
(312) 922-9410
www.fieldmuseum.org

Home to Sue, the largest, most complete T. rex fossil ever unearthed, the Field Museum—named for its first major benefactor, Marshall Field—gets dino-sized points for bringing the past to life in an engaging way. Travel back 4 billion years in "Evolving Planet"; meet a mummy in the exhibit "Inside Ancient Egypt"; step into a replica of an 800-year-old pueblo in "The Ancient Americas"; and find out the truth behind Africa's man-eating "Tsavo Lions" that inspired the 1996 movie *The Ghost and the Darkness*. Focusing on the natural world are dazzling exhibits like the "Grainger Hall of Gems," where jaw-dropping bling includes a 3,400-year-old Egyptian garnet necklace and a 28.84-carat extremely rare tanzanite stone. Feel what it's like to be a bug in "Underground Adventure"; and decode the connections among all of life on earth in the "DNA Discovery Center." A popular spot for the stroller set, the museum's Crown Family PlayLab is a sort of children's museum-within-the-museum loaded with hands-on activities, a self-contained music room and art room, and daily story times. Admission $15; seniors and students $12; children ages 3 to 11 $10; some exhibits and attractions incur an additional fee; there are discounts for Illinois teachers,

Chicago residents, and active military personnel when buying tickets in person.

ILLINOIS HOLOCAUST MUSEUM & EDUCATION CENTER
9603 Woods Dr., Skokie
(847) 967-4800
www.ilholocaustmuseum.org
Architect Stanley Tigerman used discernible design elements to create a distinct "dark side" and "light side" for this sometimes shocking, often moving, and decidedly thought-provoking museum in suburban Skokie. The story of the Holocaust is told in the main permanent exhibit (recommended for visitors 12 and up), with more than 500 artifacts, documents, photos, and survivor testimonies. It describes Nazi persecution of not only Jewish people, but also Gypsies, Jehovah's Witnesses, the physically and mentally handicapped, trade unionists, and homosexuals. At the center of the building sits a haunting reminder of the Holocaust: a rail car of the type used to transport victims to concentration camps. Past this is the lighter wing, featuring stories of liberation and rebirth and providing a place to reflect. The "Miller Family Youth Exhibition" aims to give children ages 8 to 11 a comfortable atmosphere to learn about ways to make a positive change in the world, while the "Legacy of Absence Gallery" displays artistic interpretations of contemporary instances of genocide in places such as Cambodia and Rwanda. Admission $12; seniors and students 12 to 22 $8; children 5 to 11 $6. Open Mon through Fri 10 a.m. to 5 p.m. (open until 8 p.m. on Thurs), Sat and Sun 11 a.m. to 4 p.m.

INTERNATIONAL MUSEUM OF SURGICAL SCIENCE
1524 N. Lake Shore Dr.
(312) 642-6502
www.imss.org
You'll likely come away with a greater appreciation for modern medicine after a trip to this eccentric museum. Not for the easily creeped out, it features oddities and objects of medical science including organ specimens, kidney stones, an ancient Roman speculum, an Austrian amputation saw from the 16th century, glass eyes, an iron lung, and a collection of heart valves. Opened in 1954 and housed in a landmark 1917 French chateau-style mansion, this is the only lakefront mansion open to the public. One of the first exhibits installed for the museum still impresses—a dozen murals painted by Italian artist Gregorio Calvi di Bergolo that depict surgical progress through the centuries, as well as key figures that contributed to the advancement of Western medicine. The rotating "Anatomy in the Gallery" series displays contemporary artists' takes on medical themes and may leave you scratching your head. Admission $10; students and seniors $6; some exhibits require an additional fee; free on Tues. Open Sun, and Tues through Thurs 10 a.m. to 5 p.m., Fri and Sat from 10 a.m. to 9 p.m.; closed Mon (last admission one hour before closing).

LOYOLA UNIVERSITY MUSEUM OF ART
820 N. Michigan Ave.
(312) 915-7600
www.luc.edu/luma
Set back from Michigan Avenue and worlds away from its consumer culture, LUMA, as it's known, focuses on enlightening artwork of the five major faiths: Hinduism, Judaism, Buddhism, Christianity, and Islam. In

addition to hosting several traveling exhibits, its permanent collection covers European art dating from the Middle Ages, Renaissance, and Baroque periods. See if you can spot the Medusa's head on the circa-1570 Collector's Chest, a lavishly decorated chest made of silver, ebony, lapis lazuli, feldspar, bloodstone, amethyst quartz, and cold enamel; and pay homage to the terra cotta *Madonna and Child* sculpture, crafted around 1692 by the first woman sculptor recorded in Spain. The museum's LUMA collection includes contemporary and modern works of art and now includes one of the largest groupings of Neolithic sculptures in the US, as well as a lithograph called *Job in Despair* by Marc Chagall. Admission $8; seniors $6; $2 for students over 18, members of the clergy, active military and their families, Loyola community, and NARM museum members. The museum is free on Tues. Free guided tours daily at noon and 2 p.m. Open Tues 11 a.m. to 8 p.m., Wed to Sun 11 a.m. to 6 p.m.; closed Mon.

MCCORMICK BRIDGEHOUSE & CHICAGO RIVER MUSEUM

Inside the bridge tower at the northwest corner of Michigan Avenue and Wacker Drive
Main entrance is on the Riverwalk level
376 N. Michigan Ave.
(312) 977-0227
www.bridgehousemuseum.org
From boat cruises to riverfront restaurants, there are many vantage points from which to watch Chicago River activity, but none is as interesting and informative as this unique 5-level museum run by the Friends of the Chicago River. When the Beaux-Arts-style bridge opened in 1920, it was the first double-deck, double-leaf trunnion bascule bridge ever built—meaning, it has two leaves hinged

in the middle with a counterweight that continuously balances as the sides rise to allow boats to pass through. One of the first exhibits you see inside the bridge museum is the gear mechanism that makes the system work. From there, you'll spiral up through the bridgehouse where exhibits tell of the river's history and influence on the city. At the top, you're privy to one-of-a-kind views up and down the waterway. On select Wednesdays and Saturdays during spring and fall, you can watch the gears in motion during one of the 100 times from April to November that the bridge runs its 10-minute process of opening and closing. General admission $4; seniors and children 6 to 12 $3; children 5 and under free. Bridge openings $10 per person (reservations suggested). Museum open from May 15 through Oct 31, Thurs through Mon 10 a.m. to 5 p.m.; closed Tues and Wed.

MITCHELL MUSEUM OF THE AMERICAN INDIAN

3001 Central St., Evanston
(847) 475-1030
www.mitchellmuseum.org
Acquaint yourself with the culture of the indigenous peoples. Their past and present history, culture, art, and traditions are the focus of this Evanston museum established in 1977 when John and Betty Seabury Mitchell donated their extensive 3,000-item collection of Native American art and material culture. Since then, the collection has more than tripled and includes items from all North American tribes north of the Mexican border. See a birch bark canoe made by an Algonquian-speaking tribe; a writing system devised in 1821 by a Cherokee man; a Blackfoot headdress from the Plains region; stunning pottery, jewelry, and weavings made by Pueblo and Navajo people; a gut-skin

parka from the Arctic region; and masks and totem poles representative of inhabitants of the northwest coast. Weekly kids craft activities range from loom beading to basket-weaving to creating dream catchers. Check the website for current programs and exhibits. Admission $5; children, students, teachers, and seniors $2.50. Maximum $10 per family; members and tribal members are free. Open Tues through Sat 10 a.m. to 5 p.m., Thurs 10 a.m. to 8 p.m., Sun noon to 4 p.m.

MUSEUM OF CONTEMPORARY ART
220 E. Chicago Ave.
(312) 280-2660
www.mcachicago.org

In 1969, two years after this innovative museum opened in a small space on East Ontario Street, it gained recognition as the first US structure to be wrapped in tarpaulin by renowned artist Christo. It has since moved and expanded, but remains on the cutting edge of art created since 1945. Its current home, a sun-lit, 5-floor building just east of Michigan Avenue, suits the needs of exhibits that involve everything from large-scale sculptural installations to status quo–challenging documentaries. The museum presents themed exhibits from its own collection, as well as works by established, emerging, and local artists that have included Frida Kahlo, Claes Oldenburg, Rudolf Stingel, and Jenny Holzer. The MCA brings it all down to pint-sized level with its free Family Days, held the second Saturday of every month and featuring hands-on art activities. Suggested admission $12 (the MCA is one of the last Chicago museums to still have "suggested" admission, by the way); students and seniors $7; children 12 and under (must be accompanied by an adult) free; free for all every Tues. Open Tues 10 a.m.

to 8 p.m., Wed through Sun 10 a.m. to 5 p.m.; closed Mon.

i One of the Museum of Contemporary Art's most popular offerings is its First Fridays happy hour (6 to 10 p.m.) when art and mingling mix. Tickets include museum admission, DJ-spun music, and complimentary hors d'oeuvres. Admission $18 at the door, $13 in advance.

✳MUSEUM OF SCIENCE & INDUSTRY
57th St. and Lake Shore Dr.
(773) 684-1414
www.msichicago.org

Kids and adults alike wander this massive museum with wide-eyed wonder. Opened in 1933 in the only remaining building from the 1893 World's Columbian Exposition, it was the first museum in the country to feature hands-on exhibits. The MSI has since expanded into one of the world's largest science-centric museums, earning an accolade from *Life* magazine as one of the top 15 museums in the world. It fills its 400,000 square feet with exhibits focusing on science, technology, engineering, and medicine. Impossible to cover everything in a day (you'll get worn out before you do!), there are definitely some top hits. "Coal Mine" is one of the original exhibits and still a favorite, taking visitors on a simulated trip "down" 600 feet to the bottom of a mineshaft. The 1944-captured U-505 Submarine offers a fascinating look at the only German sub (U-boat) in the United States (on-board tours are available for an extra fee, and they're worth it). In "Science Storms," get the scoop on seven natural phenomena—lightning, fire, tornadoes, avalanches, tsunamis, sunlight, and atoms in motion. The "Smart Home" is a temporary exhibit, but has been annually updated for the past several years and exemplifies the latest and greatest in eco-friendly home building practices. Kids faves: "Farm Tech" for its huge tractors they can climb right into; the baby chick hatchery for utter cuteness; "The Great Train Story," where 30-plus trains run along bridges, through tunnels, past towns, and across 1,400 feet of winding track; and "The Idea Factory," a space for young ones to explore science through play. The Omnimax movie theater is also popular, presenting science-related movies on its giant, 5-story domed screen. Most days, you can join a demonstration or hands-on activity (check with the Information Desk on Main Level 2 for a list of what's going on that day). General admission $15; seniors $14; children 3 to 11 $10; Omnimax movie tickets and other special exhibits, including on-boat tours of the U-505 Submarine, incur additional costs; parking in the garage is $18. Buy tickets online to speed up entry, particularly during peak summer or winter holiday hours. Open daily 9:30 a.m. to 5:30 p.m.

NATIONAL HELLENIC MUSEUM
333 S. Halsted St.
(312) 655-1234
www.nationalhellenicmuseum.org
It's all Greek to them, and that's a good thing at this first-rate museum that just moved to a brand-new building in the West Loop's Greektown neighborhood. In a tribute to ancient Greek storytelling, the museum's collections cover everything from original Greek civilizations to contemporary culture. Through the words of Homer, Herodotus, Aristotle, and modern-day families who traveled from Greece to America, you'll get a true sense of Greek heritage and traditions,

art, and culture. Exhibits include ancient ceramics, modern art, handmade textiles, traditional costumes, vintage photos, and musical instruments. Admission $5; under 12 free. Open Tues through Fri 10 a.m. to 5 p.m., Sat and Sun 11 a.m. to 5 p.m., closed Mon.

✱NATIONAL MUSEUM OF MEXICAN ART
1852 W. 19th St.
(312) 738-1503
www.nationalmuseumofmexicanart.org
Tucked along the edge of Harrison Park in the largely Latino Pilsen neighborhood, this gem of a museum presents carefully laid-out galleries that showcase artwork focusing on Mexican culture across the country and across the border. Past exhibits have covered subjects such as the commonalities between Chicago's Mexican and African-American communities; the annual Dia de los Muertos; and Chicano art as a recognized "school" of art, gathering works mostly from the collection of Cheech Marin. Fifteen of the exhibits organized here have gone on to travel to other US and Mexican museums. A dynamic performing arts series includes film, literature, dance, culinary arts, and more. Free. Open Tues to Sun 10 a.m. to 5 p.m.

i Don't miss the outstanding gift shop at the National Museum of Mexican Art. Stocked with way more than trinkets, it carries true culturally inspired souvenirs.

NATIONAL VETERANS ART MUSEUM
1801 S. Indiana Ave.
(312) 326-0270
www.nvam.org
When you first enter this museum, you're struck by a clinking noise coming from

overhead. You glance up to see what it is. And then you're stopped cold. It's more than 58,000 dog tags, imprinted with the names of the servicemen and women who died in the Vietnam War. Titled *Above & Beyond,* the sculpture is just one of the poignant and sometimes heart-wrenching exhibits of this unique museum, the only one in the world to focus on war through art. Founded in 1981 as a series of exhibits, the museum opened in 1986, and it broadened its reach in 2003 to showcase artwork by veterans of all wars. Admission $10; students $7. Open Tues through Sat 10 a.m. to 5 p.m.

ORIENTAL INSTITUTE
University of Chicago campus
1155 E. 58th St.
(773) 702-9514
www.oi.uchicago.edu
You can borrow an iPod for a self-guided audio tour of this U of C museum, but that's about as high-tech as this place gets. After all, it's ancient civilizations of the Near East that are the draw here. Specifically the art and artifacts of long-ago Egypt, Nubia, Persia, Mesopotamia, Syria, Anatolia, and the ancient site of Megiddo. Acquired mostly through archeological excavations sponsored by the Oriental Institute itself, the thousands of items on display include clay tablets and relief carvings; a fragment of the Dead Sea Scrolls; a human-headed, 16-foot-tall winged bull from the throne-room façade of an ancient Assyrian king's palace; and a 17-foot-tall statue of king Tutankhamun. You'll be amazed by the ingenious crafts and technology that predated our high-tech gadgets of today. Several different self-guided audio tours are available in English, Spanish, and Mandarin. Free; suggested donation $7 for adults, $4 for children

under 12. Open Tues through Sat 10 a.m. to 6 p.m. (Wed open until 8:30 p.m.), Sun noon to 6 p.m.; closed Mon.

PEGGY NOTEBAERT NATURE MUSEUM
2430 N. Cannon Dr.
(773) 755-5100
www.naturemuseum.org
With its building built to blend into its landscape, the Nature Museum (as it's mostly shortened to) can teach adults a thing or two about wildlife, conservation, and care of the planet—adult programming includes lectures, classes, and temporary art and photography exhibits—but it is, indeed, most often enjoyed by younger audiences. Its two most popular exhibits are interactive romps through the "River Works," where waterplay is the attraction, and "Hands-on Habitat," where a small slide makes for time well spent to expend some toddler energy. The "Judy Istock Butterfly Haven" tops the list for everyone, as colorful winged creatures flutter carefree through the open 2,700-square-foot greenhouse (check yourself in the mirror before you leave to be sure no butterflies have decided to exit with you). Admission $9; students and seniors $7; children ages 3 to 12 $6; children under 3 free. Open Mon through Fri 9 a.m. to 5 p.m., Sat and Sun 10 a.m. to 5 p.m. (last ticket sold at 4 p.m. on weekdays, 4:30 p.m. on weekends). See the listing in Kidstuff as well.

SMART MUSEUM OF ART
University of Chicago campus
5550 S. Greenwood Ave.
(773) 702-0200
www.smartmuseum.uchicago.edu
Though it has become a leading academic art museum since its founding nearly 40 years ago, the Smart Museum of Art is as

approachable to university visitors as it is to the general public. Comfortably viewed in one visit, the open and airy galleries cover four main categories of art—contemporary, Asian, European, and modern art and design. It begins with the reception area, which welcomes with a major, changing installation of contemporary art such as Chinese-born artist Bingyi's epic rice-paper ink painting that symbolizes a waterfall flowing from earth to heaven. In the gallery of modern art and design, you'll find everything from paintings by Mark Rothko to a dining room table and chairs designed for the Robie House by Frank Lloyd Wright. A strong collection of works on paper is interspersed throughout the galleries. Free. Open Tues through Fri 10 a.m. to 4 p.m. (Thurs open until 8 p.m.), Sat and Sun 11 a.m. to 5 p.m.; closed Mon.

SPERTUS INSTITUTE
610 S. Michigan Ave.
(312) 322-1700
www.spertus.edu
What began in 1924 as Chicago's College of Jewish Studies has developed into a complete learning center, grounded in Jewish values and offering education in the form of not only degree programs, but continuing education, lectures, seminars, concerts, and films. Now based in a glittering new glass structure of geometric angles, designed by Chicago's award-winning Krueck + Sexton Architects in 2007, its light-filled ground floor features a currently evolving exhibit titled "Uncovered & Rediscovered: Stories of Jewish Chicago." On the second floor, video clips about Jewish life in Chicago continues the story, while an "interactive map" lets visitors add their own chapter. Free. Open Sun through Thurs 10 a.m. to 5 p.m.; closed Fri and Sat.

SWEDISH AMERICAN MUSEUM
5211 N. Clark St.
(773) 728-8111
www.swedishamericanmuseum.org
In the heart of the historically Swedish North Side neighborhood of Andersonville, this charming museum, founded in 1976, is worth a visit whether you're Swedish or not. In addition to rotating temporary exhibits (a recent one highlighted the Swedish smorgasbord), its main exhibit tells the story of immigration from Sweden to America, from the reasons for leaving their homeland to the lives they created once here. Essentially the story of any US immigrant during the mid-19th century, the exhibit is highlighted by authentic artifacts of items that families packed for their journey, actual passports, and Swedish crafts. On the museum's 3rd floor, the Brunk Children's Museum of Immigration is all about the trip from a kid's point of view, aimed at children ages 3 to 12. Admission $4; seniors and students $3; $10 family rate; children under 1 free; free for all every second Tues of the month. General museum hours Mon through Fri 10 a.m. to 4 p.m. (store open same hours, except Fri until 6 p.m.), Sat and Sun 11 a.m. to 4 p.m.; children's museum open Mon through Thurs 1 p.m. to 4 p.m., Fri 10 a.m. to 4 p.m., Sat and Sun 11 a.m. to 4 p.m. For more information about the Brunk Children's Museum, check out the Kidstuff chapter.

PUBLIC ART

AGORA
Grant Park
Michigan Avenue and Roosevelt Drive
(312) 742-PLAY
Stumbling upon the 106 9-foot-tall headless bronze figures at the southwest end of

Grant Park is quite a startling experience. Poised in various walking and standing positions, they seem a ghostly presence and yet stunningly beautiful. The imposing sculpture is the largest of many like this created by internationally acclaimed artist Magdalena Abakanowicz, who uses these forms as a way to express the image of the unthinking crowd.

BATCOLUMN
600 W. Madison St.
(877) 244-2246
Though some people laughed off this Claes Oldenburg obelisk when it was dedicated in 1977, the 101-foot-high lattice-design steel gray baseball bat has become a local favorite. Considering Chicago is such a baseball- and skyscraper-loving city, how could it be anything but a home run?

FLAMINGO
230 S. Dearborn St.
(877) 244-2246
Standing on four graceful legs in the center of the Loop's Federal Plaza, this abstract sculpture is not actually flamingo-pink, but a striking vermilion red. Designed by renowned American artist Alexander Calder, the 5-story sculpture—referred to most often by locals as simply, "the Calder,"—provides a spirited contrast to the trio of black, blocky Mies van der Rohe buildings that surround it. Go ahead and walk under it and around it. And for a free viewing of Calder's famous mobiles, take a step into the lobby of the nearby Willis (formerly Sears) Tower.

FOUNTAIN OF TIME
Washington Park
Cottage Grove Avenue and Midway Plaisance

Nearly lost to the ravages of Chicago's extreme weather and time itself, this imposing, 126-foot-long sculpture was completed in 1920 by Chicago architect Lorado Taft and dedicated in 1922. In 2007, a 15-year-long restoration project undertaken by The Chicago Park District and Art Institute of Chicago—and funded, in part by a Save America's Treasures grant—was completed with wondrous results. Formed out of an unusual type of hollow-cast concrete and reinforced steel, it includes a separate hooded sculpture of Father Time who stares across a reflecting pool at a mass of 100 figures representing all stages of life, war, peace, love, and loss. Inspired by Henry Austin Dobson's poem "Paradox of Time," it is said to illustrate the line that reads, "Time goes, you say? Ah no! Alas, Time stays, we go."

FOUR SEASONS
Chase Plaza
10 S. Dearborn St.
A gift to the city from its French artist Marc Chagall in 1974, this 70-foot-long, 14-foot-high rectangular box is composed of thousands of mosaic tiles in more than 250 colors. Wrapping around its four sides, the mesmerizing image depicts the four seasons as a symbol of the journey of life, with tiles hailing from Italy, France, Norway, Belgium, Israel, and right here in Chicago.

MILLENNIUM PARK
201 E. Randolph St.
Between Michigan and Columbus Avenues
(312) 742-1168
www.millenniumpark.org
The grandest additions to Chicago's public art scene find a common home in this

newest green space for the city. Frank Gehry's ribbons of steel that make up the outdoor band shell can be spotted from blocks all around, while "The Bean" (a nickname for its true title, *Cloud Gate*) makes for magical funhouse-mirror-type reflections. *Crown Fountain* is a video installation as well as a playful homage to gargoyles of old, with moving pictures of people who intermittently "spout" water onto eagerly awaiting children. On the north and south sides of the park, temporary outdoor gallery space makes room for eye-catching, large-scale works by artists such as Mexican artist Yvonne Domenge, whose site-specific "Interconnected: The Sculptures of Yvonne Domenge" graces the plazas through October 2012. Read more about Millennium Park in Attractions and in the Parks & Recreation chapter.

MIRÓ'S CHICAGO
Brunswick Building Plaza
69 W. Washington St.
Spanish sculptor Joan Miró created this playful, quirky, somewhat ethereal work that stands between the Cook County Administration and the Chicago Temple buildings. Resembling a female figure to some extent, but with a clear glance to the heavens, the sculpture reflected the artist's fascination with, as he once described, "the spectacle of the sky," and was apparently originally titled *The Sun, the Moon and One Star*.

MONUMENT TO THE GREAT NORTHERN MIGRATION
Dr. Martin Luther King Jr. Drive and 26th Place
Sculpted by contemporary artist Alison Saar, this 15-foot-high bronze man wears a suit made of shoe soles to symbolize the northern journey that African-American men and women traveled from the South to the North following the Civil War. Facing the north, his right hand is raised as a greeting to his newfound home, while his left hand holds a tattered suitcase. This work stands at the border of the historic Bronzeville neighborhood, where many African Americans settled first.

MONUMENT WITH STANDING BEAST
100 W. Randolph St.
(877) 244-2246
Unveiled in 1984, this four-element sculpture by French artist Jean Dubuffet is only one of three Dubuffet works of this scale on display in the country. Meant to conceptualize an animal, a tree, a portal, and an architectural form, the white fiberglass pieces outlined in black were described by Dubuffet as "drawing which extends into space" and were intended to appeal to viewers of all backgrounds.

MURALS OF PILSEN
Centered around 18th Street and Ashland Avenue
As one of the most significant Mexican-American communities in the country, Pilsen brims with art galleries as well as public murals that bring to vivid life the stories, issues, struggles, and triumphs of the people who live here. Walk in any direction to discover handmade works of art like the glass tile–mosaic façade at Orozco/Cooper elementary school (1645 W. 18th Place) and, on the exterior of muralist Hector Duarte's local studio (1900 W. Cullerton), a mural of the artist himself.

THE PICASSO
Daley Plaza
50 W. Washington St.

Pablo Picasso left Chicagoans in the dark when it came to what, exactly, his 50-foot-tall, 160-ton steel sculpture was supposed to be. But that's part of its mystique. Everyone has an answer: bird, baboon, woman, Picasso's own Afghan hound, or simply an abstract expression of Picasso's famous Cubist style. Whatever it is, since its celebrated unveiling in 1967, it has become a treasured and beloved Loop icon. Commissioned by the city under Mayor Richard J. Daley, the design of the sculpture was bestowed as a gift by the then 82-year-old Spanish artist who had never actually visited Chicago. It now serves as landmark, meeting place, center of Daley Plaza events throughout the year, and performance venue with "Under the Picasso" dance and music events taking place there throughout the year (and in the lobby of the Daley Center during winter months; 312-744-3315).

THE RUNNERS
Grounds of O'Hare International Airport

Welcoming visitors to Chicago is one of the most recent public art installations in the city, presented in May 2011. The winning design from an international competition in 2006, this 18-foot-high, 40-foot-long gleaming stainless-steel sculpture is by award-winning Greek artist Theodoros Papagiannis and is a gift from the Athens Committee of Chicago Sister Cities International Program.

Papagiannis says that his five runners symbolize immigration, friendship between Athens and Chicago, the Marathon and the road to the Olympics, and the movement of time where past and present unite.

SKOKIE NORTHSHORE SCULPTURE PARK
Along McCormick Boulevard from Dempster Street to Touhy Avenue, Skokie
(847) 679-4265
www.sculpturepark.org

Once an eyesore of nothingness, 2 miles of land along the north branch of the Chicago River now comprise a scenic park featuring more than 60 large outdoor sculptures and others that are brought in on a temporary basis each year. Ranging from straightforward (two painted running horses) to strange (a menacing, three-legged spider-looking object) to simply abstract, together they make for a museumlike display as you stroll or bike the connecting paths. Detailed sculpture booklets and kid-geared guides can be downloaded from the website, and one Sunday each month from May through October, free public tours provide information on a selection of the sculptures. By the way, if you'd like one for your own backyard, all the temporary sculptures are for sale. Parking between Dempster and Main Streets, Howard Street and Touhy, and at the boat launch east of the river off of Oakton Street.

TOURS

It's an eye-opening experience to take a tour of your own city. You see things you'd never noticed before and learn about places you took for granted. You get differing perspectives on what you thought to be black-and-white, and you come away with a deeper appreciation of the place you call home. For visitors, a tour goes a step or two beyond that. Tours can introduce you to a new place, enticing you to hone in on a specific interest; or they'll delve into the details of a particular topic. They can efficiently organize a whole wish list full of places to see into a fun, focused excursion. They can take you to the must-see spots and the hidden gems. Thanks to an amazingly professional community of experienced guides here, tours are educational without being boring, and reveal interesting insights that you could only get from a local. They cover a lot of information in a short amount of time and set the stage for further explorations.

There are so many tours in Chicago these days that you can choose one that satisfies exactly what you're looking for—a bike ride that drops kickstands at several restaurants; a bus tour in search of ghosts from Chicago's past; a walking tour of Art Deco architecture that dots the Loop; a boat trip that speeds up to 45 miles an hour; or a sampling tour of various sweet spots. There's a tour for every interest, age, budget, season, and ability.

OVERVIEW

This chapter is broken down into four broad categories. "Architecture & History" includes a bit of everything and on all types of transportation—foot, bike, bus, trolley, and Segway. "Boat Tours" groups together the many Chicago River and Lake Michigan tours. "Food Tours" deserve their own section because the list is long and growing in this food-loving town. And "Arts & Theater" is last with a few insider looks at both. Note that most tour prices given do not include taxes. Some companies require advance reservations, but if you're set on one and it's the day-of, go ahead and call anyway because sometimes a new tour time will be added with enough interest or someone will cancel and open up a spot.

ARCHITECTURE & HISTORY

ABSOLUTELY CHICAGO SEGWAY
337 E. Randolph St.
(877) 866-0966, (312) 552-5100
www.chicagosegways.com

Cover 8 miles of outdoor sightseeing without ending up too pooped to pose for photos. You can do it by gliding—on a Segway. Professional guides lead the way along the lakefront through Grant Park, alongside Millennium Park, and to the Museum Campus. Your wheels provide a fun way to see some of the city's best public art and historic architecture too. Light up your night with an evening tour that starts with Buckingham Fountain's colorful water and light display, then roll over to a quiet viewing spot to take in the Navy Pier fireworks. Another tour in the dark, the Haunted Tour stops for tales of Chicago's own dark side of death, gangsters, and ghosts. Tour attendees must be 14 years or older and anyone under 18 must be accompanied by an adult. Prices $60 to $65. Tours run daily throughout the year, with a limited schedule in cold months.

BIKE AND ROLL CHICAGO
Millennium Park
239 E. Randolph St.
(312) 729-1000
www.bikechicago.com

Operating year-round rentals from its Millennium Park HQ, Bike and Roll sets up shop in nine additional citywide locales starting in April. In other words, they make it pretty darn easy to get going with one of their bicycle or Segway tours, including their most popular Amazing Lakefront Tour (in both bike and Segway versions) that hits beaches, lagoons, architecture, and more. The Presidential Tour rides "in the footsteps of Chicago's favorite son," and the 7:30 a.m. Early Bird Segway Tour of Historic Hyde Park & Kenwood presents the city scene in the morning hush before the rush. Create your own trip by renting one of the beach cruisers, mountain bikes, road bikes, tandems, kids' bikes, inline skates, or Segways—take them for a spin by the hour, half-day, full day, or even the whole week. Tour prices range from $35 to $69 for adults and include the bike or Segway, a helmet, bottle of water, and snack. Tours run from Apr 1 to Oct 31.

BLACK COUTOURS
(773) 233-8907
www.blackcoutours.com

With an emphasis on groups, this company plans tours both in Chicago and beyond that focus on black heritage, history, culture, and entertainment. Though trips are created to suit your individual needs and interests, Black Coutours provides a basic plan with its Soul Side of the Windy City excursion that features Bronzeville, DuSable's settlement, an African-American home showcase, and other points of interest. Call for pricing and scheduling information.

✴BOBBY'S BIKE HIKE
465 N. McClurg Ct. (at Illinois Street)
(312) 915-0995
www.bobbysbikehike.com

Jeremy Lewno started his bike-tour operation (named for his late father) in 2002 and made it totally hip and cool to tour the city streets, helmet on head and foot to pedal. His most popular two-wheeling guided trek is the leisurely 7-mile Lakefront Neighborhoods Tour, which ventures in and out of several North Side communities, breaking for glimpses of historic and famous spots, with accompanying narration. Work up more of a sweat—and an appetite—on the Bikes, Bites & Brews Tour, adding food sampling and gastronomically geared stories. The easy-peasy, 4.5-mile Tike Hike doles out info in kid doses (aimed at 10 and under) and gives out prizes too. On the more advanced 22-mile Historic Hyde Park Tour, you'll tool past President Obama's abode, along with architecturally significant University of Chicago structures, and the Museum of Science and Industry. Want to take your own path? Separate rentals are available. Tour prices vary from $30 to $60 for adults (discounts for students, seniors, and children), and include deluxe cruiser bicycles with baskets—and kid seats when requested. Online registration secures your spot and gets you 10 percent off walk-up prices. Parking is available for a validated discounted rate

Close-up

Tickets: Free; Guides: Priceless

No one knows Chicago better than the folks who live here. And a bunch of them are happy to show you around for a few hours—without as much as accepting a tip. Known as the **Chicago Greeter** service and run by the Chicago Office of Tourism and Culture, these totally free tours can be arranged to take you around a specific neighborhood or geared toward individual interests like public art, fashion, or films. Once you request a Greeter, you'll be matched up with an appropriate volunteer who will contact you to confirm and to find out about any special requests. There are several catches: You can only be a group of six or fewer; you must book 7 to 10 days in advance; sometimes Greeters are booked up during busy times; and travel is all by foot or public transportation.

But . . . if you didn't book in advance, that's OK; you still have another option: the **InstaGreeter.** Volunteers stand at-the-ready at a booth in the Chicago Cultural Center (77 E. Randolph St.) on Friday, Saturday, and Sunday from 10 a.m. to 4 p.m. for first-come, first-served one-hour strolls through downtown. But wait, there's even more that's free for the touring (the following four are all available Memorial Day weekend through Columbus Day weekend): At Millennium Park (Welcome Center, 201 E. Randolph St.), Greeters await your arrival every day at 11:30 a.m. and 1 p.m. for an hour tour of the park (limited to 10 people, first come, first served). There are also three InstaGreeter outposts: In President Obama's old stomping grounds in Hyde Park, they're at the Hyde Park Art Center, 5020 S. Cornell Ave., every Saturday between 10 a.m. and 3 p.m. On alternating Saturdays from 10 a.m. to 3 p.m., they are stationed in Old Town at The Second City, 1616 N. Wells St.; or in Pilsen at the National Museum of Mexican Art, 1852 W. 19th St. For more information, call (312) 744-8000 or visit www.chicagogreeter.com.

of $16 at the garage at 322 E. Illinois St. Tours are offered Mar through Nov.

✳CHICAGO ARCHITECTURE FOUNDATION TOURS
224 S. Michigan Ave.
(312) 922-3432
www.architecture.org
The go-to org for all things architectural, the Chicago Architecture Foundation has the city (and farther afield) fully covered, from its oldest structures to its newest, every style and every size, and the history, lore, trivia, and controversy that go along with them. Forget about pithy, canned commentary: CAF docents have to go through seriously rigorous education and training before leading the way on one of the more than 80 tours offered. Here for the first time? Two tours we recommend: the River Cruise aboard Chicago's First Lady yachts, which takes you along the Chicago River, under its bridges, and past dozens of the Windy City's wonderful architectural sites, with historical and witty narration; and the Highlights by Bus tour, which works perfectly for cooler days, making its way through several neighborhoods, the compelling campuses of the University of Chicago and Illinois Institute of Technology, along lakefront parks, and into

the Loop. Get a little more in-depth on tours such as the "Devil in the White City" Companion bus tour, Frank Lloyd Wright by Bus, Historic Downtown, hour-long lunchtime tours of building interiors, and many more. A super user-friendly website lets you search by type (boat, bus, Segway, walking, group), by focus, and by date or day. Tour prices vary (offering discounts for members) and generally meet at the Chicago Architecture Foundation, but not always, so double-check before you head out. Multiple tours take place every day.

CHICAGO DETOURS
Tour locations vary
(312) 350-1131
www.chicagodetours.com
Launched in 2010 by former tour guide and guidebook researcher Amanda Scotese, this newbie to the circuit offers something a bit edgier. Along with fascinating background on Chicago music, theater, and architecture, Scotese scours archives to incorporate iPad-driven documentary footage and historic photographs. In a wintertime tour called "The Loop: Explore Without Freezing," you'll take a 2-hour tour of architectural and cultural sights—all indoors, thank you very much. You can do it during summer too (when it's simply called the "Inside the Loop" tour). Prices for tours by foot and by bus range anywhere from $25 to $70, with children under 12 generally free. Tours take place throughout the year.

✳CHICAGO ELEVATED
(773) 593-4873
www.chicagoelevated.com
Tour owner extraordinaire Margaret Hicks began her guide life as a docent with the Chicago Architecture Foundation. Launching

her own business took advantage of the skills she learned there, and added in her own spirit of comedy—she's done improv for many years and recently authored the book, *Chicago Comedy: A Fairly Serious History.* Hicks' most popular tour is perfect for winter wanderings, taking groups down into the series of heated underground walkways and tunnels of Chicago called the Pedway. She also leads a trek through Printers Row, once the Windy City's red-light district; a Loop architectural tour; and her Who Needs a Boat? Riverwalk Tour. Tours each cost $15 (and sometimes she even offers them for free). Tours typically run throughout the year, but check online or call first to get her updated schedule. Hicks is happy to arrange private or customized tours as well.

CHICAGO NEIGHBORHOOD TOURS
Meet at the Chicago Cultural Center
77 E. Randolph St., Randolph Cafe
(312) 742-1190
www.chicagoneighborhoodtours.com
A visit to this city of neighborhoods wouldn't be complete without seeing a few of them. Fortunately, the Chicago Office of Tourism and Culture makes it easy with 24 specific tours, including Back of the Yards and Bridgeport, Wicker Park and Ukrainian Village, Uptown and Argyle Street, Albany Park, Little Italy, Andersonville, and more. The neighborhoods vary each week, and every tour features fascinating history, highlights, people, places, and sometimes a few surprises. The Taste of the Neighborhoods is wildly popular (i.e., it sells out fast) with its excursion to two ethnic restaurants and one stop for dessert. Tours are $30; seniors, students, and children ages 8 to 18 $25, except Taste of the Neighborhood Tours, which are $50 and $45 respectively. Neighborhood

tours run from late Mar through early Dec, Sat at 10 a.m. (arrive at 9:30 a.m.), and on Thurs and Fri from Memorial Day through Labor Day at 10 a.m.

CHICAGO RED CAP TOURS
Tours begin on the east side of Michigan Avenue, across from the Wrigley Building
(312) 927-0689
www.chicagoredcaptours.com

A former futures trader, Bill Elliott found his second calling as a convivial tour guide whose motto is, "The more we know, the more we see." He started out guiding groups on Steve's Segway Tours and now his passion for and in-depth knowledge of his native town shines through on his own two-hour Historic Buildings of the Loop tour and a 90-minute Romance of the City Tour. While the tours have a typical route, Elliott has no problem extending it a bit longer if he still has something to show you, and you've still got time. He'll head out whether there's one person or a group, giving it his all and giving you more than your money's worth. Historic Buildings tours are $20 for adults and $5 for children under 14 (free for infants) and run Mon through Fri at 1 p.m. (Elliott asks that you arrive a few minutes early, so the tours can start promptly); Romance of the City tours are $15 for adults, $5 for children and are scheduled by appointment only. Get in touch with Elliott by e-mail or phone to make a reservation, then pay when you get to the tour.

CHICAGO TROLLEY & DOUBLE DECKER CO.
(773) 648-5000
www.chicagotrolley.com

Ditch your car, or better yet, take public transportation, then see the downtown city sights in style with this company's Signature Tour, a hop-on, hop-off type deal. You can do the whole route in about 2 hours or take all day, if you'd like. Either way's A-OK with the drivers, who cover 13 miles, stop at 14 locations throughout the city, and entertain passengers with comical commentary—if you like their shtick, give them a tip, because most of them are starving actors and comedians by night. Double-decker buses or trolleys come by every 5 to 10 minutes or so, with slightly longer lag times during off-season months. Say you're staying at the Sheraton Chicago. You can catch a ride right there, then hop off at Navy Pier, do some fun stuff, then hop back on later to ride over to the Mag Mile for some shopping. Upgrade to an Explore Chicago 3-day pass for $6 more, which provides the opportunity to add a trio of Chicago neighborhood tours to the main tour. All tickets include extra goodies like a Hershey's chocolate bar and sample of Garrett popcorn. Admission for the Explore Chicago 3-day pass $35; children ages 3 to 11 $17. Admission for just the Signature Tour (good for one day) $29; children ages 3 to 11 $17; 10 percent off all prices online. Signature Tour runs daily beginning at 9 a.m. (except Thanksgiving Day, and Christmas Eve and Day); Neighborhood Tours run Memorial Day through Labor Day.

i Show your Chicago Trolley & Double Decker Co. tour ticket at the Park Shop at Millennium Park for 15 percent off all purchases.

CHICAGO'S FINEST RIVERWALK TOUR
(312) 202-0745
www.chicagosfinestriverwalktour.com

You know how sometimes a tour group is so big you can't hear the guide if you stand too far away? That won't be a problem with these Riverwalk tours, because founder Dan O'Connell limits each outing to 15 people. He also simply has a way with people, perhaps because this is O'Connell's second career. After retiring from a big-time corporate post, he decided to put his love of Chicago and its colorful history to work for him. He peppers his 2-mile, 2-hour historic tours along the Chicago River with tales of the characters who have a place in Chicago history books—for good or bad. Think you learned something? Take his optional trivia challenge, with prizes for winners. Tickets $15; seniors $10; children under 12 $8, and under 3 free; $40 for a family package (four or more older than 3). Tours take place Mon through Fri 11 a.m. and 3 p.m., (Thurs offers an additional 6 p.m. tour), and Sat and Sun 10 a.m. and noon. Tours are seasonal, generally mid-March through Dec 1.

CITY SEGWAY TOURS—CHICAGO
(877) SEG-TOUR (734-8687)
www.citysegwaytours.com
This world-class and worldwide operation was one of the first to offer tours via Segway. Good idea, we think. After all, in 2 or 3 hours, you roll a route through town that would take much longer to walk. On the shorter tour, the focus is on the rad ride, while the 3-hour tour adds in more stops and more history of the cultural institutions, parks, and skyscrapers you glide by. Open to participants 12 years and older, the tours all include a 30-minute orientation and cost $60 for 2 hours and $70 for 3 hours. Tours run year-round, Nov 1 through Mar 30 daily at 11 a.m.; Apr 1 through Oct 31 at 10 a.m., 11 a.m., 2 p.m., and 6 p.m.

GRAYLINE CHICAGO
(800) 966-8125
www.graylinevacations.com
Fourteen tours offer options for every interest and budget. Short on time? Sneak in a 2-hour Panoramic and Scenic North Side Tour that hits the Loop and Magnificent Mile, then heads further north to get glimpses of Wrigley Field, Lincoln Park, and Lake Shore Drive's iconic Totem Pole. Delve more in-depth on a four-hour Inside Chicago Grand Tour—you can even add a stop for pizza, or a view from the Hancock Observatory for an extra fee. When you've got all day, the 9-stop Hop-On Hop-Off Trolley Tour is a top choice for covering lots of downtown ground without spending precious time and energy walking from place to place or money on cabs that's better spent at the attractions and shops. No need to worry about a designated driver on The Blues by Night tour—they'll pick you up and plop you down at Buddy Guy's Legends, and the price includes dinner, the show, and an after-dinner nightcap at another blues club. Eying some of those popular shopping destinations outside city limits (like Schaumburg's huge Woodfield Mall)? Grayline will take you there too. Combine an Inside Chicago tour price with curbside pickup from Midway or O'Hare airports. Tour prices vary, and some tours must be booked two or three days ahead. Most tours run daily.

MIES VAN DER ROHE AND IIT:
AN ARCHITECTURAL TOUR
3201 S. State St.
www.miessociety.org
The folks at the Illinois Institute of Technology are understandably proud of their campus. It includes some of the world's best examples of work by influential and

legendary architect Ludwig Mies van der Rohe. See it best on a self-guided or docent-led 90-minute tour that both spotlight his crowning achievement, the national landmark S.R. Crown Hall, which fittingly houses the school's architecture program. Besides other Mies buildings, you'll get the scoop on structures from more modern-day starchitects Rem Koolhaas and Helmut Jahn. All tours $10. Self-guided audio iPod tours (and the iPods if you don't have one) are available daily from 10 a.m. to 3 p.m. at the Campus Information Center at the McCormick Tribune Campus Center, 3201 S. State St., the meeting place for guided tours, which leave daily at 10 a.m.

O'LEARY'S CHICAGO FIRE TRUCK
Boarding at 505 N. Michigan Ave. (at Illinois Street)
(312) 287-6565
www.olearysfiretours.com
Need a rescue from the norm? The hot ticket in town is this fire truck tour. Booked by charter only for groups of up to 26 (small groups by special request), the tours are run by retired Chicago fire department Captain George Rabiela. He knows his way around this town and his ride-ons give passengers a unique vantage point for some sightseeing and history, particularly about that little fire in 1871 that burned the city to the ground. $250 per hour for up to 26 people; 2-hour minimum.

SECOND CITY NEIGHBORHOOD TOUR
Meet at 1616 N. Wells St.
(312) 337-3992
www.secondcity.com
Written and led by Margaret Hicks (who's also the force behind the Chicago Elevated tours), this entertaining 90-minute tour takes you to stops around Chicago's famed Second City theater. Hear about the history of the surrounding Old Town neighborhood, discover the "secret" haunts of The Second City actors who have performed throughout its 50-plus years, and wind up back at the theater for a browse around the lobby filled with historic photos of comedic legends who carved their funny careers at this venerable skit-comedy club. Tours are $15. They run generally from June through Oct every Sun at 1 p.m. and Wed at 4 p.m.

*STEVE'S SEGWAY TOURS
350 E. Monroe St. (bottom of the ramp)
(312) 946-9467
www.stevessegwaytours.com
When Steve Beier left his job at another Segway tour outfit and started his own company in 2007, he made sure customer service was a top priority. That means when you call for information, you actually get Steve on the phone. And it means, besides a ride on the latest version of the Segway led by expertly trained guides, he and his staff happily accommodate special requests, can do private tours, often slash prices for struggling college students who are flexible on their schedule, offer the super-charged "red-key tour" for returning Segway-ers who want to zip around at top speed (12.5 miles per hour), and will gladly suggest things to do and places to go after your tour (so feel free to ask). Remember to bring a credit card for a damage waver. Pricing is $60 for 2-hour evening tours, $70 for 3-hour daytime tours; numerous discounts are offered, so be sure to check online or call to inquire. Tours run year-round; in summer reservations are strongly recommended; and in winter they are required.

i On the private owner-operated tours, it's always nice to tip your tour guide. They work extra-hard for your money, typically personalizing the experience and updating it all the time.

✳UNTOUCHABLE TOURS
Depart from the 600 block of North Clark Street
In front of the Rock 'n Roll McDonald's
(773) 881-1195
www.gangstertour.com
Your guide's name will be "Shoulders" or "Southside," or maybe "Al Dente," and he expects you to listen up to his stories of "da good ol' gangster days" of Chicago. Well, maybe they weren't so good, but they do provide some pretty entertaining history. Ride along with "dees guys" on their 2-hour bus tour, and you'll pass a church with bullet holes in it, former speakeasies and red-light districts, old gang hangs, and the theater where FBI's most wanted John Dillinger was shot. It's all light-hearted fun, but it's also fascinating and informative. Tours are $30 per person. They run daily, with more tours during the summer months.

WEIRD CHICAGO TOURS
Meet at the Hard Rock Cafe entrance, 53 W. Ontario St.
(888) GHOSTLY (446-7859)
www.weirdchicago.com
Weird, indeed. Owners Troy Taylor and Ken Melvoin-Berg consider Chicago the most haunted city in America—and they will gleefully show you why. These offbeat 3-hour tours scour the strange and sometimes dark side of Chicago: sites of murder, crime, ghostly appearances, gangster goings-on, and more. In addition to their original Weird

& Haunted Tour, there's the Devil & the White City Tour, which points out serial killer H.H. Holmes' actual "murder castle"; the Blood, Guns & Valentines Crime Tour (beware the gory details); the Hell Hath No Fury Tour, a look at the "weird, wonderful and wicked women" of Chicago; the Red Light District Sex Tour, which is not for the prude of heart; and the Conspiracy & Assassins Crime Tour. Each one leaves a lasting impression, so don't blame us if you have nightmares afterward. Tours cost $30 per person; $20 for children 10 to 12 years old; children under 10 are not recommended, but discretion is up to you (no babies or infants in strollers permitted). Tours take place throughout the year in heated, but not air-conditioned buses. Check the schedule online and buy tickets in advance, as many of these tours sell out quickly.

BOAT TOURS

✳CHICAGO ARCHITECTURE
FOUNDATION RIVER CRUISE
ABOARD *CHICAGO'S FIRST LADY*
Boards at Riverside Gardens
Lower level, southeast corner of Michigan Avenue and Wacker Drive
(800) 982-2787
www.architecture.org
The official fleet of the Chicago Architecture Foundation's acclaimed 90-minute, docent-led architecture river tour, *Chicago's First Lady* cruises along past more than 50 important buildings that line the water, accompanied by history and architectural info. Watch from the lower indoor deck or take in the breezes up top. Tickets $35. Tours run daily.

MERCURY THE SKYLINE CRUISELINE

Boards at Riverside Gardens
Lower level, southeast corner of
Michigan Avenue Bridge and Wacker
Drive
Tickets are available at the ticket
window daily each morning
(312) 332-1366, (312) 332-1368
www.mercuryskylinecruiseline.com

The bright blue awning along the Riverwalk is your beacon for this longtime Chicago boat cruise company that appeared in the 2006 Vince Vaughn-Jennifer Aniston flick *The Break-Up*. Choose from several 90-minute tours, including the popular Urban Adventure Tour, highlighting info about Chicago's past and present—pair it with a trip to the John Hancock Observatory for a small up-charge. The Chicago By Night Tour includes a stop to view the Buckingham lights show, and the all-paws-aboard Canine Cruise permits pups to come along for the ride (leashes required), complete with provided water bowls, a newspapered bathroom, and plenty of ear-tickling, tail-wagging freedom. A Fireworks Cruise runs on Wednesday and Saturday evenings in July and August, and there are special kid-oriented pirate-themed cruises too. Tickets $25 to $35; children under 12 $10 to $15; children under 3 are free; dogs $7. Tours generally run from late May to early Sept (the Canine Cruises starts in mid-July, and the Urban Adventure continues through mid-October).

i One of the most spectacular times for booking a boat tour is during Chicago's annual Air and Water Show, when you get front-row, unobstructed views of the playful antics of the planes that zoom and zip overhead. Be sure to book those well in advance.

MYSTIC BLUE CRUISES

Board at Navy Pier
600 E. Grand Ave.
(888) 333-9150
www.mysticbluecruises.com

It's fiesta time on the open water with a *Mystic* lunch, brunch, or dinner cruise. DJs spin dance music on two of the three decks; a third makes for marginally quieter mingling; and the open-air observation deck is nice for taking a breather between them. Food is served buffet-style, with mains including roasted brisket, turkey meatloaf minis, and penne with vodka cream sauce. At dinner, dip into the chocolate fondue bar for dessert. And for you night-owl party people, the popular Blue After-Dark cruise shoves off post-midnight and pumps up the volume with club music on every level (21 and over for this one). Specialty cruises like the Full Moon dinner cruises and New Year's Eve Fireworks dinner cruises are also available. As they say, where else can you party like a "yacht" star? Prices vary, starting at $36.90. Cruises run year-round, weather permitting.

ODYSSEY CRUISES

Board at Navy Pier
600 E. Grand Ave.
(866) 957-2320
www.odysseycruises.com

Glimmering during the day and glowing at night, the city skyline presents quite the lovely backdrop for a sophisticated lake cruise aboard this sleek vessel. Three-course, sit-down meals with top-notch table service and live bands (of the light rock and classic faves kind) round out the romance factor. The food ranks nearly as high as the panoramic views, with dinner dishes like caramelized duck en croûte, mushroom-braised short ribs, and bread pudding. Toast to something special or just each other on the Champagne Cruise, where your first glass of bubbly is on the house, and mouth-watering menu items include strawberries and cream french toast, house-griddled Belgian waffles, maple-glazed chipotle chicken, carved-to-order black pepper–crusted sirloin, and the deliciously decadent chocolate fountain. Prices vary, starting at about $42. Running year-round, the *Odyssey* pulls out the red carpet for holiday cruises such as Mother's Day, Father's Day, Valentine's Day, Thanksgiving, and New Year's Eve.

i Several outdoorsy outfits offer kayaking and canoe tours. See the Parks & Recreation chapter under Water Sports for more information.

SEADOG CRUISES
Board at Navy Pier
600 E. Grand Ave.
(888) 920-2600
www.seadogcruises.com
Feel the need for speed? Satisfy it in spades aboard one of these exhilarating loops along Lake Michigan. Combine the regular run with a little learning on the 75-minute Architectural Cruise that travels from the lake through the Chicago River Lock system, up the river and back; or just go for the gusto on the 30-minute Extreme Thrill Ride that cranks this puppy up to 45 miles per hour on the open water, with dizzying 180- and 360-degree spins—tours stop just long enough for a few fun facts and rock-and-roll tunes. The 30-minute Speedboat Lake Tour isn't quite as crazy, but includes info and quick zips across the lake. *Note:* You may or may not get wet depending on conditions and where you sit. No age requirement, but all passengers must be 48 inches or

taller to ride the Seadog Extreme. Tours start at $19.95 and run through Oct, weather permitting.

SHORELINE SIGHTSEEING
Board at Navy Pier
600 E. Grand Ave.
(312) 222-9328
www.shorelinesightseeing.com
Shoreline's Lake Michigan Skyline Tours fit into any busy schedule, taking you out for 30 informative minutes of Chicago's history and notable buildings, plus our inimitable skyline. Travel a little further and a little longer on the 1-hour Architecture River Cruise. More than 70 years in business, the company also offers front-row seats to Navy Pier fireworks, plus Sunset Lake Tours, and Beer Tasting Cruises. Shoreline's water taxis shuttle locals and visitors alike between Navy Pier and a handful of popular stops including the Museum Campus, Willis Tower, and Michigan Avenue Bridge. Dogs are allowed on all cruises, as long as they're leashed. Buy tickets in advance online and save 5 percent; just be sure to remember to take your confirmation number when you go to the dock. Tickets for the Skyline Tour $16 to $18, seniors $14 to $16, children 12 and under $7 to $8; Architecture River Cruise $26 to $33, seniors $23 to $30, children $13 to $16; Fireworks and Architecture combo tour $29 to $32, seniors $25 to $29, children $14 to $16; and Lake Fireworks Tour $24 to $26, seniors $22, children $12. Tours operate generally May through Oct.

SPIRIT OF CHICAGO
Board at Navy Pier
600 E. Grand Ave.
(866) 957-2324
www.spiritofchicago.com

Every so often one of the servers attending to the candlelit tables aboard the *Spirit* breaks into song or dance. It's part of the, well, spirited atmosphere of this 600-person yacht. Seating is done the old-fashioned cruiseliner way, pairing small groups together at a table for communal dining. But after filling your plate at the lunch, brunch, or dinner buffet (go back for seconds or thirds, if you'd like), you won't be sitting for long, because DJs work the crowd, spinning dance hits, rallying passengers for line dances, and generally keeping it all extra high energy. Several outdoor decks afford plenty of lake-gazing and stunning photo-ops. On select Sundays, the Gospel Lunch Cruise adds a spiritual touch to the spirited good time. Other specialty cruises include a Senior Cabaret Lunch featuring sing-along show tunes; Fireworks Dinner Cruises that coincide with Navy Pier's pyrotechnic displays; Chicago History Lunch Cruises, adding narration to the views and buffet; the Pride Moonlight Cruise, taking place the weekend of Chicago's gay and lesbian Pride Parade; and the Air and Water Show Cruise. Tour prices vary, starting at around $40. Many tours run year-round.

i *Odyssey, Spirit, Mystic Blue,* and *Seadog* cruises are all operated by Entertainment Cruises. Its website allows you to compare vessels, and search dates, times, types of cruises, and prices to find the best one for you (www.entertainmentcruises.com/chicago).

TALL SHIP ADVENTURES
Windy: **Located at Navy Pier**
(312) 451-2700
Red Witch: **Located at Burnham Harbor**
Lake Shore Drive, exit 18th Street
(312) 404-5800
For a schedule of themed cruises, call
(312) 451-2700
www.tallshipadventuresofchicago.com
Make like a real sailor aboard one of these unique ships. The 77-foot schooner *Red Witch* boasts a distinctive 2-masted topsail and dark red hull and its daily 2- to 3-hour cruises make you feel like one with the lake breeze—feel free to lend a hand on deck, or just sit back and relax. Fun fact: *Red Witch* takes its name from an epic story called "Wake of the Red Witch," which was made into a John Wayne movie in 1949. The *Windy* (Chicago's official Tall Ship) is a larger, 4-masted boat, coming in at 148 feet, sporting a grand interior cabin, and offering 1- or 3-hour cruises, including themed events like Real Pirates of the Inland Seas; Spirit Ships and Haunted Harbors; and Rum Runners. Both schooners can be chartered: the *Red Witch* for 7 to 49 passengers, the *Windy* up to 150 people. A brand-new 50-foot sloop called the *Pianissimo* can be chartered privately or shared by up to six passengers. *Red Witch* prices vary from $40 to $65; $20 to $35 for children. *Windy* prices vary from $24 to $45; seniors $15 to $35; children 2 to 11 $10 to $20. Sailing season runs from early May through early Sept.

✳**WENDELLA BOAT RIDES**
400 N. Michigan Ave. (at the Wrigley Building)
(312) 337-1446
www.wendellaboats.com

Launched in 1935 by Swedish immigrant Alberg Borgstrom, this still-family-owned business is now a beloved Chicago institution. Wendella offers a 75-minute architectural river tour, a 90-minute combo lake and river tour, and a sunset tour, as well as two specialty tours: a 2-hour wine-tasting architectural cruise, and a 90-minute fireworks tour. A cash bar and snacks are available. Tours cost $26 to $28; seniors $25 to $26; children over 3 $13 to $14; under 3 free. Tours run daily during warm months.

i In addition to tours, Wendella runs a convenient water taxi from both Metra and Amtrak train stations to points on Michigan Avenue, LaSalle Street, and Clark Street, and Chinatown's Ping Tom Park.

FOOD TOURS

CHICAGO CHOCOLATE TOURS
Office: 500 N. Michigan Ave., Ste. 300
(312) 929-2939
www.chicagochocolatetours.com
Chocoholics unite with giddy delight on these tours of some of Chicago's best and most delicious chocolate shops, bakeries, and cafes. The geographically categorized walking tours hit about five sweet stops each, for everything from traditional bonbons to outrageous cupcakes and a new cupcake-focused tour. While you're satisfying those confectionary cravings, tour guides slip in a taste of Chicago history and architecture, along with fun chocolate-related facts and trivia. All tours run about 2½ to 3 hours and cost $40 per person. Tours run daily. Check the website or call for scheduled times and accompanying meeting places.

Reservations are strongly recommended, as tours tend to sell out.

CHICAGO DINE-AROUND
Advance reservations required, or visit the website for pickup location information
(312) 437-3463 (DINE)
www.chicagodinearound.com
With so many amazing restaurants in Chicago, it's hard to choose which to hit and which to miss. But this progressive dining tour makes your life a little easier—and more filling too—by chauffeuring you in coach-bus comfort to three different restaurants, one for each course. Start with hors d'oeuvres and wine at the first, then main course at the second, and finally dessert and coffee at the third. Besides the food, you get diverse dining companions, no parking woes, and interactive informative narration between destinations. So sit back, chow down, and enjoy the ride (and the food). Tickets are $85 per person and include tax and gratuities. Tours depart every Fri and Sat evening at 6 p.m. and generally last for 3 hours. Private tours can be arranged for any other night. Booking online can reserve your spot and sometimes save money depending on promotions.

i Consider taking a food-related tour at the beginning of your visit to give you time to return to any neighborhood or particular eatery that piqued your palate and your interest.

CHICAGO FOOD PLANET FOOD TOURS
Meeting places vary
(800) 979-3370
www.chicagofoodplanet.com

Indulge your inner foodie on one of three different, sample-filled walking tours. The Near North excursion introduces you to local favorites including a genuine Jewish deli, a heaven of fudge and chocolate, and a lesser-known Chicago-style pizza place. On the Bucktown-Wicker Park trip, you'll meander through this super-hip neighborhood, stopping for gourmet bites at some of its outstanding food markets and restaurants. In Chinatown, the smells nearly outweigh the tastes at places serving up traditional teas and dim sum, top-rated Szechuan cuisine, and authentic Peking duck. Each 3-hour tour is paired with narrative of the neighborhoods and fills you up enough for lunch. Tours don't end the same place they start, but guides will direct you on how to get you back to where you need to go. Also, tickets must be purchased in advance and only by credit card. Near North and Bucktown-Wicker Park tours cost $45, $30 for adolescents, $15 for children; Chinatown $60, and $35 for all children. Near North Food Tour runs daily Mar through Nov with first tour departing at 11 a.m.; Bucktown-Wicker Park Food Tours head out every Tues through Sat from Apr through Nov, first departure time at 11:30 a.m.; Chinatown tours take place on Mon only Apr through Nov starting at noon.

*CHICAGO PIZZA TOURS
Meet near Madison Street and Wabash Avenue
(800) 979-3370
www.chicagopizzatours.com
After devouring all the delectable pizzas on this tempting tour, you'll be too stuffed to walk. Thank goodness you won't have to; the "Dough Force One" bus transports you through the city from one scrumptious taste to the next. Owner Jon Porter has done the extremely difficult pizza-eating research himself, whittling down the many contenders to a list of about 10 spots that he rotates for tours—which means if you want to go twice, you'll have a perfect excuse, because you'll probably visit different places. Whether it's the hand-tossed thin crust of Apart Pizza, the crispy-chewy results of Coalfire's 800-degree coal-fired oven, or the tried-and-true deep-dish of Gino's East, you will ultimately try four different pies, living up to this tour's motto to "See Chicago one slice at a time." Tours are $60 for everyone over 2 years old and $80 if you do the Pizza & Cocktails version; advance reservations are highly recommended. You'll get the exact start location when you reserve. Tours run frequently, but you can check the online calendar or call for specific dates.

CHICAGO SAVVY TOURS
Fine Arts Building
410 S. Michigan Ave., Ste. 424
(312) 731-8000
www.chicagosavvytours.com
www.secondcitypizzatours.com
www.thefranklloydwrighttour.com
Pizza, Frank Lloyd Wright, public art, and coffee. They're all the subject of a specialty tour from this diverse tour operation. For a fascinating overview of Chicago's rise to one of the world's greatest architectural cities, take the Signature Architectural and Historical Walking Tour, winding through town to 40 buildings in 90 minutes. Focus on Frank Lloyd Wright with several bus tours of his structures in and around the city. Master Mies on the Mies van der Rohe Tour. Or head indoors on the Chicago Spaces Tour, visiting a dozen dramatic interiors dating from 1885 to 2009. Hungry? Stuff yourself silly with four different slices of pizza on the 2½-hour

Second City Pizza Tour, or satisfy your sweet tooth on the Coffee & Pastry Tour. Tickets vary from $25 to $48 for adults depending on the tour. Tours run throughout the year, with more times and days during the summer. Check the website or call for a schedule.

ELI'S CHEESECAKE WORLD
6701 W. Forest Preserve Dr.
(773) 205-3800
www.elischeesecake.com
When the late Eli Schulman first opened his legendary Streeterville restaurant Eli's The Place for Steak in 1966 (sadly, it closed in 2005), his menu didn't actually include the now even more famous cheesecake. The rich, creamy concoction only debuted in 1977, but when it made its big-time appearance at the city's first Taste of Chicago festival in 1980, it shot to sweet-treat stardom and heavenly history. Now, the cheesecakes come in all sorts of flavors (the Totally Turtle is our pick) and are served at area restaurants, shipped all over the world, given as gifts, and generally beloved by locals. On the Sneak Peek tour of Eli's Chicago bakery, you'll learn about the history, philosophy, and art of making a cheesecake that meets Eli's standards; then, when you don't think you can handle it any longer, they'll give you a slice to taste the sensation for yourself. On weekends, the Discover Eli's tour serves up information only and does not include a visit to the bakery, but still concludes with a luscious sample. Sneak Peak tours for groups of 10 or fewer are Mon through Fri at 1 p.m. (registration requested by 12:30 p.m.) and cost $3; reservations are required for larger groups. The shorter Discover Eli's tour is offered Sat and Sun at 1 p.m. and is free for all. Children under 5 must be able to walk or be in a stroller for the Sneak Peak tour.

*FORK & THE ROAD TOURS
Meeting places vary per tour
www.forkandtheroad.com
Remember that signature Yogi Berra quote, "If you see a fork in the road, take it"? Dimitra Tasiouras and Sharon Bautista did just that when a lightbulb idea sparked the creation of these two-wheeling food tours. Combining their passion for great food with their love of cycling, the duo first started in 2008 with a hankering for gelato and a willing pack of pedaling friends; by the end of that summer, they decided to officially launch their spoke-and-snack tour company. Since then, they've created tours focused on delis, Latin meat, sandwiches, Mediterranean, Asian, and, of course, a Tour de France. Tours $50 to $60. Some things to keep in mind: If you don't have a bicycle, they always start at locations near a bike rental agency; you must wear a helmet; ride pace is about 8 to 10 miles per hour and can vary from about 10 to 20 miles; tours still go on in light rain; tours are open only to riders 18 and older.

SLICE OF CHICAGO PIZZA TOURS
Meet at Pizzeria Uno
29 E. Ohio St.
(312) 623-9292
www.sliceofchicagopizzatours.com
Anyone can tell you who makes the best deep-dish in Chicago—whoever they think makes the best deep-dish pizza in Chicago. But you get to make up your own mind on this tasty tour that takes you to three popular pie joints. At each stop, the pizza is hot and ready for digging into and for deciding which crust, cheese, and sauce you'd rank number one. Plus, you get a hearty helping of pizza history, and burn off a few of the calories as you walk the approximately 1.2 miles among restaurants. Beverages aren't

TOURS

included in the price, but you're encouraged to take your own water bottle. Parking is available for a discount at 50 E. Ohio St. (get your ticket validated at Pizzeria Uno). Tickets are $45 per person. Tours run Thurs through Sun at 11:30 a.m. and 4:30 p.m. Advance reservations are required and early booking is recommended, as tours sell out quickly.

i The Chicago Loop Alliance offers three free downloadable Loop the Loop self-guided tours: Public Art Loop, Theatre Loop, and Landmark Loop. Get them from www.chicagoloopalliance.com.

TASTEBUD TOURS
Office: 550 N. Kingsbury, #218
Millennium Loop Tour meets at Pizano's, 61 E. Madison St.
Gold Coast Loop Tour meets at Pizano's, 864 N. State St.
Savor Chicago Tour meets at Mr. Beef, 666 N. Orleans St.
(219) 929-6648
www.tastebudtours.com
With 3 hours allotted, these food explorations allow time to sit, chill out, enjoy, and even shop a little. Founded by Lynn Jaynes and his wife Karon, their Millennium Loop, Gold Coast, and Savor Chicago tours each visit five to seven locations. From classic Chicago-style hot dogs to trendy charcuterie to gourmet cakes, as well as deep-dish pizza and Italian beef sandwiches, they guarantee enough tastes to comprise a filling lunch. The range will tantalize every tastebud you've got—along with a little tickling of your noodle with commentary about Chicago history, culture, and entertainment,

and Chicago food history, culture, and entertainment too. Tours depart in rain, snow, sun, and otherwise; strollers and wheelchairs are not well accommodated in the tight spaces they sometimes visit; and vegetarian diners should call ahead for substitutions. Prefer a private experience? The Jayneses are game for that too. Tickets are $44 for all participants over the age of 2. Tours run year-round every day and start at 11 a.m.

ARTS & THEATER TOURS

ART EXCURSIONS
(630) 671-9745
www.artexcursions.com
Chicago-based husband-and-wife art historians Dr. Michelle Paluch-Mishur and Professor Jeff Mishur personally host their tours, sharing their vast knowledge and affection for art with small groups on their tours that travel around the country. In Chicago, they feature a Chicago Art and Architecture Tour with a highlight being the new Renzo Piano-designed Modern Wing at the Art Institute. But their big draw is the private guided experiences for individuals, couples, small groups, families, children or anyone else with an appreciation for art that needs a little attention. Interested in public sculpture in Chicago? They can do that. Contemporary art? No problem. Architecture? That too. Call for current tours and prices.

i Heading to a Chicago art or history museum? Most of them offer tours, whether it's an overview of a collection or targeted to a particular exhibit. Check the specific websites or call ahead if you're interested.

AUDITORIUM THEATRE
50 E. Congress Pkwy.
(312) 922-2110
www.auditoriumtheatre.org
It's quite a theatrical thrill to attend a performance at the grand Auditorium Theatre. It's even more amazing when you know what makes this National Historic Landmark so acoustically outstanding, so stunningly beautiful, and such a gem of architectural excellence. Tours point out the design and functional elements that Dankmar Adler and Louis Sullivan combined to create their masterpiece and chat about its colorful past when it hosted everything from operas to political conventions. Tickets are $10 and may be purchased 30 minutes before the tour at the theater or at Ticketmaster.com (with a handling fee). Tours generally run Mon at 10:30 a.m. and noon, and Thurs at 10:30 a.m.

BROADWAY IN CHICAGO'S HISTORIC THEATRE TOURS
Meet at Oriental Theatre
24 W. Randolph St.
(312) 977-1700
www.broadwayinchicago.com
Oohs and ahhs are expected on these tours that include two of three historic Loop theaters: The Oriental Theatre, the Cadillac Palace, and the Bank of America Theatre. Each early 20th-century space is extravagantly ornamented and beautifully restored, showing off elegant lobbies with marble, gold leaf, lavish mosaics, and a rich history of heydays and celebrities, downturns and renewals. Tickets $10 (with a handling fee if purchased through Ticketmaster). Tours take place every Sat at 11 a.m.

*CHICAGO FILM TOUR
Meet on the west side of Clark Street, between Ohio and Ontario Streets
(312) 593-4455
www.chicagofilmtour.com
Fancy yourself a film buff? Or just curious about things like where exactly Rob Lowe and Demi Moore met in the classic 1980s flick *About Last Night* or the hotel where Harrison Ford fled for justice in *The Fugitive*? Then you'll want to take a roll with this lighthearted, movie-manic tour. You'll bus it for about 2 hours across 30 miles to see more than 30 sites where over 50 movies were filmed. And just to jog your movie memory, the tour includes video clips on multiple screens aboard the bus. Feel free to bring your own snacks and drinks—we recommend buttered popcorn and a pop, of course. Tours are $30 and leave every Thurs through Sun at 10:30 a.m. and 12:30 p.m. The season is Apr through Nov, but group tours are offered year-round.

CHICAGO POETRY TOUR
Start at Chicago Cultural Center
78 E. Washington St.
(312) 787-7070
www.poetryfoundation.org
Whether your poetic preferences run toward Shel Silverstein or Sylvia Plath, anyone can relate to a look at Chicago's history through its poetry. These self-guided walking tours are produced by and downloadable from the Poetry Foundation, feature narration by NPR's Scott Simon, and include archival recordings of famous Chicago poets such as Gwendolyn Brooks and Vachel Lindsay. A route map is also downloadable to guide you. Free. A brand-new Poetry Foundation building at Dearborn and Superior Streets is also open to the public.

TOURS

i The Frank Lloyd Wright Preservation Trust organizes top-notch tours of Wright's Home and Studio (including one for kids), and the surrounding Wright-filled suburb of Oak Park (708-848-1976; www.gowright .org).

CHICAGO THEATER STORIES WALKING TOUR
Meet at southwest corner of Michigan Avenue and Randolph Street
(773) 508-4894
www.theatreclubchicago.com/about/ tour.htm
More than just a discussion of prominent Chicago theaters, these strolls delve into the stories of the people who graced the city's historic stages and the events that affected the course of Chicago theater and theatergoing. The 60-minute tours cost $18 and are held Sat and Sun at 11 a.m. and 1 p.m.; 90-minute tours cost $25 and run Sat and Sun at 3 p.m. Reservations are required for all tours. Group tours are also available 7 days a week. Contact for price and availability.

THE CHICAGO THEATRE MARQUEE TOUR
175 N. State St.
(800) 745-3000
www.thechicagotheatre.com
Find out what made this Beaux-Arts theater the flagship of the Balaban and Katz theater chain when it opened in 1921 and how it has since become the city's oldest standing movie palace of that era. Check out its landmark vertical sign and marquee, its replica of the Arc de Triomphe, the lavish lobby inspired by a Versailles chapel; and, depending on the performance schedule, stand on the stage in the footprints of Frank Sinatra, Liza Minelli, and Prince, among many other legendary performers. Tickets may be bought at the box office or through Ticketmaster: $12; children 12 and under and groups of 10 or more $10 per person (through Ticketmaster prices incur a handling charge). Tours take place Jan through Mar and Oct through Nov on Tues, Thurs, and Sat at noon; from Apr through June, as well as Sept and Dec, they are hosted every Mon through Thurs at noon and Sat at 11 a.m. and 12:30 p.m. In July and Aug, tours are daily at 11 a.m. and 12:30 p.m.

PERFORMING ARTS

Before tackling this chapter, I thought about how to distinguish it from other sections. After all, "the arts" could feasibly encompass everything from the culinary arts to the visual arts, from local music acts to comedy troupes. So, to give it a shape and style of its own, I confined the category to traditional theater, music, and dance venues and ensembles. Plus, I included art and indie movie houses in a sidebar. You'll find all the other aspects of arts in other chapters; for instance, comedy clubs and blues clubs are in Nightlife; art museums are in Attractions & Museums; and a bit of information about Chicago art galleries is in the Shopping chapter.

First, about those theaters: There are more than 200 of them in Chicago, from storefront theaters presenting shoestring productions to incredible Loop venues showing million-dollar Broadway-style spectacles. Chicago's theater scene pulses with an energy all its own, making it one of the best places to be an actor at any stage of one's career and perhaps even more thrilling to be an audience member. Find out why Lookingglass Theatre won a Tony for best regional theater; snag tickets to a production at the Steppenwolf, where a long list of now-famous actors earned their stripes; see Shakespeare done right at one of the top tourist attractions in the state; catch a Tony-winning musical at a historic Loop theater; or get down-and-dirty and up-close-and-personal with some of the most cutting-edge ensembles on stages across the country today.

The Chicago dance and musical groups included here garner international acclaim and represent all forms of dance, from classic to contemporary, ballet to tap, and music from an a cappella choir to the Chicago Symphony Orchestra.

Because Chicago has so many amazing live-performance venues, those are scattered throughout too. They are the places that play the welcoming host, whether to a rock band or to an off-Loop theater troupe, and their calendars are always full of fascinating and entertaining events. When it makes sense, costs are included, but in most cases, no prices are given, as they vary depending on what's going on and when. Now, go ahead, take your seats and enjoy the show.

MUSIC & DANCE VENUES

ARAGON ENTERTAINMENT CENTER
1106 W. Lawrence Ave.
(773) 561-9500
www.aragon.com

Today, run by a leading Latino event marketing and entertainment company, the Aragon sees lines down the block most weekends for a leading list of both Hispanic and English-language bands. But this wasn't always the case. When William and Andrew Karzas unveiled their spectacular ballroom in 1926 (at an astronomical $2 million), it soon became the number-one classiest destination for dapper young men and lovely young women to meet, mingle, and show off their moves to live tunes over the years by the likes of Frank Sinatra, Tommy Dorsey, Glenn Miller, and Guy Lombardo. The backdrop was a copy of a Spanish palace courtyard (the name comes from a province in Spain), with starry sparkling lights dotting the high-domed ceiling, crystal chandeliers, and mosaic tiles. However, by the mid 1950s, attendance was already declining when a fire next door damaged the dance hall and closed it for several months. After that, it passed through several owners and assorted uses—skating rink, boxing venue, flopped disco hall called the Cheetah Club in the 1960s, then, after a major restoration, a rock and roll venue in the 1970s. The music and the crowd have changed over the years, but the Aragon is still making history.

ATHENAEUM THEATRE
2936 N. Southport Ave.
(773) 935-6860
www.athenaeumtheatre.com
First built in 1911 by adjacent St. Alphonsus Church as a rec center replete with theater, gym, and bowling alley, the updated Lakeview building now features one main stage theater that can seat about 1,000, plus several smaller studio spaces. It rents space to local dance and theater companies, as well as cabaret acts and musical performers.

CHARTER ONE PAVILION
1300 S. Lynn White Dr.
(312) 540-2668
www.charteronepavilion.com

Lake Michigan's at your back, and the city skyline decorates the horizon on the other side of this open-air rock, pop, and light rock venue—Stone Temple Pilots; Earth, Wind & Fire; Ke$ha. It's all temporarily set up each summer on Northerly Island, just south of the Museum Campus. The outdoor environs can mean perfection on a warm night or it can prove to be the pits when the bugs are biting or it rains and the show goes on anyway. Parking over in the Soldier Field lot is generally included with your ticket price, and there's a shuttle to take you over, or you can do the 10-minute walk on your own. VIP tickets get you access to a tented bar, nicer bathrooms (as opposed to trailers), premium parking, and dedicated drink service. Speaking of which, complaints abound about the high price of beer here, but you won't mind too much when that balmy lake breeze sweeps in. Learn more about Northerly Island itself in the Parks & Recreation chapter.

*CIVIC OPERA HOUSE
20 N. Wacker Dr.
(312) 827-3580
www.civicoperahouse.com
Home to the lauded Lyric Opera of Chicago, this grandiose 1929 part–Art Nouveau, part–Art Deco theater underwent a total facelift in 1996 from top—fresh paint and elaborate stenciling on the auditorium ceiling—to bottom—reupholstered seats, new carpeting, and, well, bigger bathrooms. Although already a stunner, the improvements made it even more impressive to sit in one of the 3,563 seats and watch the divas do their thing on the largest stage in downtown Chicago. Entry is duly majestic through colonnades that line the Wacker Drive side and into a great, gilded lobby. From architectural boat tours, you can get

a glimpse of its hulking 45-story backside. Originally known as the Lyric Theatre of Chicago, the opera company was founded in 1954 and has regaled audiences with its monumental renditions of everything from Leonard Bernstein's *Candide* to Giuseppe Verdi's *Aida* to Charles Gounod's *Faust*. It all makes a night at the opera a night you'll certainly remember.

✳THE DANCE CENTER OF COLUMBIA COLLEGE CHICAGO
1306 S. Michigan Ave.
(312) 369-8330
www.colum.edu/dancecenter
This top-notch state-of-the-art performance space at art-centric Columbia College Chicago hosts a wide range of local, national, and international dance companies, with a bent toward the contemporary. Acts have included Reggie Wilson, Merce Cunningham Dance Company, The Seldoms, Joe Goode Performance Group, and the Lyon Opera Ballet.

✳HARRIS THEATER FOR MUSIC AND DANCE
Millennium Park
205 E. Randolph Dr.
www.harristheaterchicago.org
Alan Cumming, Mikhail Baryshnikov, Lang Lang, and Kathleen Battle have all headlined at this theater in Millennium Park. And it's no wonder it's trusted by such world-class talent: The outstanding sightlines of the 1,525-seat auditorium mean everyone feels part of the show; the high-caliber acoustics mean everyone can hear what they're supposed to hear; and the convenient location surely can't be beat. A family series opens up younger eyes and ears to some amazing musical and dance performances as well.

HOUSE OF BLUES
329 N. Dearborn St.
(312) 923-2000
www.hob.com
This national chain location owned by Live Nation has its fair share of faults (unexpected fees, delayed door times, hit-or-miss acoustics), but when all is said and done, this music mecca in Marina City has remained, since opening in 1996, a pretty cool space to take in a packed calendar of pop, indie rock, gospel, punk, rockabilly, and everything in between. The 55,000-square-foot, richly decorated interior is based on an opera house in Prague, and the 1,800-person capacity with mainly standing room makes this small River North hall a top venue. Seating options like private opera boxes go to the lucky or those willing to spend a bunch more (reserved minimum-drink seats, for example). Plus, every night of the week, the HOB's 250-seat Back Porch restaurant features live music. Read more about the Marina City complex in the Architecture chapter.

✳OLD TOWN SCHOOL OF FOLK MUSIC
Maurer Concert Hall
4544 N. Lincoln Ave.
(773) 728-6000
www.oldtownschool.org
Ever had an urge to learn guitar, piano, or harmonica? Or to take Irish, swing, flamenco, or belly dance lessons? You can do all that here (kids' classes too; see the Kidstuff chapter)—and you can also see how the professionals do it. Founded in 1957, Old Town's mainstay is its 2-tiered 420-seat auditorium where no seat is more than 45 feet from the stage, and a full menu of folk-plus-more features performers such as James McMurtry, the John Scofield Trio, Kurt Elling, the Ditty Bops, and Marcia Ball. The friendly confines

with coveted cocktail tables even allow you to bring in food and drinks (beer and wine included) bought at their cafe. If you're coming to town especially for a concert or still need somewhere to bunk down, Old Town has deals with several area hotels, so check the website. Wednesday is world music night when concerts are a steal at around 5 bucks. Coming soon, the venue will just get better as a new facility across the street opens with an additional 150-seat theater, three dance studios, and 16 more classrooms.

PARK WEST
322 W. Armitage Ave.
(773) 929-1322
www.parkwestchicago.com
This Jam Productions venue that opened in the 1920s now sports a funky 1970s logo and hosts all genres of bands, from Lucinda Williams to 1980s one-hit-wonder cover band Tributosaurus, to kids' fave Ralph's World. Concertgoers appreciate the intimate good-seats-all-around setting in the curved layout, and those in the know get here early to grab one of the candlelit tables to set down those drinks. Cocktail servers come around regularly, or just head back to the bar. Just beware the $20 minimum credit card policy.

RUTH PAGE CENTER FOR THE ARTS
1016 N. Dearborn St.
(312) 337-6543
www.ruthpage.org
A dance school, as well as an important incubator for emerging talent, this realized vision of the late American dance innovator Ruth Page subsidizes performances in its 200-seat theater, allowing companies to showcase their work without being overburdened by expenses. About 20 to 30 Illinois dance companies annually rent the space in the 1927 Gold Coast building.

SYMPHONY CENTER
220 S. Michigan Ave.
(312) 294-3000
www.cso.org
It's no small matter that Symphony Center serves as the splendid home base for the superbly talented Chicago Symphony Orchestra (see separate listing in the following section)—and now helmed by internationally acclaimed conductor Riccardo Muti. But this celebrated destination is much more than that too. Listed on the National Register of Historic Places, the building itself is a marvel, dating back to 1904 and a design by Daniel Burnham. More than 150 performances take place here each year, ranging from a dedicated jazz series to children's concerts to Civic Orchestra performances to chamber music; plus visiting artists; a new-music series; Friday Night at the Movies events that project classic movies like *Casablanca* as the CSO performs the score live; and Beyond the Score, which features a live concert accompanied by audiovisual and narrated commentary that delves into the composition's story. In other words, seeing a show here is a big deal.

MUSIC & DANCE COMPANIES

CHICAGO A CAPPELLA
Office: 2936 N. Southport Ave., 2nd Floor
Office phone: (773) 281-7820; tickets:
(800) SING-WOW, (773) 755-1628
www.chicagoacappella.org
This nine-person classical ensemble has been singing up a storm since its founding by Jonathan Miller in 1993. Its repertoire focuses on music composed in modern

Close-up

Screen Time

There are mega-plexes aplenty (several in the city, an abundance in the 'burbs), but for something that's beyond the norm, here's your ticket.

Brew and View. Cheap tix. Cheap booze. Second- and sometimes third-run flicks. If that works for you, then this is your place. Set in the rather rundown, formerly fancy 1912 Vic Theatre (originally built for vaudeville), this is by no means a silence-is-golden place: Expect drunken 20-somethings to heckle, sing, and quote along with the movie. Tickets $5 for up to three movies. Check online for schedule and for a quick survey that awards you $1 off for completing it. 3145 N. Sheffield Ave.; (773) 929-6713; www.brewview.com.

Davis Theater. A bit grungy after 80 years (save for its new rocking seats and brightened lobby), the Davis still makes the cut for its low prices on first-run flicks, nostalgia for old-time moviegoing, good deals on popcorn, and its hip locale in Lincoln Square, where you'll find delicious dining (and clean bathrooms—theater facilities are not known for their cleanliness). Shows before 6 p.m. are $5.50; after 6 p.m., $8; seniors and children 2 to 11 $5.50; children under 2 are free. 4614 N. Lincoln Ave.; (773) 784-0893; www.davistheater.com.

Facets Multi-Media. For more than 37 years, true movie buffs have been making tracks to this off-the-beaten-path nonprofit arts organization, whose screenings skew to the artsy, indie, experimental, cult, documentary, and foreign variety. Its accompanying video store does likewise, with tens of thousands of hard-to-find titles, and a new Netflix-like membership program that allows you to search online for a never-ending supply right to your house no matter where you are in the country. Tickets average $9. 1517 W. Fullerton Ave.; (800) 532-2387, (773) 281-9075; www.facets.org.

Gene Siskel Film Center. Named for the Windy City's late beloved movie critic Gene Siskel, this School of the Art Institute of Chicago (SAIC) public program attracts more than 80,000 viewers to a fascinating lineup of nearly 1,500 of the world's best, most overlooked, most talked-about, most controversial, stirring, and inspirational films, including movies of the Black Harvest International Festival of Film and Video, the European Film Festival, Festival of Films from Iran, and two series presented in conjunction with the School of the Art Institute of Chicago. It also hosts the only Oscar night party in Chicago sanctioned by the Academy of Motion Picture Arts and Sciences. Tickets $10; students $7; students, faculty and staff of the SAIC and Film Center members $4; children under 6 generally not permitted in the theater. 164 N. State St.; (312) 846-2800; www.siskelfilmcenter.org.

The Music Box. Described as "atmospheric" and deemed first-date romantic with its twinkling ceiling stars and clouds, the lovely little Music Box was built in 1929 as a movie theater—unlike many grand theaters of its time that boasted big stages, this 750-seater only saved room for an orchestra pit and organ chambers in case sound films didn't get off the ground. Nowadays, an organ is often played between films on Saturday and Sunday evenings, and the theater screens about 300 independent and foreign titles a year in the main theater and in a newer, smaller one. Tickets $9.25; Mon special $5 admission and buy one, get one popcorn and soda. 3733 N. Southport Ave.; (773) 871-6604; www.musicboxtheatre.com.

times, but also reaches back as far as the 9th century. Catch one of its four subscription series concerts for music that might include spirituals, jazz, or even the Beatles.

CHICAGO CHAMBER CHOIR
Tickets: (312) 409-6890
www.chicagochamberchoir.org
Presenting several major concerts annually—including a joyful winter holiday show—this choir group of several dozen singers spreads its love of music by bringing choral performance to communities that lack live music in their lives, including inner-city schools and homeless shelters. Tickets for main performances are $18; students, children 12 and under, and groups of 10 or more $15.

✳CHICAGO HUMAN RHYTHM PROJECT
Office: 2936 N. Southport Ave.
Presenting at various venues
(773) 281-1825
www.chicagotap.org
A little shuffle, ball, change, anyone? And that's just the tip of the tap iceberg when it comes to the things these dancers can do with their bodies. Four major calendar events presented by the Emmy Award–nominated CHRP include the tap-happy Rhythm World, described as "the oldest and most comprehensive festival of American tap and contemporary percussive arts in the world." But CHRP doesn't stop with just their own feet. Besides performances of the ensemble BAM!, the company also presents a full slate of other artists, and holds workshops and classes, so audiences can get in on the beat too. With a background of charitable giving—proceeds from the first performance back in 1990 were donated

to a meals-on-wheels program serving people affected by HIV/AIDS—the group now awards scholarships, provides outreach residency programs, and hosts conferences about the world of tap. Next up: establishing the first-ever permanent cultural institution dedicated to American tap and contemporary percussive art.

CHICAGO SINFONIETTA
Office: 70 E. Lake St., Ste. 226
(312) 236-3681
www.chicagosinfonietta.org
A dearth of opportunities for minority classical musicians, composers, and soloists motivated Paul Freeman to form his own orchestra in 1987. Since then, the Chicago Sinfonietta has been driven by a goal of "musical excellence through diversity," achieving raves wherever it plays and introducing new, underserved audiences to classical music through its outreach programs. In 2011, Mei-Ann Chen stepped into Maestro Freeman's role as music director and continues to lead a subscription season at Symphony Center and a 4-concert season at Wentz Concert Hall in Naperville (630-637-SHOW), as well as collaborations with other artistic companies including serving as the official orchestra of the Joffrey Ballet (see listing below). Ticket prices vary.

i Looking for the best local bands? Cool-kid clubs abound around town. To find a list, pick up weekly publications the *Chicago Reader* (www.chicagoreader.com) or *TimeOut* magazine (www.timeoutchicago.com), or check online at www.metromix.com.

It Happened Here

Chicago is one of Hollywood's favorite off-site shoot locations. With friendly people to work with, an eager and talented lot of actors, and actual changes in weather, it makes sense. Here are some famous films that used at least part of the Windy City environs as scenery.

1959: *North by Northwest*
1967: *In the Heat of the Night*
1973: *The Sting*
1979: *Ordinary People, The Blues Brothers, My Bodyguard*
1982: *Risky Business*
1983: *Sixteen Candles*
1985: *About Last Night, Ferris Bueller's Day Off, Running Scared*
1986: *The Color of Money, The Untouchables*
1990: *Home Alone, Backdraft*
1993: *The Fugitive*
1994: *While You Were Sleeping*
1996: *My Best Friend's Wedding*
1999: *High Fidelity*
2001: *Ocean's 11*
2002: *Barbershop*
2004: *Batman Begins*
2006: *The Time Traveler's Wife*
2007: *The Dark Knight*
2008: *Public Enemies*
2010: *Transformers 3*
Scheduled 2013: *Superman: Man of Steel*

✳CHICAGO SYMPHONY ORCHESTRA & CHORUS

220 S. Michigan Ave.
(312) 294-3000
www.cso.org

From the violins to the tubas, the harp to the trumpets, the dozens of musicians who make up this celebrated orchestra know how to get the notes on the page to resonate with audiences' hearts and souls. And they do it a lot, what with more than 150 concerts annually—on their own and in collaboration with artists from around the world—at their Symphony Center HQ and at Ravinia Festival in suburban Highland Park, their summer home since 1905. Italian conductor Riccardo Muti is just the tenth to take the reigns as music director since the CSO was established in 1891. Its sibling singers, the Chicago Symphony Chorus was founded in 1957, and since then, the two organizations have made beautiful music together, racking up more than 60 Grammy Awards over the years. Take a listen and hear for yourself. See the Symphony Center listing in the section on Music & Dance Venues above.

PERFORMING ARTS

CHICAGO'S MUSIC OF THE BAROQUE
Office: 111 N. Wabash Ave.
(312) 551-1414
www.baroque.org
Music by some of the most popular classical music composers is performed by Music of the Baroque, including Pachelbel, Bach, Handel, Vivaldi, and Haydn. This professional 60-person chorus and orchestra is led by one of the world's greatest Baroque conductors, Jane Glover, who doubles as artistic director of opera at London's Royal Academy of Music. The ensemble performs a series of concerts at various locations around the city, including the Harris Theater in Millennium Park.

FULCRUM POINT NEW MUSIC PROJECT
Office: 30 E. Adams St., Ste. 1201
(312) 726-3846
www.fulcrumpoint.org
Pushing hard beyond expected limits of new classical music, the 20 members of this group, including its director Stephen Burns, clearly have fun on the job. More than just bringing the music to the masses, they astound even die-hard traditionalists as they merge classical instruments with electronic, theatrical lighting, art and photography, and sometimes deconstructed rock tunes. Fulcrum originated in 1998 and continues to evolve, presenting themed concerts at locations around the city, including the Field Museum, Art Institute of Chicago, National Museum of Mexican Art, and most commonly at the Harris Theater. If you don't think you like classical music, this ensemble will make you think again.

GIORDANO JAZZ DANCE CHICAGO
Office: 614 Davis St., Evanston
(847) 866-6779
www.giordanodance.org

Technically superb and artistically brilliant, this world-class dance company does not disappoint. With impossible aerobic energy, muscular agility, and graceful movements, the 10 dancers seem to barely take a breath—and neither will you as you watch them in action. Formed by the late choreographer Gus Giordano, who also authored the seminal *Anthology of American Jazz Dance,* and currently led by Artistic Director Nan Giordano, the company's repertoire continues to amaze at performances throughout the world and right here at the Harris Theater and other dance venues.

*HUBBARD STREET DANCE CHICAGO
Office: 1147 W. Jackson Blvd.
(312) 850-9744
www.hubbardstreetdance.com
A request to teach tap classes led Lou Conte to open his own dance studio more than 35 years ago. It didn't take long before his professional company took shape. Hubbard Street Dance Chicago soon began to attract choreographers of the highest caliber, and now boasts a long list of accolades as one of the best and most versatile contemporary dance troupes in the country and around the world—as well as one of the only year-round performing companies. Bold collaborations with other renowned cultural organizations have urged Hubbard Street to constantly rethink and rework its own repertoire and have led to amazing experiences for its audiences. If you've got some aspirations of your own, the Lou Conte Dance Studio still obliges with more than 60 classes each week in everything from ballet to jazz, tap to African dance.

*JOFFREY BALLET

Office and school at 10 E. Randolph St.
Performances at Auditorium Theatre
50 E. Congress Pkwy.
(800) 982-ARTS (2787), (312) 386-8905
www.joffrey.org

You know you're good when you're the first dance company ever to appear on TV, the only dance company to grace the cover of *Time* magazine, and the only one to inspire a major movie (*The Company,* directed by Robert Altman). Such high honors for a company that, after beginnings in New York and L.A., has its feet firmly pointed in Chicago. Lucky us. Founded by Robert Joffrey in 1956, and directed by the eminent Gerald Arpino from 1988 to 2007, the Joffrey is now under direction of Scotland-born dancer Ashley C. Wheater. Besides a yearly season of world premieres and full-length favorites and a frequent touring schedule, the classically trained dancers enchant audiences of all ages each winter holiday season with their glorious telling of *The Nutcracker.* Twirl over to the Joffrey's sparkling new Academy of Dance for a free tour every second and fourth Wednesday of the month at noon (call 312-386-8921 by the Monday prior to reserve).

LUNA NEGRA

Performances at the Harris Theater, Pritzker Stage in Millennium Park, and the Museum of Contemporary Art
(312) 337-6882
www.lunanegra.org

Take the precision of ballet, add the innovations of contemporary dance, and the dynamic energy of Latin, and you get this exciting young company led by artistic director Gustavo Ramirez Sansano. Through its performances and its educational work in communities both nationally and internationally, Luna Negra brings a new voice to dance.

RIVER NORTH DANCE CHICAGO

Office: The Ruth Page Center
1016 N. Dearborn Ave.
(312) 944-2888
www.rivernorthchicago.com

Prepare for your jaw to drop at the beautifully bold and taut, often sensual, and frequently surprising performances of this contemporary jazz company. Having recently celebrated its 20th anniversary, River North has proven itself to be a leading force on the Chicago dance scene. With multiple awards for original choreography by artistic director Frank Chaves and co-artistic director emerita Sherry Zunker, as well as others, the vibrant company soars in performances in the Chicago area—including its annual Valentine's Day weekend engagement at the Harris Theater—and around the country.

THODOS DANCE CHICAGO

Office: 860 W. Blackhawk St., Ste. 305
(312) 266-6255
www.thodosdancechicago.org

Named one of Chicago's "top ten hidden talents" by the *Chicago Tribune,* Melissa Thodos has a remarkable list of achievements to her name, including forming this energetic contemporary dance ensemble in 1992. Not only a performing company, but also a nurturing environment for members' growth as performers, educators, and choreographers, Thodos specifically seeks dancers who have a history of teaching and aspirations of choreography—member works get the spotlight in the annual "New Dances" series each summer. Their powerful and engaging

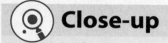 # Close-up

Off-Loop Gems

Chicago Tribune theater critic Chris Jones weighs in with his expert opinion on where to see some of the best theater companies you've never heard of. Refer to the sidebar to get all the pertinent information about the theaters Jones mentions.

Insiders' Guide: What makes Chicago such a prolific theater town?

Chris Jones: The visitor has three kinds of choices when it comes to theater here: There's one scene that's the big downtown scene to see major Broadway shows in a setting and within a group of theaters there's not an equal to—outside of New York, Chicago's theater district has the highest concentration of theaters. The second are world-class residential companies that would include theaters like the Goodman, Steppenwolf, and Court Theatre—well-known nonprofits doing world-class theater. The third part would be to get out into the neighborhoods where young artists are doing new works, often innovative staging, often with very little money, but with the spirit that Chicago has been known for.

IG: Have you seen things change over the years?

Jones: No question there's more theater in Chicago than there was a decade ago. It has now reached a point where people come from all over the world to see theater—that's a fairly new development and there's been such an increase in the quantity and quality. We're seeing more shows go from Chicago to Broadway—Steppenwolf, for example—and an increasingly important center for new work and a generator of original ideas. Chicago is recognized as one of the hottest theater cities in America.

IG: Do you think actors come here over New York?

Jones: New York remains the center of the industry, but for young actors wanting to be seen, to start their own company, say what they want to say and be seen saying it, then Chicago is the place for that—and there's a tradition of newspapers trying to get out and about and see some of this work; that is important.

IG: What are some of your favorite established small theater companies?

Jones: The Steep Theater on Chicago's North Side, very conveniently located, a classic storefront theater, putting on gutsy new plays with the train rumbling overhead. The House Theatre in Wicker Park—real daring originality, increasingly cool and really moving. Lifeline Theatre in Rogers Park—for great family programming and gritty programming. For Chicago-style musicals, Theo Ubique Cabaret Theatre [pronounced thee-oh oo-bah-kway] with full-on musicals in the tiniest space where you

performances can be seen throughout Chicago and often in collaboration with other arts organizations, such as the Chicago Symphony Orchestra, Remy Bumppo Theater, and Fulcrum Point New Music Project. In addition to dedicated work in schools, Thodos also takes its show on the road and has shown off its innovative moves at the Edinburgh Fringe Festival, the International Istanbul Dance Festival, Jacob's Pillow Dance Festival, and in venues around the country.

can barely swing a cat, and they do it consistently with really high standards; and the American Theater Company tends to do high-quality work, very gritty. For new work in a historical setting, Victory Gardens in the historic Biograph Theater [known as the place where John Dillinger was shot by the FBI]—always a good choice in a building with history and tradition, presenting new and exciting work; they are really good. Up on Belmont, you've got two buildings, Stage 773 and Theater Wit; they have between them six different theaters and always something there that people can go to and see what's there if you want to take a chance. If you want Chicago-style raw, blood and guts, in-your-face theater, Profiles Theatre is a long-established theater that's been a storefront for about 20 years. Also, A Red Orchid Theatre, one of the established storefronts, and if visitors are staying in downtown hotels, relatively easy to get to; Michael Shannon [who was an early member] is playing [General Zod] in the upcoming *Superman* ["Man of Steel"].

IG: Are there any emerging or younger companies that you're keeping your eye on?
Jones: The New Colony, an itinerant company; Griffin Theatre, a great small company that's opening a new theater of their own in about a year. And talking about venues, the Chopin Theatre in Wicker Park seems to be occupied by always interesting performers.

IG: When visitors are in town, what's your one go-to theater recommendation?
Jones: If they're here for one night, my recommendation is Second City [see Nightlife] because it's a very high level of entertainment and it really is a theater, though people think it's just a comedy club, and very affordably priced.

IG: Any others to mention?
Jones: If you're interested in new hot African-American companies, you could look at the Black Ensemble Theater, which is soon to open a new building, and attracts a really diverse audience. For more drama, the Congo Square Theatre Company, probably the leading African-American theater company, growing, very reliable, highly professional. On the Latin scene, Teatro Vista, which works in partnership with the Goodman.

IG: Anything else to note about Chicago theater?
Jones: It's one of the great reasons to come here; it's more truthful than theater elsewhere and more affordable than elsewhere—you can usually get a good ticket to a good show for $25—particularly if you use HotTix—and you're often seeing the stars of tomorrow.

i Snag HotTix half-price day-of-performance theater tickets in person Tues through Sun at two locations, as well as online: 72 E. Randolph St., 163 E. Pearson St., and at www.hottix.org.

BIG NAMES & BIG SHOWS

APOLLO THEATER
2540 N. Lincoln Ave.
(773) 935-6100
www.apollochicago.com

Chris Jones Recommends

American Theater Company
1909 W. Byron St.
www.atcweb.org
(773) 409-4125

Black Ensemble Theater
4520 N. Beacon St.
(773) 769-4451
www.blackensembletheater.org

Chopin Theatre
1543 W. Division St.
(773) 278-1500
www.chopintheatre.com

Congo Square Theatre Company
2936 N. Southport Ave.
(773) 296-0830
www.congosquaretheatre.org

Court Theatre
5535 S. Ellis Ave.
(773) 753-4472
www.courttheatre.org

Griffin Theatre Company
3711 N. Ravenswood Ave.
(773) 769-2228
www.griffintheatre.com

The House Theatre
Performances at the Chopin Theatre
1543 W. Division St.
(773) 769-3832
www.thehousetheatre.com

Lifeline Theatre
6912 N. Glenwood Ave.
(773) 761-4477
www.lifelinetheatre.com

The New Colony
Dank-Haus German Cultural Center
4740 N. Western Ave., 2nd Floor
(773) 413-0TNC (0862)
www.thenewcolony.org

Profiles Theatre
4147 N. Broadway
(773) 549-1815
www.profilestheatre.org

A Red Orchid Theatre
1531 N. Wells St.
(312) 943-8722
www.aredorchidtheatre.org

Stage 773
1225 W. Belmont Ave.
(773) 327-5252
www.stage773.com

Steep Theatre
1115 W. Berwyn Ave.
(866) 811-4111
www.steeptheatre.com

Teatro Vista
3712 N. Broadway, #275
(312) 666-4659
www.teatrovista.org

Theater Wit
1229 W. Belmont Ave.
(773) 975-8150
ww.theaterwit.org

Theo Ubique Cabaret Theatre
Performances at No Exit Cafe
6970 N. Glenwood Ave.
(800) 595-4849
www.theoubique.org

Victory Gardens Biograph Theater
2433 N. Lincoln Ave.
(773) 871-3000
www.victorygardens.org

Practically under the Brown Line El tracks, this powerhouse of a small-ish theater (no relation to New York's Apollo) has amassed an impressive track record of hits since opening in 1978. David Mamet's *Sexual Perversity in Chicago* (inspiration for the movie *About Last Night*) shot to fame here—starring none other than John Belushi—as well as *Waiting for Lefty, Steel Magnolias,* and *Pump Boys and Dinettes.* The Apollo has served as home to plays produced by Steppenwolf like *Balm in Gilead* with John Malkovich and Gary Sinise before they made it big; it has hosted crowd-pleasing musicals like *Always . . . Patsy Cline* and presented the Midwest debut of the wildly popular *The Vagina Monologues.* But perhaps its most exciting production ever is the still-running *Million Dollar Quartet,* the rock-and-roll story of the day in 1956 that legends Johnny Cash, Jerry Lee Lewis, Carl Perkins, and Elvis Presley recorded together. After a multiple-extended run here, the show stormed Broadway, snagging a Tony nomination for Best Musical and a Tony Award for actor Levi Kreis who played Lewis. There are curtains for kids too, with several long-running productions here by the Emerald City Theatre Company. With just 440 seats in 11 pitched rows, the Apollo makes any show sing.

AUDITORIUM THEATRE
50 E. Congress Pkwy.
(312) 922-2110
www.auditoriumtheatre.org
From regular performances by the Joffrey Ballet to a Beach Boys concert to a production of *Fiddler on the Roof,* the Auditorium Theatre proves hard to peg for its broad scope of offerings. It could also just as easily be listed for its architecture alone. Designed by Dankmar Adler and Louis Sullivan and opened in 1889, the 17-story building that houses the theater was a marvel of stunning proportions—110,000 tons of granite and limestone spanning half a city block; 4,200 seats (there are now 3,877), 55 million pieces of mosaic tile, the tallest building in Chicago at the time, and the largest in the country. It was one of the first buildings to offer heat and air-conditioning and one of the first that was wired for electricity; it still uses the same kind of electric clear-glass carbon-filament bulbs it did when it opened. Perhaps the most famous aspect of this National Historic Landmark is its perfect acoustics, making it the ideal place to see a show of any kind.

i Factor in parking costs when you attend a downtown show, but hold onto your ticket stub, as most area parking garages extend a discount to theatergoers. Check online to find out which is closest to your theater.

BRIAR STREET THEATER
3133 N. Halsted St.
(773) 348-4000
www.blueman.com
Currently the longstanding home of Chicago's PVC tube-playing, paint-splattering, Cap'n Crunch-munching, silent, but zany Blue Man Group, this 600-seat theater was built in 1901 as the stables for Marshall Fields' delivery service horses. It was converted to a theater space in 1984 and takes people on quite a ride these days. Tickets to Blue Man Group range from $49 to $69.

BROADWAY IN CHICAGO
Office: 17 N. State St., Ste. 810
Tickets and info: (312) 977-1700
Customer service: (312) 977-1702
www.broadwayinchicago.com

It's hard to believe that Broadway in Chicago was only created in 2000. It has become such an integral, essential, and vibrant part of downtown that it seems to have been around forever. More than 1.7 million people see BIC shows a year, now presented at five theaters, including the Cadillac Palace Theatre (151 W. Randolph St.), Bank of America Theatre (18 W. Monroe St.), Oriental Theatre (24 W. Randolph St.), Auditorium Theatre (50 E. Congress Pkwy.), and the newest addition, the Broadway Playhouse (Water Tower Place, 175 E. Chestnut Ave.). While the Broadway Playhouse presents smaller-scale shows, and the Auditorium Theatre focuses on dance and music concerts, the other three are the top spots to catch big sprawling productions of classic and new musical favorites like *Wicked, Chicago: The Musical, West Side Story, Mary Poppins,* and *Spring Awakening.* In fact, Chicago theaters and their audiences have served as crucial testing ground for the pre-Broadway runs of *The Producers, Spamalot, Movin' Out,* and *The Addams Family.* Plus, each theater has a history of early 20th-century glory, later decline, and then wonderful recent resurrection to original, ornamented splendor, evoking oohs and ahhs for design of the theater as much as what's on stage there. Learn more about several of the theaters on a Historic Theatre Tour, listed in the Tours chapter.

i Watching with a group? Consider adding $30 to each Broadway in Chicago theater ticket and you'll get a private suite available 45 minutes before curtain and during intermission; complimentary light bites and drinks; private restrooms and coat check; and all-around special treatment.

*CHICAGO SHAKESPEARE THEATER
Navy Pier
800 E. Grand Ave.
Office: (312) 595-5656
Tickets: (312) 595-5600
www.chicagoshakes.com

The Bard gets top billing at this Tony Award–winning theater whose productions have included *Romeo and Juliet, As You Like It,* and *A Midsummer Night's Dream.* But with a 48-week season and more than 600 performances, Shakespeare isn't the only thing going at this dual-staged space. The CST Family Series plays to a younger audience with fables, fairy tales, interactive music concerts, musical theater like *Aladdin* and *The Adventures of Pinocchio*—as well as respectful abridged versions of Shakespeare. And the World's Stage Series brings shows to Chicago from foreign lands, including acclaimed theaters from Russia, India, Lebanon, and South Africa. Whether you pair a performance with a stop at Navy Pier's lofty Ferris wheel is entirely up to you. For more about Navy Pier, see the Attractions & Museums chapter.

i Shakespeare Theater-goers get guaranteed parking at Navy Pier even when the garage says it's "full." Just tell them you're there for Shakespeare and then remember to get your parking ticket validated for 40 percent off.

CHICAGO THEATRE
175 N. State St.
Office: (312) 462-6300
Guest Relations: (800) 745-3000
Tickets via Ticketmaster: (312) 902-1500
www.thechicagotheatre.com

The frequently photographed, 6-story vertical marquee of this French Baroque–style theater twinkles with 8,915 light bulbs. It's a prelude to the extravagant 5-story lobby and mural-filled 3,600-seat auditorium and why this historic theater was called "the Wonder Theatre of the World" when it opened in 1921. It was, in fact, the prototype of majestic movie palaces to come. After being shuttered for a short time, it was graciously restored and reopened in 1986 and now hosts a musical and comedic list of who's who including Ellen DeGeneres, Aretha Franklin, Paul Simon, Dolly Parton, Chelsea Handler, and Diana Ross, and shows of the now-annual Just for Laughs comedy festival. The smaller Chicago Theatre Downstairs extends the venue capacity. For information about tours of the theater, check out the Tours chapter.

GOODMAN THEATRE
170 N. Dearborn St.
(312) 443-3800
www.goodmantheatre.org
One of Chicago's top nonprofit regional theaters doing highly acclaimed world-class work, the Goodman is in the thick of the Loop Theatre District and considered one of the big players. But it had some rocky times in the past. It began in 1922 with a donation from the Goodman family to the Art Institute to construct a theater in honor of their aspiring playwright son Kenneth, who had died in the flu epidemic of 1918. Though the theater itself shut down after less than a decade, an accompanying drama school continued on, with graduates including Geraldine Page, Karl Malden, and Joe Mantegna. In the late 1950s, the professional acting company slowly began rebuilding, and the school was taken over by DePaul University. A turning point in the Goodman Theatre's history came when the dynamic Robert Falls stepped in as artistic director in 1986. Among the many stellar world premieres, American classics, and acclaimed revivals, Falls also began an early and still-standing collaboration with actor Brian Dennehy. The famous screen actor has appeared in multiple Goodman productions including *Death of a Salesman* and *Long Day's Journey into Night*, both of which went on to Tony-winning Broadway runs. Falls also brought in other bright talent to develop works and form what's now referred to as the Artistic Collective. In 2000, the Goodman moved into its current thoroughly modern quarters—a changing color pattern of light blocks illuminates the exterior at night—which features a main stage theater and the smaller Owen Theatre. The Goodman is famous for pushing the dramatic envelope and for its annual production of Charles Dickens' *A Christmas Carol*, a local holiday tradition for several decades.

i The Goodman Theatre sells remaining mezzanine tickets for the current day's performances at half-price beginning at 10 a.m. online (enter promo code Mezztix) or in person beginning at noon. For students with ID, 10Tix are available for 10 bucks.

✳LOOKINGGLASS THEATRE
Water Tower Water Works
821 N. Michigan Ave.
Office: (773) 477-9257
Tickets: (312) 337-0665
www.lookingglasstheatre.org

And Even More Theaters . . .

. . . that we thought you should know about:

Chicago Center for the Performing Arts. Four small stages featuring a variety of improv, standup, musicals, cabaret, and drama. 777 N. Green St.; (312) 733-6000; www.theaterland.com.

Light Opera Works. Musical theater from around the world, presented in English. Cahn Auditorium, 600 Emerson St. and McGaw YMCA Children's Center, 1420 Maple Ave., Evanston; (847) 869-6300; www.light-opera-works.org.

The Mercury Theater. Traveling shows of any variety in a refashioned 1912 silent movie house. 3745 N. Southport Ave.; (773) 325-1700; www.mercury theaterchicago.com.

Noble Horse Theatre. And now for something totally different: shows on horseback. 1410 N. Orleans St.; (312) 266-7878; www.noblehorsechicago.com.

Raven Theatre Company. Focusing on American classics, both comedy and drama, and the occasional world classic. 6157 N. Clark St.; (773) 338-2177; www.raventheatre.com.

Redmoon. Amazing spectacles of pageantry, acrobatics, and large-scale puppetry, as well as site-specific performances. 1463 W. Hubbard St.; (312) 850-8440; www.redmoon.org.

Remy Bumppo. Presenting thought-provoking works by the world's greatest playwrights. 2257 N. Lincoln Ave.; (773) 404-7336; www.remybumppo.org.

Royal George Theatre. Lincoln Park theater with four stages and a variety of fun-loving fare like the ongoing *Late Nite Catechism*. 1641 N. Halsted St.; (312) 988-9000; www.theroyalgeorgetheatre.com.

Writers' Theatre. Where the words and the actors take center stage in classic and contemporary plays in an intimate setting. 325 Tudor Ct. and 664 Vernon Ave., Glencoe; (847) 242-6000; www.writerstheatre.org.

Original works and original adaptations are at the heart of this daring, surprising, and thought-provoking nonprofit theater, which won the 2011 Regional Theater Tony Award. Formed in 1988 by a group of college grads, including David Schwimmer (of *Friends* fame), it kicked off with and took its name from their self-produced version of *Alice in Wonderland*. The Lewis Carroll fantasy also inspires their mission and values to "change, charge, and empower." Using their theater space in infinitely flexible configurations, the imaginative ensemble has been known to incorporate dance, music, high-wire acts, and high-tech into their performances, many of which have won Jeff Awards—and the recent *Trust*, which was filmed for the silver screen (starring Clive Owen and Catherine Keener) before debuting on stage, and both of which were co-written and co-directed by Schwimmer.

i Get to the theater on time, because many theaters enforce a seating policy that limits entry after the lights have dimmed. Some may seat you after the first scene, others at their discretion in the back of the theater and allow you to move to assigned seats only during intermission.

STEPPENWOLF THEATRE COMPANY
1650 N. Halsted St.
(312) 335-1650
www.steppenwolf.org

Ever heard of Gary Sinise (a.k.a. Lt. Dan)? He and high school pal Jeff Perry and Perry's college friend Terry Kinney banded together back in 1974 to form an intrepid theater troupe. They quickly incorporated and gathered a few more actors for their first full season of plays in 1976, which they presented in the basement of a church in Chicago's North Shore suburb of Highland Park. Those nine members included the three original guys, plus H.E. Baccus, Nancy Evans, Moira Harris, John Malkovich, Laurie Metcalf, and Alan Wilder. Now several moves, endless accolades, a National Medal of Arts, and nine Tony Awards later, nearly all of them are still counted among the 43-member ensemble that comprises this internationally regarded, ground-breaking theater. The roster also includes well-known screen actors such as Joan Allen, William Petersen, and John Mahoney—and they really do come back now and then for appearances at the state-of-the-art theater complex that opened in Lincoln Park in 1991.

ARCHITECTURE

Chicago's astronomic growth following the Great Chicago Fire of 1871 led to many of the world's building innovations. Like the first skyscrapers, a practical answer to the downtown area's increasing land values. Why not build up instead of out? Many of the architects who are known as part of the first Chicago School of architecture were the ones who designed these lofty towers. They started with load-bearing masonry walls and moved into iron and steel and then the glass-and-steel structures that foretold even taller things to come.

Just 20 years after the destruction of the city, Chicago was selected as the site of the sought-after world's fair. And while it was mostly the level of financial backing that beat out New York for the right to host the event, the planners put their money where their mouths were and proved that the selection committee had made the right decision. Despite hiccups and tragedies during the process (co-organizer John Root died suddenly in 1891, for example), Chicago's World's Columbian Exposition of 1893 was a resounding success. Much gratitude was bestowed on its director, John Burnham, who commissioned some of the era's greatest architects to design the fair's many structures: Richard Morris Hunt; Charles McKim, Mead and White; Henry Ives Cobb; and Adler and Sullivan, to name a few. Though some decried the overall neoclassical Beaux-Arts plan with its plaster of Paris–clad buildings as a sad step backward for architecture, most visitors were decidedly wowed by what became known as the White City—and by Chicago.

From there, the city continued to prove itself as a creditable hotbed of architectural creativity. One particularly lasting legacy: Chicago and the close suburb of Oak Park were where Frank Lloyd Wright and his followers began developing the Prairie School of design. Interest in this style lasted from the late 19th to early 20th centuries, ending soon after World War I, as America took a more conservative turn. Today, the Prairie School–designed homes are a hot commodity.

A Second Chicago School of architecture appeared in the 1940s and continued right through to the early 1970s, most influenced by Mies van der Rohe, his large-scale commission of the Illinois Institute of Technology campus, and his many students who followed in his rectilinear footsteps. It was what led to some of Chicago's most impressive skyscrapers standing today, including the Hancock and Willis (formerly Sears) towers.

Wherever you look in Chicago, whatever direction you take to explore, its mighty architectural legacy greets you. It might be as you crane your neck up to see what's standing at the top of the Chicago Board of Trade or as you meander the blocks of the beautiful Astor Street. The sites here offer a place to start your architectural journey of Chicago.

OVERVIEW

Whittling down the endless architecturally interesting places in Chicago was not an easy task. This chapter could have easily encompassed the entire city and included sites in every neighborhood, or I could have categorized places by time period or style, but I found it best to focus on downtown and the Loop. This area alone has such a wide range and close concentration of noteworthy buildings that it serves as a great introduction and representation of Chicago architecture as a whole.

The category "Historic Districts & Homes" gives you a taste of what's beyond the city center and even a bit of what's hidden amid it. Take the book with you as you visit the places that interest you, so you can compare the history and descriptions of what you see; it's always so much more impressive to see these places in person. Or check the Chicago Architecture Foundation's website to find out when its docents are leading guided tours of the locations listed; their tours include visits to every one of these (and many more), except for Clark House, which has its own tours.

DOWNTOWN LANDMARKS

CHICAGO BOARD OF TRADE
Address: 141 W. Jackson Blvd.
Architect: Holabird & Root
Year Completed: 1930
Designations: Chicago Landmark, National Register of Historic Places, National Historic Landmark
A soaring example of Art Deco architecture, this Holabird & Root building stands proudly at one end of the LaSalle Street financial corridor. Through historic preservation—including removal of unappealing 1950s dropped ceilings in the lobby—and stylistic replication (of elevators that needed replacing, but were redesigned with Art Deco sensibility), an update in 2006 infused it with renewed glory. Still referred to as the "board of trade building," it actually now houses the CME Group, which is a merger of CBOT and the Chicago Mercantile Exchange. Take a look up to glimpse the woman standing atop the building; she's a 6,500-pound aluminum sculpture of Ceres, the goddess of agriculture. The CME Group website has some visitor info at www.cme group.com.

860–880 NORTH LAKE SHORE DR.
Architect: Mies van der Rohe
Year Completed: 1951
Designations: National Register of Historic Places, Chicago Landmark
Exemplifying the minimalist style of the architect who's famous for his "less-is-more" philosophy (though he insists he never said that), these two high-rise residential towers of glass and steel—dubbed the "glass houses"—were the first by Mies (as he's known) in Chicago to receive landmark status. They were also a forerunner of many glass-and-steel followers, but none as noteworthy as these. Located along luxe Lake Shore Drive, the 26-story twin structures lie across from Lake Michigan and offer some of their home-owners amazing views. Though the private residences aren't open to the public, feel free to walk by and peer into the lobby, or get a good look from the beach, or, for anywhere between $200,000 and $650,000, just purchase one of the 255 units yourself and live in the lap of history.

HAROLD WASHINGTON LIBRARY
Address: 400 S. State St.
Architect: Hammond, Beeby and Babka
Year Completed: 1991

Though not really old enough to have any historic distinctions, Chicago's central library is still quite distinct. The result of a 1987 design competition (in which it beat out a glassy modern thing by Helmut Jahn, by the way), the building's bold Neo-Classical stylings borrow from Beaux-Arts, Greek, and Roman. The 756,640-square-foot library ranks as the largest public library building in the world and boasts 5-story arched windows on three sides of the redbrick façade. You can't miss the seven huge gargoyle-like sculptures around the perimeter of the roofline, including a 20-foot-tall great horned owl—get a good look at this crown of sorts from the Loop El trains that ride nearby (the Library stop gets you within a quick walk of the building). Interior spaces are equally impressive with marble mosaics and museum-quality artwork; at the top is the Winter Garden, a glittering space lit with a 52-foot glass-paneled dome that makes a stunning setting for special events. Pick up materials at the first-floor info desk that will take you on a self-guided tour of the structure; or download the guide at www .chicagopubliclibrary.org. Find out more about Chicago's public library system in the Appendix.

JAMES R. THOMPSON CENTER
Address: 100 W. Randolph St.
Architect: Helmut Jahn
Year Completed: 1985

Whether you think this postmodern behemoth falls into the category of ridiculously awful or eye-catchingly innovative, you've got to admit, it has an unmistakable presence in the Loop. All futuristic with its blue glass—which causes annual outrage for its extreme temperature swings inside— red structural beams, and salmon-colored and silver design elements, the 17-story government office building (the governor's office is here) glitters against many traditional and more unassuming buildings all around. Two sides parallel bordering streets, while a third angles inward as it goes up, leaving space for an open plaza, which contains Jean Dubuffet's four-piece *Monument with Standing Beast* sculpture. The interior is a must-see—an immense, 16-story atrium with hallway balconies circling overhead, glass elevator shafts, and view down from a 72-foot-diameter cutout from the lobby level into a marble mosaic flower on the concourse level. Shops, restaurants, an Illinois art gallery, and access to El trains are also on the lower floors. Find information about the building, exhibits, directions, and more at www.state.il.us/cms/1_jrtc. Find out more about the Dubuffet sculpture in the Attractions & Museums chapter.

JOHN HANCOCK CENTER
Address: 875 N. Michigan Ave.
Architect/Engineer: Fazlur Khan/ Skidmore, Owings & Merrill
Year Completed: 1969
Designations: Member of the World Federation of Great Towers

Originally considered a sore thumb for its bold, black exterior and enormous (for the time) size, this northern anchor on the Magnificent Mile is now one of the world's most recognized and beloved skyscrapers and still the 12th tallest. The steel X-bracing on its façade not only gives the Hancock its prominent look, but enables the interior to remain free of columns and central support that many other tall buildings require. Its equally iconic tapered design—narrowing 105 feet from east to west and 65 feet from north to south—gives it the sturdiness it needs to shoot up 1,127 feet and 100 stories; a row of lights around the top can be seen from all over the city and changes color depending on the season and celebration (green on St. Patrick's Day, for example). And just to be safe, the caissons extend right into the bedrock below. While lower floors serve as retail, restaurant, and office space, the upper levels are home to the rich and famous, with 700 luxury units. Fun fact: The diagonal bracings block views from two windows on each floor, but these rooms are considered status symbols and actually cost more. Visit www.johnhancockcenterchicago .com. For information about the 94th-floor Hancock Observatory, check out the listing in the Attractions & Museums chapter.

*MARINA CITY
Address: 300 N. State St.
Architect: Bertrand Goldberg
Year Completed: 1962
Often seen in movies, ads, and even on an album cover (Wilco's *Yankee Hotel Foxtrot*), these twin residential towers, affectionately called the "corncob towers" were the result of Goldberg's goal to keep people in the city, rather than lose them to suburban flight. Besides the 900 residential units (450 per tower), the "city-within-a-city" complex originally included 896 parking spaces per building, laundry facilities, a movie theater, gym, swimming pool, ice rink, bowling alley, stores, restaurants, and a marina. When they opened, the buildings achieved two global firsts: They were the tallest residential structures and the tallest built from reinforced concrete. They also became a model for

mixed-use high-rise buildings throughout the country. While not all of the original features remain—the House of Blues took over the theater, for example—many still do, and located on prime real estate along the Chicago River, the condos are still coveted. Each wedge-shaped unit includes at least one 175-square-foot arched balcony, which creates Marina City's instantly identifiable flower-petal design. Visit www.marina-city .com. A listing for the House of Blues is included in the Arts chapter.

MERCHANDISE MART
Address: 222 Merchandise Mart Plaza
Architect: Graham, Anderson, Probst & White
Year Completed: 1930
With superlative status as the world's second-largest building (only the Pentagon is bigger), "the Mart," as it's called by locals, encompasses a whopping 4.2 million square feet, spans 2 blocks and reaches 25 stories along the Chicago River. The imposing and impressive irregular trapezoid-shaped structure with its grand Art Deco aspects was built by Marshall Field & Co. to consolidate and increase its wholesale business. Although it didn't do much for Marshall Field's bottom line—no thanks to the Depression— the building has remained a trendsetter of style through its hundreds of furniture and apparel showrooms and trade shows. In 1945, the Kennedy family bought the Mart (sold again in 1998) and began an ongoing modernization, revitalization, and move toward increased public access. Added in recent years was LuxeHome, a gathering of upscale home decor boutiques. Tours are available on Fri at 1 p.m. for $12; seniors and students $10. Call (312) 527-7762 for more information; www.merchandisemart.com.

✳MICHIGAN AVENUE BRIDGE

Address: Chicago River at Michigan Avenue
Architect: Edward Bennett
Year Completed: 1920
Designation: Chicago Landmark

In his 1909 "Plan for Chicago," Daniel Burnham envisioned a bridge connecting Chicago's north and south sides. His "Plan" co-author Edward Bennett made it happen in grand Beaux-Arts style. It was the first double-decker, double-leaf trunnion bascule bridge built, meaning it is hinged with counterweights that balance the two sides of the street as they lift for boats to pass through. See the Attractions & Museums chapter for more information on the museum that's now housed inside the bridgehouse.

MONADNOCK BUILDING

Address: 53 W. Jackson Blvd.
Architects: North half was Burnham & Root; south half, Holabird & Roche
Year Completed: 1891; 1893
Designations: National Register of Historic Places, Chicago Landmark

The transformation of skyscraper construction can be seen in the two halves of this largely unornamented 16-story Loop office structure—when it was completed, it was the largest office building in the world and, for a short time, the tallest. The north half employs early skyscraper techniques and was one of the last built almost completely with load-bearing brick walls—a massive 6 feet at the base. Illustrating a newfangled approach, the south half features an early example of steel skeleton construction. Named for a mountain in the Boston-based developers' native New England area, the building once had four separate sections, each with its own mountain name. Recent restoration efforts have received acclaim from preservation organizations, and this historic building still houses 300 office suites, each with oak and glass entrances. Visit www.monadnockbuilding.com.

✳THE ROOKERY

Address: 209 S. LaSalle St.
Architects: Burnham & Root; Frank Lloyd Wright (1905 lobby remodel)
Year Completed: 1888
Designations: National Register of Historic Places, National Historic Landmark, Chicago Landmark

With steel-framed skyscrapers still in their early stages, John Root designed this 11-story financial district office building as a hybrid of masonry and steel foundation and support. On the exterior, it exhibits both beauty and bulk: its brick and granite hint at styles including Moorish, Venetian, Indian, and Arabian. In contrast, the bright interior shows off intricately detailed ironwork and gilded marble and a spectacular iron staircase that spirals up from the 2nd floor to the 12th. An ingenious central light court seems to reach to heaven with its glass ceiling, and the ground floor lobby remodeled by Frank Lloyd Wright introduces Prairie Style elements in the stair rails and light fixtures. Over the years, building managers covered glass-block floors with vinyl and windows with tar paper and paint. Luckily for us, multimillionaire bonds trader Thomas Baldwin III bought the historic building in 1988 and instigated a meticulous restoration project that has brought the light and love back to the Rookery. What's in the name? It's said to refer to the crows that roosted at the site's former building, a temporary City Hall. Visit www.therookerybuilding.com.

Religious Icons

Many ethnic and cultural communities grew around their church or temple. A drive around town will reveal many of those that still serve a dynamic congregation. Here's just a short list of 8 outstanding examples of religious structures.

All Saints Episcopal Church and Rectory. 4550 N. Hermitage Ave.; (773) 561-0111; www.allsaintschicago.org. A unique example of the Stick Style of architecture, this Ravenswood church was built in 1883, with the Tudor rectory added in 1905.

First Baptist Congregational Church. 60 N. Ashland Ave. (1613 W. Washington Blvd.); (312) 243-8047; www.fbcc-chicago.net. Founded by abolitionists in 1851, the congregation built this church in 1871 in the Gothic Revival style.

Fourth Presbyterian Church. 126 E. Chestnut St.; (312) 787-4570; www .fourthchurch.org. Holding a prominent position at the northern end of the Magnificent Mile, this 1914 structure is a combo of English and French Gothic.

K.A.M. Isaiah Israel Temple. 1100 E. Hyde Park Blvd.; (773) 924-1234; www .kamii.org. After the merging of the first Jewish settlers in the city who organized Kehilath Anshe Maariv (K.A.M.) and the second group, which founded Isaiah Israel, this Byzantine-style reform temple constructed in 1924 now houses the oldest Jewish congregation in Chicago.

Old St. Patrick's Church. 700 W. Adams St.; (312) 648-1021; www.oldstpats .org. Founded by Irish immigrants and dedicated in 1856, this Romanesque structure was one of few to survive the Great Chicago Fire in 1871—it dodged it by two blocks—making it the oldest public building in Chicago.

St. Gelasius Church Building. 6401-09 S. Woodlawn Ave.; (773) 363-7409. Though just a shell and teetering on the edge of destruction (restoration plans put the cost at more than $6.7 million), this Chicago Landmark built in the 1920s by renowned ecclesiastical architect Henry J. Schlacks still has visual impact for its Renassaince Revival style in gray limestone.

Temple Sholom. 3480 N. Lake Shore Dr.; (773) 525-4707; www.sholomchi cago.org. Directly located on the Inner Drive of Lake Shore Drive, this reform congregation's home is an interesting Byzantine-style octagonal structure built in 1930.

The Historic Chicago Temple Building. 77 W. Washington St.; (312) 236-4548; www.chicagotemple.org. Smack-dab in the middle of the Loop, this church-slash-historic-skyscraper was built by the famed duo of Holabird & Roche in 1924. The 27-story structure not only houses the church, parsonage, and unique Chapel in the Sky, but also offices and the Silk Road Theatre Project.

*SULLIVAN CENTER/CARSON PIRIE SCOTT BUILDING

Address: 1 S. State St.
Architect: Louis Sullivan
Year Completed: 1899; with additions in 1906 by Burnham and Root, and 1961 by Holabird and Roche
Designations: Chicago Landmark, National Register of Historic Places, National Historic Landmark

Wide bay windows allowed light into this State Street building and also made it possible to showcase merchandise in window displays at sidewalk level—a novel idea at the time. Originally built by Sullivan for the Schlesinger & Mayer company, the structure was sold in 1904 to Carson Pirie Scott, whose retail department store occupied the historic space until it shuttered its doors in 2007. Left vacant, the building then underwent renovations that have revived its beauty inside and out. Its most recognizable feature is its decorative ironwork and rounded corner piece. At first glance, it seems this ornate and delicately detailed entranceway was a departure from Sullivan's "form follows function" motto, but it duly served the purpose of drawing attention from passersby to the shopping destination. In 2011, Target announced plans to lease 125,000 square feet of the 600,000-square-foot interior. We hope they won't paint a big bull's-eye on it.

TRIBUNE TOWER

Address: 435 N. Michigan Ave.
Architect: Howells & Hood
Year Completed: 1925
Designation: Chicago Landmark

To celebrate its 75th year of publication in 1922, the *Chicago Tribune* sponsored an international design competition for its new headquarters, for which they expected no less than "the most beautiful office building in the world." This 36-story Gothic limestone building with its eight flying buttresses above the 24th floor won among 256 entries. Though critics point out that its victory over other more modern designs may have set back architectural innovation in Chicago, they can't argue that it commands attention at the south end of the Magnificent Mile. Based on the Rouen Cathedral in France, its entrance features whimsical nods to the architects: carved images of Robin Hood and a howling dog (for Howells). Around its exterior base, the walls are dotted with dozens of stones from famous buildings and monuments around the world including the Taj Mahal, the White House, the Petrified Forest, and even the moon. Peer in at the live radio broadcasts from the ground-floor WGN studio, whose call letters unabashedly stand for "World's Greatest Newspaper." Visit www .chicagotribune.com.

WATER TOWER & PUMPING STATION

Address: North Michigan Avenue between Pearson Street and Chicago Avenue
Architect: William Boyington, designer
Year Completed: 1869
Designation: National Register of Historic Places, Chicago Landmark, American Water Landmark

These Gothic sandcastle-like limestone landmarks were originally built to pump clean water from intake bins at Lake Michigan's shoreline to Chicago residents (the water tower equalized the water pressure). They also served a loftier purpose as a gathering place and beacon of hope when these two structures remained standing while the city around them burned to the ground in the 1871 Great Chicago Fire. The pumping station continues to serve its initial purpose, while the tower now shows up in many a wedding photo and houses a free gallery featuring works by local photographers. Refer to the Arts chapter to find out about the Lookingglass Theatre that is located in the Pumping Station.

WILLIS (FORMERLY SEARS) TOWER
Address: 233 S. Wacker Dr.
Architect: Skidmore, Owings & Merrill
Year Completed: 1973
At 1,454 feet, this soaring skyscraper is still the tallest building in the Western Hemisphere and the second tallest building in the world (the United Arab Emirates' Burj Khalifa is first at 1,729 feet). Within its 110 stories are 16 city blocks' worth of rentable space. Its innovative glass and steel design by Fazlur Khan features nine interlocking tubes that create a majestic feel as the body steps back as it rises, culminating in its final, highest-reaching section. Check out the striking 3-story lobby to see a large-scale mobile by Alexander Calder; or zip up to the 103rd-floor Skydeck for a look down on the world. Ever wonder how the building's more than 16,000 windows get washed? The engineers thought of that too: Six roof-mounted robotic washers rev into action eight times a year. And, by the way, though Sears has moved its HQ to the 'burbs, locals will likely resist ever calling this Willis Tower (for the newest name-rights tenant), so feel free to continue to refer to it as the Sears Tower. Visit www.willistower.com. Get details about the Skydeck Chicago in the Attractions & Museums chapter.

✳WRIGLEY BUILDING
Address: 400 N. Michigan Ave.
Architect: Graham, Anderson, Probst & White
Year Completed: South tower, 1921; north tower, 1924
A favorite for its glittering aesthetics, this Spanish Revival–style office building is most brilliant at night, when floodlights add an extra sparkle to its white terra-cotta cladding. Home to the gum giant, its unusual triangle-shaped footprint means that none of the building's four corners form a right angle. Located at the southwestern end of the Magnificent Mile along the Chicago River, it's a highlight of architectural river tours—you can even check the time on its colossal clock tower, whose dials are nearly 20 feet in diameter. Visit www.thewrigley building.com.

HISTORIC DISTRICTS & HOMES

ALTA VISTA TERRACE DISTRICT
Address: 3800 block of North Alta Vista Terrace
Architect: Various
Year completed: 1900–1904
Designation: Chicago Landmark
One of the last developments by clever real estate investor Samuel Eberly Gross, this charming block of 20 historic homes (18 two-story and 2 three-story) has a distinctly European feel in the middle of Lakeview. Meant to replicate London rowhouses, each home even has photo-op-worthy doors. They're not all identical, as each structure features variations on Classical Renaissance motifs, columns, pediments, and other decorative elements, but each structure has a twin in plan at the diagonally opposite end of the block.

✳ASTOR STREET HISTORIC DISTRICT
Address: 1200 to 1600 blocks of Astor Street (and cross streets)
Architect: Various
Years completed: 1880–1940
Designations: Chicago Landmark

Established in the 1880s as an enclave in the already posh Gold Coast, the residents here wanted a name befitting of their fortunes, and so named it after John Jacob Astor, who died in 1848 and was considered the country's first multimillionaire. The homes here range from Art Deco to Queen Anne, Romanesque to modern, and include the historic Charnley-Perksy House (see listing below). Recently, a 20-room, 20,000-square-foot mansion in the area (boasting a separate 5,000-square-foot coach house) listed for $22 million, a record asking price for a single-family home in Chicago. While you might not be able to live here, you can certainly stroll or tour the neighborhood and soak in some of that upscale ambience.

CHARNLEY-PERSKY HOUSE
Address: 1365 N. Astor St.
Architect: Louis Sullivan and Frank Lloyd Wright
Year Completed: 1892
Designation: National Register of Historic Places, National Historic Landmark, Chicago Landmark

Located in the Gold Coast's Astor Street district, this understated, symmetrical structure with its prominent wooden balcony belies its historical significance. Built for lumberman James Charnley, it remains the only residence that combined the architectural efforts of Louis Sullivan and Frank Lloyd Wright, who was Sullivan's fledgling draftsman at the time. After several owners and its near-destruction (because of the Depression,

plans to build a high-rise here were fortunately scrapped), architectural firm Skidmore, Owings & Merrill purchased it and restored it to its original look. In 1995, Chicago philanthropist Seymour Persky donated money to the Society of Architectural Historians to purchase the site. Now, tours give visitors a rare interior look at the two famed architects' skilled woodwork, signature ornamental patterns, forward-thinking design, and clues to what Wright would produce in later years. Wright modestly called this "the first modern house." Now run as a museum, the house is open for tours on Wed at noon, Sat from Apr through Nov at 10 a.m. and noon, and Sat during Dec through Mar at 10 a.m. only. Wed tours are free; Sat are $10; seniors and students $8; children 5 to 12 $5. Visit www .charnleyhouse.org

CLARKE HOUSE
Address: 1827 S. Indiana Ave.
Architect: Unknown
Year Completed: Circa 1836
Designation: Chicago Landmark

Considered by many historians to be the oldest residence in Chicago (there's one on the outskirts of the city at 5624 N. Newark Ave. that has a section dating to 1833), this Greek Revival–style structure was built by wealthy hardware man Henry B. Clarke, and was actually moved twice, finally landing here in the Prairie Avenue District. Tours run by the Glessner House Museum (see listing below) illustrate what life was like for a middle-class family in Chicago during the city's formative years. First-come, first-served tours take place Wed through Sun at noon and 2 p.m. Admission is $10; seniors and students $9; children ages 5 to 12 $6; children under 5 free; free for all on Wed. Visit www.clarke housemuseum.org

GLESSNER HOUSE MUSEUM
Address: 1800 S. Prairie Ave.
Architect: Henry Hobson Richardson
Year Completed: 1887
Designation: National Register of
Historic Places, National Historic
Landmark, Chicago Landmark

The only remaining Chicago building built by renowned Boston architect H. H. Richardson, the fortresslike Glessner House, built for farm equipment manufacturer John Glessner, was a surprising departure from other more Victorian-styled homes of the city's elite that lined South Prairie Avenue in the late 19th century. Exemplifying Richardson's penchant for using rugged, rough stone, the sturdy, front façade reveals little of the cozy interior, which is flooded with light from a central courtyard. Though the house racks up 17,000 square feet, the creative layout makes it feel homey. Oak paneling, stately fireplaces, and the Glessner family's preserved collection of English and American furnishings and decorative arts make this a must-stop. Guided tours are available Wed through Sun at 1 and 3 p.m. Admission is $10; seniors and students $9; children ages 5 to 12 $6; children under 5 free; free for all on Wed. Tour both Clarke and Glessner houses for a discounted combined price. Visit www.glessnerhouse.org.

HYDE PARK–KENWOOD HISTORIC DISTRICT
Address: Bounded on the north by 47th
Street, on the south by 55th Street,
Blackstone Avenue on the east, and
Drexel Boulevard on the west
Architect: Various
Year Completed: 1860s–1890s
Designation: Chicago Landmark

Before it was annexed to Chicago in 1889, this area emerged as a lovely suburb south of the city. With plenty of land to go around back then, single-family homes were the norm, as were the large lot sizes they sat on. Among the more than 1,600 structures in the district, about 460 have some kind of historical or architectural significance. Architectural styles include Italianate (typically among the oldest); Queen Anne; Tudor; Gothic (specifically on the University of Chicago campus) and many other revival styles that were the preference of the day, such as Romanesque, Georgian, Renaissance, Baroque, and Classical. Kenwood, in particular, boasts the works of Frank Lloyd Wright—including two of his famous "bootleg homes"—and Howard Van Doren Shaw who built homes for Chicago industrial moguls such as meatpacker Gustavus Swift and lumber merchant Martin Ryerson. The Chicago Architecture Foundation runs several walking and bus tours that include these historic 'hoods.

JANE ADDAMS HULL HOUSE
Address: 800 S. Halsted St.
Architect: Charles J. Hull
Year Completed: 1856
Designation: National Historic
Landmark, Chicago Landmark

Preserved and operated by the University of Illinois at Chicago, this landmark building (typically referred to simply as Hull House) became a hub of pioneering social welfare reform work by Noble Peace Prize–winner Jane Addams. The original social settlement home and the Arts and Crafts-styled Residents' Dining Hall together now serve as a museum commemorating the work of Addams and her colleagues who accomplished everything from improving public health and education, advocating for free

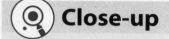

Close-up

University Appeal

Two downtown college campuses boast some of the city's most extraordinary architecture. At the **Illinois Institute of Technology,** it's mostly **Mies van der Rohe** who gets the attention. After all, as head of the university's Department of Architecture from 1938 to 1958, the Bauhaus founder designed the master plan for the campus, which now showcases 20 of his structures, making it the largest assemblage of Mies-designed buildings in the world. Such significance led to the listing of IIT's entire academic campus on the National Register of Historic Places. Don't miss Mies's glass box **S.R. Crown Hall,** home to the College of Architecture. Making more recent marks here are Dutch architect **Rem Koolhaas,** whose metal-and-glass **McCormick Tribune Campus Center** includes a vivid orange-steel tube that encloses 530 feet of Green Line El track. **Helmut Jahn,** who studied under Mies, gets the credit for the newest residence halls, three 5-story buildings wrapped in corrugated steel that merge an urban sense with intimate natural spaces. For information about tours, call the Mies van der Rohe Society at (312) 567-7146, www.miessociety.org, or refer to the Tours chapter.

The architectural star of the **University of Chicago** campus is **Frank Lloyd Wright**'s **Robie House,** a local and national landmark and listed on the National Register of Historic Places. Completed in 1910, it exhibits Wright's quintessential Prairie Style elements, from its graceful low, overhanging roof to its dominant horizontal lines to its free-flowing interior spaces and the furnishings he designed to be seamlessly integrated into them. Together with the Frank Lloyd Wright Preservation Trust, U of C oversees ongoing restoration of the home and opens it to the public for daily tours (5757 S. Woodlawn Ave.; call 708-848-1978; www.gowright.org). A stroll around the campus as a whole takes you through its 211 acres of old-growth trees, ivy- and gargoyle-covered and Gothic buildings that are based on Oxford University and several designed by acclaimed 19th-century architect Henry Ives Cobb. The **Rockefeller Memorial Chapel** is a model of this style as well, build in the 1920s and featuring a working 10,000-pipe organ and 72-bell carillon. Other bigwig designers involved with the more modern developments here include Mies van der Rohe, Eero Saarinen, Raphael Vinoly, and Cesar Pelli. Pick up campus maps at the 1915 Holabird & Roche–designed Rosenwald Hall Visitor Center, 1101 E. 58th St.

speech and fair labor practices, establishing Chicago's first public playground, and helping to desegregate the city's public schools. Exhibits delve into the work and its impact. The museum is open for tours Tues through Fri, from 10 a.m. to 4 p.m., Sun from noon to 4 p.m., closed Mon and Sat. Visit www .hullhouse.org.

OAK PARK

A detour just west of Chicago takes you to this suburban bonanza of **Frank Lloyd Wright** architecture. The Wisconsin-born Wright came to Chicago in 1887 when he was just 20 years old and quickly snagged an apprenticeship with architect Louis Sullivan. They did some amazing work together (notably, the James Charnley House), but

Wright was determined to make his own mark, so he dabbled on the side, got fired, and eventually set up shop in Oak Park in 1898 where he lived for 20 years and honed and perfected his signature Prairie Style, designing 125 structures out of that office. Many of them still stand proud along the streets here and most of them are still private residences. Several structures have been designated National Historic Landmarks—the **Heurtley House** (318 Forest Ave.), **Unity Temple** (875 Lake St.), and Wright's own former **Home and Studio** (951 Chicago Ave.), which is the best first stop when you visit. Here, you can purchase a self-guided audio tour of the neighborhood, as well as of the Home and Studio itself, where a careful restoration has returned it to original glory. For more information, visit www.gowright .org or call (312) 994-4000.

PRAIRIE AVENUE HISTORIC DISTRICT
Address: 1800 and 1900 blocks of South Prairie Avenue; 1800 block of South Indiana Avenue, and 211 to 217 E. Cullerton St.
Architect: Various
Year Completed: Circa 1890s–1900
Designation: Chicago Landmark
If you considered yourself among the rich and important of Chicago back in the late 19th century, then you had to have a Prairie Avenue address. Although many of the luxurious homes of Chicago's elite that once lined these streets have been bulldozed, there's a handful left that hint at what history held. Remaining are the homes of the Clarks and Glessners (see separate listings), piano company founder William W. Kimball (1801

S. Prairie Ave.), hardware company owner Joseph G. Coleman (1811 S. Prairie Ave.), and Marshall Field Jr. (1919 S. Prairie Ave.).

✳PULLMAN HISTORIC DISTRICT
Address: Area around 112th Street and Cottage Grove Ave.
Architect: Solon S. Beman and others
Year Completed: 1880s
Designation: National Historic Landmark, Chicago Landmark
Considered the first planned industrial complex in the country, Pullman was the brainchild of sleeping car magnate George Pullman. He built this far south side community—in 1896 called "the world's most perfect town"—to house his employees in rental units, complete with church, school, recreational facility, parkland, and factory buildings. He had his employees do the construction, of course, so the town of more than 1,000 homes and the public structures was built in just 4 years, by 1884. The plan worked just fine for about a decade until sales slumped; Pullman reduced salaries, but not rent. Workers went on strike, Pullman left town, and his perfect village fell apart. It now stands as a quiet relic to the Pullman past, but also as a vibrant modern neighborhood. Tours showcase the former Hotel Florence, the Market Square, Arcade Building, and Greenstone Church, which features the original 1882 pipe organ. Start at the Visitor Center (11141 S. Cottage Grove Ave.; 773-785-8901) for exhibits as well as self-guided or, every first Sun from May to Oct at 1:30 p.m., docent-guided walking tours ($7; seniors $5; students $4).

PARKS & RECREATION

Famed landscape architect Jens Jensen once said, "I have always thought that if the city cannot come to the country, than the country must come to the city." And that is exactly what he and others helped do for Chicago—through their efforts to maintain and nurture the natural, they left a legacy of green spaces, shady parks, big open athletic fields, and beautiful gardens. So, although Windy City residents might not all be lucky enough to have their own private backyards, it doesn't matter much when they have a park or playground (or two) just down the block, plus expanses of beachfront, gardens, and public space at Grant Park and Millennium Park, not to mention the forest preserve at the city's outer boundaries. The following is just a selection of Chicago areas where the country comes to break up the big buildings, letting us all breathe a little deeper and play a little longer.

PARKS & GARDENS

ALFRED CALDWELL LILY POOL
Fullerton Parkway and Cannon Drive
(312) 742-PLAY (7529)
www.chicagoparkdistrict.com
Just a quick hop from the Lincoln Park Zoo, this lovely hidden gem boasts National Historic Landmark status for its rare Prairie-style design by acclaimed landscape architect Alfred Caldwell, a protégé of Jens Jensen. A restoration of the 1½-acre pool was completed in 2002, providing even more reason to visit this picturesque spot, where water lilies and other aquatic plants mingle and sway, sunlight dapples oak, hawthorn, and wildflowers, a recorded 200 species of birds pop in for a rest, along with frogs, turtles, and butterflies, and a waterfall trickles over rock formations that are meant to hint at the Midwest's glacial history. From May to October, a docent is available for tours and questions on the hour and half-hour on Fri and Sun from 1 p.m. to 4 p.m., and on Sat from 9 a.m.

to noon. Free. Open May through Oct, 7:30 a.m. to 7:30 p.m., weather dependent.

✳CHICAGO BOTANIC GARDEN
1000 Lake Cook Rd., Glencoe
(847) 835-5440
www.chicagobotanic.org
Stop and smell the roses—and hyacinths, irises, pansies, daffodils, daisies, and dozens of other types of flowers, flowering plants, trees, and shrubbery that fill 385 sprawling acres. Free admission; parking $20 for cars and $25 for vans; on Tues, senior citizens park for $7. On Sun, from spring through early fall, a trolley runs from the nearby Glencoe Metra train station and is $2 round-trip per person. Open daily 8 a.m. to sunset. See more information in the Attractions & Museums chapter.

CHICAGO PARK DISTRICT
(312) 742-PLAY (7529)
www.chicagoparkdistrict.com

Chicago parents sometimes think that they should move to the suburbs so they can have a yard. And then they remember: There are yards around every corner in Chicago— public parks with playgrounds, baseball fields, indoor and outdoor pools, beaches, lagoons, or gardens. There are, in fact, more than 7,600 acres of parkland and 570 parks operated by the Chicago Park District. As Chicago started taking root as a city in the 1830s, the young government bestowed upon itself a motto that had meaning and staying power: "Urbs in horto," Latin for "City in a Garden." Through the combined work of dedicated residents and forward-thinking officials, the Lincoln, South, and West park commissions were formed in 1869. Together, they helped to set aside great swaths of land for development as public parks and insti- gated the construction of the country's first field houses (some of them now considered historic, architecturally significant structures). By 1934, 22 park districts were operating in Chicago—and all suffered from the Depres- sion. To consolidate costs, the umbrella Chi- cago Park District that we know now was created. Currently under its stewardship are famous attractions such as Garfield Park Conservatory, Grant Park, Oak Street Beach, and Lincoln Park, but also so many small neighborhood parks, it's too much to list— look for some of the more distinctive parks mentioned in this chapter. The Park District is responsible, not only for the upkeep of the parks themselves, but the hundreds of activities and programs that take place there every day, from drop-in toddler play times to soccer lessons to day camps to a bonanza of low-cost or free festivals throughout the year. In 2011, the Chicago Park District added a big task to its job description when it took over as organizer of the immensely popular Taste of Chicago in Grant Park.

i Looking for a unique event loca- tion? Chicago Park District ven- ues come through for everything from toddler birthday parties to black-tie weddings. Check the www.chicagopark district.com Events page for detailed information.

CHICAGO RIVERWALK
Wacker Drive between Michigan Avenue and Franklin Street

As part of a master plan under former Mayor Richard Daley to develop Chicago's "second shoreline," this riverwalk remains a work in progress, but the work that's been done makes it worthy of warm-weather strolls, alfresco meals at outdoor cafes, or just a peaceful contemplation as the boats go by. Or go ahead and hop a ride on one of the many river and lake tours that push off from spots along the Riverwalk. Smell some- thing fishy? That's the so-called Fish Hotel, located near the Dearborn Street Bridge, a manmade hangout for finned creatures, complete with submerged plantings and flowering native plants that lend a little homey decor. Between Wabash Avenue and State Street sits one of the largest Vietnam veterans' memorials outside of Washington, D.C., featuring a fountain and the names of Illinois soldiers killed or missing in action. And connecting the Riverwalk to the lake- front bike path is a trellised walkway under Lake Shore Drive that's ornamented with murals illustrating Chicago's growth as a city and various city achievements throughout the years. If you'd like to learn more about this waterway, head over to the Bridgehouse

Museum (see Attractions & Museums). Open generally mid-May through mid-October, 6 a.m. to 11 p.m.

FOREST PRESERVE DISTRICT OF COOK COUNTY
Office at 536 N. Harlem Ave., River Forest
(800) 870-3666
www.fpdcc.com

Chicago takes great pride in the fact that, in addition to our man-made skyscrapers, there's plenty of Mother Nature–made beauty around town, including the 68,000-acre forest preserve that hugs Cook County, in which Chicago is included. It all might have been bulldozed away if it were not for the foresighted and tireless efforts of several environmental commissions, advocacy groups, and individuals in the early 20th century who saw the need for and benefit of free and preserved natural spaces. These days, we almost take it for granted that just beyond downtown, there are none of the things we normally associate with city living: picnicking, cross-country skiing, golfing, boating, bird-watching, fishing and ice-fishing, and miles and miles of trails to hike and bike. Free. Open daily sunrise to sunset.

GRANT PARK
From Lake Michigan west to Michigan Avenue
Randolph Street south to the Museum Campus
(312) 742-PLAY
www.chicagoparkdistrict.com

Encompassing a variety of formal gardens and a dozen baseball fields, as well as ornate Buckingham Fountain and the world-class institutions of the Museum Campus (see Attractions & Museums), the 320-acre Grant Park is one-of-a-kind, and well deserving of its nickname as Chicago's "front yard." It started taking shape in 1835 when a public park was first formed. It grew much larger when rubble from the Chicago Fire of 1871 was moved there. Although Chicago "planner" Daniel Burnham envisioned museums and civic buildings along the parkland, mail-order mogul Aaron Montgomery Ward sued to preserve its open stretches of land—and we're grateful that he did. Ward now has both a garden and a park in the River North neighborhood named after him in tribute to the cause he fought and its stunning green results.

HUMBOLDT PARK
1440 N. Sacramento Ave.
(312) 742-7549
www.chicagoparkdistrict.com

One of the parks outlined by William Le Baron Jenney in 1869 in a plan for the wide boulevards of Chicago, Humboldt Park was later designed by renowned landscape architect Jens Jensen. Located in the largely Puerto Rican far west side neighborhood that bears the same name, the park boasts several unique qualities, including a scenic stream and a lagoon with the city's only non-lakefront sandy beach—open to swimming and popular for its stocked fishing spots. The 207-acre park also features a circular and serene formal garden where you'll find a pair of bronze bisons that were originally cast for the 1893 World's Columbian Exposition. Visit the Chicago Park District website to download a self-guided audio tour of Humboldt Park that lasts about an hour and includes stopping points along the way. Just be careful if you go in the evening, as the park can get a bit edgy. Free. Open daily dawn till dusk.

INDIAN BOUNDARY PARK
2500 W. Lunt Ave.
(773) 764-0338
www.chicagoparkdistrict.com
You might miss this tucked-away park unless you live in the surrounding West Ridge neighborhood. But it's worth finding it. Besides typical parkland, you'll discover a lazy duck-filled lagoon and the 1929 Tudor-style field house designed by Clarence Hatzfield and now a Chicago Landmark and listed in the National Register of Historical Places. It's the site of numerous art and music classes, events, plays, and concerts. For kids of all ages, the wow factor comes when they get a glimpse of the castlelike wood play structure built by 1,500 community volunteers over 5 days in 1989. It's a maze of ins and outs, ups and downs, and nooks and crannies too small for grown-ups and perfect for imaginative kids (just know that after a rainy day, those crannies can get a bit muddy).

*JACKSON PARK
57th Street south to 67th Street
Stony Island Avenue east to Lake Shore Drive
(773) 256-0903
www.chicagoparkdistrict.com
Venturing along the paved paths and quaint bridges of the 600-acre Jackson Park reveals a welcomingly unkempt variety of woodland, prairie, shrubland, and several lagoons—anglers can find a shady, quiet spot for tossing a line here. The hum of cars whirring down adjacent Lake Shore Drive is drowned out by the voices of ducks, geese, and birds—bird-watching is big, in fact, with a count of about 250 species that make a migratory landing here. Keep walking and you'll come upon the Osaka Garden,

a Japanese-style garden that was originally envisioned by Frederick Law Olmsted in his landscape plan for the 1893 World's Columbian Exposition. After several dips into near disappearance and subsequent resurrections, the Osaka Garden is once again a lovely stop with decorative stones and bridges (some graffiti too, unfortunately). An 18-hole, par-70 golf course is located at Richards Drive (773-667-0524), and Jackson Park is also the east-side bookend to Washington Park, connected by the Midway Plaisance, the site of midway exhibits at the World's Fair. Though the attractions are all gone, if you look north, you'll get a backside view of the grand Museum of Science and Industry, the only remaining building built for the fair.

*LAKEFRONT TRAIL
Approximately from Hollywood Avenue south to 71st Street
(312) 742-PLAY (7529)
www.chicagoparkdistrict.com
Hit this 18½-mile paved linear path for a mostly uninterrupted stretch along the Lake Michigan shoreline. It connects neighborhoods from Rogers Park to Hyde Park for biking, running, walking, and marvelous people-watching. Wherever you pick up the path, you'll pass interesting sights: sunbathers lounging at beaches, games of recreational beach volleyball, pups bounding into the water to fetch balls at the doggie beach (Belmont Avenue), intense chess matches at the retro-styled chess pavilion (North Avenue), picnicking and grilling, dining at the only lakefront outdoor restaurant (Oak Street Beach Cafe; 312-915-4100), and views of the daredevil-piloted planes and jets of the annual summer Air and Water Show (see Events). Rent two-wheelers, tandem bikes, or four-person surrey bikes at several

stops along the way too. If you'd rather not compete for space on the fairly narrow trail (speedster cyclers can sometimes rule the road here), then we suggest you get out early when it's magically quiet and you can watch the sunrise over the lake.

i For information on joining organized runs along the Lakefront Trail, contact the Chicago Area Runner's Association at (312) 666-9836; www.cararuns.org. Find friends for cycling from the Chicagoland Bicycle Federation at (312) 427-3325; www.biketraffic.org.

LINCOLN PARK
Lakefront from Ardmore Avenue south to Ohio Street Beach
(312) 742-7726 (Lincoln Park Cultural Center)
www.chicagoparkdistrict.com

The mother of all Chicago parks, Lincoln Park extends for an impressive 1,208 acres along the lakeshore. First known as Lake Park, it was renamed in honor of the 16th president soon after his assassination in 1865 and includes several sections of landfill. It also encompasses the Lincoln Park Zoo and Lincoln Park Conservatory; numerous beaches, lagoons, harbors, and ponds; a golf course and a driving range; the Theatre on the Lake; several prominent statues (including one of Honest Abe himself); the Peggy Notebaert Nature Museum, and the Chicago History Museum.

i Check this out: Near Waveland Avenue east of Lake Shore Drive in Lincoln Park stands the 40-foot-tall Kwanusila Totem Pole. It was created in 1986 by Tony Hunt, the hereditary chief of the Kwakiutl tribe of Fort Rupert, British Columbia, and it's a replica of a 1929 pole that had deteriorated.

✳LURIE GARDEN
Southeastern edge of Millennium Park
(312) 742-1168
www.luriegarden.org

A 5-acre plot set aside amid the rest of the Millennium Park bustle, this urban oasis transforms with the seasons, each one displaying its own sense of beauty and life. Come in winter to enjoy the hush of freshly fallen snow and icicles that dot the 15-foot-high evergreen "shoulder" hedge— a symbolic nod to Carl Sandburg's famous description of Chicago as the "City of Big Shoulders." In spring, colorful bulbs emerge, along with happy honeybees and migratory birds. Summer bursts with a rainbow of splendid color; and fall brings a bounty of butterflies and gently swaying ornamental grasses. Two distinct areas—dubbed the "light" and "dark" plates for their contrasting types of growth—are divided by a diagonal pedestrian boardwalk that hovers over a series of stepped pools. Dip your toes in and breathe in the calm. Then get a bird's-eye view of the entire award-winning design as you stand atop the Nichols Bridgeway, which crosses Monroe Street to the Modern Wing of the Art Institute. Free. Open daily 6 a.m. to 11 p.m.

Learn about the thought behind the look of the Lurie Garden on a free 20-minute tour. Fri 11 a.m. to 1:30 p.m. and Sun 10 a.m. to 1:30 p.m. from May to Sept. Meet at the south end of the boardwalk.

MILLENNIUM PARK
201 E. Randolph St.
Between Michigan and Columbus Avenues
(312) 742-1168
www.millenniumpark.org

Built over what used to be a combination of plain ol' parkland, exposed subterranean rail yards, and parking lots, Millennium Park has arguably become Chicago's best big investment—we're talking $475 million of investment, just a wee bit over the originally estimated $150 million. But those cost overruns and 4-year construction delays are all just water under the Frank Gehry–designed BP Bridge now—technically, the bridge passes over Columbus Drive to the Daley Centennial Plaza. Chicagoans and visitors alike flock to Millennium Park for its urban green zone of grass and gardens, and for its interactive public art: *Cloud Gate* (nicknamed "The Bean"), the pair of water-spouting glass-block towers, the outdoor concert pavilion. Free (some activities incur a fee). Open daily 6 a.m. to 11 p.m. (Also see Attractions & Museums chapter.)

NORTHERLY ISLAND PARK
1400 S. Lynn White Dr.
(312) 742-PLAY
www.chicagoparkdistrict.com
After a controversial, middle-of-the-night destruction of its airstrips in 2003 orchestrated by the former Mayor Richard Daley, this once municipal airfield was reverted back to its original purpose as a natural habitat, now operated by the Chicago Park District. Jutting out into Lake Michigan as a 91-acre peninsula that parallels the shoreline, the parkland features strolling paths, and a field house that's open on weekends from November to April and daily during the late spring and summer. Several year-round festivals take place here as well, and Charter One Pavilion's temporary 7,500-seat outdoor stage is erected each summer for alfresco concerts. Get more information about the music venue in the Arts chapter.

✳NORTH PARK VILLAGE NATURE CENTER
5801 N. Pulaski Rd.
(312) 744-5472
www.chicagoparkdistrict.com
Once you discover this friendly 46-acre natural haven northwest of downtown, you'll return again and again for wanderings along rustic trails that weave through the nurtured savanna, wetlands, prairie, and woodlands. You'll have them practically to yourself on cool days, and on summer visits the beehives buzz with mesmerizing activity—watch them work up close, but not too personal, in the glass-enclosed hive inside the center's small main building. In here you'll also find a collection of fossils for hands-on exploration, and the library where children's books about nature and animals fill shelves of a cute nook, and a bin full of animal puppets provides mini-imaginations with all they need to put on a show through the curtains of a little play puppet theater. During special events like the maple festival, "city wilds," winter solstice, and harvest festival, a variety of folk bands, storytellers, arts and crafts, and outdoor vendor booths attract an increasing number of fans. Most events and activities are free. The nature center is typically open daily 10 a.m. to 4 p.m.

OZ PARK
2021 N. Burling St.
(312) 742-7898
www.chicagoparkdistrict.com
It may have been Hollywood that cemented the fame of L. Frank Baum with the 1939 silver-screen version of his book *The Wonderful Wizard of Oz*, but he called the Windy City his home in the late 19th century. This park is a few miles east of where he settled and pays homage to his legacy, not only with

its name, but four sculptures that mark the boundaries of the park, designed by artist John Kearney over the course of about a dozen years. The first to come was the Tin Man in 1995, unique in that it's constructed of old car parts. The others—the Scarecrow, Cowardly Lion, and the universal favorite, Dorothy & Toto—are all made of bronze. A baseball diamond, basketball court, small walking path, and the aptly titled Dorothy's Playlot and lovely Emerald Garden complete the celebration of this beloved author.

PING TOM MEMORIAL PARK
300 W. 19th St.
(312) 746-5962
www.pingtompark.org
Before Chinatown's late civic leader and life-long resident Ping Tom rallied to establish some parkland in Chinatown, it didn't have much. Now, this tranquil 13-acre riverfront park, a reuse of an old railroad yard, features a playground, picnicking areas, and a decidedly distinct Chinese style of landscaping, including pagoda-like covered shelters. Five more acres were recently acquired, with plans that include developing water access for boats, fishing opportunities, and a parking facility.

WASHINGTON PARK
Cottage Grove Avenue west to Martin Luther King Jr. Drive
51st Street south to 60th Street
(773) 256-1248
www.chicagoparkdistrict.com
The western partner to Jackson Park (separated by the wide Midway Plaisance), Washington Park fills a 371-acre expanse and features Lorado Taft's epic *Fountain of Time* sculpture. Listed on the National Register of Historic Places, it is also home to the DuSable Museum of African American History.

BEACHES

63RD STREET BEACH
6300 S. Lake Shore Dr.
(312) 742-PLAY (7529)
www.chicagoparkdistrict.com
This Jackson Park beach stands out for its landmark beach house, a 1919 cast-in-place concrete Classical Revival pavilion that was renovated in recent years, using an aggregate from quarries that produced the same kind of stone that originally created its exterior. An added courtyard fountain provides summer fun for kids and a scenic backdrop to weddings that are often held here.

☀FOSTER AVENUE BEACH
5200 N. Lake Shore Dr.
(312) 742-5121
www.chicagoparkdistrict.com
For east and west coasters looking for a beach worthy of their oceanfront partners, Foster Avenue Beach obliges with a decent spread of sand, big enough for tossing a Frisbee and for families to spread out their blankets, buckets, and sand toys. And though the sand was dumped here as fill, it's appreciated by bathers for its texture—softer than the rockier sand that's found naturally along the shore. Upping the comfort level are a new-ish beach house with decent enough bathroom facilities and loads of grassy areas for laying down picnics. Groups planning on staying all day often tote in full-on tables, tents, chairs, and grills. There's parking at a small lot and along the street here, but don't plan on getting any of it if you get here later than about 11 a.m. in the summertime.

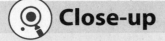 **Close-up**

Feathered Friends

A happy accident led to one of the city's best bird-watching hideaways. During the height of the Cold War era of the 1950s through the 1970s, the US Army leased a tucked-away spot at Montrose Beach to hide Nike missiles—they planted honeysuckle to aid the ruse. By the time the Army vacated, birds had already decided this was a lovely place to take a breather. The land happens to extend into Lake Michigan, making it even more attractive for the flyers. Pretty soon, bird-watchers caught on, tiptoed in and have been returning ever since to catch sight of up to 300 different species of birds. It's been nicknamed, appropriately, the **Magic Hedge,** for its magical pull for both birds and birders alike. A little further east lies yet another surprise of Mother Nature: the **Montrose Beach Dunes** that formed because beach maintenance crews couldn't quite get to it, so it was left alone, with beautiful results. Here, too, birds and other wildlife thrive. Don't forget your binoculars. Get here via the Montrose Avenue exit off Lake Shore Drive or the Lakefront Trail; (312) 742-PLAY; www.chicagoparkdistrict.com.

NORTH AVENUE BEACH
1600 N. Lake Shore Dr.
(312) 742-PLAY (7529)
www.chicagoparkdistrict.com
Hands-down the city's most popular beach, the expansive North Avenue teems with 20-somethings who come to ogle and be ogled. But it's also action-packed with loads of sand volleyball courts (a frequent site of tournaments), a roller hockey rink, the annual Air and Water Show, the Polar Plunge (for the brave—or crazy), a chess pavilion, bike rentals, and typically an outdoor workout facility in the summer. You can even grab some quick eats here at the concessions of the ship-shaped red, white, and blue beach house whose rooftop Castaways Bar and Grill (773-281-1200) has a happening summer happy-hour scene.

OAK STREET BEACH
1000 N. Lake Shore Dr.
(312) 742-5121
www.chicagoparkdistrict.com

It's not just the sand that's hot here. We're talking hot bods and those who appreciate them. That's why, despite its petite size, Oak Street is considered the most fashionable and most famous of Chicago's beaches, and it makes sense, being right off the Magnificent Mile. In fact, it's about as close to South Beach as Chicago gets—complete with several dozen palm trees imported from Miami and stuck right into the sand. The benefit over Florida? No sharks. If you're not working on your tan, you might be working out, as Oak Street is a favored triathlon training ground because of its expanse of deep water. You'll also find the only beachfront restaurant here, the Oak Street Beach Cafe.

BIKING

ACTIVE TRANSPORTATION ALLIANCE
9 W. Hubbard St., Ste. 402
(312) 427-3325
www.activetrans.org

By "active transportation," they mean by foot, bike, and public transportation. They advocate for it by helping to create legislation that protects cyclists, pedestrians, and transit riders; and they support it by organizing bicycling clubs and developing more bike trails and better sidewalks; and they simply celebrate the cycling life with events like Chicago's Memorial Day weekend annual Bike the Drive (www.bikethedrive.org), which closes down Lake Shore Drive to cars, allowing cyclists to take a turn for a change.

CHICAGO CYCLING CLUB
Various locations
(773) 509-8093
www.chicagocyclingclub.org
Established in 1994, the CCC offers about 200 different rides generally about three or more times each week from April through October; there are also winter rides on Christmas and New Year's Day. They range from leisurely social tools around town with rest stops and meals, to longer and faster rides for cyclists in training. Monthly meetings offer up bike tech tips and socializing with spoke-minded folks. Membership is $20 for individuals, $25 for families. Meetings occur at various Chicago locations; check the website for updated information

ICE SKATING

MCCORMICK TRIBUNE ICE RINK
Millennium Park
At Michigan Avenue between
Washington and Madison Streets
(312) 742-1168
www.millenniumpark.org
New York has Rockefeller Center; Chicago has Millennium Park. Each winter, an ice rink

pops up along the Michigan Avenue side of the park, and skaters line up to figure-eight—or slowly shuffle—their way around the small oval rink. With the city at your toes, it makes for perhaps the most exciting skating rink in town. Skating has historically been free, though that might change in the future; skate rental is $10 or just bring your own pair. Open daily during winter.

MCFETRIDGE SPORTS CENTER
3843 N. California Ave.
(773) 478-2609
www.chicagoparkdistrict.com
This active rec center features the Chicago Park District's only indoor ice-skating rink. Whether hosting ice-hockey games, ice-dancing rehearsals, or beginning ice-skating lessons, this rink is always hot. Named for a former park district president, McFetridge also boasts the park district's sole indoor tennis courts. Open daily.

MIDWAY PLAISANCE PARK
1130 Midway Plaisance (east 59th Street
at Woodlawn Avenue)
(312) 745-2470
www.chicagoparkdistrict.com
An outdoor ice-skating rink (inline skating in summer) lies just where the first Ferris wheel once stood as part of the 1893 World's Columbian Exposition. The Midway Plaisance, the broad band of greenery that connects Washington and Jackson parks, was part of the grounds for this World's Fair. It held midway amusements, restaurants, international exhibits, and more. It's now a popular spot for strolling and exercising— and ice skating.

RINK AT WRIGLEY
Corner of Clark Street and Waveland Avenue
(312) 617-7017
www.rinkatwrigley.com
What's an urban baseball stadium to do during the winter? Open a skating rink in the parking lot. That's what Wrigley Field did a couple of years ago, and it's been a home run with fans. It may not be the biggest rink in the world, but it's the most spirited. Admission Mon through Thurs is $5, $3 for children; Fri through Sun $10, $6 for children. Call or check the website for hours.

SOCIAL SPORTS CLUBS

CHICAGO SPORT & SOCIAL CLUB
770 N. Halsted St., Ste. 306
(312) 850-8196
www.chicagosocial.com
Get your game on and register for one of the thousands of teams for everything from basketball to soccer, kickball to softball, and the world's largest beach volleyball league—more than 20,000 participants in 1,200 teams nearly every summer take to the sands of Montrose, North Avenue, and Oak Street beaches. Plus, when you join as a team or individual, you're one of the 75,000 members privy to year-round social and charity events to fill your social calendar. So go ahead and suit up or drink up, or both. Fees vary per sport and event.

PLAYERS SPORTS GROUP
3617 N. Ashland Ave.
(773) 528-1999
www.playerssports.net
This sports club has grown to more than 45,000 players since its beginnings in 1993, and now offers a variety of sports leagues that change per season and include the expected, like basketball, tennis, softball, and the offbeat such as cornhole and dodgeball, plus several tournaments, and plenty of opportunities to mix and mingle. You have to be age 19 and up to play in a variety of levels, and 21 to partake in the social activities. Fees vary per sport and event.

SPORTS MONSTER
4237 N. Western Ave.
(773) 866-2955
www.sportsmonster.net
This Chicago outpost of the 15-city-strong company features a range of sports leagues including basketball, broomball, bowling, ultimate Frisbee, soccer, and volleyball, as well as classes and clinics for activities such as running, rock climbing, and dancing. Consider yourself more of a Muppet than a monster? No worries. All levels are welcome. Plus, Sports Monster promotes individual registration as much as team registration. Fees vary per sport and event; membership fee too.

WINDY CITY FIELDHOUSE
2367 W. Logan Blvd.
(773) 486-7421
www.windycityfieldhouse.com/sports
In addition to hosting outside companies' league events, this huge, multipurpose, warehouse-size facility runs some of its own, both recreational and competitive, and at all levels. Join as an individual or round up the crew for a team. Fees vary.

CHICAGO GOLF COURSES

DIVERSEY DRIVING RANGE
141 W. Diversey Pkwy.
(312) 742-7929
www.cpdgolf.com

Convenient to downtown and right off Lake Shore Drive, this dual-level driving range is located on a scenic stretch of Lincoln Park within sight of Lake Michigan. It's open no matter the weather, and when the weather's right for wimpy golfers, it's packed. It's fairly no-frills, though it has been improved over the years and boasts heating lamps and has a parking lot. Club rental and lessons are available. Buckets $9 for 50 balls and $14 for 100. The $25 Advantage Card takes $1 off each bucket.

DIVERSEY MINIATURE GOLF
141 W. Diversey Pkwy.
(312) 742-7929
www.cpdgolf.com

Practice your putts at this popular 18-hole mini golf course associated with and adjacent to the Diversey Driving Range. It's not super-fancy, but it's clean family fun and has a couple of challenging moments (as well as the oft-errant wood chip from the surrounding park). Admission $8 (with Advantage Card $7); seniors and children 17 and under $6. Open daily.

JACKSON PARK
6401 S. Richards Dr.
(773) 667-0524
www.cpdgolf.com

Chicago's only 18-hole public course lies amid mature trees within historic Jackson Park and makes use of every club in your bag. At 5,463 yards, the par-72 course features par 5s that top out at 560 yards down to par 3s at about 200 yards. Complaints aside that include noise from kids playing at fields nearby, sub-par maintenance, slow-moving players (i.e., beginners, so give them some slack), several streets to cross, and dodging goose droppings, this is a fine

facility for a price that really can't be beat. Its renovated clubhouse rents power carts and offers quick concessions, and there's a driving range here too. Course rates are $20 on weekdays, seniors and juniors rate (available with Advantage Card only) $15, twilight games $17; weekends are $23 for all, twilight games $18. Open daily.

ROBERT A. BLACK GOLF COURSE
2045 W. Pratt Blvd.
(312) 742-7931
www.cpdgolf.com

Up north and tucked away a bit, this 9-hole, par-33 course presents a perfect outing for groups and golfers working on their game. It plays at a medium speed, with wide fairways and fairly flat terrain; no water, but sand bunkers offer extra challenge. Course rates are $19 weekdays, $14 with Advantage Card; seniors and juniors rate (with Advantage Card only) $10; weekends $21, $16 with Advantage Card; seniors and juniors (with Advantage Card only) $16. Open daily.

*SYDNEY R. MAROVITZ
3600 N. Recreation Dr.
(312) 742-7930
www.cpdgolf.com

The lake breeze can be a lovely thing or a challenging factor of this par-36 course—call it the Waveland course if you want to sound like a local—that parallels Lake Michigan for 3,240 yards. Tee up early (we're talking before sunrise) and you'll get in your 9 holes within a couple of hours; after that, it often gets frustratingly slow on warm days. But it still remains a favorite. A ladies' league forms during the summer. Course rates are $23 weekdays, $18 with Advantage Card; seniors and juniors rate (with Advantage

Card only) $11; weekends $26; $21 for all with Advantage Card. Open daily.

TENNIS

CHICAGO PARK DISTRICT COURTS
(312) 742-PLAY (7529)
www.chicagoparkdistrict.com
Under the Chicago Park District umbrella are dozens of outdoor tennis courts. They vary in number and quality, but they are a treat for all levels of players. Some popular spots include Athletic Field Park (at Lake Shore Drive and Addison Street, 773-478-2889), McFetridge Sports Center (California near Irving Park Drive, 773-478-2609), and downtown's Daley Bicentennial Plaza (Randolph Street and Columbus Drive, 312-742-7648). Rates vary from free on up.

CHITOWN TENNIS LEAGUE
www.chitowntennis.com
Didn't quite make it to Wimbledon this year? That's OK. You can be the winner of your local tourney on a ChiTown tennis league. Just join online and ChiTown hooks you up with like-minded players, and coordinates schedules and playoff season on local courts from spring through summer. Not so much into the competitive aspect? Join the Partner Program and you'll be connected with up to 20 players who match your skill level and are close enough to you to meet up. You can even request doubles. With such service—and annual donations from the company based on a percentage of profits to the Cancer Research Institute—what's not to, ahem, love? $16 to $35 to join, depending on the program.

✳MIDTOWN TENNIS CLUB
2020 W. Fullerton Ave.
(773) 235-2300
www.midtown.com
The number-one name for year-round tennis in a decidedly not-year-round tennis town, Midtown boasts a generous 18 indoor courts, plus platform tennis and a dedicated tennis practice space. It's an immaculate and highly regarded facility for top players including the likes of Andre Agassi, Billie Jean King, and Venus Williams, who have all torn up the courts here. And the club is just as welcoming for beginners—of all ages. The extensive junior instruction program starts kids as young as 3 in the USTA-created 10-and-under tennis system, while the Tennis in No Time program pulls in adults (it's great for meeting people) for a refresher or to develop new skills. Some lessons are open to nonmembers, but membership gets you access to the fitness center, kids' club, Pilates classes, and more. The pro shop can sell you a racquet or just string yours. Bonus for Chicago: There's free parking.

WATER SPORTS

CHICAGO RIVER CANOE & KAYAK
Chicago: (773) 704-2663; Skokie
Lagoons: (847) 414-5883
www.chicagoriverpaddle.com
Rentals, guided paddles, canoe and kayak lessons, and even 4-week cardio kayak workout classes are organized by this established outfit. City sightseeing trips take you on a semi-strenuous 6-mile kayak trip through the skyscraper "canyon" of downtown, while the easier Moonlight Dinner Paddle guides participants up to a riverfront park for a pleasant picnic meal. Other tours start from the Skokie Lagoons and traverse this scenic

wildlife waterway. Rentals are $15 an hour for a single, $20 per hour for a tandem. Lessons and tour prices vary; cardio classes $80 for first-time joiners, $50 for returning. Generally running from late Apr through early Oct.

CHICAGO SAILING
Dock B, Belmont Harbor North
3526 N. Recreation Dr.
(773) 871-7245
www.chicagosailing.com
This enthusiastic, 20-plus-year-old company helps start beginning skippers on their sailing journey, and helps more advanced sailors polish up their rusty skills. Mix and mingle with your fellow mateys at the floating Club Sail events held several times a week, including Tuesday night's cookout; or book a luxury charter for a laid-back personal cruise. For those who've already got the nautical know-how, you can also rent from among the fleet. Prices vary.

CHICAGO YACHT CLUB
400 E. Monroe St.
(312) 861-7777
Belmont Station: 300 W. Belmont Ave.
(773) 477-7575
Sailing School: (773) 477-4952
www.chicagoyachtclub.org
Founded in 1875, the Chicago Yacht Club now ranks as one of the oldest and definitely one of the best regarded yacht clubs in the world. Besides more than 100 races, social events, and club activities that it runs, there's a top-notch sailing school, which provides

lessons throughout the summer for juniors and adults. Pricing varies.

KAYAK CHICAGO
(630) 336-7245
www.kayakchicago.com
With more than 20 years of kayaking experience and even more as an avid outdoorsman, Dave Olson sets the right course for kayak tours and lessons. Get out on a Fireworks Paddle to ooh and ahh at Navy Pier's weekly summer pyrotechnics from the quiet of the Chicago River. The Architectural Tour gives you a little history for your efforts, and the Lake Paddle gets you offshore with views of the skyline. For something a little different, try out paddleboarding. Rent recreational kayaks with no prior experience, or sea or surf kayaks if you've already passed the appropriate classes. Pricing varies.

WATERIDERS
950 N. Kingsbury (north end of the Riverwalk)
(312) 953-WATR (9287)
www.wateriders.com
New downtown evening and Evanston Historical Lakefront kayak paddles add to this outfit's lineup of Chicago River tours, which feature narration of some architectural, gangster-era, and historical facts about Chicago. All levels are welcome, and if you want to toughen those muscles, join the kayak workouts on Monday and Tuesday evenings. A wide range of kayak rentals are also offered. Pricing varies.

SPECTATOR SPORTS

A longtime baseball fan once told me that he didn't root for one Chicago baseball team over the other, because it was so rare to have two Major League teams in one town that we should be happy if either does well. That makes so much sense, though not too many locals are bound to follow it—Chicagoans do love their cross-town rivalry between the South Side Sox and North Side Cubs. But it's true. Chicago is lucky to have two baseball clubs, each boasting huge fan bases, despite only a few championship wins between them over the years. We also have incredible (at least for watching, if not winning) professional basketball, football, soccer, and hockey teams, all well supported, well loved, and well attended. Women's sports are gaining ground here too, and not too far from the city are a horse-racing track and a NASCAR raceway. It's easy to get caught up in the enthusiasm at a live game whether you're a die-hard fan or one-time watcher. If you're root, root, rooting for the home team, we're right there with you; and if you're cheering on the opposing team, then just don't tell us.

BASEBALL

CHICAGO CUBS
Wrigley Field
1060 W. Addison St.
(773) 404-CUBS (2827)
www.chicagocubs.com

As much about the stadium they play in as the team itself, the National League Chicago Cubs have held a special place in the hearts of Chicagoans (predominately those living on the North Side) for decades. Affectionately nicknamed the Lovable Losers for their persistent World Series-less record since 1908, they attract swarms of positive-thinkers who try to convince themselves that "This is the year," along with legions of visitors who come to experience a game at the "friendly confines," the second-oldest ballpark in Major League Baseball. Seating capacity is about 41,000, and it's typically sold out (unless they're not doing well and it's a cold day in May), including the famous bleachers that leave attendees baking in the sun (bring a hat if these are your seats). If it's your first time to the stadium, head over to Fan Services for a special commemorative photo. The Cubs have seen many outstanding players, including Sammy Sosa, Mark Grace, Ryne Sandberg, Ernie Banks, Billy Williams, and Ron Santo (the latter three have statues at the field). And truly, most games are a good time whether the team wins or loses. Beer, Vienna-beef hot dogs, the changed-by-hand scoreboard, and the 7th-inning stretch with its rousing round of "Take Me Out to the Ballgame"—a nod to the late great Cubs announcer Harry Caray, whose image also graces a Wrigley statue. If you can't get game tix, grab a seat at the onsite Captain Morgan Club (773-404-4750), as close to the action as you can get and where you can still share the action amid a rowdy crowd. Or take a stadium tour (see Attractions for more tour information). Individual game tickets range from $8 to well over $100, depending on the opponent and seat selection. Street parking is hard to come by with resident permit-only parking in the closest vicinity. You can order parking passes online for the small Cubs-run lots, and you can find plenty of neighboring residents and business owners charging to park in their own lots, but we recommend taking the Red Line El train, which stops practically on top of the stadium at the Addison stop and, on game days, is practically a party on board. The Cubs season starts early April and either ends early October or continues beyond that (fans always have fingers crossed). Read more about Wrigley Field in the Attractions & Museums chapter.

CHICAGO WHITE SOX
US Cellular Field
333 W. 35th St.
www.chicago.whitesox.mlb.com
Nostalgia at a White Sox game was lost when the South Side team's 80-year-old Old Comiskey Park was scrapped for its flashy new, 41,000-plus-seat stadium in 1991. But the White Sox still have one huge up on the Chicago Cubs—a World Series title. It came in 2005 under manager Ozzie Guillen who was in charge of the American League club until near the end of the 2011 season. It also helped erase the scar of its old 1919 betting scandal that led to the team's notorious past nickname, the Black Sox. These days, games at "the Cell" offer fan-friendly extras like water spritzers for cooling down on hot days; a kids' area with baseball clinics, batting cages, and practice pitching areas (sneakers necessary); the Speed Pitch to test your tossing speed; fun photo-ops with player cut-outs; and the White Sox legends sculpture plaza featuring Minnie Minoso, Carlton Fisk, Charles Comiskey himself, and others. Concessions here offer up the standard dogs and suds, but also venture into veggie burgers, deli sandwiches, quesadillas, ice cream, and the Rookie's Club, serving up kid faves like PB&J. Individual tickets range from about $15 to $90, depending on day, time, and opponent—the most expensive seats are for Chicago's famous Cross-Town Classic rivalry games against the North Side Chicago Cubs that decide which crowd can go home crowing. Parking in official lots is $23, but we suggest the Red Line El train, which takes you within walking distance at its 35th Street stop; the Green Line is just a couple of blocks east of the Red Line; and the Metra now has a stop at 35th Street along its Rock Island Line. The Sox season runs from early April through September, or longer if they make it to another playoff.

BASKETBALL

CHICAGO BULLS
United Center
1901 W. Madison St.
(312) 455-4000
www.nba.com/bulls
Entering the NBA for the 1966 to '67 season, the Bulls were a struggling-to-fair and occasionally top team that won a couple of Division titles. Then came the mid-1980s and all that changed with a rookie named Michael Jordan. Almost immediately, Jordan became the team's greatest player—and soon acknowledged as arguably the greatest of all time. Together with fellow Basketball Hall of Fame inductee Scottie Pippen, Jordan led the Bulls to three consecutive NBA championships before he retired from basketball and tried his athletic prowess at pro baseball instead. Chicago gave

him a mammoth send-off, then welcomed him back with equal enthusiasm when he decided to return to his first love. He proved himself again with three more titles before saying good-bye for good—and leaving a legacy that includes a retired jersey number (23, which also appears on a grand gate outside his suburban Chicago residence), a mile-long list of records and firsts, and a mystique that continues to follow him and the team he put on the global sports map. While the Bulls may not have that much "air" anymore, it still has players that impress and still puts up a high-energy game at the vast United Center, the largest arena in the US and also home to the Chicago Blackhawks. Besides the 20,000-plus stadium seats, there are a slew of swanky suites, including day-of-event rental and executive suites. Score a shot (of the photograph kind, that is) with the b-ball god himself at the Michael Jordan statue. Tickets range from as low as $10 on up to about $950 (children under 36 inches tall are free, but must sit on a lap), with an average being about $50 to $70—prices fluctuate depending on the opponent. During the season, the box office is open Mon through Sat from 11 a.m. to 6 p.m. and through halftime on all game days. Paid parking is available at United Center lots; #19 United Center Express CTA buses can also take you from downtown to the stadium, and some bars offer shuttle service.

FOOTBALL

CHICAGO BEARS
Soldier Field
1410 S. Museum Campus Dr. (at Lake Shore Drive)
(847) 615-BEAR (2327)
www.chicagobears.com

Regardless of whether you cheer or boo the newfangled Soldier Field stadium that debuted in 2003—sometimes described as looking like a spaceship landed inside the original 1924-built, Greek-colonnaded structure—fans can't wait to get there for a game by their beloved Bears. The North Division "Monsters of the Midway" have been playing at Soldier Field since they moved here from Wrigley Field in 1971. They've become famous for many things including the player they called Sweetness (the late Walter Payton) and his 13 seasons as the team's leading rusher, among other amazing feats. They're known for their Super Bowl XX win in 1986 and the hoopla before and after that it spurred (did you know the Super Bowl Shuffle got a Grammy nomination?). They're remembered for their hot-tempered former coach Mike Ditka, their rabid fans, and their epic tailgating. Individual tickets are sold through Ticketmaster (if you can score one at all) and at StubHub.com, where season ticket-holders resell their tickets for prices that range from about $75 to $385 (children under 32 inches tall are free, but are required to receive a lap pass, available at Gate 10; strollers are prohibited). Tickets typically go on sale in July for the season. Parking is $46 in Museum Campus lots. The Bears take to the gridiron starting early September and continue through early January and longer depending on their standing. In other words, it's almost always cold during games, so if you're going, dress warmer than you think you should.

ℹ️ Go behind the pigskin action on Soldier Field tours that take you to the field, the Doughboy memorial statue, the United Club, the famous original colonnades, and the visitors' locker room. Tickets $15; seniors $7; children 10 and over $10, children 9 to 4 $4; free for kids 3 and under. Check the website for upcoming dates.

ICE HOCKEY

CHICAGO BLACKHAWKS
United Center
1901 W. Madison St.
(312) 455-7000
www.chicagoblackhawks.com
When the Central Division NHL Blackhawks won the Stanley Cup in 2010, Chicago celebrated with a fan-tabulous ticker-tape parade that attracted more than 2 million people. It was actually the fourth title the team has taken home since debuting in 1926, but the first since 1961. It certainly solidified the Hawks' reputation as a team to be reckoned with, and it also grew in esteem in the sports-happy Windy City, which had a fairly negative view of the team during much of the 1990s and into the early 21st century—not only because they lost so much, but because late owner Bill Wirtz had enacted strange and strangling policies like no televised home games in Chicago. We're glad that era's over; when Wirtz died, his son, Rocky, took over and swiftly turned things around, boosting the team into a winning franchise and winning over fans with loads of marketing, televised games, and light-hearted extras like Zamboni races and games played at an iced-over Wrigley Field. Tickets start at $40 ($27 for standing room) and go up from there the closer you get to

the rink. The Hawks play typically from late September through early April, with playoffs potentially extending that.

SOCCER

CHICAGO FIRE
Toyota Park
7000 Harlem Ave., Bridgeview
(888) MLS-FIRE (657-3473)
www.chicago-fire.com
One of the newer additions to Chicago's sports scene, the Chicago Fire made its Major League Soccer debut in 1998—its formation was announced on October 8, 1997, the 126th anniversary of the Great Chicago Fire of 1871. They've been smoking hot ever since, with an MLS Cup Championship their first year out, plus conference and division championships as well. Although the stadium is a bit far afield, the fiery fandom offers a taste of that wild European football sensibility. Tickets range from $15 to $70 (and $225 for field-side). Tailgating is free. The Fire takes to the field from March through October.

INDOOR FOOTBALL

CHICAGO RUSH
Allstate Arena
6920 N. Mannheim Rd., Rosemont
(855) 787-4946
www.arenarush.com
Co-owned by 'da Bears former coach Mike Ditka, this Arena Football League team might not have the huge fan base of the Bears, but it may have a happier one. After all, game-goers aren't numb from the cold, the shorter 50-yard field means way more reason to jump out of your seats with excitement (scores regularly get to numbers like 50 or 60), the smaller stadium gets you

much closer to the action, the tight-skirted Adrenaline Rush cheerleaders attract roars of approval, and tickets don't cost an arm and a leg. Tickets $10 to $60. Parking ranges from $11 to $20; tailgating doesn't cost anything. The season runs from mid-March through late July.

CHICAGO SLAUGHTER

Sears Centre Arena
5333 Prairie Stone Pkwy., Hoffman Estates
Ticket hotline: (888) 732-7784, Slaughter front office: (847) 310-3190
www.chicagoslaughter.com
Part of the 22 current teams of the Indoor Football League, which formed from a 2008 merger between the Intense Football League and the United Indoor Football Association, the Slaughter was founded in 2006 and joined the IFL in 2010. Former Bears Football star Jim McMahon is an owner. Beyond the play, there's a pre-game hour of kid-friendly festivities including a bounce house, face-painting, live bands, and visits with the mascot, Sarge. Stick around after the game, too, for autographs on the field from the players, coaches, and Slaughter Girls. Tickets $8 to $35; tailgating is free and, as they say, "encouraged" (don't be surprised if a coach or player stops by for a burger). Home games typically take place mid-February through mid-June.

WOMEN'S SPORTS

CHICAGO BANDITS

Rosemont Stadium
27 Jennie Finch Way (Bryn Mawr Ave. and Pearl St.), Rosemont
(877) 7BANDIT (722-6348)
www.chicagobandits.com

This fastpitch softball team started off with a bang in 2005, taking home title of Regular Season Champions and then snagging a Championship Series victory in 2008. It probably didn't hurt that the owners had early on recruited four Olympic players, including gold medalists Leah O'Brien-Amico and Jennie Finch, who was named USA Softball Athlete of the Year in 2009—though she retired in 2010. With her 6-foot-2 blond and leggy looks, Finch is still something of a fastpitch poster girl (notice the stadium address); she now holds fastpitch camps across the country. The Bandits got a brand-new stadium for the 2011 season, making it the first professional softball stadium in the Chicagoland area. The women's windmill-style pitches really are super speedy, hitting upwards of 75 miles per hour (equivalent to 100 miles per hour for baseball), which make games a kick to watch, along with the close-to-the-action feel (capacity is about 2,000), and post-game autograph sessions. Tickets $9.75 to $13.25 for a single game (group discounts are available—group ticket prices run $7 to $9.50). The season starts in June and runs through August.

CHICAGO SKY

Allstate Arena
6920 N. Mannheim Rd., Rosemont
(866) SKY-WNBA
www.chicagosky.net
The Chicago Sky came on as an expansion team to the Eastern WNBA conference in 2005; its team name and logo were announced, fittingly, at the Adler Planetarium. In such a sports-crazy town like Chicago, it was about time that we had a team in the WNBA, which was founded nearly a decade earlier in 1996. Early investors included Michelle Williams of Destiny's Child

fame and Beyoncé Knowles' father, Matthew Knowles. Although the Sky have yet to soar to championship heights, they score big with fans who enjoy the quick pace of the two 20-minute halves and simply appreciate the team's talented women who wow audiences with their powerhouse dunks, slams, jumps, and steals. Plus, the players get high points off the court for their charitable Chicago Sky Cares Foundation, which helps build girls' self-esteem and positive self-image by partnering with area organizations like the Girl Scouts and Girls on the Run. Tickets $15 to $500 (most in the $15 to $40 range). Season from early June through mid-September.

WINDY CITY ROLLERS
UIC Pavilion
525 S. Racine Ave.
(312) 413-5740
www.windycityrollers.com
Ruth Enasia, Yvette Yourmaker, Beth Amphetamine, Karmageddon, Deb Autry, Mya Ssault, Sargentina. These are some of the whimsically fear-inducing assumed names of Chicago's roller derby queens. Believe it or not, the Windy City team is one of nearly 90 across the country in four different regions, all part of the recently formed Women's Flat Track Derby Association. With their wicked moves, lightning-fast feet, blocks, whips, and merciless knock-downs, this game is one of the wildest to watch. Brains, brawn, and beauty all in one high-octane event. Tickets $22 with facility fee; students and seniors $15; children 12 and under $10; track-side seats available at $15 to $35.

HORSE RACING

ARLINGTON PARK RACETRACK
2200 Euclid Ave., Arlington Heights
General: (847) 385-7500;
tickets: (847) 385-7427
www.arlingtonpark.com
It's a good bet you'll have a grand time at this historic horse-racing facility—and you'll barely make a dent in your purse with tickets starting less than $5. Arlington opened in 1927 and held the world's first million-dollar race, the now-famous Arlington Million, in 1981. Tragedy struck in 1985 when the grandstand burned down, but crews managed to erect a temporary structure and the Million, nicknamed the Miracle Million that year, was held here for its fifth run. Making it through a couple of closures, buyouts, new beginnings, and big-time races—the 2002 Breeders' Cup marked its Midwest debut here—Arlington has come out ahead. It's not only because of its beautiful park setting, top-notch amenities, and live racing schedule, but also for its busy calendar of family-friendly events and promotions, from post-race concerts to giveaways, Father's Day barbecues to Independence Day fireworks. General admission tickets—which include access to the Grandstand and the Park—range from $4 to $15 depending on the race, while seating adds to that price, and Arlington Million seat tickets range from $25 to $100. General parking is free; preferred parking ($5) and value ($10) are also available. Check the track's online tips on which parking area is closest to your seats. Racing runs from early May through late September.

RACING

CHICAGOLAND SPEEDWAY & ROUTE 66 RACEWAY

500 Speedway Blvd., Joliet
Speedway: (888) 629-RACE (7223);
Raceway (815) 727-RACE
www.chicagolandspeedway.com

On its sprawling 930 acres, the nearly 70,000-seat Speedway, which celebrated its 10th anniversary during its 2011 season, features a 1.5-mile, D-shaped, tri-oval track for NAS-CAR Sprint Cup, NASCAR Nationwide, and NASCAR Camping World Truck Series events; the Route 66 is a quarter-mile drag strip and half-mile dirt oval track. Together, these sister tracks comprise 1,300 acres of racing and offer full-throttle action for season ticket-holders and now single-day ticket-holders. Head to Champions Park for pre-race revving up, as you browse the monuments in honor of the winners of the Speedway's NASCAR Sprint Cup and IndyCar Series since the Speedway opened. Got a little Mario Andretti in you? Get behind the driver's seat with the NASCAR Racing Experience or Mario Andretti Racing Experience (877-722-3527), and the Richard Petty Driving Experience (800-237-3889). Single-day tickets $16.50 to $140 depending on the race. Open during events; check for schedule.

KIDSTUFF

There's a ban on bored kids in Chicago. Well, maybe not officially, but there might as well be. Just take a look at all the options. It's a list you can't help but love. With more families choosing to stay in the city rather than move out to the suburbs, the choices just keep getting better too. That's not to say that the suburbs aren't allowed in the chapter—there are some amazing attractions within a half hour or so of down-town that are definitely kid-crowd-pleasers. So whether you've got a 2-year-old who goes gaga for princesses or an 8-year-old who bends it like Beckham, there's a place for them in this city made for fun.

OVERVIEW

It was tough to find a way to break up this kid list into meaningful groups. The first one is admittedly a fusion of fun stuff, so be sure to scan all the entries, because they range from the ever-popular American Girl Place, to an art-centric destination outside the city meant for mini mess-makers, to a mammoth amusement park. Other categories cover sports classes, perfect for families who are relocating; children's theater and music; and attractions with a focus on young visitors. We've tried to include all current hours and pricing, but as these tend to change, it's always good to call or check online first. Some favored spots for birthdays may close if there's a private party, while some have seasonally dependent hours of operation. We know that traveling with kids can often mean traveling with their unwieldy strollers too, but many of these kid-oriented locations do offer stroller parking; it's worth calling to find that out before you discover that you are forced to leave it outside. Some places boost the fun factor with special events like live bands, appearances by costumed story characters,

or even moms' nights out (also good to check calendars for special events like these). A few of these spots require at least a half a day to fully enjoy, particularly those that are beyond the city, while some of these spots are perfect for squeezing into a busy schedule.

FANTASY & PURE FUN

AMERICAN GIRL PLACE
Water Tower Place
835 N. Michigan Ave.
(877) 247-5223
www.americangirl.com
Guys, this one's for the dolls. This Mag Mile store was the company's first retail location and is now one of 11 in the country. You can't avoid the merchandise mania here, and the prices are high for items like match-ing doll and girl clothes, doll furniture and accessories, books, posters, and of course, more dolls—personal shoppers are avail-able to help fill your basket. But if you want to limit the number of bright red American Girl shopping bags you leave with, then just

Online Resources

www.chicagokids.com: An excellent, frequently updated calendar of events and list of resources for everything from birthday party spaces to kid classes.

www.chicagoparent.com: The online component to the popular free magazine, with articles from each issue, plus parent bloggers, news, contents and giveaways, and more.

www.dailycandy.com/kids/chicago: From the phenomenon that is Daily Candy, this hip and happening site highlights one fabulous product, service, event, or place every day and shoots it out to email subscribers.

www.kidgrade.com/chicago: Where moms and dads can review and read reviews of places to eat, shop, and play with your kids—or, as descriptions and ratings may reveal, to leave little ones at home.

www.npnparents.com: A membership organization dedicated to connecting families throughout the city, from expectant parents to those with elementary-age children and beyond. A valuable school directory, anonymous discussion forum, exclusive discounts to Chicago-area businesses, and access to free events nearly every week are some of the perks that come with membership.

www.onthegochicago.com: Local mom Cindy McCarthy blogs about her adventures through the city with her two toddlers. She visits first-hand, then offers up her take on neighborhoods, restaurants, museums, road trip destinations, and more.

www.timeoutchicagokids.com: *TimeOut Chicago Kids* started as a section of *TimeOut Chicago*, branched out into its own print publication, and now has this super-duper website, complete with feature articles, listings and reviews galore, and its fun and practical Hipsqueak blog.

concentrate on the experiences that allow children to dine in a cafe where dolls get their own mini chairs and place settings; strike a pose with their doll in the photo studio; or head to the hair salon whose stylists give dolls the ultimate updos. Special events take place throughout the year. Fees vary for activities. Open Mon through Thurs 10 a.m. to 8 p.m., Fri and Sat 9 a.m. to 9 p.m., Sun 9 a.m. to 6 p.m.

EXPLORE & MUCH MORE
3827 N. Southport Ave.
(773) 880-KIDS (5437)
www.exploreandmuchmore.com
Aimed at kids ages 0 to 8 (though it tends to attract an under-5 crowd), this two-level space is the brainchild of a pair of parent physicians who wanted a safe, educational, and fun indoor place for kids to play. They enlisted the help of a prolific children's

museum designer and came up with the perfect mix of make-believe and activity components, like a fully stocked kitchen with wood furniture and BPA-free plastic utensils, a slide and perfectly small bouncy house, and look-at-this kinds of things, like the maze of see-through pipes that send scarves racing through it. Fee is $12 for the first child; $9 each for siblings; children under 1 and adults are free. A 10-visit punch card is $108 and $81 for siblings. Open Mon through Fri 9 a.m. to 1 p.m. and 2 to 5 p.m.; open on weekends if there are no private parties (birthdays here are popular); check the website for specific weekend hours.

✳EXPLORITORIUM
4701 Oakton St., Skokie
(847) 674-1500, ext. 2700
www.skokieparkdistrict.org
Being part of the Skokie Park District (read: inexpensive entry) and just a quick drive north of the city (i.e., free parking) make this indoor amusement center for little ones a big hit. Once they're in, they're off and running. From the tube and tunnel climbing structure to the water table to the climbing wall to the dress-up area replete with stage set. A book nook and tables stocked with coloring supplies offer a little down time— though it doesn't last for long. Nonresidents (children and adults) $5; residents are $3; children under 1 free. Open Mon, Tues, and Fri 9 a.m. to 5 p.m.; Wed noon to 5 p.m.; Sat 9 a.m. to 1 p.m.; closed Thurs and Sun.

FAMILY GROUNDS CAFE
3652 N. Lincoln Ave.
(773) 281-0785
www.familygroundscafe.com
Chicago parents (especially of the stay-at-home variety) were practically drooling with anticipation while they waited for this ingenious space to open just a block from the Brown Line Addison El stop. When it did, it was swarmed and soon had to institute an online reservation system. But it's all good. After all, what could be bad? A light-fare cafe with local Intelligentsia coffee to keep caregivers perky and set up with free Wi-Fi, while kids busy themselves in the separate 1,500-square-foot indoor dreamland, including a playhouse that has changing themes, a train table, car table, construction zone, arts and crafts activities, dress-up clothes, mini basketball court, and a stage for regular storytelling and music times. Though it's not a drop-off kind of place (a sign warns, "Unattended children will be given an espresso and a free puppy"), it does make it easy to relax while kids don't. Reservation time-block play admission for 1 hour 45 minutes is $5.95 (adults and children who are crawlers and up): these are available Mon through Fri starting at 9 a.m. or 11 a.m., and Sat starting at 8:30 a.m., 10:30 a.m., or 12:30 p.m. Drop-in play time admission is $10.95 for the first child (crawlers and up), $5.95 for each sibling; adults are free: these run Mon through Fri 1 to 6 p.m. Memberships can also be purchased, and special events may affect pricing.

FANTASY KINGDOM
1422 N. Kingsbury St.
(312) 642-KIDS (5437)
www.fantasykingdom.org
Imaginations soar at this king- and queen-dom for kids 6 and under. One minute your little one is pushing a pint-sized shopping cart full of food, the next he's in the police station or cooking for you in the kitchen. First, she races to dress up in the Cinderella costume, the next thing you know, she's a

firefighter in the fire station. Multiple miniature spaces, plus two train tables, two slides, a separate space for the under-2 crowd, and intermittent entertainment (like a "pirate" who plays hide and seek with the kids and rewards their efforts with stickers and a story) make this a favorite for cold and rainy days. Plus, there are tables and chairs (and high chairs) to take a breather for lunches and snacks, a fridge to store milk, free Wi-Fi, and free coffee until noon Monday through Friday. The only downside is that it's usually closed on Saturday and Sunday for private parties (but the parties are a blast, so we understand). Daily admission $12; free for adults and siblings under 1. Multi-month and multi-visit punch passes are available and offer a discount on admission. Open from Labor Day through Memorial Day Mon through Fri 9 a.m. to 5:30 p.m. (in Apr, May, and Sept, depending on weather, it may close by 4:30 p.m., so call ahead); Memorial Day through Labor Day open Mon through Fri 9 a.m. to 3 p.m. (on rainy days, it generally stays open until 5:30 p.m.).

HOBBITLAND
1504 N. Western Ave.
(773) 698-8634
www.hobbitland.com

Decorated with fanciful murals painted by one of the owners, this cheerful Ukrainian Village indoor space offers open play time for kids to get their creative juices flowing with wooden toys, games, kitchen things, art projects (a huge blackboard is cool), story times every Wednesday at 10 a.m., and art projects (for members only) every Thursday. Three-visit stamp cards are $30 for one child, $45 for two. Five-visit pass cards are $50 with one child, $75 with two; 10-visit passes are $95/$145; and 30-day memberships are also available: $65 with one child; $95 for two. Open Mon, Wed, and Thurs 9 a.m. to 5 p.m. (closed between 2 and 3 p.m.); Tues 9 a.m. to 3 p.m.; Fri 9 a.m. to 2 p.m.; closed Sat and Sun for private parties.

KID CITY
1837 W. Grand Ave.
(312) 829-6775
www.kidcitychicago.com

Kitted out with kid cars, a grocery store, train tables, reading area, playhouse, mini cafe, and a separate cushy space for non-walkers, there are hours of fun built into this indoor space just west of downtown. For parties, the book corner turns into a cinema where kids can lounge for a movie with popcorn and juice boxes. Admission for drop-in play is $14 for the first child, $10 for siblings. Memberships offer a discount and are $105 for a 30-day and $160 for a 90-day pass (30% off for siblings). Open play hours Tues through Fri 9:30 a.m. to 6 p.m. (during summer, closing time is 4 p.m.).

LEGOLAND DISCOVERY CENTER
Streets of Woodfield
601 N. Martingale Rd., Schaumburg
(847) 592-9700
www.legolanddiscoverycenter.com

A drive into the shopping mall-land of Schaumburg also gets you to this 30,000-square-foot, indoor Lego-laden amusement park, the first one in the United States. Besides the many incredible Lego-built scenes and structures (like a mini city of Chicago), there are rides, 4-D movies, a mini factory tour and plenty of building pieces for little fingers to construct their own Lego land. Just know that the staff is pretty strict about height limits for the rides and prepare your kids accordingly. There's a small food court

KIDSTUFF

too. Admission prices $19, children 3 to 12 years old $15; there's a discount if you order tickets online. Open Mon through Fri noon to 7 p.m., Sat and Sun 10 a.m. to 7 p.m. (last admission sold at 5 p.m.; summer hours open every day at 10 a.m.).

LITTLE BEANS CAFE
1809 W. Webster Ave.
(773) 251-1025
www.littlebeanscafe.com

Combining all the things kids need—plenty of room, props, and costumes galore to tap into their fabulous imaginations (it's like an entire mini village in there)—and all the things parents want, like a full upscale breakfast and lunch menu; attention to germ-ridding; family bathrooms that have those adorable mini toilets; special events such as visits from Cinderella; classes including mom and tot yoga, art, and music; and, for maximum mom happiness, the option to pay for supervised play while she gets a manicure right then and there (offered on Mon from 2 to 5 p.m.). Daily pass $12, siblings $7; supervised play rate $20 for up to 1½ hours. Discount multi-visit passes are available: 10 visits for $100 for the first child, $50 each additional; yearly memberships are $750 and $500 for siblings. Open Mon through Fri 9 a.m. to 6 p.m., Sat 9 a.m. to 3 p.m., Sun 9 to 11 a.m. Private parties available.

MAKE-A-MESSTERPIECE
The Glen Tower Center
2050 Tower Dr., Glenview
(847) 730-5275
www.makeamessterpiece.com

Do your kids tend to make a mess? Wait, that's a silly question. Of course they do. And it's not always a good thing, is it? But at this ultimate art-as-play destination geared toward little ones ages 2 to 12, they're encouraged to get messy, and you won't even flinch. Hang up their jackets, grab a smock, and let little ones enjoy the creative stations like Bubble'ology, where colored bubbles drop down from big tubes, then pop on paper to make bubble-splatter paint pictures; the Drum Roll, which puts your mini Picasso (covered in full-on waterproof gear) inside a sound studio where they'll bang all they want on drums filled with paint; and the Lil' Sprouts center where the message is all about sustainability and the mess is all about projects with gardening in mind. A cafe offers free Wi-Fi lounging; a slide and a playhouse get kids' wiggles out; and a gift shop carries top-notch crafty games, toys, and art projects that are perfect as gifts. General admission includes unlimited creative time at open art tables, and the two play areas. Admission starts at $10 for children 3 and older ($5 for 1 to 3 years old, free for children under 1) and goes up from there depending on how many activities you choose; packages are available, but generally each special activity is an additional $5. Open Tues through Sat 10 a.m. to 5 p.m., Sun 11 a.m. to 5 p.m.; closed Mon.

MY CORNER PLAYROOM
2121 N. Clybourn Ave.
(773) 388-2121
www.mycornerplayroom.com

This Clybourn Corridor play space gives kids free rein to roam the climbing structure, dress-up area, even a rice-filled sandbox, under the enthusiastic guidance of the dedicated staff—if you'd like to give over complete kid duty, they even have a list of babysitters who will meet you here and let you skedaddle for a while. A roster of art, music, science, and kid fitness classes adds to the fun. Daily open play–only passes are $15 per child or $25 for family; play classes are an additional $5 per child or $10 for family. Monthly memberships are $50 per child or $85 for family and include unlimited in-and-out daily play by the month, as well as play classes; punch card passes are available at $135 for 10 visits and also include open play and play classes. Open play hours: Sept through May open Mon through Thurs 8 to 9 a.m. and 1 to 6 p.m., Fri 8 a.m. to 6 p.m., Sat 9 a.m. to noon; from June through Aug, open play on Fri is the same as Mon through Thurs.

PICKLE'S PLAYROOM
2315 W. Lawrence Ave.
(773) 293-7747
www.picklesplayroom.com
More than just another indoor place for kids to expend some energy while parents enjoy some "I don't have to entertain" time, this Lincoln Square spot also incorporates a children's hair salon, and 30 minutes of playtime are included with each haircut. Owner Mike Stokes, previously a stay-at-home dad, was tired of nothing-to-do days, so he conceived of this all-in-one fun-tastic space that's also big on eco-friendliness, right down to its cafe serving local baked goods, Metropolis coffees, and assorted kid drinks. Be aware that this is not a fully supervised space, so parents are still in charge of their charges. Admission for open play is $12, siblings $9; a 5-play pass is $55 (5-play sibling pass is $40), 10-play $100 (sibling $65), monthly pass $75 (sibling $50). Open Mon through Fri 9 a.m. to 5 p.m., Sat 9 a.m. to 3 p.m., Sun 10 a.m. to 3 p.m. Check the website for schedule updates.

Suit Up & Splash Down

As soon as summer hits, the spray features go on at some of Chicago's free parks.

Adams Playground Park. 1919 N. Seminary Ave.; (312) 742-7787. A gated-off area with water slides, sprays, and spouts makes this park a blast, but it's also notorious for getting a bit too crowded for comfort, so come early or on weekdays. There are also swing sets and climbing structures, as well as a huge sandbox.

Portage Park. 4100 Long Ave.; (773) 685-7235. Within this vast green space (great for picnicking), the pool and water play area is one of the favorites. Just know that you can't bring big bags of stuff into the pool area with you.

River Park. 5100 N. Francisco Ave.; (312) 742-7516. Recently revamped, this water park gets high marks for its variety of features, from a run-through-if-you-dare straight-down sprayer to little spouters for little sprouts. Watch toddlers around bigger kids.

Welles Park. 2333 W. Sunnyside Ave.; (312) 742-7511. Located within a recently constructed shiny new playground, the spray feature here is just one of the attractions and provides a nice cool-down for hot days. Watch out for the muddy patch that develops behind the water.

PUMP IT UP OF CHICAGO
821 W. Eastman St.
(312) 664-7867
www.pumpitupparty.com
This local outlet of a national franchise is a huge hit for birthday parties that take over the giant inflatable slides, mazes, and bouncy houses, and a challenging climbing wall. But it's also open at varying times for Pop-In Playtime and makes for an exhausting (in a good way) indoor outlet for your kids' seemingly endless energy—in other words, decide what you're going to do when they nap later. Separate play hours just for littler ones (children 42 inches and under) takes the craziness down a notch and also provides scooter-cars. Admission is $10 per child for Pop-In Playtime, free for adults. Open daily, but hours vary depending on whether private parties or groups have reserved the space; be sure to call or check online for updated hours. Every Tuesday and Thursday from 5:30 to 7 p.m. is open for Family Jump Time.

SIX FLAGS GREAT AMERICA
1 Great America Pkwy., Gurnee
(847) 249-4636
www.sixflags.com/greatamerica
The biggest outdoor amusement park near Chicago is also a longtime favorite. Admission prices may be steep, but it does get you access to the 14 roller coasters, the interactive Buccaneer Battle, the new Kidzopolis for the littlest ones, and a waterpark. Locals will recognize the beloved Little Dipper mini-coaster from Chicago's old Kiddieland grounds; the American Eagle may not be the most high-tech, but the creaky wooden track adds to the fear factor; the Demon and the Logger's Run are also classic oldies but goodies. For something a tad more terrifying, hop on Batman the Ride, an inverted, outside-looping coaster; or the wild head-first-flying Superman. Skip the biggest crowds by visiting on a weekday or during Apr, May, June, or Sept. Admission starts at around $40 for kids, and parking is extra, but the website lists discount packages. Open seasonally and during the annual Halloween Fright Fest. Call or check online for specific hours.

MUSEUMS & ZOOS

✳CHICAGO CHILDREN'S MUSEUM
Navy Pier
700 E. Grand Ave.
www.chicagochildrensmuseum.org
From its beginnings in 1982 as a small exhibit in the former Chicago Public Library (now, the Chicago Cultural Center), this 3-floor extravaganza of educational and entertaining exhibits has become one of the major anchors at Navy Pier and one of the top children's museums in the country. In addition to super-creative temporary exhibits (like the recent "Forts" that provided all the essentials for constructing the ultimate secret den), permanent (and frequently updated) exhibits include "WaterWays," which gives kids permission (and smocks) to get wet (hand-dryers are available, but we suggest bringing an extra shirt); "Play It Safe," which teaches kids about safety through fun stuff like crawling out of a faux-smoky house, sliding down a fire pole, and steering the fire truck; and "Kids Town," emphasizing pretend play in areas like a grocery store and car wash, and spaces to crawl through—here's where crawlers have the most fun too, and where caregivers will find a private nook for nursing or feeding. Special hands-on art and movement activities take place throughout the day, so be sure to check the schedule.

Admission $12 for children and adults; seniors $11; children under 1 free; free for all Thurs 5 to 8 p.m. and free for visitors 15 and under the first Sun of every month. Parking at Navy Pier is extra. Open daily 10 a.m. to 5 p.m.; Thurs stays open until 8 p.m.

KOHL CHILDREN'S MUSEUM
The Glen Tower Center
2100 Patriot Blvd., Glenview
(847) 832-6600
www.kohlchildrensmuseum.org
Originally a quaint little place in the Chicago suburb of Wilmette, this kids' museum's popularity went viral when it moved into a hugely expanded space in what's known as The Glen, about 5 miles north. Now ranked as one of the country's top 10 children's museums by *Parents* magazine, the 23,000-square-foot Silver LEED-certified space boasts 17 interactive learning-based exhibits that include a pretend Potbelly Sandwich Works shop; pretend grocery store (expect to wait in line for this on busy days); "City on the Move," which incorporates math, technology, and science with magnets, pulleys, balances, and more; and "Powered by Nature," which shines the fun on renewable energy sources. As far as amenities go, these folks have thought of everything: diaper dispensers in the bathroom, lockers, infant areas and nursing stations throughout the museum, an outdoor seasonal habitat, and a cafe. The museum store is great for gifts and offers free wrapping. Plus, there's free parking. Now, if they could only make it a little bigger to better accommodate their adoring crowds. Admission $8.50 for adults and children; seniors 55 and older $7.50; free for children under 1. Open Mon 9:30 a.m. to noon (until 5 p.m. from June through Aug), Tues through Sat 9:30 a.m. to 5 p.m., Sun noon to 5 p.m.

✳LINCOLN PARK ZOO
2001 N. Clark St.
(312) 742-2000
www.lpzoo.org
The great thing about this zoo is it's free, so if your little one only lasts 30 minutes, you won't feel bad. And if they want to spend all day checking out the wild animals that roar, leap, chirp, and moo, then you certainly get your money's worth. Of course, two of the most begged-for stops for kids are the mini train and the carousel, which are not free (LPZoo Express Train $2.50, carousel $2.75), but the photos you'll take of them beaming with excitement make it OK. The Farm-in-the-Zoo is a free favorite, where certain times allow brave young animal-lovers to feed the cows and pet the goats. Bring a picnic lunch or get it from the cafe, which offers ample seating inside and out. Free; extra fee for some activities; parking on the east side of the zoo starts at $17 for up to 3 hours, but there's free (hard-to-find sometimes) street parking and buses nearby. Open 365 days a year. For more information about the Lincoln Park Zoo, see the Attractions & Museums chapter.

PEGGY NOTEBAERT NATURE MUSEUM
2430 N. Cannon Dr.
(773) 755-5100
www.naturemuseum.org
With its building built to blend into its landscape, the Nature Museum (as it's mostly shortened to) can teach adults a thing or two about wildlife, conservation, and care of the planet, but it is, indeed, generally aimed at younger audiences. For kids, its two most popular exhibits are interactive romps through the "River Works," where waterplay is the attraction, and "Hands-on Habitat," where a small slide makes for time well

spent to burn up some toddler energy (no need for conservation on that front, right?). Perhaps the most renowned exhibit is the "Judy Istock Butterfly Haven," a 2,700-square-foot greenhouse where hundreds of colorful winged beauties and several species of birds flutter through the tropical setting (it feels deliciously warm during winter doldrums). Admission $9; students and seniors $7; children ages 3 to 12 $6; children under 3 free. Open Mon through Fri 9 a.m. to 5 p.m., Sat and Sun 10 a.m. to 5 p.m. (last ticket sold at 4 p.m. on weekdays, 4:30 p.m. on weekends). For more about the Peggy Notebaert Nature Museum, check out the Attractions & Museums chapter.

SWEDISH AMERICAN MUSEUM CENTER
5211 N. Clark St.
(773) 728-8111
www.swedishamericanmuseum.org
On the 3rd floor of this Andersonville museum, the small Brunk Children's Museum of Immigration (aimed at ages 3 to 12) presents a hands-on kid's perspective of the journey that Swedish children might have taken from their homes in Sweden to the New World 150 years ago. In the front area, little ones can dress up in clothes a little Swedish boy or girl would have worn back then, play in the Swedish farm and home, then get a play passport and ticket for the across-sea journey and "enter" America on the other side of the museum. Here, they learn to farm, fish, and tend to their new home. It's rarely crowded in this kid-sized gem, making it a great change of pace from the city's bigger and flashier attractions. Admission $4; seniors and students $3; $10 family rate; children under 1 free; free for all every second Tuesday of the month. Children's museum

hours are Mon through Thurs 1 to 4 p.m., Fri 10 a.m. to 4 p.m., Sat and Sun 11 a.m. to 4 p.m. General museum hours are Mon through Fri 10 a.m. to 4 p.m. (the gift shop is open the same hours, except Fri until 6 p.m.), Sat and Sun 11 a.m. to 4 p.m. For more on the Swedish American Museum Center, see the Attractions & Museums chapter.

SHOW TIME

ADVENTURE STAGE CHICAGO
Performances at Vittum Theater
1012 N. Noble St.
(773) 342-4141
www.adventurestage.org
Don't expect sugar-coated shows here. Philosophically complex, thought-provoking, discussion-inspiring dramas have included *And a Child Shall Lead*, about a group of children in a Jewish ghetto during the Holocaust who create poems, music, poetry, and more; *Katrina: The Girl Who Wanted Her Name Back*, a stirring story that followed the New Orleans disaster complete with live, 6-piece jazz band; and a rendition of the best-selling young adult book *Holes*. In fact, we'd dare say this could easily double as adult theater that features young protagonists. In other words, be prepared to be as engaged and self-reflective as your kids will be. Children under 5 are not permitted into the theater, and many performances target ages 9 or older. Adventure Stage also holds classes and workshops. Tickets generally $12 to $20.

✳CHICAGO CHILDREN'S THEATRE
Performance locations vary
Office: 1464 N. Milwaukee Ave., Second Floor
(773) 227-0180
www.chicagochildrenstheatre.org

Musical Interludes

These venues and events offer concerts of all types for kids of all ages.

Beat Kitchen
By night, it's a bar and adult music venue; by day (typically Sunday at noon), a pancake place and mini music-lover's locale. Performers have included the Okee Dokee Brothers, the Dreamtree Shakers, and local fave Mr. Singer and the Sharp Cookies. Tickets start at $5 per person. 2100 W. Belmont Ave.; (773) 281-4444; www.beatkitchen.com.

Chic-a-Go-Go
Celebrating total off-the-wall silliness that's just this side of freaky, this public-access TV music and dance show welcomes guests of all ages to join its taping sessions (generally every month). Going strong for more than 15 years, the quirky, shoestring-budget production has attracted a stream of strange costumed regulars, along with musical guests (equally strange at times). It's definitely a unique experience. Tapings at Chicago Access Network Studios, 322 S. Green St.; www.roctober.com/chicagogo.

Harris Theater
This state-of-the-art music and dance theater in Millennium Park gives kids a chance to experience it with three to four annual performances ranging from Dan Zanes to tapper Derek Grant. Tickets $10. 205 E. Randolph St.; (312) 334-7777; www.harristheaterchicago.org.

Old Town School of Folk Music
Besides its full plate of kids classes, Old Town gets big hugs for its Concerts for Kids series, held in its intimate theater. Past performers have included Justin Roberts, Elizabeth Mitchell, Ella Jenkins, and some of Old Town's own top-notch instructors. Tickets 4544 N. Lincoln Ave.; (773) 728-6000; www .oldtownschool.org.

Symphony Center
The world-renowned Chicago Symphony Orchestra hosts a family matinee series sponsored by Kraft that introduces kids to classical music without the typical adult-oriented setting. Come an hour early for free pre-concert fun. Tickets $8 to $66. 220 S. Michigan Ave.; (312) 294-3000; www.cso.org.

This theater company might move around, but it's always a solid choice for young-people programs. Its first production in 2006, *A Year with Frog and Toad*, was presented at the Goodman Theatre, and was such a rousing success that the company leaped into the following year with four plays. It has since performed at the Victory Gardens Biograph Theater, the North Shore Center for the Performing Arts, and the Ruth Page Center for the Arts. Wherever they go, the shows are absolutely professional and widely acclaimed. The company's unique Red Kite Project creates productions and even hosts a camp specifically for children on the autism spectrum. Ticket prices vary.

*EMERALD CITY THEATRE
Performances at the Apollo Theatre
2540 N. Lincoln Ave.
Classes at 2933 N. Southport Ave.
Tickets: (773) 935-9336; theatre school and general inquiries: (773) 529-2690
www.emeraldcitytheatre.com
Break your kids' TV habit with a visit to a live show by this longtime favorite local company geared for 3-year-olds and up. Receiving raves from the toughest critics in town (that would be toddlers, of course), the troupe has performed musical versions of everything from *Pinkalicious* to *Charlie and the Chocolate Factory*, and *Don't Let the Pigeon Drive the Bus* to *Snow White*. Frequent pre- and post-show activities like arts activities, and photo and autograph sessions, let kids feel like they're part of the play. Emerald City also brings out the future Broadway star in your child with a full spectrum of classes for kids up to 13 years old, plus summer camps, after-school programs, and birthday parties. Ticket prices for performances start at $16 for adults, $13 for children.

LIL' BUDS THEATRE
1210 W. Bryn Mawr Ave.
(773) 334-4543
www.lilbudstheatre.org
Both youth actors and professional actors unite to perform in the two main stage shows from this family theater company—one, a rollicking winter holiday musical and the other a spring play. Classes and workshops for children ages 3 through 18 include basic acting skills, creative drama, sketch comedy, and improv. Performance ticket

prices vary; call for more information about class prices and schedule.

MARRIOTT LINCOLNSHIRE CHILDREN'S THEATRE
10 Marriott Dr., Lincolnshire
(847) 634-0200
www.marriotttheatre.com
Giving young theatergoers the same treatment as its grown-up audiences, this long-standing suburban theater has a children's musical series of both original works and classic stories. Recent shows have included an abridged *The Wizard of Oz* and a version of Aesop's fable *How Can You Run with a Shell on Your Back?* Tickets $15. Performances take place most days at 10 a.m. and sometimes there's a second show at 12:30 p.m.

MERRY MUSIC MAKERS
3171 N. Ravenswood Ave., #212
(773) 929-4MMM (4666)
www.merrymusicmakers.net
Using the nationally recognized Music Together and I Can Sing! programs for children from birth to age 6, the musical experiences include classes for mixed-age students (birth through 5); French and Spanish immersion music classes; a class specifically designed just for infants (up to 8 months old); a Supportive Environment session for children with special needs or development delays; and singing lessons that focus on concepts such as breath support and harmony. Classes are offered throughout the year, come with CDs and songbooks, and generally run 10 or 12 weeks. Call or see the website for specifics and for information about attending a trial class for free. Besides the central Lakeview location, Merry Music Makers holds classes in Andersonville (5445 N. Clark St.), Edgebrook (6736 N. Loleta Ave.),

Southport Corridor (3827 N. Southport Ave.), and in the nearby suburb of Park Ridge (10 Main St.).

MUSIC PLAYHOUSE
3829 N. Southport Ave.
(773) 572-8054
www.themusicplayhouse.com

It's the spirit and clear love of what she does that has made Chicago city director Julie O'Connell the perfect leader for this small company that has three locations nationwide. Offering 10-week Music Pups classes 6 days a week for children from birth through 5 years old (perfect for siblings of different ages), the brightly painted studio is a bright spot in any kid's—and caregiver's—day. Each session includes sit-down and stand-up songs, plus practice with rhythm and tone, as well as a chance for free-dance and experimentation with a variety of instruments. A take-home songbook and CD let kids practice what they're learning at home too. We're pretty sure moms, dads, and nannies have as much fun as the little ones. Tuition $160 for the first child, $110 for each sibling (siblings under 6 months at the start of the session are free). Sessions run throughout the year, and open houses are held at the start of every session. Call or check online for the full schedule.

OLD TOWN SCHOOL OF FOLK MUSIC
4544 N. Lincoln Ave.
909 W. Armitage Ave.
(773) 728-6000
www.oldtownschool.org

Since 1985, this legendary music venue and school has offered its famous Wiggleworms early childhood music sessions for little tykes ages 6 months through 3 years (in addition to the two locations above, there are several other branch locations that host Wiggleworms). Want to start even earlier? The 30-minute Lullabies classes introduce finger-play songs, a little dancing, call-and-response songs, and a comfortable environment for babies who are nursing, feeding, giggling, crying, and, of course, sleeping. Kids can't get enough? For 3- and 4-year-olds, there's the Wigglegrads class. A varied roster of other classes for kids from toddlers through teenagers include art, piano, violin, dance and movement, and theater. There's even a teen open mic on most first Saturdays of the month. Classes are held throughout the year at both locations. Pricing varies; call or check online for details.

SPORTS CLASSES

CHICAGO PARK DISTRICT
(312) 742-PLAY
www.chicagoparkdistrict.com

From archery to volleyball, boxing to fencing, the Chicago Park District has it all. At its more than 570 parks across the city, there is always something going on—and at a very reasonable price. It's easy to find a program that fits your children's interests; the tricky part is getting them into the class. While Chicagoans praise the Park District for its ongoing improvements and its wide variety of offerings, we curse it for the limited spaces versus the vast number of residents who'd like to participate. The website announces when programs are available for browsing—and the system is pretty easy to navigate, as you can search by park, age, type of program, or zip code. Just create an account, log in, and save the programs you'd like to register for. Then, on the day that registration opens at 9 a.m., you'd better have your finger hovering over the "submit" button to get a spot, as the

For Your Information

Some super kid-friendly attractions are included in other chapters because they entertain all ages, but we wouldn't want you to forget about them when planning a family day out, so here's a quick reference list to 9 of them we feel merit mention here too:

most popular programs and park locations get filled within minutes. There are usually spots saved for walk-in registration, though that requires you get in line at least an hour before doors open. Still, with its faults, the Chicago Park District does provide a huge benefit for residents. Prices vary. Sessions run throughout the year. Read more about the Chicago Park District in the Parks & Recreation chapter.

LIL' KICKERS CHICAGO
2640 W. Bradley Place
(877) 545-5457
www.lilkickerschicago.com
A low coach-to-kid ratio, a true developmentally correct curriculum (i.e., not a well-meaning parents' ad-hoc version of one), and a focus on learning through skills instead of competition has shot this soccer program's success into the stratosphere. Based on the four Cs—comprehensive, noncompetitive, child-centered, and creative—the program allows tots as young as 18 months

to participate. They start as Bunnies, learning soccer basics and working on gross motor skills; then they can move on up through Thumpers, Cottontails, Hoppers, Jackrabbits, and Big Feet (for 5- and 6-year-olds), each class building new skills and offering new goals. For bigger kids through age 9, the Micro Classes get more complex and prepare participants for competitive play. Annual membership of $36 per child or $72 per family required for enrollment; tuition starts at $168 for 12 classes ($14 per class). Additional locations are at 2343 S. Throop St., and 1535 N. Dayton St.

LIL' SLUGGERS
Bash Sports Academy
2617 W. Fletcher St.
(312) 945-1585
www.lilsluggerschicago.com
Forget boring waits for action on the field; in a Lil' Sluggers Baseball class, kids ages 2 to 8 are constantly moving and doing. Director Jeff Kapp knows a thing or two

about organized baseball, having begun playing in high school and turning semi-pro for several years after college. In small groups, experienced coaches teach the real concepts, motions, and rules of baseball through fun drills that get kids hitting, running, throwing, catching, and fielding. Don't worry, the littlest learners use a whiffle ball, then they move onto a foam-type baseball, then advance from there until they're using a regular tee ball. The older kids are prepped for tee ball teams or Little League. Sessions run 10 weeks for $225. Call or look online for current schedules. Two other locations are at Menomonee Club, 1535 N. Dayton St., and at the Windy City Fieldhouse, 2367 W. Logan Blvd.

MIDTOWN TENNIS CLUB
2020 W. Fullerton Ave.
(773) 235-2300
www.midtown.com
Rated by the US Tennis Association as one of the top junior tennis programs in the country that follow the QuickStart format, Midtown is also one of the world's largest indoor tennis facilities—a bonus for fickle Chicago weather. Kids ages 3 to 12 get court time with the top-notch, upbeat junior instruction that takes it down to their level, complete with smaller court sizes, bigger rackets, and slower balls. Fun-based drills break skills into bite-sized pieces and help improve the ABCs of tennis—agility, balance, and coordination—for your nascent Nadals and up-and-coming Clijsters. Ten-week sessions start at $165. Classes run all year; call or check the schedule for details. Find out about adult programs about Midtown Tennis Club in the Parks & Recreation chapter.

SHOPPING

Whether you're a window-shopper or a shopaholic, the Windy City satisfies with retail around nearly every corner and everywhere you look. Some neighborhoods are definite destinations. In the eight blocks of North Michigan Avenue between Oak Street and the Chicago River known as the Magnificent Mile, there are more than 450 stores alone, including those stacked into the eight-level Water Tower Place, considered the nation's first vertical mall. Along the snug strip of Oak Street from North Michigan Avenue to State Street lie some of the glitziest boutiques—think Hermès, Prada, and Barneys New York. With limited street parking, this posh Gold Coast area even offers its own valet service. In Bucktown, Wicker Park, and Ukrainian Village, it's all about the hip factor, while Lincoln, Southport, and Armitage avenues boast a trendsetting assortment of indie shops.

From a rare literary find at Printers Row bookstore to a relic of recording history at Permanent Records, from a fuzzy Folkmanis puppet at Timeless Toys to a haute custom gown at Ikram, Chicago shopping runs the gamut. The stores listed here give you a good dose of what you'll find, some of the best of the best and the hidden gems, but by no means the full spectrum. If you can't decide where to begin, consider taking a Shop-Walk tour (773-255-7866, www.chicagoshopwalk.com) to get the lay of the boutique land. These tours, run by style expert Danielle Lutz, provide daily 2- or 4-hour group or private excursions to five different neighborhoods. Or simply embark on your own exploration. Happy shopping!

BOOKSTORES

BARNES & NOBLE
1441 W. Webster Ave.
(773) 871-3610
www.bn.com
There are two of these big-box stores in the city, and about two dozen in surrounding suburbs. They specialize in a little of everything, with genres ranging from mystery novels to biographies, self-help to science fiction, travel to children's books. Plus, they sell an impressive selection of magazines, toys and games, some DVDs, journals, stationery, and cards you won't necessarily find at

your local drugstore. Most stores also have author visits, story times, cafes, and free Wi-Fi. Hours vary, but generally open every day until at least 9 p.m. A second Chicago location is at 1130 N. State St. (312-280-8155).

THE BOOK CELLAR
4736-38 N. Lincoln Ave.
(773) 293-2665
www.bookcellarinc.com
From author readings to joke-telling workshops, book clubs to speed-dating events, this Lincoln Square bookstore embraces its

diverse community with more than just its carefully edited book selection. Besides the regular reads, the tightly packed space (read: leave strollers outside) carries a wide assortment of local authors. Pick one up, then grab a Julius Meinl coffee and Southport Grocery vanilla cupcake or light sandwich in the cafe and enjoy the ambience. Open daily; Sun and Tues have limited hours.

> **i** For many Chicago-area locals, a trip to Water Tower Place is practically a pilgrimage. And it's a top spot for visitors too. Be sure to stop at the concierge desk on the street level to get the scoop on sales, perks, and special deals throughout the mall (835 N. Michigan Ave.; (312-440-3166; www.shopwatertower.com).

CHICAGO COMICS
3244 N. Clark St.
(800) 509-0333, (773) 528-1983
www.chicagocomics.com
Searching for an old *Archie & Friends*, *Batman*, *Avengers*, or *Doctor Who*? From classic books to up-and-coming newcomers and one of the most extensive selections of indie titles in the Midwest, this neatly jam-packed store, founded in 1991, is where comic book fiends get their fix. Behind the counter, comic gems of yesteryear hang, while huge bins hold backstock books. Can't find your favorite? If it's not sitting in their basement storage, the dedicated staff will special-order it for you—or get it from their sister store Quimby's (see listing). Kapow! Open daily starting most days at noon.

EUROPA BOOKS
832 N. State St.
(312) 335-9677
www.schoenhofs.com
Just off the beaten Mag Mile path, you'll find this slice of literary Europe. Though not quite as storied as its Harvard Square sibling Schoenhof's Foreign Books (founded in 1856), Europa is equally worldly with its focus on foreign-language literature, periodicals, and educational series. Special emphasis is given to French, Spanish, Italian, and German, but there are also items in Hebrew and Latin. Service can be hit-or-miss, but the unique finds keep ex-pats, culturally curious, foreign visitors, and language learners coming back. Open daily.

OPEN BOOKS LTD.
213 W. Institute Place
(312) 475-1355
www.open-books.org
A bookstore with noble goals, this nonprofit used bookstore uses its proceeds to promote literacy in Chicago and beyond. It began in 2006 with an initial 10,000 donated books stored in founder Stacy Ratner's basement; by 2008, more than 200,000 books filled a warehouse. In 2009, the store opened, allocating space for writing and reading programs on the second level. The welcoming, whimsically decorated store—a coffee table that looks like stacked books, purple and red walls and bookshelves—now boasts about 50,000 books for sale at any given time, plus game nights, book review-writing open to anyone, author readings, children's story times, and more. Open daily.

PRINTERS ROW FINE & RARE BOOKS
715 S. Dearborn St.
(312) 583-1800
www.printersrowbooks.com
It makes perfect sense that the resident dog at this antiquarian and rare bookshop would be a Great Pyrenees—it's supposedly the

oldest dog breed in the world. It's also no surprise that the bookstore is located in a historic 1883 building, which was built as the headquarters for the M.A. Donohue Publishing Company, and its books proudly sit in mismatched old wood display cases and behind cut-glass doors. Like fine wines, the books here have aged gracefully and gained in status—and price. Try $8,000 for a first edition of Charles Dickens' *A Christmas Carol,* or $6,000 for a rare copy of *Donald Duck* signed by Walt Disney. There are plenty of less expensive tomes to be found here, too, covering 16th- to 20th-century American and British literature and Chicago history, along with signed letters from the likes of Nelson Algren and Ray Bradbury, and a good selection of out-of-print titles. Open Tues through Fri 10 a.m. to 7 p.m., Sat 11 a.m. to 5 p.m., and by appointment; closed Sun and Mon.

QUIMBY'S
1854 W. North Ave.
(773) 342-0910
www.quimbys.com

Founded in 1991 with the intent to carry "every cool, bizarre, strange, dope, queer, surreal, weird publication ever written and published," this Wicker Park store with the Chris Ware mascot (a mouse that's also named Quimby, but not named for it) delivers what it promised. You may be surprised, shocked, or even offended by some of it, but that's all part of the First Amendment philosophy of owner Eric Kirsammer (who also owns Chicago Comics). Find everything from lowbrow art books like *Bodies of Subversion: A Secret History of Women and Tattoo* to adult (read: X-rated) graphic novels to consignment zines and some seriously off-beat kids stuff (*Never Mind Your P's And Q's: Here's the Punk Alphabet, Black Book of Colors*). Open daily, usually from noon.

✳SANDMEYER'S BOOKSTORE
714 S. Dearborn St.
(312) 922-2104
www.sandmeyersbookstore.com

Brick walls, exposed wood ceiling beams, and creaky wood floorboards give this South Loop mainstay a rustic feel, just perfect for cozying up with a new release, bestseller, or old classic. The mom-and-pop shop has been selling them all since 1982 and has become the kind of bookstore that gets you excited about buying a bunch of books to stack by your bedside. There's also a generous children's book selection, and, if you ever have trouble finding what you're looking for, just ask owners Ulrich or Ellen Sandmeyer. Open daily.

SEMINARY CO-OP BOOKSTORES
Seminary Co-op
5757 S. University Ave.
(800) 777-1456, (773) 752-4381
www.semcoop.com

There are bookworms and then there are the 17 students at the University of Chicago who decided to turn their love of reading into a business. In 1961, they each chipped in 10 bucks and founded a bookstore. Today, the Sem Co-op, located in the basement of the Chicago Theological Seminary adjacent to the campus, carries an acclaimed selection of academic volumes. It has also grown into a triple-threat triumph, with two other independent bookstores: The 57th Street Bookstore (1301 E. 57th St., 773-684-1300) prides itself on its stellar mystery and children's sections (among many others). At the Newberry Library's A.C. McClurg Bookstore (60 W. Walton St., 312-255-3520), set within the wonderful Newberry Library in the Gold Coast, the focus is on the history of Chicago, the Midwest, and Native American culture, and is also a trove of hard-to-find cards and gifts. Seminary and 57th Street open daily; Newberry location closed Sun and Mon.

UNABRIDGED BOOKSTORE
3251 N. Broadway St.
(773) 883-9119
www.unabridgedbookstore.com
If the name doesn't clue you in to what this Lakeview indie shop is all about, just take a step inside. Lots of insider staff recommendations, a book of the month, and usually a surprising themed table—"Chilling Scandinavian Mysteries," for example—make it a must-visit for any book lover. Though owner Ed Devereux opened his store in 1980 to showcase gay and lesbian literature, he has always upheld a dedication to all genres, including general fiction, travel, home design, poetry, cooking, and his award-winning children's section. Don't miss the sale books too. Open daily.

WOMEN & CHILDREN FIRST
5233 N. Clark St.
(773) 769-9299
www.womenandchildrenfirst.com
There's a whole lot of estrogen soaring through the stacks of this feminist-focused Andersonville bookstore, founded in 1979. Each staff member purports to be "a reader, a feminist, and a bookseller," and they give extra attention to books by and about women. There is also a phenomenal children's book nook—story times here are very popular—as well as lesbian and gay fiction and nonfiction. Open daily.

WOMEN'S CLOTHING & ACCESSORIES

AKIRA
1814 W. North Ave.
(773) 489-0818
www.shopakira.com
It's high style (not to mention, high heels) without the highfalutin' price tags at this trend-setting local chain. Opened in 2002 at this original Bucktown location by college pals Erikka Wang, Jon Cotay, and Eric Hsueh, Akira instantly changed Chicago's fashion landscape. They now boast 14 locations in the city and suburbs, including stores for men's clothing and shoes, with more on the way. Wang is always on the lookout for the next best thing and comes up with fashion-forward finds like strappy, chunky-heeled shoes from Qupid, a Blaque Label asymmetrical chiffon tube dress, Urban Behavior cargo pants, and a gold-plate-and-leather cocktail ring from House of Harlow 1960 Jewelry Collection by Nicole Richie. Store hours vary; most open daily.

✳ART EFFECT
934 W. Armitage Ave.
(773) 929-3600
www.shoparteffect.com
This rambling Armitage Avenue boutique happily crosses the line between gift shop and women's clothing store. For yourself, pick up a frilly Odd Molly Hawthorne blouse, Havaianas flip-flops, a V-neck Three Dots tee or a short-sleeve, uneven-hem Ella Moss dress. Then check everyone else off your list with gifty things like a cheese tasting party kit, MOR body products, a Jonathan Adler porcelain menorah, or Smencils scented pencils—kids go ape over flavors like bubble gum, root beer, and cotton candy. You might just keep those for yourself too. Open daily.

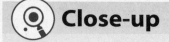

Close-up

Trolling for Treasures

Antiquing is not reserved just for quaint country towns. In fact, a strip of Chicago's **Belmont Avenue**—from Damen to Western avenues generally—boasts the largest concentration of antiques stores in the Midwest. For treasures from the past, pop into any one of them, including **Father Time Antiques** (2108 W. Belmont; 773-880-5599; www.fathertimeantiques.com) for time pieces and jewelry; **Good Old Days** (2138 W. Belmont; 773-472-8837; www.goodolddaysinc.com), selling furniture, old-style radios, vintage ad signs, and more since 1971; **Lazy Dog Antiques** (1901-1903 W. Belmont; 773-281-3644; www.rubylane.com/shop/lazydogantiques) and **Miscellania** (2323 W. Belmont; 773-348-9647) for a wide variety of antiques from around the world; and **Night and Day Vintage** (2228 W. Belmont; 773-327-4045; www.nightanddayvintage.com), specializing in vintage clothing and accessories.

BLAKE
212 W. Chicago Ave.
(312) 202-0047
You'd better know where you're going when you head to Blake, because there's no welcome sign and no window display and you need to buzz to be allowed in. Fitting entry considering the showroomlike layout of this home for ready-to-wear high fashion—there's just one size per garment out for viewing, for starters. Opened in 1984 by dynamic duo Marilyn Blaszka and Dominic Marcheschi, Blake boasts one of the most complete lines of big-time Belgian designer Dries Van Noten, along with other notables such as Givenchy, Marni, and Balenciaga. If you're serious about fashion and have some serious cash to drop, you'll find just what you're looking for. Open Mon through Sat; closed Sun.

CASA DE SOUL
1919 W. Division St.
(773) 252-2520
www.casadesoul.net

Self-described "creative director" Kennedy Ashinze did a little soul-searching, chucked his stockbroker day job in 2004, and turned to a life of style. He has since made a name for himself with his Wicker Park shop and garnered fans of his funk sensibility seen through clothing. Though there's a smattering of menswear, like club-casual tops by Freshjive, most of the racks reel in women with a globally hip, decidedly urban feel. And mixed in with the Elroy Apparel organic cotton dresses and flirty jackets by 2two, there are art mags, high-end headphones, and the latest musical offerings from musicians like Fela Kuti. Open daily.

CERATO BOUTIQUE
3451 N. Southport Ave.
(773) 248-8604
www.ceratoboutique.com
Unabashedly Chicago-centric and fearlessly feminine, this Southport shop is named for a Bach flower remedy (Dr. Edward Bach created a series of flower-based homeopathic dilutions, each with a different purpose). Cerato is said to boost confidence in your inner

voice and intuition. With total confidence in the abilities of local designers, Cerato looks right here for its offerings. From Avery Layne's mod-ish dresses to Brynn Capella's Italian leather handbags to Elise Bergman's sweet-sexy collection of handmade pieces and the costume-jewelry-turned-stunning statement accessories by Jen Cook. Forget following the crowd, Cerato makes it trendy to be yourself. Open daily.

DOVETAIL
1452 W. Chicago Ave.
(312) 243-3100
www.dovetailchicago.com
Somethings old are transformed into some-things new at this delightful vintage boutique in West Town. Little crystal-y chandeliers and made-over grandma-type furnishings create the perfect setting for Julie Ghatan's and Jen-nifer Clower's repurposed and re-energized wardrobe pieces for men and women, plus jewelry, mid-century home furnishings, and art. Open Wed through Sun (opening usually at 1 p.m.); closed Mon and Tues.

THE DRESSING ROOM
4635 N. Lincoln Ave.
(773) 728-0088
www.thedressingroomchicago.com
The oft-changed windows of this petite Lincoln Square shop tempt with cute-trendy dresses, jackets, and tees. Owners and Lin-coln Square locals Barbara Ruiz and Sarah Sanchez carry women's wear that works for dames who are done with super-tight and too-short everything, but haven't deferred to mom jeans or muumuus—and don't feel like spending a small fortune. Find a great selec-tion of jeans, funky tees, and fun skirts, along with Hanky Panky undies, and fleece-lined wool gloves and leggings. Be sure to check

their Facebook page for seasonal specials. Open daily.

EMBELLISH
4161 N. Lincoln Ave.
(773) 525-4400
www.embellishchicago.com
Need to add a little pizzazz to your life? Then you need a little Embellish in your life. This cozy North Center store is an accessory-lover's dream come true—jewelry by D-Amato, men's wallets by Hippo Hand-crafted, bags by Nino Bossi, or locally created and uniquely styled hats from Squasht. And most everything comes with a jaw-drop-pingly low price tag. Open daily.

FLORODORA
330 S. Dearborn St.
(312) 212-8860
www.florodora.com
You might not expect to find a super-cute independently owned boutique right in the Loop. But there it is. When Michael Blos-som opened Florodora—named for a 1900 Broadway musical famous for its "Florodora Girls"—in the historic Monadnock Building in 2007, he received widespread applause from style-conscious women around town. It has remained a go-to spot for dresses, vintage-inspired coats, romantic summer frocks and flirty skirts. Since prices lean to the steeper side, be sure to keep the store's semiannual "Scandal Sale" on your radar. Open Mon through Sat; closed Sun. Florodora Shoes too, 348 S. Dearborn St.

HANDLE WITH CARE
1706 N. Wells St.
(312) 751-2929
www.handlewithcareboutique.com

Just as there are two sides to every story, there are two sides to this longtime Old Town boutique: One is designer-casual with loftlike decor, the other, designer-dressy with a fancier feel. Both are rather designer-priced, if you know what we mean. But it's the select pieces from names like Rebecca Taylor, Trina Turk, Shoshanna, and alice + olivia that have made for loyal customers since the shop opened in 1981. Open daily.

IKRAM
15 E. Huron St.
(312) 587-1000
www.ikram.com

Although Ikram Goldman's stunning haute-couture boutique was a standout from its start, when word got out that one Michelle Obama entrusted Ikram with outfitting her, fashionistas everywhere took note. And while Goldman never speaks of her fashionable friendship with the First Lady, Chicago is certainly proud of the connection. It's an understandable one, too, what with names like Jean Paul Gaultier, Rodarte, Givenchy, Yohji Yamamoto, and Sonia Rykiel gracing her sophisticated shop. Goldman also carries one of her purportedly personal favorites for the high-society set, Jimmy Choos. The shop recently moved from Rush Street into this much larger space.

KNEE DEEP VINTAGE
1425 W. 18th St.
(312) 850-2510
www.kneedeepvintage.com

This Pilsen shop isn't about second-hand. It's vintage. And it is not trash. On the contrary, it's most definitely treasure. In the form of wearable old T-shirts from the 1950s or 1980s, cashmere sweaters, authentic navy jackets, and a fabulous assortment of shoes

that add a bit of "cool" to any outfit. The great thing, too, is that it's not a sprawling store that sucks the energy out of your shopping hunt; it's meticulously organized with salespeople who are genuinely excited about helping you find your treasure. Open daily (generally starting at noon).

KRISTA K
3458 N. Southport Ave.
(773) 248-1967
www.kristak.com

In 2002, Krista Kaur Meyers carved out a sizeable niche for herself on Chicago's trendy Southport Avenue shopping strip. It didn't take long for Krista K to add more space and then expand with Krista K Maternity a half-block north (3530 N. Southport Ave.). The attraction? An entire floor dedicated to top-end denim from the likes of Splendid, James Jeans, and Paige Denim; and a separate top floor selection that includes finds like a drape dress by Haute Hippie, a flowy pleated polyester blouse by Elizabeth and James, or open-toe high-heel suede booties by Pedro Garcia, made in Spain. Open daily.

MICHELLE TAN
1872 N. Damen Ave.
(773) 252-1888
www.michelletan.com

Considering the swiftly earned fashion chops of Michelle Tan—a year after her 1999 graduation from the International Academy of Design and Technology, she launched her first line and won the "Style Maker and Rule Breaker" award from Fashion Group International—she could have moved her shop to Fifth Avenue or Beverly Hills. But she decided to remain true to her Chicago roots. Glittering white walls and shelves bestow attention on Tan's own blacks, creams, browns, and navies in her clothing and handbags, all of which have been described as "deconstructionist" and "romantic." A big supporter of local designers, Tan also saves rack room for pieces by other burgeoning local designers. Open Tues through Sun; Mon by appointment. Also at Block 37, 108 N. State St.; (312) 701-1818; open daily.

MS. CATWALK
2042 N. Damen Ave.
(773) 235-2750
www.mscatwalk.com
At this candy-stripe-painted Bucktown shop, you can pick up a little something for a strut around town without howling at the prices. Lace and ruffles, silky sleeves, puff-bottomed jackets, and a vintage-ish selection of tees all create a flirty, fun look from designers like Esley, RYU, Ya, and Fumblin Foe. Open Wed through Sun; closed Mon and Tues.

P+L BOUTIQUE
2956 N. Clark St.
(773) 248-3758
www.pandlchicago.com
Named for husband and wife team Paul Chiemmongkoltip and Leena Thairuammit, this Lakeview shop has a motto that sets the stage: "Happywear for women and men"—and now kids too. Thoughtfully selected designs from around the world include heathered pima cotton cowl neck sweaters from Alternative Apparel, a sleeveless wraparound sweater-dress from Spain's Skunkfunk, and hipster loafers for guys from British-based J Shoes. One glance at the prices, and you will look as happy as your clothes. Open daily.

PENELOPE'S
1913 W. Division St.
(773) 395-2351
www.shoppenelopes.com
Another pioneering power couple, Joe Lauer and Jena Frey opened their super-cool clothing and hip housewares destination—named for their pet Pug—in 2002, when this strip of Division Street was derelict, offbeat, and bereft of fashion boutiques. Now, Penelope's is surrounded by worthy followers, but it still stands strong, carrying coveted lines for women and men by Sessun, APC, Built by Wendy, and Dunderdon, with vintage-y and European flair and a solid in-the-know appeal. Open daily.

P.45
1643 N. Damen Ave.
(773) 862-4523
www.p45.com
In 1997, when partners Tricia Tunstall and Jessica Darrow (who has since departed) opened their fashion-forward boutique in then-sketchy Bucktown, they paved the way for the neighborhood's now-famous multitude of indie shops. It is now an anchor of style amid shops that come and go and it still gets raves for savvy style picks from local, national, and international designers. A swish interior redo in 2008 gave the store an airy feel with sugar maple floors and gleaming white walls and counter. While this might not be your stock-up shop—a hoodie by Inhabit sold for nearly $400, a Native American-like necklace from Lizzie Fortunato Jewelry for around $300, and a natural hemp sunhat for over $255, for example—it is the place to get those signature pieces you'll never regret. Open daily.

ROBIN RICHMAN
2108 N. Damen Ave.
(773) 278-6150
www.robinrichman.com

In an interior that could be described as rustically romantic, fashion maven and School of the Art Institute grad Robin Richman sells the stuff she loves. And it has been the model for her success since she opened her Bucktown store nearly a dozen years ago. Interspersed on antique French tables and Lucite shelves, under glass cake covers and complemented by metal skirt forms, she displays an internationally diverse collection of designers. Everything from artistic shoes to vintage-styled hats and mittens to drapy menswear-inspired women's clothing and leather-focused jewelry. Open Tues through Sun; closed Mon (open Mon in summer).

*SOFIA
72 E. Oak St.
(312) 640-0878
www.sofiavintage.com

Originally opened in a Gold Coast office building, Sofia struck a chord with fashion-conscious Chicagoans looking for that perfect mix of vintage and couture. So local sister act Ashley Zisook and Allison Zisook Goldstein moved to swanky Oak Street digs down the street from Prada, Wolford, and Hermès. Though their address has changed, they have not given up their motto of encouraging clients to "live lovely." Named in honor of the inimitable Sophia Loren, Sofia now carries a selection of emerging designers and classic favorites: color-dyed M2F Denim shorts, cardigans from the Winter Kate line from Nicole Richie (look for her signature in one of the dressing rooms), and Chanel dog tags and handbags. Select

vintage pieces round out the effortlessly chic look. Open daily.

THE SOMETIMES STORE
1167 W. 19th St.
(773) 396-7979
www.sometimesstore.com

Three friends plus an empty bedroom (thanks to a breakup with a boyfriend), plus a whole bunch of vintage clothing, equaled a big idea for Christine Bejasa, Alysse Dalessandro, and Kirsten Kilponen. They decided to open a shop (Bejasa has since moved to New York and has a branch there too). It's open, you guessed it, sometimes, and it changes locations pretty frequently too, but it's always a limited selection that's always super-affordable. Just sign up for their e-mails and find out when they're ready for another sale. If you love yarns of yesteryear from the 1940s through '90s, you'll be happy you did.

SQUASHT BY LES
2556 W. Chicago Ave.
(773) 292-4123
www.squashtbyles.com

Lesley Timpe's time studying fashion in Spain gives her line of women's clothing and accessories a certain European touch. She began her Chicago business by selling to other boutiques, but realized her own dream when she opened her Ukrainian Village boutique in 2010. She focuses on natural and organic fabrics and vintage prints in her hand-crafted dresses, blouses, handbags, headbands, and her signature sassy reversible sewn hats that run the gamut from traditional black herringbone to funky faux fur–lined. She also carries pieces by other designers such as Megan Lee Designs and jewelry by Scarlett Garnet and Veronica Riley

Martens. Open Wed through Sun; Mon and Tues by appointment.

*THREADLESS
3011 N. Broadway
(773) 525-8640
www.threadless.com

If its Facebook page is any indication—a staggering 254,000-plus fans—this is one hot T-shirt shop. It also hints at the wide net Threadless has thrown. More than just a store, it's truly an interactive, influential community of more than 1 million members around the world. A community that submits original T-shirt designs, votes for designs, buys the winning designs, and even submits photos of themselves in the finished tees. The business began by word of mouth, gained cult following, and grew into a mainstream mainstay in the Lakeview neighborhood. New designs are available for voting every week, with the newest winners sold at the store on Friday and online a few days later. The lucky chosen designers receive cash, and customers get the best in offbeat, whimsical, wacky, occasionally obscene, but always imaginative T-shirts for men, women, and kids. Open daily. Also at 1260 W. Madison St.

TRIBECA
1035 W. Madison St.
(866) 300-7713
www.shopattribeca.com

This West Loop shop is perfect for those "find-it-for-less" kinds of wardrobes. Kim Hiley scours the coasts for the best on-trend, of-the-moment fashions that keep comfort in mind and brings them back here. Like tunic dresses from Orion London, sassy going-out tops from Tracy Reese, and dresses by Susana Monaco. Find the perfect office-to-night-out outfits, feminine summer shirts that give you that effortlessly L.A. look, and winter-warm sweaters that keep you fashionable through the frost. Open daily.

TRILLIUM
1744 W. Division St.
(773) 698-8162
www.trilliumchicago.com

The simple and lovely trillium flower gets translated into this minimalist space with dark hardwood flooring and a spotlight on the weekly-changing selection of boyish girly clothes, accessories, and shoes. Owner Erica Cook focuses on designers like Steven Alan, Joie, Twinkle by Wenlan, and Billy Reid who offer easy ways to layer, like bright striped tanks or flirty dresses under flouncy cardis, or colorful Swedish Hasbeens high-heeled clogs with a simple, sophisticated pair of jeans. Open Tues through Sun; closed Mon.

*TULA
3738 N. Southport Ave.
(773) 549-2876
www.tulaboutique.com

When Tula owner Laura Westgate announced in August 2010 that her then 4-year-old Southport shopping corridor boutique would close due to the down economy, there was such a universal cry from customers to keep it open that she reconsidered. Instead, she broadened her price points and cut back a bit on store hours. Thanks to loyal supporters, you can still visit this charming hidden-away spot for timelessly beautiful wardrobe pieces like a luscious cardigan from L.A.-based Pete, and a flowery chiffon top from Hanii Y. Open Tues through Sun; closed Mon.

VIVE LA FEMME
2048 N. Damen Ave.
(773) 772-7429
www.vivelafemme.com

The service: welcoming, customer-focused, funny. The clothes: impeccable, flattering, on-trend, and curve-friendly. Yes, this Bucktown boutique caters to women sizes 12 to 24 and does so with respect and understanding. Owner Stephanie Sack serves as a stunning model for her picks from designers including Comfy USA, Zen Knits, and Kiyonna. In here, size really doesn't matter; it's all about style. Open daily.

WORKSHOP
818 W. 18th St.
(312) 226-9000
www.workshop-chicago.com
www.freidesigns.com

With studio in the back and organically minded retail space up front (check out handmade old-growth wood display pieces), local designer Annie Novotny's Workshop is a perpetual work in progress. Her sustainable sensibility translates to a unique aesthetic—for example, she's been inspired by colors and patterns from the photographs of rural farmers from the Depression—and feminine, floaty flair that has an equally modern mind. Her School of the Art Institute background means she has a certain giddiness about accessories like buttons made out of her vintage fabric scraps and one-of-a-kind jewelry by local arty friends. Although she sells to retailers around the country, all of her items are sewn in Chicago by workers who receive a fair and living wage. Open Wed through Sun.

MEN'S CLOTHING & ACCESSORIES

APARTMENT NUMBER 9
1804 N. Damen Ave.
(773) 395-2999
www.apartmentnumber9.com

Some of today's designers like Paul Smith, Phillip Lim, Earnest Sewn, Rag & Bone, and Band of Outsiders give young, style-conscious guys just the right not-trying-too-hard good looks. Opened by sister team Sarah and Amy Blessing, their Bucktown shop carries them all and achieves a surprisingly manly physique with its concrete floors and rustic wood accents. It also carries accessories, including casual-day cufflinks, grownup jeans, sunglasses, and messenger bags. Open Tues through Sun; closed Mon.

BELMONT ARMY
855 W. Belmont Ave.
(773) 549-1038
www.belmontarmy.wordpress.com

When the logo is a silhouette of a leggy woman holding a machine gun of some kind, you know this is not your average store. And since its opening about 15 years ago, it has not and never will be average. Among its 5 floors and 10,000 square feet, you'll find an eclectic mix: earthy leather Timberland boots, Chrome messenger bags, true army surplus on the 3rd floor (top floor is vintage), skater-friendly sneaks, goofy adult-sized feetie pajamas, and Goth-geek unicorn corpse pendants. Don't let the shaggy staff and no-frills atmosphere fool you: This is not inexpensive stuff, but it's likely hard to find anywhere else. Open daily.

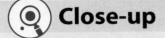

Close-up

An Old Gem

Chicago has said a sad farewell to some shopping institutions, namely Marshall Field's on State Street. But one family-owned business has toughed it out through the decades and remains a stalwart landmark to this day. It's **C.D. Peacock,** a celebrated jewelry store founded in 1837, the same year that Chicago incorporated as a city. Originally called the House of Peacock for founder and third-generation jewelry and watch repairman Elijah Peacock, the sophisticated shop took on the initials of his son Charles Daniel in 1889. Having survived the Great Chicago Fire of 1871 (all the valuables were stored in a fireproof vault), the store grew and moved several times and now has four locations in the city and suburbs. C.D. Peacock has always decked out Chicago's most esteemed movers and shakers, including George Pullman, Potter Palmer, and Marshall Field and continues to ornament celebrities nationwide (Mick Jagger is said to be a customer). From its impeccable Hearts on Fire diamonds to the timeless 1837 Collections honoring the company's history to the fine cultured pearls of legendary Mikimoto and luxury watches by Cartier, Chanel, and Patek Philippe, C.D. Peacock still sparkles. And with such longevity, you can be sure they'll be able to honor that lifetime mounting guarantee. The downtown store is at the Shops at North Bridge, 520 N. Michigan Ave.; (312) 644-5355; www.cdpeacock.com.

✳**CRAM**
3331 N. Broadway
(773) 477-1737
www.cramchicago.com

Recently expanded, this Boystown shop is named (backward) for owner Marc Engel who first opened the high-end Chasalla on Oak Street. He has created a casual-yet-cool look—a chalkboard wall, metal pipes used as racks, repurposed dressers for tables, and a couple of old wood Pepsi boxes to hold accessories. Designers are both American and European (Diesel, Ben Sherman, G-Star, Cheap Monday, Penguin, Lacoste), with a variety of both budget-friendly and happy splurges. There is a selection of women's wear too. Open daily.

HABERDASH
1350 N. Wells St.
(312) 440-1300
www.haberdashmen.com

On his blog, Haberdash owner Adam Beltzman features both a romantically in-depth history of jeans and a glossary of denim-related terms. You see, Beltzman, a former lawyer, is a thinking-man's style-guider. He thinks gym clothes belong in the gym, and he uses the words "dapper" and "gentleman" without pause. But far from being stuffy, this Old Town boutique is woody-warm and welcoming, featuring blazers, comfortable work shirts, slacks, wool pullovers and chunky cardigans, and solid leather shoes meant to look sharp and last long. Another slightly hipper, younger brother store is in River North at 607 N. State St. (312-642-8551). Open daily.

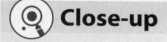

Close-up

Primp and Pamper

From Swedish massages to sassy hairdos, check out 8 of our favorite spots to get prettied up from head to toe.

Circle Salon. Glass of wine, hot towel for your hands, cookies, scalp massage, stool to rest your feet during haircuts. It all adds up to a welcoming feel at this retro-chic Bucktown beauty palace. Stylists make education a top priority and do both cuts and color. But the part we like best? Their eco-friendliness, using products from Davines, natural bamboo brushes, and energy-efficient dryers. 2135 W. Division St.; (773) 715-1026; www.thecirclesalon.com.

Exhale Spa. This upscale Gold Coast destination (one of a handful around the country) is possibly best known for its unique Core Fusion classes—a super-charged strength-training workout that leaves legs shaking and arms aching (it's all good). But it also offers top-notch facials, massages, acupuncture, Thai therapy, and expert nutritional counseling. 945 N. State St.; (312) 753-6500; www.exhalespa.com.

Halo for Men. With 6 locations around Chicago (including this Loop spot), Halo has become the guys' go-to guardian angel of personal aesthetics. "The Man" signature treatment comes with shampoo and conditioning, haircut and style, paraffin hand wax, hand massage, hot towel, and facial toner. There's even a version for kids, aptly called "The Boy." Plus, get beard trims, hot lather shaves, hair color, and more. 70 W. Madison St.; (312) 606-4256; www.halochicago.com.

Juko Nail and Skin Rescue. Glam up fingers and toes at this cheerful, airy storefront in Wicker Park. Bring your own vino and make it a party. Waxings too. 2130 W. Division St.; (773) 772-2990; www.jukochicago.com.

MONTOPOLI CUSTOM CLOTHIERS
714 S. Dearborn St., #7
(312) 987-0987
www.montopolichicago.com

Off the rack? Phooey. It's all hand-picked fabrics from around the world, custom-fit and perfectly suited for you and only you at this 55-year-old bespoke clothing maker. The tailors will come to you or you can visit the relaxing Printers Row showroom. Either way, the experience is gold standard and the result is Rolls-Royce, whether in work shirts, a suit or a formal tuxedo they're creating.

Remember that old saying, "It's better to look good than to feel good"? At Montopoli, you feel good because you look good. Tailoring takes 4 to 8 weeks to complete. Appointments recommended.

SHRINE HABERDASHERY
47 E. Oak St., 2nd Floor
(312) 675-2105
www.shrinestyle.com

Depending on the time of day, customers are offered a cup of coffee or a glass of whiskey as they enter—just a hint at the doting

Marietta's Day Spa and Salon. You don't go to this tucked-away Gold Coast spot for fancy bells and whistles; you go for the friendly down-to-earth service that covers all the self-indulging you need in one place: massages, hair styling, manis and pedis, waxing, and facials. 58 W. Maple St.; (312) 337-4827; www.mariettasdayspa .com.

Salon 1800. A tried-and-true Lincoln Park spot for more than 20 years (it got its own makeover a few years ago), this full-service salon along Armitage Avenue (read: boutiques galore just down the block) offers everything from hair coloring to microdermabrasion, Fantasy Tans to deep muscle massages. Be sure to check their website for special deals. 1133 W. Armitage Ave.; (773) 929-6010; www.salon1800.com.

Thousand Waves Spa. No boys allowed at this lovely little Lakeview retreat. Though you can just pay for use of the petite hot tub, dry sauna, and steam room, it all feels much better after one of the amazing massages or an herbal body wrap. A relaxation room makes for perfect quiet lounging. A special program provides women with cancer with five free massages. 1212 W. Belmont Ave.; (773) 549-0700; www .thousandwavesspa.com.

Urban Oasis. Living up to its name in spades, this temple of TLC focuses only on body treatments: massages, acupuncture (at the North Avenue location), and chiropractic (at Maple Street). From the moment you step into the serene and muted space and are taken to your personal changing room, you're transported to a totally Zen zone. Heavenly massages include aromatherapy, deep tissue, Ashiatsu, trigger point, prenatal, and Thai. Every 60- or 90-minute service includes 20 minutes in a private shower—choose steam, body spray, or rain shower (our favorite). 12 W. Maple St., 3rd Floor; (312) 587-3500; and 939 W. North Ave.; (312) 640-0001; www .urbanoasismassage.com.

(in a good way) service at this Gold Coast men's accessories boutique. The global pursuits of owner Rafik have resulted in an elite (read: expensive) and often exclusive selection for only the most debonair and daringly well-dressed of dudes: demon-head copper cufflinks from Japan that top $1,000; Francesco Maglia tartan-print umbrellas, Italian leather briefcases, handmade imported silk ties, and felt brimmed hats that beg to be tipped. Open daily.

JEWELRY

ERIN GALLAGHER
1013 W. Webster St.
(866) 582-6709
www.egjewelry.com

Yes, Erin Gallagher's instincts for stunning jewelry are well-known across town and now across the country too, but it's her eco-friendly conscience that truly sparkles. Most of the metal she uses is recycled, and stones are conflict-free. You can purchase one of Gallagher's own stunners—from bib necklaces to strings of pearls, chain bracelets to diamond rings—or belly up to the gem bar to choose your own chain, where prices start as low as $15, and produce your own precious trinket (they're ready in about 3 weeks). Other services rock too: Host a party, get a discount on bridal party jewelry, and search her totally intuitive website by gem color, birthstone, metal color, and neckline to find the perfect piece. Open Wed through Sun; open Mon by appointment, closed Tues.

LESTER LAMPERT
57 E. Oak St.
(312) 944-6888
www.lesterlampert.com
In 1995, the Field Museum honored Lester Lampert's then-75 years of business with a 9-day show displaying 100 of the jewel master's most notable baubles from throughout the years. This family-owned shop is still going strong, creating trademarked designs (for instance, their sliding diamond ring) and selling them along with other exquisite lines at their 4-floor Oak Street store. The jewelers on staff specialize in custom work, from engagement rings to standout special occasion pieces. Prices reflect the history and high quality. They also provide appraisals and estate consultations. Open Mon through Sat; closed Sun.

BEAUTY PRODUCTS

*AROMA WORKSHOP
2050 N. Halsted St.
(773) 871-1985
www.aromaworkshop.com
Everyone should have a signature scent, and while there are perfumes aplenty, it's hard to decide on just the right one. That's where the Aroma Workshop comes in. At this tiny Lincoln Park storefront, you sniff out the

perfect blend among nearly 100 different pure essential oils and perfume oils from African musk to clove, lilac to ylang ylang. Need help? Owner Tedd Neenan has ample knowledge with certification from the Pacific Institute of Aromatherapy, and he's happy for you to smell every one before deciding. Just be sure to allow enough time. After you've got the right concoction, it can be used as a cologne, a body lotion, bath salts, and more. And don't worry if you run out: The shop saves your recipe for next time. Want to learn more? Take a class here that teaches you about fragrances that help ease joint pain, muscle aches, and stress.

BRAVCO
43 E. Oak St.
(312) 943-4305
www.bravcobeauty.com
Oak Street has its posh boutiques and exclusive day spas, but it also has Bravco—a jam-packed bath and beauty catch-all that makes product junkies swoon. And we're not talking drugstore cheapo stuff, either, but rather salon-worthy brands like Crew, Bumble and bumble, Keratin, Dermalogica, Kerastase, and Original Sprout—typically for less than you'd pay at the salon. Open daily.

MERZ APOTHECARY
4716 N. Lincoln Ave.
(773) 989-0900
www.smallflower.com
Every cabinet, cubby, nook, and cranny of this Lincoln Square landmark brims with intriguing things like Dr. Singha's Feng Shui Spray, Greens Today Original Superfood Formula, New Chapter LifeShield Mushroom formulas, the store-branded Smallflower Trading Co.'s Royal Saffron soap, and other homeopathic, herbal, natural, European, and otherwise

interesting wellness products. Custom-built with leaded glass windows, parquet floors, and solid oak cabinets to replicate a European apothecary, Merz dates back to 1875 when Pete Merz opened his pharmacy. Abdul Qaiyum bought it in 1972 and then, in 1982, moved it to its current location, but he maintained the time-honored tradition of providing "the best service and products to help our customers lead happier, healthier lives." The only downside: It's so good and so well known (bus tours sometimes stop by) that it's often super-crowded. Open Mon through Sat; closed Sun. Open daily at its location in the Palmer House Hilton, 17 E. Monroe, (312) 781-6900.

CHILDREN'S STORES

BABYDOLLS BOUTIQUE
3727 N. Southport Ave.
(773) 525-2229
www.babydolls-boutique.com
You'll go gaga for this precious Southport corridor shop with its feminine feel and super-cute selection of baby, mommy, and expectant-mom gift items. Owner Vanessa Rodriguez, the first Mexican-American entrepreneur in this neighborhood, carries eye-catching jewelry and handbags, popular Cloud B products like the Sleep Sheep, picture-perfect frames and keepsake albums, rattles and all-cotton aden + anais swaddlers. Plus, part of the proceeds from Rodriguez's own line of handmade baby dresses, christening gowns, and onesies (called Pink & Blue are the new Black) goes to local charities that help needy children and moms-to-be. Open daily.

✳BUILDING BLOCKS
3306 N. Lincoln Ave.
(773) 525-6200
www.buildingblockstoys.com
From classic ABC blocks to Plan Toys' more creative block sets, farm-sound blocks to bath blocks, and blocks in a bevy of different foreign alphabets, this Lakeview store bursts with blocks—not to mention a huge assortment of other great toys and a whole lot of toy-loving energy. Looking for a birthday present for a 3-year-old boy or a 9-year-old girl? The longtime staff can point you to top sellers, their personal favorites, and the newest fads. Fire engines with lights and sounds, sticker books, kids' music CDs, a full line of tiny Calico Critters, dolls and doll clothes, Groovy Girls, and Bruder trucks; they're all here. Bring your kids in at your own risk. Also in Wicker Park at 2130 W. Division St. (773-235-1888). Open daily.

PSYCHO BABY
1630 N. Damen Ave.
(773) 772-2815
www.psychobabyonline.com
For kids with a little rock and roll in their souls (or genes), this Wicker Park kid shop opened by two moms in 2003 is a must. Chuck the pink frills and go with a Run DMC T-shirt, a onesie that says, "Boob Man," a skull-and-crossbones sun hat, or a zebra-print dress with glitter detailing. There are also some pink frilly things and typical blue boy stuff, but it's all made by rad brands like Rowdy Sprout, Appaman, and Chaser LA. Prices might seem steep, but the big points for being seen with your cool kid make up for it. Come for a kickin' storytime with "Really Nili" Wed morning. Open daily.

SECOND CHILD
954 W. Armitage Ave.
(773) 883-0880
www.2ndchild.com

You barely have time to wash and fold your kids' clothes before they've moved onto the next size. It can be a whirlwind, not to mention a money pit, to constantly update their wardrobes. And that's where Amy Helgren comes in. She got the idea for her Lincoln Park consignment store in 1987 after the birth of her second child, who couldn't simply wear the hand-me-downs from her bigger sister because she was a different size and born in a different season (hence, the name). Being selective about what she allows into her tiny, packed-to-brimming store means that you'll find gently used or even new gear and garb for infants through children's size 14, as well as maternity, with labels like Ralph Lauren, Tea, Jacadi, Catimini, North Face, and Joe's Jeans. End-of-season sales offer deep discounts; get there early. Open daily.

TIMELESS TOYS
4749 N. Lincoln Ave.
(773) 334-4445
www.timelesstoyschicago.com

Let your kids occupy themselves at the train table while you browse this Lincoln Square favorite for princess and pirate dress-ups, board books, Plan Toys, miYim organic plushies, kid-friendly kites, puppets galore, and Melissa & Doug puzzles. Just beware the craziness here during Christmas holiday shopping, know that they offer only store credit for returns, and don't blame us if your child doesn't want to leave that train table when you're ready to go. Open daily.

HOME & GARDEN

JAYSON HOME & GARDEN
1885 N. Clybourn Ave.
(800) 472-1885
www.jaysonhomeandgarden.com

InStyle, House Beautiful, Real Simple, and *Redbook* magazines have all featured items from this decorator's dream store. And it's no wonder. A hand-rubbed mahogany Essex buffet table, leather upholstered ottoman, vintage Suzani feather pillows, a solid wood candle-bulb chandelier, faux zebra-hide rugs, and exotic orchids. This Lincoln Park store's high-end selection of unique imported and antique goods, sophisticated home furnishings, flowers, and plants is everything you need to make your own home and garden gorgeous and magazine spread–worthy. Open daily.

MATERIAL POSSESSIONS
704 N. Wabash Ave.
(312) 280-4885
www.materialpossessions.com

For more than 30 years, this Gold Coast store has been a go-to for upscale gifts, particularly from their gift registry. Find hand-painted Cantaria dinnerware, Nambé tulip-bud vases, handmade Limoges porcelain trays and plates inspired by Persian rug patterns, luxe bed linens and pillows by Ann Gish, and understated jewelry. Open daily.

✳P.O.S.H.
613 N. State St.
(312) 280-1602
www.poshchicago.com

The word "posh" originated with early 20th-century steamship journeys from England to India. Wealthy travelers could afford to book cabins for the 30-day trip that kept them out of the sun—"Port Out Starboard Home." It's

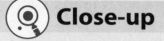

Close-up

Galleries Galore

Got a blank wall or a mantle that needs some fancying-up? No matter your style, you're sure to find just the right piece at one of Chicago's many art galleries. For sheer concentration of options, the River North area can't be beat. From roughly Chicago Avenue south to Kinzie Street, Orleans Street east to Dearborn, there are nearly three dozen, showcasing everything from Outsider Art at the **Judy A Saslow Gallery** (300 W. Superior St.; 312-943-0530; www.jsaslowgallery.com) to the 20,000-square-foot **Gruen Galleries** (226 W. Superior St.; 312-337-6262; www.gruengalleries.com) featuring contemporary American and European sculpture and paintings. **The Golden Triangle** (330 N. Clark St.; 312-755-1266; www.goldentriangle.biz) houses a massive collection of Asian and European antiques and furniture, and **ArchiTech Gallery** (730 N. Franklin St.; 312-475-1290; www.architechgallery.com) offers a unique array of architectural art. Get a complete listing of galleries, plus find out about the artists, exhibit openings and other events, as well as the greater Chicago gallery scene (in Pilsen, the West Loop, Bucktown and Wicker Park, Michigan Avenue, and beyond) from *Chicago Gallery News,* a magazine published three times a year in January, April, and September, and online at www.chicagogallerynews.com.

the perfect moniker for this utterly quaint store that carries the most wonderful home enhancers, many hailing from across the pond. It's a delightful mix of charming flea-market finds; commercial china intended for, but never used at, hotels, country clubs, and restaurants around the world; and a carefully edited selection of new items. Among the finds: a vintage, wall-mounted French Kitchenalia coffee grinder, a pair of painted cast-iron Westie dog bookends, restored and replated silver-plate soup spoons from England (some stamped with a hotel crest), and a set of whimsical yellow plates decorated with French gnomes. It's hard to choose; we want it all. Open daily.

POST 27
1819 W. Grand Ave.
(312) 829-6122
www.post27store.com

Angela Finney-Hoffman dreamed of owning her own furniture store by the time she was 27—but it wasn't until 2008, after some time designing furniture and lighting for acclaimed designer Holly Hunt in Chicago and after ("post," get it?) her 27th year when she finally went out on her own. She has since made her own name for herself with her ever-changing display of mid-century modern, plus reclaimed and repurposed pieces, locally grown accessories, and even some clothing items. Inspired, but don't know for what? Ask Finney-Hoffman for an in-home consultation. Open Tues through Sun; closed Mon.

✳SCOUT
5221 N. Clark St.
(773) 275-5700
www.scoutchicago.com

You'll stumble upon this Andersonville boutique, you'll be pulled in, you'll browse, you'll feel right at home. And then you'll bring something from here to your own home. It happens all the time, because devoted owner Larry Vodak knows how to "scout" out those antique-y, forlorn but fabulous, and hidden gems of furniture and lovely decorative pieces. And he knows that they don't just have to look good, but they have to have soul too. From the design junkie to the design flunkie, Scout can help you find that perfect table, bookcase, chair, or lamp. And then you'll probably be back for something else to go with it. Open Tues through Sun; closed Mon.

TABULA TUA
1015 W. Armitage Ave.
(773) 525-3500
www.tabulatua.com

Don't just set your table, decorate it with artful pieces that reflect your personality. Grace Tsao-Wu's Lincoln Park shop has been a favorite of party hosts around the city for more than 15 years, and she also has a thriving wedding registry business. Because she scours the world for pieces you wouldn't find at any old department store, Tsao-Wu's vibrant selection includes glass pitchers made in Italy by Match Pewter, sweet sponge-decorated pottery from UK-based Emma Bridgewater, meticulously crafted porcelain china from Germany, Budapest-based Anna Weatherly's delicately painted porcelain designs, and Royal Crown Derby fine bone china that's been made in England since 1750. Plus, there are handmade knives, kitchen and serving utensils, drinkware, condiment sets, placemats, sake and sushi sets, and more. Open daily.

SHOES & ACCESSORIES

✳1154 LILL
904 W. Armitage Ave.
(773) 477-LILL (5455)
www.1154lill.com

In 1999, Jennifer Velarde was sewing handbags in her studio apartment at 1154 W. Lill St. in Chicago. After showcasing the bags, along with fabric swatches she made them from, at a local street fair, an idea was born. An idea that has become nothing less than a retail sensation: customized bags designed by the customer herself. Popular with girls' nights out, bridal parties and as gifts, Lill is now a bustling Armitage Avenue boutique, offering 30 styles of bags and accessories and an endless array of exquisite fabrics to mix and match to make your perfect bag. Choose a clutch, wristlet, "mom" bag, shoulder purse, or work tote and carry it with pride, knowing that you actually designed it yourself. And don't worry if the fabric options overwhelm, the staff knows how to steer you right, so you won't be disappointed. Open daily.

✳ALAMO SHOES
5321 N. Clark St.
(773) 784-8936
www.alamoshoes.com

In our self-serve, quick-serve, toss-away culture, it's a pleasure to find a family-owned business that values its customers and takes time to serve them right. An Andersonville favorite that even has free parking, Alamo carries brands of the best and comfiest kind like Keen, Teva, Born, Mephisto, Earth, Rockport, ecco, Merrill, and Birkenstock. And the service is of the real-life, actual salesman type. They never hover, but they're always around when you need them. In fact, many of the employees have been around for much of this store's 30 years, so they know their stock and will make suggestions if you're overwhelmed, pull out alternatives from the stacks in the back room, and never make you feel silly if you try on a dozen pairs before choosing the right one. They specialize in sending customers home with a perfect fit, whether super-narrow or extra-wide, and the same goes for kids, who also get balloons on the way out. Open daily.

CITY SOLES
1566 N. Damen Ave./2001 W. North Ave.
(888) GO-FUNKY, (773) 489-2001
www.citysoles.com
Dress your feet up in the hippest styles from around the world at this Wicker Park shop. Men's and women's shoes range from ballet flats to platform knockouts, casual everyday to special occasion. The extensive stock changes frequently, so if you're aching for that metallic leather Corso Como bootie or vegetable-dyed Cydwoq boot, a black patent leather sky-high heel from Cavage or a Brazilian-made vegan shoe by NeuAura, you'd better box it up and go before it's gone. Scan their sale shoes to save a few bucks, as hip feet don't come cheap here. Open daily.

CLICK
3729 N. Southport Ave.
(773) 244-9141
www.clickshoes.net
"Shoe salesman" can have a negative connotation, but not at this feminine and lighthearted Southport store where the staff seriously adores shoes and truly wants to spread the love. Come in to browse the winning mix of sexy and casual, sporty and flirty, casual and downright delicious—and don't be shy about asking for help or buying those fabulous open-toe, high-heeled sandals or spirited two-tone wedges or pumps with rhinestone detail. Don't worry, you'll find something to wear them with. Click goes crazy every year with its buy one, get one for a penny sale. Open daily.

HOUSE OF SOLE
1237 S. Michigan Ave.
(312) 834-0909
www.houseofsole.net
In 2007, Tiffany Bullock kicked aside her finance and banking career and put her money where her feet are. In her contemporary-chic South Loop boutique, you'll find the perfect merging of cool and comfy. Prices reflect the high quality of brands like Spain-based Chie Mihara, Dav Western-styled rainboots, super-soft leather Fidji made in Portugal, and the bohemian-chic GeeWaWa. Complete your outfit with Bullock's selection of purses, clothes, tights, and jewelry. Open daily.

KATHRYN KERRIGAN
2031 N. Damen Ave.
(773) 235-7150
www.kathrynkerrigan.com
Chicago-area native Kathryn Kerrigan once struggled to find fashionable prom shoes for her size 11 feet. Now she makes it a snap for other tall women to do so with her eponymous haute line of flats, pumps, boots, ballet-style shoes, and sandals. Sold in sizes 9 through 13 at her Bucktown shop and from size 5 online (European sizes 35 to 46), the shoes are handcrafted in Spain and Italy and reflect the elegant and classic sensibilities Kerrigan learned from her socialite, flapper-era grandmother Dottie Kerrigan. Giving larger-framed women an extra leg up, Kerrigan's store is owned by and across the

street from Stephanie Sack's Vive La Femme clothing boutique. Kathryn Kerrigan also has a store in Libertyville at 14047 Petronella Dr., Ste. 105 (847-557-5067). Open Tues through Sun; Mon by appointment.

LORI'S SHOES
824 W. Armitage Ave.
(773) 281-5655
www.lorisshoes.com

Locals who love shoes know Lori's. Since Lori Andre opened her first 650-square-foot shop in 1983, it has grown to become a 4,500-square-foot temple to toesies and expanded to include several suburban locations as well. But the Armitage Avenue boutique is the first and best. From Spanish espadrilles from Andre Assous to Italian leather sandals from Zamagni, Lori's carries dozens of the trendiest, most fashion-forward styles for feet around. Most shoe boxes don't hide behind a secret door; they're out on the floor, stacked high with the shoes displayed atop. It makes it easy to know if they've got your size, but tricky to maneuver when it's busy, which it almost always is (hint: leave your huge tote bag at home and park that stroller outside, please). Open daily.

STATIONERY & GIFTS

ELEVENZEES
1901 W. Division St.
(773) 772-1150
www.elevenzees.com

Opened by mom and son team Patty and Chad Johnson, this Wicker Park shop's cute name comes from the English tradition of having a snack and tea between breakfast and lunch, known as "elevenses." Here, it translates to a carefree spirit and an eclectic array of gifts for hostesses, housewarmings,

new moms, and that friend who seems to have it all. Items in the cozy space include adorable Trumpette socks for baby, sweetly scented candles from Archipelago, stationery from Meri Meri, lacy underthings from Hanky Panky, and scrumptious exotic chocolates from Vosges. Located within the store is Temple Beautiful, where you can indulge your spirit with energy workshops, tarot card readings, Reiki, and more. Open daily.

✳ENJOY, AN URBAN GENERAL STORE
4723 N. Lincoln Ave.
(773) 334-8626
www.urbangeneralstore.com

We dare you to leave this store without uttering a chuckle or two. After all, Rebecca Wood's Lincoln Square store has a serious sense of humor, carrying silly stuff like bacon air fresheners; "Stop Copying Me" onesies for twins; a birthday card that reads, "Today's your birthday and we should do special birthday things like eat pie and swear"; a Minor Miracle mug that reveals an image of the Holy Mother after you've finished your hot drink; a *Psycho* image shower curtain; packages of three Little Missmatched socks; and a Mr. T In Your Pocket key chain. But Enjoy has a sentimental side too, with inspiring books and art panel prints, beautiful frames, sterling silver necklaces, and journals and memory books. Open daily.

GAY MART
3457 N. Halsted St.
(773) 929-4272

Less "gay" than offbeat, this Boystown shop caters to boys who don't want to grow up, with comic book action figures and movie figurines like Batman, Spiderman, the Hulk, and characters from the *Wizard of Oz*. You'll also find some gay pride paraphernalia like

Good to Go

Grab up gourmet gifts, pack for a picnic, stock your fridge, or plan for a party at one of these gastronomically oriented shops.

The Chopping Block. Well known for its top-notch recreational cooking classes for everyone from close friends to couples, kids to corporate teams, the Chopping Block also has shelves full of dreamy foodstuffs, plus kitchen utensils and gadgets. In Lincoln Square at 4747 N. Lincoln Ave.; (773) 472-6700; and in the Merchandise Mart at Kinzie and Wells Streets; (312) 644-6360; www.thechoppingblock.net.

The City Olive. The olive reigns at this Andersonville boutique. Owner Karen Rose, a former nurse who hopes to spread the healthy word about olive oil, invites visitors to taste any of the oils—virgin, infused, and flavored—that hail from around the world, and many of the vinegars and other foods (tapenades, jams, spices, mustards) before buying. Plus, olives aren't just for eating; she sells olive-based cosmetics and soaps too. 5408 N. Clark St.; (773) 878-5408; www.cityolive.com.

The French Market. Crepes, pastoral artisan cheeses, Belgian fries and beer, cheesy popcorn, decadent chocolates, cooked-to-order pasta, and organic produce all find a home in this West Loop European-inspired indoor food market with more than 30 vendors, many of which are local entrepreneurial businesses. 131 N. Clinton St.; (312) 575-0306; www.frenchmarketchicago.com.

Gene's Sausage Shop. From Louisana-born andouille to Poland's zywiecka, this longtime favorite for meaty treats offers more than 40 smoked-in-house sausages and 30 types of deli meats. You can't miss the huge cow that marks this meat-lover's spot. In Lincoln Square at 4750 N. Lincoln Ave.; (773)-SAUSAGE; and the original location at 5330 W. Belmont Ave.; (773) 777-6322; www.genessausageshop.com.

Joong Boo Market. You might not understand all the descriptions at this Asian produce market, but if you've got an adventurous palate, go for it—and be prepared for some super-spicy stuff (kimchi, anyone?). Don't miss the perfectly thin-skinned dumplings. 3333 N. Kimball Ave.; (773) 478-5566; www.joongboomarket.com.

Nuts on Clark. No frills, just bins, bags, and shelves stacked with snacks both salty and sweet. For more than 30 years, this Wrigleyville shop has been selling gourmet cheese and caramel popcorn, dried fruits, candies, nuts of all kinds, and chocolate-covered everything. 3830 N. Clark St.; (773) 549-6622; www.nutsonclark.com.

Provenance Food & Wine. Pair high-quality, low-priced wine with delectable goodies like homemade crackers, pasture-raised meats, and fresh-baked breads. The "Taste Chicago" basket is lovingly filled with locally made deliciousness, both sweet and savory. In Logan Square at 2528 N. California Ave.; (773) 384-0699; and Lincoln Square at 2312 W. Leland Ave.; (773) 784-2314; www.provenancefoodandwine.com.

T-shirts and rainbow wind socks, along with the occasional kinky item (i.e., it's probably not the place to bring young children). Generally open daily (closed Tues during the winter).

GREENHEART SHOP
1911 W. Division St.
(312) 264-1625
www.greenheartshop.org
You can't miss the pink-and-white striped awning embellished with a large green heart—and you shouldn't. With its focus on sustainable businesses, fair trade, and eco-friendly goods, and its nonprofit status, you'll not only find extraordinary gift items from more than 60 different countries—oil drums–turned-artwork from Haiti, olive oil from Palestine, cards from Rwanda, and recycled wine-bottle glassware from northern Wisconsin—you'll also add a drop in the do-good bucket. The Ukrainian Village store is a retail extension of the Center for Cultural Interchange (CCI), a not-for-profit organization founded in 1985 to promote cultural understanding among nations, environmental consciousness, and world peace. Open daily.

RENEGADE HANDMADE
1924 W. Division St.
(773) 227-2707
www.renegadehandmade.com
Just up the street from Greenheart is another gem of handicrafts. This one focuses on works by hundreds of artists from around the world who have something to sell, sometimes beautiful, frequently folksy, often quirky, always one-of-a-kind. Renegade began as a hugely successful local crafts fair—and still is—so the brick and mortar store is an offshoot of that. Here, you can browse for handmade belts, vegan soap bars, crocheted scarves, knit baby moccasins, birchbark votive candle holders, and a bevy of other giftables, all without worrying about the weather. Open daily.

ROTOFUGI
2780 N. Lincoln Ave.
(773) 868-3308
www.rotofugi.com
A sort of toy store for grown-ups, this wonderfully wacked-out part-retail, part-gallery space boasts a loyal following for many a good reason. Starting with owners Kirby and Whitney Kerr, who clearly love their curating kookiness and appreciate the people who come to check it out. The plethora of vinyl figures—Japanese anime-type monsters, the Simpsons, Marshall the marshmallow boy, "wickedly awesome" Chinese zodiac animals—changes often, as does the rotating mix of modern-pop gallery work. What's in the name, you ask? A combination of the word "roto," taken from the roto-casting molding process for many vinyl toys, and the name of their beagle-shih tzu Fugi (who's usually padding around the store). Open daily.

SPARE PARTS
2947 N. Broadway
(773) 525-4242
www.shopspareparts.com
For more than 20 years, this welcoming shop has been a favorite for picking up purses, backpacks, briefcases, and messenger bags. Exclusive lines by Village Tannery and well-known brands like HOBO and Burton mean price ranges vary. With husband-and-wife team Donte and Vanessa Mearon, you know you'll also find a mix of items for both men and women. Of note for the guys: the

cufflinks made from wood salvaged from stadium seats including Notre Dame's and ties made from vintage Chicago and New York maps. Jewelry from local designers, baby accessories, stylish scarves and hats, and artwork by Donte himself complete the picture. Open daily.

UNCLE FUN
1338 W. Belmont Ave.
(773) 477-8223
www.unclefunchicago.com
When you need a little pick-me-up, forget the caffeine and head to this "little shop of har-hars." It'll bring you back to your carefree days, it'll make you giggle, guffaw, maybe groan; it'll put you in a kick-up-your-heels mood that you can bag up and take home with you. After all, life is always funnier when you've got a stink bomb, some fart powder, an Astro Boy clock, Pez candy, bacon lip balm, handshake buzzers and, fittingly a "Stooges in Your Pocket" noisemaker. Feel better? We thought so. Open daily.

RECORD SHOPS

PERMANENT RECORDS
1914 W. Chicago Ave.
(773) 278-1744
www.permanentrecordschicago.com
Call this place P-Rex for short and you'll sound like an insider at this thriving Ukrainian Village shop. Give the resident cat Zaireeka (a Flaming Lips reference) a friendly pat, and you're a pal for life. But you're a welcome visitor no matter what, because owners Lance Barresi and Liz Tooley want it to be that way. In a time when true record stores are fast disappearing, the pair opened this vinyl- and indie-label mecca—and have made it work by keeping on top of what their customers

want, buying direct from bands whenever they can, stocking rare finds and what they like, then enthusiastically sharing it all with their clientele. They also have their own indie label and understand that high-tech listening and buying go hand in hand with old-time media. Their website and e-commerce site are stellar, their weekly newsletter has a loyal following, and they happily electronically alert people to concerts around town. Open daily.

RECKLESS RECORDS
3126 N. Broadway
(773) 404-5080
www.reckless.com
Get over the sometimes music-snobbish staff and revel in the excellent selection of new and used records, CDs, DVDs, video games, and even some VHS tapes and cassettes for those who can't shake the 1980s. Concert posters decorate the windows and walls, and some performances take place right here in the Lakeview store. With items meticulously categorized, the organization is far from reckless, though your purchasing might be as you discover new releases from local and national acts the likes of Deathspell Omega, Furze, Brain Idea, and Wolfgang Voigt; and old favorites like Burt Bacharach, Harry Belafonte, Captain & Tennille, Olivia Newton-John, and Barbra Streisand. Happy hunting! Also in Wicker Park at 1532 N. Milwaukee Ave.; (773) 235-3727; and the Loop at 26 E. Madison; (312) 795-0878. Open daily.

TRANSISTOR
5045 N. Clark St.
(312) 863-1375
www.transistorchicago.com
Hard to peg into any one retail hole, this inventive Andersonville store has music in its

heart and art in its soul. Paintings, live-music photography, and mixed-media fill the black walls. Conversation-starter buys include jewelry made from hexagon hardware nuts or stamps from around the world, and clocks fashioned from hard drives and vinyl records. Plus, letterpress cards, calendars, a button vending machine, and hard-to-find coffee-table books from publishers like Princeton Architectural Press, Black Dog, and Phaidon; indie and electronica CDs and vinyl including PJ Harvey, The National, Depeche Mode, Roxy Music, and New Pornographers. Bit of a musician yourself? Check out the synths, turntables, headphones, high-end speakers, monitors, mixers, and unusual instruments (Beep-It optical theremin, perhaps?). And if you just want to come and hang out, that's A-OK. Owners Rani Woolpert and Andy Miles host everything from live daily webcasts, live music performances every Friday evening, free film screenings, and tutoring and group instruction on a variety of musical and artistic topics. And did we mention the Ping-Pong table? Open daily from 1 p.m.

ANNUAL EVENTS & FESTIVALS

Chicago is a four-season city, and lucky for us, its festivals are too. Below is just a sampling of the many events that take place throughout the year. Most are family-friendly, and many are free or simply require a small donation that usually benefits the host neighborhood association. Chicagoans love to eat, and its many food fests reflect that, along with the our penchant for a big parade—some parades are listed here, but for info on even more, like the Polish Constitution Parade, the Puerto Rican Parade, and the Disability Pride Parade, just head to the City of Chicago's event database at www .explorechicago.org; here, you can also search by date, type of event or festival, and free events. Consider taking public transportation to most of these events, because parking is just a hassle, especially when a festival closes several blocks of streets.

JANUARY

FLOWER SHOWS
Lincoln Park Conservatory
2391 N. Stockton Dr.
www.chicagoparkdistrict.com
(312) 742-7736

Garfield Park Conservatory
300 N. Central Park Ave.
www.garfieldconservatory.org
(773) 638-1766
Beginning of Jan and end of Jan through early May
At the beginning of the year, these two conservatories are wrapping up their festive displays of winter holiday flora, featuring vibrant poinsettias. At the end of the month, they give visitors a stunning sneak-peek at spring, with a changing palette of pretty pinks, purples, yellows, and lots of lush greenery to ease the winter doldrums and stir thoughts of sunnier days.

FEBRUARY

CHINATOWN LUNAR NEW YEAR PARADE
Wentworth Avenue and Cermak Road
(312) 326-5320
www.chicagochinatown.org
Early Feb
Ring in the Lunar New Year with this colorful parade through Chicago's tight-knit Chinatown community. Along with marching bands, festooned floats, lion dancers, and the annual Miss Friendship pageant, a highlight is the fabulous 100-foot-long paper-and-silk dragon. While you're in the area, be sure to stop into the many authentic Asian markets for souvenirs and the season's famous moon cakes. Free.

MARCH

CHICAGO FLOWER & GARDEN SHOW
Navy Pier
Festival Hall
600 E. Grand Ave.
(312) 595-5400
www.chicagoflower.com
Early Mar, spanning 9 days
Spring starts early in Chicago—at least indoors, with seemingly billions of blooms that turn Navy Pier's Festival Hall into a glorious scene that would make Monet jealous. In fact, there are dozens of artistic gardens to see: from the feature gardens that follow each year's changing theme to the tablescapes that offer flowery inspiration for entertaining, and the colorful horticulture competition, featuring the best-of-the-best houseplants, window boxes, and garden-geared photography. Need more motivation? The marketplace rounds up more than 100 vendors to plant ideas in your head for your own garden. Not quite the green thumb? Educational seminars inform and illuminate on everything from landscaping to organic gardening. And a Kids' Activity Garden gives budding bloomers a place to express themselves. Entrance fee weekdays $15; weekends $17; children 4 to 12 $5 all days.

ST. PATRICK'S DAY PARADE
Columbus Drive and Balbo Avenue,
north to Monroe Street
(312) 942-9188
www.chicagostpatsparade.com
Saturday before St. Patrick's Day
There are more than a million people who claim Irish roots in the Windy City, but everyone gets a little green on St. Patrick's Day. Paint a shamrock on your face and join the 350,000-plus onlookers at this massive downtown parade that boasts a waving lot of politicians and other city VIPs, plus a kilted clan of bagpipers and the chosen St. Patrick's Day Queen. For added green-day excitement, start off at the Michigan Avenue Bridge (get there at about 9:30 a.m.) to catch a glimpse of Chicago's famous dyeing of its river. The Chicago Journeymen Plumbers started the odd tradition back in 1962 and it's grown into a holiday favorite, but don't ask how they get that perfect shade of Kelly green, because it's a guarded secret. Free. Parade starts at noon.

APRIL

EGG-STRAVAGANZA AT SOLDIER FIELD
1410 S. Museum Campus Dr.
(312) 235-7000
www.soldierfield.net
Weekend before Easter
Each Easter season, gridiron action at Soldier Field takes a backseat to a good old-fashioned egg hunt. Actually, the organizers make it pretty easy to find the eggs (after all, where can they hide them on a football field?), but the kids won't mind when they open their loot of candy. Plus, there are face-painters, balloon artists, a live concert, and of course a much-anticipated visit from the big bunny himself. An Easter breakfast can be added to the event for a fee. The egg-grab is free.

MAY

BIKE THE DRIVE
Lake Shore Drive
Start at Columbus Drive and Jackson
Boulevard
North to Bryn Mawr Avenue, south to
57th Street
(312) 427-3325
www.bikethedrive.org
Sunday of Memorial Day weekend

It's a one-day-only novelty to be able to pedal down Lake Shore Drive. And it's quite a site to see when it happens—but even more fun to do. No cars, just bikes, tons and tons of all types, riders of all ages, and smiles on everyone's faces. Run by the Active Transportation Alliance as a fund-raiser for their programs and advocacy, the ride starts at the break of dawn, 5:30 a.m., so that the drag can reopen to vehicles by 10 a.m. The whole route is 30 miles, but you're not required to bike the whole thing, and several rest stops along the way provide snacks, water, and bike repairs. Bring your own bike or rent one for a discount from Bike and Roll Chicago and Bobby's Bike Hike (see the Tours chapter). When you're done riding, head over to the participants' festival at Jackson Boulevard and Columbus Drive where there's breakfast ($7), live music, a kids' activity area, and booths of goodies. Advance registration is $42 for non-Active Transportation Alliance members ($37 members); children 17 and under $15; day-of registration is $55. There are discounts for registering by a certain date, and if you sign up for more than one Active Transportation Alliance ride and/or become a member, it's also cheaper.

GREEN CITY MARKET
South end of Lincoln Park
Between Clark Street and Stockton Drive
Early May through late October
(773) 880-1266
www.greencitymarket.org

When you see some of the best chefs in the city purchasing their produce for the day here, you know it's gotta be good. And it is. Since its tiny beginnings in 1998, it now draws more than 175,000 people each season. You can pick up fresh, local, and sustainably grown and produced fruits and veggies, flowers and plants, cheeses, baked goods, and meats. Or just come for lunch—homemade bread and artisanal cheese will do the trick nicely, or order up a divine crepe, made while you wait. Top chef demonstrations take place throughout the season, and there's usually a live musical act or two each day. Its Lincoln Park setting makes it all sublime. It runs every Wed and Sat from 7 a.m. to 1 p.m. During off-season months, from Jan through Apr (typically two Saturdays each month), the Green City Market takes cover in the lobby and South Gallery of the Peggy Notebaert Nature Museum (2430 N. Cannon Dr.). Free.

MEMORIAL DAY PARADE
State Street from Lake Street south to
Van Buren Street
(312) 744-3315
Memorial Day

Honoring fallen heroes, Chicago's Memorial Day Parade has been a big deal since it began in 1870, and is now one of the largest in the nation. Wave hello to the mayor and other politicians, along with marching bands, and veterans' groups. Start time is noon.

JUNE

57TH STREET ART FAIR
57th Street
Between Kenwood and Kimbark
Avenues
(773) 493-3247
www.57thstreetartfair.org
First weekend in June
A beloved tradition for more than 60 years in the Hyde Park area, this juried art fair (the oldest in Chicago) got its start when silversmith Mary Louise Womer created an event where local artists could show and sell their original works. It has since blossomed into a much-lauded art extravaganza that attracts over 20,000 visitors to browse and buy from more than 250 artists of all types, plus kids' activities, and munchies to keep up your energy. Free.

ANDERSONVILLE MIDSOMMARFEST
Clark Street
Between Foster and Catalpa Avenues
(773) 728-2995
www.andersonville.org/midsommarfest
Second weekend in June
Andersonville itself is so hip and fun that the festival just gives you an excuse to go there—along with about 50,000 other people. Going on for more than 45 years, this event rocks out with two days of local bands, food, kid fun, and vendor booths. The area's Swedish roots come out for the party with Nordic folkdancers, the traditional Maypole dance, and a Swedish women's choir. $5 donation; seniors and children 12 and under free.

CHICAGO BLUES FESTIVAL
Grant Park
Jackson Boulevard and Columbus Drive
(312) 744-3315
www.explorechicago.org
Second weekend in June

Shemekia Copeland, B.B. King, John Primer, Eddie "The Chief" Clearwater, Koko Taylor, and Willie "Big Eyes" Smith. They've all banged out the blues at this blast of a festival that makes the most of its place in the Blues Capital of the World. It started in 1984 with a tribute to Muddy Waters a year after his death and continues to honor blues legends who have made musical history, both past and present. Three days of concerts on four stages, all for free. Can't get blue over that. Food and beverage tickets sold separately.

FAMILY FUN FESTIVAL
Millennium Park, Chase Promenade North
North Michigan Avenue and East Randolph Street
(312) 742-1168
www.millenniumpark.org
Mid-June through mid-Aug
Chicagoans have got to hand it to retail giant Target: It sure does spread its wealth as sponsor of free admission times at museums and of this popular summertime kid corral. Sing-alongs and live bands twice daily; story times at the stocked book nook; rotating activity zones from area orgs like the Lurie Garden, the roving Chinese-American Museum of Chicago, Chicago History Museum, and Chicago Architecture Foundation; plus blocks, hula-hoops, and beanbag tosses all out for the playing. The big white tent makes it weather-resistant (watch for puddles here and there when it rains hard), and its Millennium Park location makes it perfect for post-play picnics. Free.

GAY & LESBIAN PRIDE PARADE
From Belmont and Halsted to Sheridan and Diversey
(773) 348-8243
www.explorechicago.org
www.chicagopridecalendar.org
Last Sunday in June
The more outrageous the better at this annual spectacle, one of the largest gay pride parades in the country. Cars of supporting politicians, and festooned floats from community organizations, businesses, media, and more make their way through Boystown, attracting a raucous and jampacked cheering crowd of equally colorful onlookers. It's the highlight of the GLBT Pride Fest weekend. Free.

MAIFEST CHICAGO
Lincoln and Leland Avenues
(773) 545-4800
www.mayfestchicago.com
First weekend in June
Lincoln Square embraces its German roots with this traditional welcoming of the arrival of spring. Along with the anticipated kegtapping and crowning of the May Queen, it features live bands, German folk music, and dancing around the decked-out May Pole. Free.

RAVINIA FESTIVAL
200 Ravinia Park Rd., Highland Park
Tickets (847) 266-5100
www.ravinia.org
The oldest outdoor music festival in the country got its start back in 1904 as an amusement park. It is now a summer must-do, attracting about 600,000 visitors each summer who flock here for a listen to music ranging from Rufus Wainwright to Jennifer Hudson, the Doobie Brothers to the Chicago Symphony Orchestra (this is its summer home). Pack a picnic for lawn seating under the stars or purchase food at one of the many food vendors and restaurants and take it back to your blanket. For the big bucks, you can get tickets for seats under the covered pavilion (you can still dine on the lawn first). Ticket prices vary. Outdoor parking is available at the facility, as well as free park-and-ride buses and a Metra line train that adds a stop at festival grounds during Ravinia season only. The concert series runs from early June through mid-September.

RIBFEST CHICAGO
Lincoln Avenue at the intersection of Irving Park and Damen Avenue
(773) 525-3609
www.ribfest-chicago.com
Second weekend in June
Carnivores converge on the Northcenter neighborhood for this finger-licking spread of the best ribs the city has to offer. With upwards of 50,000 hungry souls, you might have to fight for a bite, but don't worry, with two dozen restaurants slinging out a total of about 50,000 pounds of ribs, there's enough to go around. Plus, there are two stages of local and national live bands, a Kids Square with loads of activities for getting sillies out, and a celebrity-judged "Best Ribs" winner. $5 donation.

TASTE OF CHICAGO
Grant Park
(312) 742-4387
www.chicagoparkdistrict.com
Last week in June through July 3
The mother of all Chicago festivals, this one is a dizzying gastronomic delight, with 60 restaurants serving up six different items each, ranging from pizza and pasta to pad

Thai and giant turkey legs, Eli's cheesecake to original rainbow ice cream cones. The feeding frenzy began small in 1980 and has expanded to attract more than 3 million visitors each year. You want to try everything, don't you? Well, you can at least fit in a few more nibbles with the smaller, 2-bucks-or-less "Taste Of" portions served at each stand. And if you fear this is a dieter's nightmare, just look for green apple icons on the menus, denoting a healthier option. To rein in costs, in 2011, The Taste (what you should call it if you want to sound like a local) gathered four annual lakefront music festivals—Viva Chicago Latin Music Festival, the Chicago Country Music Festival, Celtic Fest Chicago, and the Chicago Gospel Music Festival—to entertain here, replacing previous big-name acts that performed in the past. The merging also put the focus back on Chicago and its diverse and delicious food. Designated Taste parking lots include free trolley service to the festival. Food and beverage tickets are sold in strips of 12 for $8, and large dishes run typically seven or eight tickets.

THEATER ON THE LAKE
2401 N. Lake Shore Dr.
(312) 742-7994
www.chicagoparkdistrict.com
Mid-June to early Aug
Chicago is lucky to live by the lake, and it makes full use of all its facilities—including this 1920 Prairie Style–inspired building, which served until 1939 as a recuperation ward for babies with tuberculosis or other diseases, then later as a USO Center. In 1952, it took on a theatrically oriented persona, and in 1996 became the site of this popular 8-plays-in-8-weeks program run by the Chicago Park District. Professional companies from some of the city's best off-Loop theaters are chosen to perform one of their plays here for one weekend each. Subscribers get a real deal at $110 for all shows in the intimate, enclosed-but-breezy (i.e., bring a sweater) theater; individual tickets are $17.50. Parking is available for a fee at the Lincoln Park Zoo, located at Fullerton Avenue and Cannon Drive.

WELLS STREET ART FESTIVAL
Wells Street, between North Avenue and Division Street
(773) 868-3010
www.chicagoevents.com
Second weekend in June
Just beyond the curlicued entrance gate to Old Town, this prestigious juried art festival is ranked one of the best in the country. In Chicago, it happens to be known as one of the artsiest outdoor summer party scenes, too. Roam more than 250 fine art exhibitors; get in your bids at the silent auction for original works of art; taste foods from local restaurants; rock out to music on the main stage where past musical acts have included 10,000 Maniacs, American English, and a Dave Matthews tribute band, the Trippin Billies. Donation: $7 before 5 p.m. and $10 after 5 p.m. Adding to the art array (as well as the food, fun, and music) is the Old Town Art Fair, which also takes place this weekend and is just a short walk away, with its main gate at Lincoln Avenue and Wisconsin Street; for more info on that one, check out www.oldtownartfair.org.

JULY

CHICAGO SUMMERDANCE
Grant Park, Spirit of Music Garden
601 S. Michigan Ave.
(312) 742-4007
www.chicagosummerdance.org
Early July through mid-Sept

More than 100,000 people each summer shake their groove thing under the stars on the Spirit of Music Garden's open-air dance floor (made of totally recycled materials, by the way) in Grant Park. They come in groups, as couples, and solo. They come early for free dance lessons in everything from tango to salsa, mambo to jitterbug. Then they stick around for the live bands to strut their newly learned stuff. The SummerDance schedule often includes stints at other parks throughout the city and at Navy Pier, and a Winter-Dance takes place at Millennium Park. Thurs through Sat 6 to 9:30 p.m., and Sun 4 to 7 p.m. Free.

SHEFFIELD GARDEN WALK & FESTIVAL
Webster and Sheffield avenues
www.sheffieldgardenwalk.com
Second to last weekend in July
Chicago's urban gardeners combine efficiency and artistry to give their small spaces big impact. This summertime festival shows off some of the best blooms of the city on a stroll through the charming, historic neighborhood around Sheffield Avenue. Pick up a guidebook with map and garden details and start exploring; if you've got the stamina for it, take a peek at all 100 private gardens, or just make your way to a handful. A Kids Corner features a mini Ferris wheel, petting zoo, pony rides, and more, while gardening experts are on hand to answer your growing questions. Live music from national and local bands, and food too. Donation $7; after 3 p.m. $10.

TASTE OF LINCOLN AVENUE
Lincoln Avenue, between Fullerton Parkway and Wrightwood Avenue
(773) 868-3010
www.wrightwoodneighbors.org
Last weekend in July

Going on nearly 30 years, this scaled-down little sis to the Taste of Chicago attracts more than 50,000 attendees and has raised over $1.5 million for its causes including helping to fund area parks and schools. Five stages feature musical acts all day, both local and national in name (Freddy Jones, Otis Clay, Soul Asylum, to name a few). A block-long Kids' Carnival scores with inflatable slides, face-painting, petting zoo, magicians, singers, and more. In between all the action, there's plenty of food to suit all tastes, as well as a wine garden. Donation $7 to $10.

AUGUST

CHICAGO AIR & WATER SHOW
North Avenue Beach
Viewing easily from Fullerton Parkway to Oak Street
(312) 744-3315
www.chicagoairandwatershow.us
Third weekend in Aug
They soar, they spin, they fly in formation, they generally defy logic. Those are the pilots of this amazing show, the largest free show of its kind in the US, attracting upwards of 2.2 million wide-eyed attendees. Typically showing off their flying prowess are the US Air Force Thunderbirds, the US Army Parachute Team Golden Knights, the Aeroshell Aerobatic Team, Chicago Fire Department Air/Sea Rescue, and a powerful display of military aircraft. Free.

NORTHALSTED MARKET DAYS
Halsted Street, between Belmont Avenue and Addison Street
(773) 868-3010
www.northalsted.com
Mid-Aug

The people-watching doesn't get much better—or much wilder—than at this Boystown street fair where scandalously skimpy and flamboyantly fun outfits are the norm. But feel free to come casual because, spanning four city blocks, lined with more than 400 food and arts-and-crafts vendors, this 2-day event is welcoming no matter what you wear. Three stages of live entertainment have featured famous acts such as Gloria Gaynor and Lisa Lisa. Suggested donation.

SEPTEMBER

57TH STREET CHILDREN'S BOOK FAIR
57th Street
Between Kenwood and Kimbark avenues; main entrance is under the giant balloon arch on 57th Street and Kimbark Avenue
57bookfair@gmail.com
www.57cbf.org
Third Sunday in Sept
The best in kid lit gets pulled together for this reading rainbow of booksellers and community organizations. Little ones can't help but fall in love with books when they're paired with a parade where story characters come to life in costume (in the past, there's been Curious George, Clifford, Winnie the Pooh, and Madeline); live music and dance; arts and crafts activities; and a story room where authors chat about their books with an awed little audience. Free.

CHICAGO JAZZ FESTIVAL
Chicago Cultural Center, Millennium Park and Grant Park
www.chicagojazzfestival.us
Labor Day weekend
The city's longest-running music festival is now a Labor Day weekend tradition, featuring acts in three different locations that culminates with two days in Grant Park. International and local musicians have included Cassandra Wilson, Roy Hargrove, and Orbert Davis. Free.

WORLD MUSIC FESTIVAL
Multiple venues
www.worldmusicfestivalchicago.org
Mid-Sept
The "world" part of this event is no euphemism—many of the performers travel just for this event from across the globe. In fact, since the ambitious festival began in 1999, it has showcased more than 500 music and dance artists and ensembles from more than 75 countries. Typically, there are close to 100 acts and nearly all are free. Check online for specific lineup and locations.

OCTOBER

CHICAGO MARATHON
Route starts at Grant Park
(312) 904-9800
www.chicagomarathon.com
Second Sunday in Oct
Whether aiming for your personal best or just to complete the course, the Bank of America Chicago Marathon is a favored one for its flatness factor, attracting participants from every state and more than 100 countries. With a route that weaves its way through 29 of Chicago's neighborhoods, it's quite a way to tour the city too. A pre-race pasta dinner and post-race party add an enormous social element. Not a runner? Pick a spot along the course and cheer on the throngs as they pass—the website gives a good general rule of thumb as to when the runners reach each mile marker and where to stand for good viewing.

NOVEMBER

MAGNIFICENT MILE LIGHTS FESTIVAL
Michigan Avenue, between Oak Street
and the Chicago River
(312) 409-5560
www.themagnificentmile.com
Saturday before Thanksgiving

Bundle up and brave the chill because this is the ultimate in kick-offs to the winter holiday season. All-day festivities include live music and family-friendly fun, plus plenty of shopping. But the anticipation is all about the parade, led by Mickey Mouse and Minnie Mouse, who have the honor of lighting more than a million twinkling lights on 200 trees that line the historic avenue. Following Mickey are over 30 floats, giant balloons, spirited marching bands, celebs, and the biggest star of them all, Santa himself. It all culminates with a fireworks display at the procession's southern end. Free.

DECEMBER

CHRISTKINDLMARKET
Daley Plaza
50 W. Washington St.
(312) 494-2175
www.christkindlmarket.com
Thanksgiving through Christmas

Daley Plaza is transformed into a charming German market for the winter holiday season. Covered booths are chock-full of gifts to check everyone off your list, including delicate painted tree ornaments, nutcrackers, wooden toys, German beer steins, wool sweaters and mittens, and Swarovski crystal. The booths' distinctive red-and-white striped awnings replicate those used at the original 16th-century Christkindlesmarkt in Nuremberg, Germany, and many of the vendors themselves fly in from Germany specially to present their wares at this festive annual event. Throughout the day, hear caroling, visit Santa, admire the giant city Christmas tree, and warm up and fill up with bratwurst, schnitzel, gingerbread, pretzels, and a mug of *glühwein,* Germany's signature hot spiced wine. Free (food prices are additional).

DAY TRIPS & GETAWAYS

here are dozens of places to visit within a quick drive of Chicago, so if you have some extra time on your trip, take advantage by heading out on one of these added adventures. If you're moving to Chicago, then these excursions are perfect for a day or weekend away after you've settled in (believe it or not, Chicago residents sometimes need a change of scenery). I've left out most specific pricing and hours, as these descriptions are intended as mini guides, quick reads that are jam-packed with information on how to get to each destination, where go, where to eat, and where to stay. All the pertinent contact details are there for you to take it that step further when you're ready to hit the road.

GALENA, ILLINOIS

A few hours west and slightly north of Chicago is this quaint and quiet city, at one time the lead-mining capital of the world. Today its romance factor ranks high, with more than 85 percent of the area's 19th-century buildings listed on the National Register of Historic Places. It also avoided major flattening by Midwest glaciers, and boasts hills high enough for skiing.

Getting There

Take I-90 west toward Wisconsin. From there, take the I-39/SR 20 exit toward Rockford. Follow US-20 west into Galena. The visitors' center is on the first floor of the Old Train Depot immediately on the right after turning.

Attractions

Start at the **Galena/Jo Daviess County Convention & Visitors Bureau** (101 Bouthillier St.; 877-GO GALENA; www.galena .org) where you can pick up resources and find out about the popular **Galena Trolley**

Tours (314 S. Main St.; 815-777-1248; www .galenatrolleys.com) that operate four different outings every day from Apr through Nov and on a limited schedule Feb through Mar. The one-hour narrated Non-Stop Tour covers nearly all of Galena's historic district, while the 2½-hour Tour of Homes pauses for further exploration of three historic mansions, the Dowling House, the Belvedere, and Ulysses S. Grant's Home.

You can also visit each of these homes on your own. The **Belvedere Mansion and Garden Tour** (1008 Park Ave.; 815-777-0747; www.belvederemansionandgardens.com) takes you into this 1857 Italianate home designed for steamboat magnate J. Russell Jones, who became ambassador to Belgium. Among the 22 rooms of ornate Civil War–era decor are the emerald velvet drapes made famous in *Gone With the Wind,* bought in an auction and added here. Tours run mid-May through mid-Nov. It's worth purchasing a discount combo ticket that also includes a peek into the historic **Dowling House** (220

Diagonal St.; 815-777-1250), built in 1826 and considered Galena's oldest residential structure. The 1860 Italianate **Ulysses S. Grant Home** (500 Bouthillier St.; 815-777-3310; www.granthome.com) gives you a sense of the Civil War hero and 18th president's daily life, displaying furnishings and other pieces that really did belong to the Grant family. Now a National Historic Landmark and on the National Register of Historic Places, the home is open for free tours May through Oct.

Another aspect of Galena's past comes to life at the **Old Blacksmith Shop** (245 N. Commerce St.; 815-777-9129; www.galenahistorymuseum.org), claiming title as Galena's last remaining blacksmith shop. Throughout the year, contemporary blacksmiths still use the space for work. The renovated structure is open Fri through Mon from May to Oct, and a donation is requested at the door.

One of Galena's newer claims to fame is as part of the Illinois wine-growing region. Here, the standout is **Galena Cellars Vineyard & Winery** (4746 N. Ford Rd.; main office at 515 S. Main St.; 800-397-WINE; www.galenacellars.com), a family-owned winery that has been producing—and winning awards for—its vino since its first cherry wine came out of the barrels in 1976. It now offers 40 varieties that run the gamut from dry reds to dessert to sparkling wines. Tours are available daily from May through Oct, and Sat and Sun in Nov. If you're around in June, find out if the area's **Top of Illinois Wine Festival** is going on (www.topofilwinefest.info).

Wondering about that skiing? It really happens—at **Chestnut Mountain Resort Downhill Skiing/Snowboarding** (8700 W. Chestnut Rd.; 800-798-0098; www.chestnutmtn.com). The resort's 19 runs cover 220 acres and all levels, and a snowboard park features half-pipes, quarter-pipes, table tops, and rails. The bonus for being in a small town in the Midwest? There are rarely lines for lifts.

Dining & Drinking

Galena isn't a big city, just 3,300 people or so, but it does have some worthy restaurants among its few dozen. At **The Flying Horse** (216 S. Commerce St.; 815-777-4800; www.theflyinghorse.com), a white-tablecloth style merges with a friendly attitude. The menu features fresh seafood and grilled steaks, and an "A to Z martinis" list, which literally includes 26 creative libations. In a historic 1838 building in downtown Galena, you'll find **Fried Green Tomatoes** (213 N. Main St.; 815-777-3938; www.friedgreen.com), which has nothing to do with the movie, and everything to do with contemporary Italian dishes, including its popular namesake fried green tomato appetizer. The first traditional Japanese restaurant in Galena, **Little Tokyo** (300 N. Main St.; 815-777-8883; www.littletokyoofgalena.com) serves up superb fresh fish and artisanal sake.

Kick back with a handcrafted beer at **Galena Beer Company** (227 N. Main St.; 815-776-9917; www.galenabrewery.com) where owners Warren and Kathy Bell typically have five beers on tap—Hefeweizen, amber ale, stout, IPA, and a cream ale—plus several seasonal brews. Their inventive tapas menu, fancy sandwiches, and salads complement nicely. On Fri and Sat nights and Sun afternoons, they offer horse-pulled buggy rides too.

Where to Stay

Being the historic and romantic destination that it is, Galena is chock-full of bed and breakfasts and cozy little inns. **The**

Goldmoor Inn (9001 W. Sand Hill Rd.; 800-255-3925, 815-777-3925; www.goldmoor .com) is an anniversary favorite, located on a scenic bluff overlooking the Mississippi River. Choose from three cottages, two authentic log cabins, and 12 suites, each luxuriously appointed in varying themes. As the oldest operating hotel in Illinois, the 1885 **DeSoto House Hotel** (230 S. Main St.; 800-343-6562, 815-777-0090; www.desotohouse.com) honors the past, naming its 55 Victorian-style rooms for people who played a part in Galena's history.

You'll get plenty of rest, relaxation, and recreation at the **Eagle Ridge Resort & Spa** (444 Eagle Ridge Dr.; 800-892-2269, 815-777-5000; www.eagleridge.com). Sheltered among 6,800 acres of rolling countryside, it features four championship golf courses, boat and bike rentals, the Stonedrift Spa, and hot air balloon rides at sunrise and sunset.

KOHLER, WISCONSIN

Those fancy low-flow toilets and stylish marble sinks that you see have to come from somewhere—and it's right here in their namesake Kohler, Wisconsin, where John Michael Kohler founded his company in 1873. Kohler originally began producing farm implements, but made his first bathtub in 1883, and the rest, as they say, is interior decorating history. Learn about that history while you indulge in the posh treatments offered in this scenic resort town.

Getting There

About 2½ hours north of Chicago, your trip to Kohler starts north on I-90/I-94 (it's labeled as west). Stay on US-41 north toward Waukegan until the highway merges back with I-94. Then stay toward I-43 north toward Green Bay. Take exit 12B toward Sheboygan/Kohler, following the ramp left toward SR 23 west, then take the exit for County Road Y to Kohler, take a right and follow the signs.

Attractions

It was tubs and toilets that made this town, so you really must make time to go deeper into the company's water-full ways at the **Kohler Design Center & Factory Tours** (101 Upper Rd.; 920-457-3699; www.destination kohler.com). Originally a recreation hall for Village of Kohler residents, it now showcases the best of the best with design vignettes and the huge, humorously titled "Great Wall of China." It's open daily and free (until you start thinking about buying something), as are the 3-hour factory tours, which run Mon through Fri starting at 8:30 a.m. (age 14 and up only). Not so free, but worth every pretty penny are the services at the award-winning **Kohler Water Spa** (501 Highland Dr.; 800-344-2838; www.destinationkohler.com). Soak till your body becomes Jell-O in the latest and greatest Kohler baths, or choose from a full menu of massages, manis and pedis, facials, body treatments, hair treatments, and energy therapies. Just know that the lounging pool is co-ed, so take a swimsuit. Shopping gets special treatment here too, at **The Shops at Woodlake** (725Q Woodlake Rd.; 920-459-1713) where you'll find more than 20 high-end boutiques. For more tees than sprees, try one of two equally challenging golf courses: **Blackwolf Run,** 1111 W. Riverside Dr.; or **Whistling Straits,** N8501 County LS. Call (800) 344-2838 for advance reservations, (866) 847-4856 for same-day.

Dining & Drinking

Kohler's dozen restaurants are all on property at the **American Club,** the **Inn at Woodlake,** or at the golf clubs. They range from the quick counter-service **Take 5 Cafe** (open daily for breakfast to early evening snacks; 920-457-4445) to the ultra-upscale **Immigrant** (open for dinner only, in peak season Tues through Sat, and off-season limited hours; 800-344-2838), where jackets are required for men, the decor reflects the heritage of early Wisconsin immigrants, and each course comes out in a perfectly leisurely fashion. For a complete list of dining choices, check online at www.destination kohler.com.

Where to Stay

You've got two options, each with its own incredible merits. At **The American Club** (419 Highland Dr.; 800-344-2838; www.des tinationkohler.com), you get fascinating history along with one of the 240 upscale rooms. The 1918 English Tudor structure was originally built to provide low-cost housing for poor Kohler immigrant employees. It had all the necessities, plus social aspects including a bowling alley, which lives on as tabletops in the lower-level Horse & Plow restaurant. Along the adjacent hallway, check out black-and-white photos and immigrant documents from Kohler's beginnings. For more modern accommodations, check into the **Inn at Woodlake** (705 Woodlake Rd.; 800-344-2838; www.destinationkohler.com), with sleek and modern style and deluxe WaterTile bodysprays and showerheads. Rooms facing Wood Lake offer the most scenic views.

LAKE GENEVA

Wealthy Chicagoans discovered this beautifully glacier-formed area in the late 19th and early 20th centuries, building wildly expensive summer mansions that eventually drew nearly as much attention as the landscape itself. Take a boat cruise for views or nonchalantly stroll your way around the 21-mile perimeter of Geneva Lake to get a glimpse of some of them.

Getting There

Head out of Chicago on I-90/I-94 west (you're heading north); follow US-41 north, which will merge back into I-94 west. Take exit 344 toward Kenosha/Lake Geneva. Turn left onto WI-50 and follow that for about 25 miles into Lake Geneva.

Attractions

The **Lake Geneva Chamber of Commerce & Visitors Bureau** (201 Wrigley Dr.; 800-345-1020, 262-248-4416; www.lakegenevawi .com) is open every day and doles out info about the lake and things to do. We definitely recommend a boat cruise, particularly the **Mail Boat Tour** (Riviera Docks, 812 Wrigley Dr.; 800-558-5911, 262-248-6206; www .cruiselakegeneva.com), which lets you in on a 140-year-old tradition that involves a nimble mail carrier who jumps off and on the moving boat, delivering and picking up mail for residences along the lakefront. Quite a sight to see and available only during summer months. You can also rent your own boat from **Lake Geneva Boat Rentals** (262-249-9647), which is next to **Big Foot Beach State Park** (1550 S. Lake Shore Dr.; 262-248-2528; www.dnr.wi.gov, www.wiparks.net), a lovely picnicking and hiking destination across from the non-lifeguarded Big Foot Beach. Another fun in the sun option: **Lake Geneva Beach** (Wrigley Drive at Center Street; 262-248-3673), which does have lifeguards and is popular with families.

Learn about this influential lake at the **Little Geneva Lake Museum** (255 Mill St.; 262-248-6060; www.genevalakemuseum .org; open seasonally) or see it all from above on a hot-air balloon ride with the **Lake Geneva Balloon Co.** (meet at Lake Geneva Pie Company, 150 E. Geneva Sq.; 262-206-3975; www.lakegenevaballoon.com), which runs from May through Oct. Keep your feet on the ground and focus your gaze on the starry skies above at the University of Chicago–owned **Yerkes Observatory** (373 W. Geneva St., Williams Bay; 262-245-5555; http://astro.uchicago.edu/yerkes), an astronomical icon built in 1897 and the largest lens-type telescope in the world. Free tours are offered every Saturday, with monthly observing sessions as well.

About 10 minutes from Lake Geneva in Elkhorn, Wisconsin, is the quirky **Watson's Wild West Museum** (W4865 Potter Rd., Elkhorn; 262-723-7505; www.watsonswild westmuseum.com) where you can watch rope-twirling pros, and browse a bounty of antique cowboy paraphernalia like spurs, holsters, bear traps, and branding irons. It's free and open daily May through Oct, but sometimes closes for private groups. Another unique spot nearby in Delavan is the year-round **Dancing Horses Show** (5065 Hwy. 50, Delavan; 262-728-8200; www .thedancinghorses.com), a dazzling display of equine excellence, plus bonus exotic bird show, water and light show; petting zoo; and pony rides. There's an admission fee for everyone over 3 years old.

Dining & Drinking

You may smell **Popeye's** (811 Wrigley Dr.; 262-248-4381; www.popeyeslkg.com) before you get there. This isn't the chicken chain, but a staple favorite in Lake Geneva for its slow-roasted rotisserie meats. At **Ryan Braun's Tavern and Grill** (430 Broad St.; 262-248-0888; www.ryanbraunslg.com), named for the Milwaukee Brewers All-Star left-fielder, the name of the game is accessible Italian and brick-oven pizzas. Head there any day for lunch or dinner, including a gluten-free menu. For a special-occasion champagne Sunday brunch, locals head to the **Geneva ChopHouse at the Grand Geneva Resort and Spa** (7036 Grand Geneva Way; 262-249-4788; www.grandgeneva.com), serving up a mouthwatering spread.

Where to Stay

The Grand Geneva Resort (7036 Grand Geneva Way; 800-558-3417; www.grand geneva.com) tops the options in terms of amenities and recreation, with six restaurants; ski and snowboard hills, cross-country and snowshoeing trails; 36 championship golf holes; horseback rides from on-site **Dan Patch Stables** (262-215-5303); body treatments and fitness facilities at the **Well Spa;** and an indoor waterpark at adjacent **Moose Mountain Falls.** Fun fact: This place began as a Playboy Club in 1968. At the **Abbey Resort** (269 Fontana Blvd.; 800-709-1323, 262-275-9000; www.theabbeyresort.com), an indoor pool, arcade, and kids' programming during the summer appeal to families, while the 35,000-square-foot **Avani Spa** gives moms and dads some "me" time. For "us" time, couples book a romantic room at the adults-only **SevenOaks** (682 Wells St.; 262-248-4006; www.sevenoakslakegeneva

.com), an elegant bed and breakfast styled after those you might find amid the English countryside.

MILWAUKEE

It's been nicknamed Brew City for a reason, but in the past couple of decades, Milwaukee has expanded its profile way beyond beer, with a world-class art museum, revived Riverwalk, and renovated structures that now house hip dining and shopping destinations.

Getting There

Take I-90/I-94, following US-41 (the Edens) north until it merges again with I-94, and get off at exit 310C to get into downtown Milwaukee.

Attractions

Pick up visitor guides, shopping guides, and maps at the **Visit Milwaukee Visitors Center** (Frontier Airlines Center, 400 W. Wisconsin Ave.; 800-554-1448; www.visitmilwaukee .org), then head out to our number one must-do, the **Milwaukee Art Museum** (700 N. Art Museum Dr.; 414-224-3200; www .mam.org), which became a global sensation in 2001 when architect Santiago Calatrava's new building debuted. Be sure to time it right to see the opening of its giant "wings" (officially titled *Burke Brise Soleil*), Tues through Sun at 10 a.m., or their closing at 5 p.m. Inside, 4 floors of galleries showcase art from throughout the ages, boasting an impressive number of works by Wisconsin native Georgia O'Keeffe. In a renovated 1924 former bank, the **Grohmann Museum— Man at Work Art Collection** (1000 N. Broadway; 414-277-2300; www.msoe.edu/

manatwork) showcases more than 800 paintings and sculptures that illustrate the evolution of organized work.

Some people might call beer-making an art. Find out for yourself at **Lakefront Brewery** (1872 N. Commerce St.; 414-372-8800; www.lakefrontbrewery.com), an innovative brewer that created the first certified organic beer in the US and hosts tours of its facilities Mon through Sat (first-come, first-served, 50 people max) that start off right with a mug of suds. For a look at another legendary Milwaukee contribution, follow the hum to the **Harley-Davidson Museum** (400 Canal St.; 877-436-8738; www.h-dmuseum.com), practically a pilgrimage for hog lovers. Trace Harley history in displays depicting everything from the first-known bike ever built to customized models, and in the Experience Gallery, where you can sit on one and get a feel for Harley power. It's open daily and guided tours are available for an extra fee.

Several attractions in one, **Discovery World** (500 N. Harbor Dr.; 414-765-9966; www.discoveryworld.org) features science and technology exhibits, aquariums, theaters, and more. Plus, the *Denis Sullivan*, a replica of a 19th-century 3-masted Great Lakes schooner, offers day sails and deck tours during the summer. The museum is open Tues through Sun. For year-round lake-trekking, climb aboard one of the **Edelweiss Boats** (205 W. Highland Ave.; 414-276-7447; www.edelweissboats.com) for themed excursions such as disco, beer and brats, a kids' pirate cruise, or a romantic dinner cruise.

Back on land, be sure to visit the **Mitchell Park Horticultural Conservatory** (524 S. Layton Blvd.; 414-649-9830; www.county parks.com), otherwise known as The Domes because of the three iconic 85-foot-high half moons of glass that contain underneath a variety of garden splendor, from cacti to jungle plants. A don't-miss for fans of Milwaukee-based *Happy Days* is the **Bronze Fonz sculpture** (along the Milwaukee River-walk, just south of Wells Street); designed by Wisconsin artist Gerald Sawyer, it's a fun like-ness of Henry Winkler's super-cool character on the old TV show, complete with leather jacket, Wrangler jeans, Skate Buckle boots, and two thumbs up.

Dining & Drinking

Milwaukee has made a name for itself in the food world with dining hot spots like **Barto-lotta's Lake Park Bistro** (3133 E. Newberry Blvd.; 414-962-6300; www.lakeparkbistro.com), whose Adam Siegel won a 2008 James Beard Award for Best Chef Midwest. His traditional French cuisine and the restau-rant's scenic setting on a bluff looking out onto Lake Michigan combine for a definite hit. Another James Beard Award winner, **Sanford Restaurant** (1547 N. Jackson St.; 414-276-9608; www.sanfordrestaurant.com) wows with chef-owner Sanford D'Amato's eclectic menu. Going the organic route is farmer-chef-owned **Roots Restaurant and Cellar** (1818 N. Hubbard St.; 414-374-8480; www.rootsmilwaukee.com), specializing in farm-to-table cuisine.

Milwaukee's German roots are revealed at the historic **Mader's Restaurant** (1041 N. Third St.; 414-271-3377; www.maders restaurant.com), home to the world's larg-est Hummel store, and at mainstay **Karl Ratzsch's** (320 E. Mason St.; 414-276-2720; www.karlratzsch.com), serving for more than a century. Another gastronomic specialty in these parts: custard. Get it at **Kopp's Frozen Custard** (18880 W. Bluemound Rd., Brook-field, 262-789-9490; 7631 W. Layton Ave., Greenfield, 414-282-4312; and 5373 N. Port

Washington Rd., Glendale, 414-961-3288, www.kopps.com). And for a good ol' beer and burger, head to **Sobelman's Pub and Grill** (1900 W. St. Paul Ave.; 414-931-1919; www.milwaukeesbestburgers.com).

Where to Stay

From historic to hip, Milwaukee's got some-thing to suit any style. **The Pfister Hotel** (424 E. Wisconsin Ave.; 800-558-8222, 414-273-8222; www.thepfisterhotel.com) offers up the history, opening in 1893 and meeting the highest of standards ever since, includ-ing a museum-quality art collection. Set in a renovated 1937 Art Deco office building, **Hotel Metro** (411 E. Mason St.; 877-638-7620, 414-272-1937; www.hotelmetro.com) blends sophistication with environmental sensitivity, not to mention a serene rooftop deck with fireplace and reflecting pool. At the **Iron Horse Hotel** (500 W. Florida St.; 888-543-4766, 414-374-4766; www.theironhorsehotel.com), you can walk to the Harley-Davidson Museum or take a ride around the area on your own "iron horse," a nickname for a motorcycle.

ROCKFORD, ILLINOIS

This midsized Midwestern community has come through a few dips and now has more to offer than you might think. And although it might average 35 inches of snow, even in winter the hospitality is warm, and the CoCo Key Water Resort is an indoor entertainment paradise.

Getting There

It's a 1½-hour mostly straight shot on I-90 west. Then take the Rockford Business 20/State Street exit (not US 20, which comes up first) to get into town.

Attractions

The **Rockford Area Convention & Visitors Bureau** (102 N. Main St.; 800-521-0849, 815-963-8111; www.gorockford.com) carries guides and offers suggested itineraries Mon through Fri. Our suggestion: Definitely make your way to the **Riverfront Museum Park,** which is a triple treat of museums. Kids will have a blast at the **Discovery Center Museum** (711 N. Main St.; 815-963-6769; www.discoverycentermuseum.org), worth several hours of amusement with 250 hands-on exhibits on two floors and ranked fourth in a Top 10 list of best children's museums by *Child* magazine. Push a little archaeology, geology, and biology at the **Burpee Museum of Natural History** (737 N. Main St.; 815-965-3433; www.burpee.org), whose top attention-getter is Jane, the 21-foot juvenile T-rex skeleton. And last but not least in this trio, the **Rockford Art Museum** (711 N. Main St.; 815-968-2787; www.rockfordartmuseum .org), focusing on 20th-century American art, American Impressionist paintings, photography, works by self-taught African-American artists, and contemporary glass.

Embrace the outdoors at **Rock Cut State Park** (7318 Harlem Rd., Loves Park; 815-885-3311; www.dnr.illinois.gov). About 10 minutes north of Rockford, this 3,092-acre open space includes two lakes, horseback riding (no rentals), mountain-biking and hiking trails, and fully equipped campgrounds. At the **Anderson Japanese Gardens** (318 Spring Creek Rd.; 815-229-9390; www.andersongardens .org), the 12 acres of flora is all meticulously handcrafted and beautifully maintained by famed Portland-based landscape designer Hoichi Kurisu.

And then there's the water park: **CoCo Key Water Resort** (7801 E. State St.; 866-754-6958, 815-398-6000; www.cocokey waterresort.com) is the largest indoor water park in Illinois, boasting an indoor-outdoor whirlpool, tube rides, water slides, a lazy river, a zero-depth wading pool, and an adjacent arcade.

UTICA-STARVED ROCK

In tiny Utica, the natural attraction is a doozy—Starved Rock, the first state park in Illinois, established in 1911. Hiking trails, Native American history, stunning views of the Illinois River, plus camping, fishing, boating, and more make it one of the most popular weekend getaways for building-locked Chicagoans who crave open space. In terms of food here, you pretty much need to pack your own.

Getting There

Take I-55 south (toward St. Louis), then Exit 250B toward Iowa and I-80 west. Take Exit 81 SR 178/Utica/LaSalle and turn left at SR 178/East 8th Road and follow signs to the park.

Attractions

It's a good idea to start your trip at the **Starved Rock State Park Visitors Center** (near I-80 and I-39 intersection and SR 178 in Utica; technically 2568 E. 950th Rd., Oglesby; 800-868-7625, 815-667-4726; www .starvedrockstatepark.org). You'll get the lay of the land in orientation videos, and can pick up trail maps and snacks. The park's 2,630 acres present a picturesque vista of rock formations, canyons, bluffs, waterfalls, and photo-op overlooks of the Illinois River. When you've hiked to your heart's content, there's bird-watching, fishing, horseback riding, and canoeing. Or just pitch a tent and take a snooze under the stars. Although the park attracts more than 2 million visitors a year, at off-season times, the sheer size of the park makes you feel like it's yours alone. If you want it quieter still, head just south of Starved Rock to **Matthiessen State Park** (off SR 178; 815-667-4868; www.dnr.state.il.us), with 5 miles of trails and a couple of canyons divided by a waterfall. Nearby **Buffalo Rock State Park** (1300 N. 27th Rd.; 815-433-2224; www.stateparks.com/buffalo_rock.htm) is similarly scenic, a 298-acre park with a unique artistic feature, the *Effigy Tumuli,* five animal-shaped mounds created out of the earth by artist Michael Heizer in 1983.

Where to Stay

Not up for camping? No problem. **Starved Rock Lodge** (SR 178 and SR 71; 815-667-4211; www.starvedrocklodge.com) offers up indoor bedding either in the original 1939-built log structure, rooms added in the late 1980s, or in cabins. Plus, the **Starved Rock Inn** (intersection of SR 6 and SR 178; 815-667-4211; www.starvedrockstatepark .org) adds rustic living in an 8-room inn. Whichever you choose, you can hang out in the Lodge's indoor pool. Or go a little wild at **Grizzly Jack's Grand Bear Resort** (2643 N. SR 178; 866-399-FUNN; www.grizzly jacksresort.com), whose rooms come with free passes to the 24,000-square-foot indoor water park and separate 36,000-square-foot indoor amusement park.

LIVING HERE

In this section we feature specific information for residents or those planning to relocate here. Topics include real estate, education, health care, and much more.

RELOCATION

If you're weighing whether to move to Chicago, a pros and cons list should make it easy—lots of pros and just a few cons. Here's what you're in for: A diverse metropolitan city with a friendly Midwest attitude. A town whose pulse beats with blues music and university classes, hot night spots and romantic restaurants, amazing cultural institutions and championship sports teams. A lake and a river that provide recreation, transportation, and shipping, and a public bus and train system that traverses the city. Further boosting appeal is Chicago's walkability (ranked #4 on the www.WalkScore.com website), with many neighborhoods boasting restaurants, shops, bars, train and bus stops, and even grocery stores just steps away from your front door.

Chicago's central downtown is as vibrant as many of its neighborhoods, and during the past several decades, buying a condo downtown has become commonplace. While the housing downturn has no doubt negatively affected Chicago's condo-building boom, it does mean that there are some great buys out there in areas that may have been prohibitive in the past. On the flip side, apartment-hunting is a bit trickier these days and pricier than you might assume, as former house-owners snatch up apartments and move to the city. Demand goes up as quantity goes down, with less new construction taking place. But a manageable cost of living and job opportunities at everywhere from huge corporations to small mom-and-pop-run businesses have kept people here. If you've already decided you're Chicago-bound, then congrats. We're happy to have you. If you're still deciding, give us a shout and we'll help convince you. Welcome to the Second City, which is always first in our book.

OVERVIEW

Moving can be stressful even for the most organized of people. New places, new faces, and lots of details to work out. This chapter is meant to ease the transition, providing the 411 on how to plan your move, get where you need to go, get a sense of your new surroundings, and get involved once you're here. Whether you've already chosen your home base or you're still looking for a place to buy or rent, the facts here help you achieve the next step—that is, becoming a Chicagoan. You'll also find information about chambers of commerce, the dreaded DMV to register your car (it's not so bad, really), Chicago's famous (or infamous) aldermanic structure, and the city's excellent library system.

INFO FOR NEWCOMERS

CHICAGOLAND CHAMBER OF COMMERCE
Aon Center
200 E. Randolph St., Ste. 2200
(312) 494-6700
www.chicagolandchamber.org

Encompassing the city of Chicago and six neighboring counties, the Chicagoland Chamber of Commerce is a massive organization that aims to attract businesses and consumers to Chicago and keep them here. With more than 2,600 members, it is one of the largest chambers in the country and has received a 5-star accreditation (the highest) from the US Chamber of Commerce. If you're intending to open a small business, membership in the chamber offers valuable networking and advocacy benefits. As a consumer, the membership directory is a great resource for looking up everything from law firms to retailers, restaurants to landscapers.

NEIGHBORHOOD CHAMBERS OF COMMERCE

A growing number of smaller chambers of commerce have taken root around town and provide more personalized and direct service for their communities. Their existence tends to indicate that the particular area has a cohesive agenda and welcoming attitude. They often host neighborhood festivals throughout the year, fund-raising events, farmers' markets, and tours. They also may provide coupon booklets or area guides that highlight their members. Of course, while it's encouraging to see area businesses participating in their chamber, the fact that some retailers, restaurants, bars, and attractions choose to abstain from membership should not be taken as a negative; there may be all kinds of reasons for joining or not joining. Some of the city's local chambers of commerce are listed within the "Neighborhoods at a Glance" in the "Area Overview" chapter of this book.

CHICAGO CONVENTION AND TOURISM BUREAU
2301 S. Lake Shore Dr.
(312) 567-8500
www.choosechicago.com
The Windy City's official one-stop-shop for global leisure travelers, meeting planners, and travel professionals is the Chicago Convention and Tourism Bureau (CCTB), which goes by the shortened moniker, Choose Chicago. It publishes a free visitors' guide, and lists restaurants, attractions, shops, theaters, museums and more on its website, which also boasts a direct online hotel reservation system.

CHICAGO VISITOR INFORMATION CENTERS
Chicago Water Works, 163 E. Pearson St.;
Chicago Cultural Center,
77 E. Randolph St.
www.explorechicago.org
You don't have to be a visitor to appreciate the multitude of free information available at these destinations for the city-curious. Run by the City of Chicago, they're open every day and offer brochures on area attractions, tours, and events; multilingual maps; a culinary concierge on hand to recommend restaurants; and free InstaGreeter tours offered by volunteers. The online component provides a good database of listings of "Things to See & Do," places to "Eat, Sleep & Shop," and "Neighborhoods."

GOVERNMENT

CITY OF CHICAGO
City Hall
121 N. LaSalle St.
(312) 744-5000; or dial 311 within Chicago for non-emergency services
www.cityofchicago.org

A complex, diverse, and metropolitan city demands a comprehensive and comprehensible website to corral all its functions, and Chicago's does just that. From auto pounds to zoning, you'll find information about all the necessary evils and the enticing benefits of city living. Apply for—or find out how to apply for—business licenses, building inspections, tax refunds, and even jobs; find or link to your alderman's office, an architect, the bus schedule, a health clinic, a lost pet, or a warming center; pay for a parking ticket or a water bill; request a recycling cart, graffiti removal, snow removal, or a bike map. The site also has valuable tools and tips for homeowners, job-seekers, people with disabilities, renters, seniors, veterans, volunteers, teens, and ex-offenders. Plus, you can look up a directory of any and all city departments; and programs and initiatives that the city sponsors on topics including education, consumer protection, the Freedom of Information Act, housing affordability, healthcare, taxes, and more. The 311 nonemergency phone service can also help with just about all these things.

Department of Motor Vehicles

Driver's License

You've got a lot going on when you first move, so Illinois gives new residents to the state of Illinois 90 days to get a new driver's license. When you do, be sure to have your driver's ducks in a row to make sure you don't have to experience the DMV twice: You'll need one document that shows your written signature, date of birth, and social security number (you can use the same document or more than one to satisfy this requirement, and this can include your current out-of-state driver's license); and two documents that prove your residency (this

could be a mortgage or lease agreement, official mail from a university, cable or gas bill, or other such item). Study up on those Rules of the Road too, because you'll have to take a written exam, possibly a driving exam, and a vision screening as well. A separate motorcycle driver's test is required. A basic driver's license fee is $30 and is valid for four years.

Chicago's Secretary of State Driver Facilities

Chicago Central
100 W. Randolph St.
(312) 793-1010

Diversey Express
The Hall Plaza
4642 W. Diversey St.
(312) 793-1010

Loop Express
69 W. Washington St.
(312) 793-1010

Chicago North
5401 N. Elston Ave.
(312) 793-1010

Chicago South
9901 S. Dr. Martin Luther King Jr. Dr.
(312) 793-1010

Chicago West
5301 W. Lexington St.
(312) 793-1010

Vehicle Registration

There isn't quite as much leniency in terms of applying for your vehicle's Illinois title and registration as there is with getting a driver's license—you're given just 30 days after establishing your residence here. This service is also provided at the state driver facilities. Have the following at the ready: name and address of the vehicle's owner; odometer reading; year, make, model, vehicle identification number, body type, date of purchase (and whether new or used); names and addresses of any lienholders; and out-of-state title or other proof of ownership. Visit the website or call ahead to determine whether there are any other circumstances that require you to have additional documents. Title fees are $99 and registration fees are $95. Also, be aware that all motor vehicles registered in Illinois must carry liability insurance. Call (800) 252-8980 or (217) 785-3000, or visit www.cyberdriveillinois.

Residents of Chicago also must purchase a city sticker each year to affix to their windshield—vehicles registered in the city without one are subject to tickets. They expire annually on June 30. There is a 30-day grace period for new residents to purchase their sticker without incurring a late fee of $40 on top of the regular $75 fee. If you've moved to Chicago between June 1 and July 15, you may obtain a city sticker online at www.chicityclerk.com; delivery is supposed to be within 10 to 14 days, so if it doesn't show up by then, give the Clerk's office a call. Otherwise, you must purchase it in person at City Clerk offices, Department of Revenue Substations (listed below), or at the 300 community vendors, which include currency exchanges that often tack on an extra fee. You're required to present documentation that proves your address. Through Nov 30, the standard $75 fee applies, but between Dec 1 and Mar 31, it is prorated to $50 and from Apr 1 through May 31, it is prorated to $25.

If you have moved onto a street with zoned residential permit parking (RPP) and plan to park your car on the street, you will need a city sticker that indicates your zone; this tacks on an additional fee of $25. These RPP zones are devised to help cut down on street-parking woes for residents who live in highly congested areas. Regardless of whether you purchase the zoned city sticker, living in an RPP zone allows you to request daily residential guest passes. Simply show proof of residency and you may purchase up to 30 daily passes every 30 days; they come in sets and cost $8 for 15. You can get 30 passes online or 15 in person at a City Clerk facility (open only Mon through Fri) or through the mail. To see if your street is an RPP area, check online at the City Clerk's website, www.chicityclerk.com.

MAIN CITY CLERK OFFICE
City Hall, Rm. 107
121 N. LaSalle St.
(312) 744-6861

Other City Clerk Facilities for Parking Permits:
- 2550 W. Addison St.
- 2006 E. 95th St.
- 4770 S. Kedzie Ave.
- 400 W. Superior St.

Vehicle Inspection

In addition to being properly documented, your vehicle's emissions control systems must be properly inspected. The federal Clean Air Act Amendments of 1990 put this requirement in motion for large, urban areas that do not meet certain federal air quality standards—unfortunately, Chicago is one of them, along with much of Northeastern Illinois. The general rule is that all vehicles must get tested every 2 years, beginning when they're 4 years old. When you move to Illinois, after you register your vehicle, you will receive a notice to test 3 months prior to your registration expiration date. There are two approved Air Team testing stations in the city (see below) and several more in outlying suburbs; they are open Mon through Fri and Sat mornings and do not require an appointment. Saturdays get busy, and lines can get long, but you can call ahead for prerecorded wait-time estimates or visit the Illinois EPA website for live station queue cameras. If your vehicle fails the test, the inspector will print out a report detailing the issues. You'll need to get your vehicle repaired and retested. For general questions about all this, call (800) 635-2380 or visit www.epa.state.il.us (click on "Vehicle Testing").

Emissions Testing Locations

- 6959 W. Forest Preserve Dr., (800) 383-7085. This is a full-service station that can test vehicles with both on-board computers (OBD) as well as those without.
- 1850 W. Webster Ave., (800) 380-6610. This is an OBD-only testing facility.

Voter Registration

COOK COUNTY CLERK
(312) 603-0900
www.cookcountyclerk.com

Because there are so many neighborhood-related issues, it's valuable to have that local voting right so you can have a say in who your congresspeople are and, on an even more local scale, who your alderman is. As in any case, to be able to vote in Illinois-specific elections, you must be a US citizen, not convicted of an offense and in jail, be at least 18 years old on or before the next election, and not claim voting rights anywhere else.

Typically, you must also have been living in your election precinct for at least 30 days before voting. However, there is a fairly new law that allows a grace period for registering and voting. This permits you to register to vote up to one week before an election. These grace-period registrations can take place only during limited days and hours at a Cook County Clerk's office (there is one in downtown Chicago at 69 W. Washington St., 312-603-0900, and five in the suburbs); the Cook County Clerk's website will tell you when you may do this. As with any in-person voter registration, you must show two forms of ID (no photo necessary, but at least one indicating your new address), and for this grace-period registration, you will then be required to vote on a touch-screen machine immediately after registering; in other words, you will vote that day instead of on Election Day.

The easiest way to register to vote in Illinois is to get it done when you get your new driver's license. You will be asked if you'd like to register to vote and if you do, you'll receive an application form to sign. You'll get a receipt, which you should keep until your official voter card arrives in the mail, and that's that.

You can also register through a mail-in application to the Cook County Clerk's office. Registration forms are available on the Clerk's website in English, Spanish, and Chinese or by calling the Clerk's office. At any time, you may also register to vote at one of the Cook County Clerk's six locations, as well as any village, city, or township clerk (a list is available on the Clerk's website). Oftentimes, politically oriented organizations may set up booths to register voters as well.

Dog Registration

Annual registration for your dog isn't just a good idea—and plenty of people get away without it—but it's actually required by a municipal code in Chicago for all dogs 4 months and older. Plus, the benefits are worth it: 1) A portion of the fee goes to helping the city's Animal Care & Control facility; 2) your dog's registration tag number helps identify him if he ever gets lost; 3) registration is also required at boarding and doggie daycare facilities; and 4) registration allows you to obtain a permit for access to dog-friendly parks.

The fees are minor, just $5 for a sterilized dog ($50 for unsterilized, because of the high rate of unwanted, unplanned litters); senior citizens get a discount. To register, your dog must be up-to-date with her rabies vaccination, and the registration expires one year after the date of the vaccine (or three, depending on what kind of vaccination your dog receives). You can register your dog online at www.chicityclerk.com or at one of the City Clerk offices listed below.

MAIN CITY CLERK OFFICE
City Hall, Rm. 107
121 N. LaSalle St.
(312) 744-6861

SATELLITE OFFICE
5430 W. Gale St.
(312) 742-5319

SATELLITE OFFICE
5674 S. Archer Ave.
(312) 745-1100

City Council

Divided into 50 legislative districts or wards, each with its own representative called an alderman, the Chicago City Council comprises the city's legislative branch of government, which is led by and answers to the mayor. The aldermen are elected for 4-year terms and have a great deal of clout within the city. They also serve their ward constituents, and their offices are the places to call for things like requesting a new stop sign or getting a yard sale permit. But on a larger scale, the aldermen meet regularly to discuss subjects such as traffic code changes, utilities, taxes, and public health.

Chicago claims to have the second-largest city council in the US (New York's has 51 members, but Los Angeles has just 15). But this is not necessarily a good thing, according to some people—aldermen salaries cost taxpayers upwards of $100,000 each, and their 20 or so committees cost another $4.5-plus million. Other detractors complain that the size of the council makes it difficult to get anything done; and a whopping 30 have been convicted of federal crimes, including bribery and embezzlement. In fact, Chicago's new mayor Rahm Emanuel has broached the idea of cutting the number of aldermen in half. However, overhauling a time-honored system will likely be met with its own set of naysayers and will take time to sink in, if it ever does.

i Find out your ward number and corresponding alderman by calling the City Clerk's Office at 312-74-CLERK (2-5375) or visiting the website at www.chicityclerk.com.

LIBRARIES

Since its beginnings in 1873, the Chicago Public Library system has evolved into a network of more than 70 libraries of all sizes and styles. From 1897 to 1991, the city's central library was housed in the ornate and beautiful building that now serves as the Chicago Cultural Center. In 1991, the new Harold Washington Library opened and, measuring in at 756,640 square feet, got itself listed in the *Guinness Book of Records* as the largest public library building in the world (read more about the library in the Architecture chapter).

i **Children age 13 and younger who can write their first and last name may get their own library cards by filling out an application signed by a parent or guardian. An ID is required as well.**

Library programs run the gamut from financial seminars to children's story hours, art exhibits to summer reading programs. The extensive website includes a full calendar of events for all the libraries, as well as an "Ask a Librarian" option; lists of bestsellers, recommended reads, Chicago-related fiction, and more; information about renting library spaces for private events; a blog that highlights books, movies, and other library-related topics; a section for kids, teens, and parents to help with homework and explore topics further; and the opportunity to create your own library account where you can place holds online and search the online database.

i **Libraries lend a limited number of free-admission passes to area cultural institutions. Located at checkout desks, they include popular spots like the Shedd Aquarium, Museum of Science and Industry, and Field Museum. They're hot commodities, turn over fast, and are due within a week.**

The city's ongoing One Book, One Chicago program began more than 10 years ago and recommends a great read for the whole city. Each library stocks numerous copies of the book and many of them—along with area bookstores and universities—host related book discussions and other events.

All Chicago libraries offer free Wi-Fi access (though the network is not secure), and most offer the use of free computers. Find your local library and so much more at www.chipublib.org or by calling (312) 747-4300.

Chicago Main & Regional Libraries

Harold Washington Library Center
400 S. State St.
(312) 747-4300

Sulzer Regional
4455 N. Lincoln Ave.
(312) 744-7616

Woodson Regional
9525 S. Halsted St.
(312) 747-6900

Utility Contacts

Natural Gas

People's Energy
(866) 556-6001
www.peoplesenergy.com

Electricity

Commonwealth Edison
(800) 334-7661
www.comedmove.com

Phone/Cable/Internet

AT&T
(800) 244-4444
www.att.com

RCN
(312) 804-2516
www.rcn.com

Comcast
(866) 886-6838
www.comcast.com

Dish Network
(800) 333-DISH
www.dishnetwork.com

Direct TV
(888) 777-2454
www.directTV.com

Trash/Recycling Pickup

Chicago Disposal
(773) 978-7878
www.chicagodisposal.com

Flood Brothers
(773) 626-5800
www.floodbrothersdisposal.com

Waste Management
(800) 796-9696
www.wm.com

HOME HUNTING

Apartment Searches

More than half of the Chicago population lives in rental units. Finding the right one for you can sometimes take a combination of patience and persistence. If you know the neighborhood you'd like to live in, it can help to take a drive or stroll around to familiarize yourself with what's there, what's within walking distance of which buildings, and which blocks seem like they have the ambience you're looking for—is it the bustle of living on a main thoroughfare or the peaceful feeling of living off the beaten path? Bring a notebook and pen with you or your smart phone to record any "for rent" signs you see posted on doors, as sometimes these units aren't advertised anywhere. You can also search through the classifieds of the *Chicago Reader* weekly newspaper or its online component, www.chicagoreader .com. Craigslist in Chicago also lists rentals, though be aware that many leasing agents also list here, which is fine, but can also be bothersome.

If you don't know where to start or can't spend the time perusing on your own, there are several companies that are more than happy to help. Their agents will even drive you around if you don't have a car or don't know your way around. Offices are typically open 7 days a week (appointments are recommended for weekends), and agents represent apartments across the city and in Evanston—everything from studios to townhomes. If you're in a rush to find a place, the apartment-search companies can get you moved in lickety-split because they cut down on your search time and can pinpoint properties that are move-in ready. Services are generally free because landlords and building managers pay a fee to have their units included in the pot of properties that agents at these companies represent. However, it's important to know that because there's a fee on the other end, it's typical that the rental prices may fall on the higher end, while landlords or managers of lower-priced rental properties may choose not to pay that fee and list elsewhere.

Some places to begin your search include:

- **The Apartment People.** Offices in Lakeview, River North, and Evanston; (800) 44-RENT-4; www.apartmentpeople.com.
- **Chicago Apartment Hunters.** 1022 W. Belmont Ave.; (773) 975-6600; www.chicagoapartmenthunters.com.
- **Rent Smart Chicago.** Six Chicagoland offices; (800) 262-5314; www.rentsmartchicago.com.
- **Apartment Savvy.** 2835 N. Clark St.; (773) 348-8921; www.apartmentsavvy.com.

Realtors

Like looking for an apartment, searching for a home to buy can be exciting, but daunting, with the added stress of getting a bank loan. As the Internet has become more sophisticated, so have the online tools for home-buyers. Although doing your own web-based home search can yield potentially perfect results, working with a licensed Realtor can help make the path smoother, from initial viewing to negotiation to signing the papers to putting the key in the front door. The Chicago Association of Realtors (CAR) represents more than 12,000 members and has a slew of information to assist in learning more about the process and finding an agent that suits your tastes.

Some of the biggest names in home sales in the area:

- **Baird Warner:** (800) 644-1855; www.bairdwarner.com
- **Coldwell Banker:** (800) 323-9565; www.coldwellbankeronline.com
- **Dreamtown:** (312) 265-8000; www.dreamtown.com
- **Koenig & Strey:** (847) 853-5000; www.koenigstrey.com
- **@Properties:** (312) 491-0200; www.atproperties.com
- **Prudential:** (866) 224-8895; www.prudential.com
- **Remax:** www.remax.com (phone contacts vary per office)
- **Rubloff:** (866) 795-1010; www.rubloff.com

MEDIA

Ideas from all sides and in between are represented in Chicago's media outlets, print, radio, and online. We pride ourselves on having two daily newspapers, as well as numerous free monthlies and numerous radio stations for every musical taste.

Daily Newspapers

CHICAGO SUN-TIMES
(312) 321-3000
www.suntimes.com
This daily paper has been in existence in some form since 1844. After a few buyouts, mergers, and scandals—as in 2004 when the paper was found to be misrepresenting its circulation count—it's back on a steady track. It began fairly liberal, took a right turn in 1984 when conservative media mogul Rupert Murdoch bought it, but has seemed to tilt back to a relatively moderate

approach. Commuters like it for its tabloid size, its local focus, heavy sports coverage, and easily digestible articles, including movie reviews by long-standing film critic Roger Ebert. Circulation of nearly 420,000 is one of the largest in the US and includes a pretty big newsstand appeal, probably due to its flashy front covers.

CHICAGO TRIBUNE
(800) TRIBUNE (874-2863)
www.chicagotribune.com
Looking at its executives, the *Chicago Tribune* would easily be considered friends of the Republican party, and it has almost exclusively endorsed Republican political candidates, but from the perspective of its columnists and editorial pages, its largely considered a toss-up in terms of bias. Looking back at history, the *Tribune* has certainly had its share of negatives aimed at both parties. It's also still considered the more "intellectual" of Chicago's two major dailies, maybe partly because of its traditional foldover, broadsheet size. Founded in 1847, the *Tribune*'s most famous editor and co-owner Joseph Medill ran it from 1855 pretty much until his death in 1899 (though he took time off for political aspirations, including a term as mayor of Chicago). Circulation for the *Trib* is a bit higher for its weekday paper than the *Sun-Times*, and its Sunday circulation is quite high, nearly 800,000 (many residents subscribe to Sunday-only delivery). Coverage in the *Tribune* tends to be slightly more national in scale than the *Sun-Times* as well. The Tribune Company also publishes the *Red Eye* and the online lifestyle guide Metromix .com, as well as its little sibling ("the voice of teen Chicago"), TheMash.com

DAILY HERALD
(847) 427-4300
www.dailyherald.com
This beloved independent and locally owned paper has been growing since its beginnings more than 120 years ago. It focuses on the suburban communities in Cook, DuPage, Kane, Lake, and McHenry counties, but covers the world too.

RED EYE
(800) TRIBUNE (847-2863)
www.redeyechicago.com
Found free for the taking at tons of kiosk boxes near public transportation, the *Red Eye* is your romance novel of newspapers. A fun, quick read, not much substance. In a typically cheeky way with an often insider-y feel, it covers pop culture, sports, restaurants, and bars, and has a column about the CTA.

HOY
(800) TRIBUNE (847-2863)
www.vivelohoy.com
The second largest Spanish language paper in the country, *Hoy* is owned by the Tribune Company.

Weekly Newspapers & Magazines

CHICAGO DEFENDER
(312) 225-2400
www.chicagodefender.com
Published every Wednesday, this flagship paper of Real Times, Inc., began in 1905 and has become one of the country's most influential African-American weeklies. Together with the Chicago Defender Charities, it has hosted Chicago's annual Bud Bulliken Day Parade since 1929, the largest parade specifically showcasing children.

CHICAGO READER
(312) 828-0350
www.chicagoreader.com
The largest-run free weekly paper in Chicago, and one of the most successful alt-weeklies in the country, the *Reader* has recently switched from broadsheet to tabloid size with a dual cover (one side focusing solely on music); the change irked some and pleased others. Famous for its in-depth reporting and unabashedly critical coverage of politics, it also is highly regarded for its comprehensive reviews and listings of the local music scene. Its classified and personal ads (particularly the "I Saw You" section) are widely read, and its column "Savage Love" has a near-cult following for its raw, real sex advice.

CRAIN'S CHICAGO BUSINESS
(312) 649-5200
www.chicagobusiness.com
This business insider pub is one of more than 30 business, trade, and consumer magazines published by privately owned Crain Communications Inc. Together, the print and online editions provide targeted, valuable data and often breaking news for the business community. Crain's is available by subscription.

NEWCITY
(312) 243-8786
www.newcitychicago.com
Staking claim as Chicago's "only locally owned and operated cultural weekly," the free *Newcity* magazine has been going strong for more than 22 years. With irreverent attitude, it covers art, film, literature, music, theater, and bars and restaurants.

TIMEOUT CHICAGO
(312) 924-9555
www.timeoutchicago.com
Debuting in Chicago in 2004, *TimeOut Chicago* was pretty much an immediate success, earning praise for its intelligent, off-beat, and interesting articles on everything from sex and dating, to opera and classical music, to gay and lesbian arts and culture. The London-based Time Out publishing company has since expanded in Chicago, launching a highly touted *TimeOut Kids*, a *TimeOut Chicago Student Guide*, an *Eating and Drinking Guide*, and smaller annual guides to the summer festivals, fall festivals, home design, and holiday gift-giving. *TimeOut* is available for purchase on newsstands and by subscription.

WINDY CITY TIMES
(773) 871-7610
www.windycitymediagroup.com
Winner of multiple awards, including from the American Civil Liberties Union and The Human Rights Campaign, *Windy City Times* covers gay and lesbian issues and interests. It's owned by the Windy City Media Group, which also publishes the news and entertainment outlet Queercast (www.windycityqueercast .com), and the glossy four-pager about the LGBT entertainment scene called *Nightspots*.

Monthlies

CHICAGO MAGAZINE
(312) 222-8999
www.chicagomag.com
After several owners, *Chicago* has found a worthy publisher in the Tribune Company, which bought it in 2002. In 2004, the magazine received an award for General Excellence from the well-regarded National

Magazine Awards. Top-notch writing features topics from the superficial—hot new lipstick colors—to the serious—the recession's effect on Chicago's architecture industry—and popular best-of issues highlighting restaurants, bars, elementary schools, doctors, and more.

CHICAGO PARENT
(708) 386-5555
www.chicagoparent.com
Growing and changing (always for the good) for the past 25 years, this award-winning publication is distributed for free in Chicago and beyond. It addresses topics that interest, surprise, and motivate parents. It lists events throughout Chicagoland and features resource guides for essentials like birthday parties and schools. The website is a wealth of information as well.

THE CHICAGO REPORTER
(312) 427-4830
www.chicagoreporter.com
A bimonthly publication of the Community Renewal Society, the *Chicago Reporter* has prided itself on high-caliber investigative reporting focusing on race and poverty since its founding in 1972.

CS
(312) 274-2500
www.modernluxury.com
Painting the town red with its high-society and high-style perspective, *CS* is one of the glossiest of free publications in town, featuring celebrity profiles, artsy fashion spreads, and coverage of openings and hot spots. In Chicago, Modern Luxury also includes *Men's Book Chicago, CS Brides, CS Interiors,* and *Front Desk* (for the visitor market).

MICHIGAN AVENUE
(312) 753-6200
www.michiganavemag.com
Upping the upscale factor in Chicago, Niche Media LLC launched its freebie *Michigan Avenue* magazine in 2010 and it's been getting plenty of attention for its flashy style, celebrity covers (think Robert Redford and Jennifer Hudson), society pages full of pretty people attending fund-raisers around town, and an insider look at lifestyles of Chicago's rich and famous.

MINDFUL METROPOLIS
(312) 281-5199
www.mindfulmetropolis.com
Get your green culture roundup, eco-friendly event details, and environmentally conscious info here. Provided free at more than 600 locations around Chicagoland and by subscription.

TODAY'S CHICAGO WOMAN
(312) 951-7600
www.tcwmag.com
Launched in 1982, *TCW* is a free publication aimed at professional women in Chicago and its wealthy North Shore suburbs. Features, columns, and departments cover jobs and money, beauty and fitness, fashion and style, and wining and dining.

Radio

91.5 FM, WBEZ
(312) 948-4600
www.wbez.org
National Public Radio

93.1 FM, WXRT
(312) 329-WXRT (9978)
www.wxrt.com
Adult alternative

93.9 FM, WLIT
(312) 540-2000
www.litefm.com
Adult contemporary

97.9 FM, WLUP
Request lines: (312) 591-ROCK and (312) 591-ROLL
www.wlup.com
Classic rock

98.7 FM, WFMT
(773) 583-5000
www.wfmt.com
Classical

99.5 FM, WUSN
(312) 649-0099
www.us99.com
Country

101.9 FM, WTMX
(312) 591-6800
www.wtmx.com
Adult new music mix

103.5 FM, WKSC
(855) 591-1035
www.1035kissfm.com
Top 40

105.9 FM, WCFS
(312) 591-1059
www.fresh1059.com
'80s, '90s and today's music

107.5 FM, WGCI
(312) 540-2000
www.wgci.com
Hip-hop and R&B

670 AM, WSCR
(312) 644-6767
www.670thescore.com
Sports (home of White Sox) and talk radio

720 AM, WGN
(312) 591-7000, (312) 591-7200
www.wgnradio.com
Talk, news, and sports radio

780 AM, WBBM
(312) 297-7800
www.wbbm780.com
Traffic, weather, news, and sports

TV

CHANNEL 2, WBBM
(312) 899-2222
www.cbschicago.com
Local CBS affiliate

CHANNEL 5, WMAQ
(312) 836-5555
www.nbcchicago.com
Local NBC affiliate

CHANNEL 7, WLS
(312) 750-7777
www.abc7chicago.com
Local ABC affiliate

CHANNEL 9, WGN-TV
(773) 528-2311
www.wgntv.com
Local syndicated channel owned by the Tribune Company

CHANNEL 11, WTTW
(773) 583-5000
www.wttw.com
Local PBS affiliate

CHANNEL 32, WFLD
(312) 565-5532
www.myfoxchicago.com
Local Fox affiliate

Blogs & Websites

http://chicagoist.com

The second venture from New York's http://gothamist.com, Chicago's blog explores the city's arts, food, culture, controversies, and quirks.

http://gapersblock.com

Named for Chicago's term for traffic delays caused by accidents, this well-organized and daily updated blog encourages readers to "slow down and check out all the cool things in the city."

www.centerstagechicago.com

Owned by the *Sun-Times,* this site is loaded with listings of restaurants, bars, theater happenings, and more, and adds useful extras like its "virtual L," which offers a roundup of what to do near each El stop.

www.metromix.com

A longtime favorite go-to for in-the-know coverage on dining, nightlife, theater, live music scenes, this *Chicago Tribune*–run web site is impressive for its extensive photos and also includes a rundown of great deals around town.

http://chicago.citysearch.com

Online recommendations and user reviews of locations across the city including restaurants, bars, spas, shops, and more. An annual Best of Citysearch competition generates some buzz.

http://dailycandy.com/chicago

Like a friend who always knows the latest and greatest, Daily Candy lets readers in on everything from a new local jeweler, a just-opened sandwich shop, or where to find the cutest new hostess gift.

www.urchicago.com

Once a print pub, this alt weekly went totally digital a few years ago and now runs interviews with up-and-coming musicians, artists, writers, filmmakers, and more, along with bold reviews of the same, along with videos, blogs, and free music downloads.

EDUCATION & CHILD CARE

When it comes to higher education, you can't get much better or broader than Chicago. Students from all over the country and the world attend schools in Chicago, and there's good reason. From a Michelin Guide–mentioned culinary school to the most diverse arts college in the country, from amazing law schools to a university boasting eight Nobel-winning faculty members. There is a program for every career focus and every budget. Here you'll find overviews of most of the major college and universities in the city, as well as many technical and community colleges. Every school welcomes prospective students for visits to get more detailed info and a first-hand feel of the campus.

Although one can find pockets of excellence in the city's public education system, Chicago has struggled to find a formula for success that carries through to every school, which is partly a consequence of simply being a big, economically diverse city. But education is a focus of the current mayor, not to mention many passionate parents, and has improved throughout the years. Navigating the elementary and high school system can be frustrating, so fortunately there are various services and organizations that help.

We hope this primer to Chicago schools gives you a jump-start on it or helps you decide where to pursue your higher education. We'll start at the beginning, with child care and preschool.

CHILD CARE & PRESCHOOL

As plenty of studies have shown, those pre-kindergarten years between ages 0 and 5 can be crucial ones for your child's development. Particularly for working parents, finding the right preschool or day-care provider, whether at home or in a facility, is an important, and often difficult decision. Luckily, Chicago offers a wide range of options in all price ranges, in all neighborhoods, and for all needs—part-time or full-time, every day, and throughout the summer. The types of schools vary as well, with nearly every church offering a preschool program, as well as the Jewish Federation of Metropolitan

Chicago. There are a half-dozen Montessori schools that accept preschoolers in Chicago, and about 25 outside the city. Several universities have associated child-care facilities, including the University of Chicago, Northeastern Illinois University, and Loyola University. There are also worthy national-chain options such as KinderCare (www.kindercare .com), Bright Horizons (www.brighthorizons .com), and Kumon Learning Centers (www .kumon.com).

The state of Illinois' Department of Child and Family Services sets standards for and licenses day-care centers, homes, group homes, and day-care agencies for the state. In Chicago, a day-care center license is required for a facility where three or more children are cared for away from their parent or guardian; a home day care does not need the city license unless it has facility for more than 16 children, but it does need the state license.

There are nearly 3,000 licensed day-care centers in Illinois and more than three times that many licensed day-care homes. Another option available for many families is the state-run, half-day Preschool for All program, which admits children ages 3 and 4 (as of 2011, it was a free service, though that may change) and is typically held in a public school. Anyone can apply to any of the PFA schools, but first preference for these coveted spots goes to at-risk 4-year-olds living within the neighborhood boundaries of the particular public school. Most PFA programs are offered twice a day, one group in the morning and the other in the afternoon; the downside for working parents is that they take place only through the school year, not the summer. An alternative to this is the Chicago Public Schools' Tuition-Based Preschool, which offers a full-day, school-year program for around $10,000, typically much less than private preschool options that offer a full day.

Several valuable resources can help parents find preschools and day-care providers. For the Chicago Public Schools PFA programs, check online at www.cps.edu and search under Schools-Preschools, call (773) 553-2010, or visit the CPS Early Childhood Education website at www.ecechicago.org. In addition, *Chicago Parent* magazine (708-386-5555, www.chicagoparent.com) publishes a yearly (advertising-driven) "Making the Grade" publication, which focuses on private options; the Savvy Source (www.savvysource.com) offers a list of preschools;

and the Neighborhood Parents Network (www.npnparents.com) has an extensive discussion forum where members chat freely about their experiences with all kinds of preschools. NPN also publishes an interactive annual school directory, which includes details about preschools and elementary schools, both private and public; NPN members may view it online or download it.

PUBLIC SCHOOL DISTRICT

There are a total of 675 elementary, high school, and charter schools in the Chicago Public Schools system, making it the third-largest school system in the nation. In 1987, the Secretary of Education William Bennett bestowed on Chicago an embarrassing description: worst public schools in the nation. Since then, reforms and changes in school board structure have definitely bettered its outlook—reducing overcrowding, making capital improvements, adding schools, and upping scores and graduation numbers—although challenges and complaints remain. Chicago's first new mayor in 22 years, Rahm Emanuel, has vowed to improve things further, and controversial issues such as approving more charter schools are part of his discussion.

i Many private and public schools offer open houses, which feature tours of the school and opportunities to ask questions; if there is no open house offered or you miss the date, most schools will accommodate private tours upon request.

In the meantime, the Chicago Public Schools continue to serve a broad spectrum of Chicago's population in its traditional elementary (grades 1 through 8) and high schools, military academies, magnet schools, special education schools, gifted centers and classical schools, contract schools, and charter schools. The system of selection and enrollment can be frustratingly complicated, confusing, and stressful, but enrollment is guaranteed regardless of overcrowding at the traditional elementary and high school in your neighborhood—each school has specific boundaries that are delineated at the Chicago Public Schools website. However, children may attend schools outside of those attendance boundaries through a computerized lottery application system. The CPS Options for Knowledge guide lists all schools with availability for the upcoming school year. The Office of Academic Enhancement (773-553-2060) distributes the guide at all public schools, park district facilities, and online at www.cpsoae.org; there is also an Options for Knowledge school fair, generally held each October. Applications are due typically in December.

Some of the most common Chicago Public School terms:

- **Charter Schools:** Schools approved by the Board of Education, but run separately, meaning different rules and regulations for teachers and students. Currently, there are approximately 70 charter elementary and high schools in Chicago.
- **Classical Schools:** Schools with an accelerated, liberal arts–focused curriculum; testing required for admittance. Chicago has just a handful of classical schools.
- **Gifted Program:** Refers to programs that are offered at Regional Gifted Centers; admission based on free testing before kindergarten or 1st grade. Admittance factors in test scores, as well as the number of available spots and desegregation

guidelines. There are a dozen gifted centers in Chicago.
- **Magnet Cluster Schools:** These are made up of four to six neighborhood schools that have attendance boundaries and accept students outside those boundaries through the standard application and lottery. They each have a different specific focus, such as fine and performing arts.
- **Magnet Schools:** A straight magnet school does not have attendance boundaries, and has a focused curriculum such as dual-language program.
- **Neighborhood School:** This is the school for which your children receive automatic admittance. It is generally, but not always, the closest school to you (attendance boundaries get a little fiddly), usually walkable. Sometimes neighborhood schools are part of a magnet cluster, but not always.
- **Selected Enrollment Elementary School:** The generic phrase for Gifted Centers and any other school requiring testing.

PRIVATE ELEMENTARY & HIGH SCHOOLS

There are loads of independent schools in Chicago, including religious schools, Montessori, and lab schools located on college campuses (mostly but not solely attended by children of university faculty and employees). Tuitions vary, with many of the most sought-after schools commanding the highest rates, and others (generally Catholic schools) offering a less-expensive option. Several resources provide excellent information about the city's many private-school choices.

ARCHDIOCESE OF CHICAGO OFFICE OF CATHOLIC SCHOOLS
(312) 534-5200
http://schools.archchicago.org

THE CHICAGO JEWISH NEWS
www.chicagojewishnews.com
(lists Jewish day schools and high schools)

ILLINOIS MONTESSORI SCHOOLS
(847) 945-7582
www.illinoismontessorischools.com

INDEPENDENT SCHOOLS ASSOCIATION OF CENTRAL STATES
(312) 255-1244
www.isacs.org

NATIONAL ASSOCIATION OF INDEPENDENT SCHOOLS
(202) 973-9700
www.nais.org

i The not-for-profit Neighborhood Parents Network, a parent resource network with more than 5,000 family members, hosts a comprehensive and much-anticipated school fair each fall where private and public schools attend and share information with parents. www.npnparents.org.

HIGHER EDUCATION

CITY COLLEGES OF CHICAGO
District Office: 226 W. Jackson Blvd.
(312) 553-2500
www.ccc.edu
The City Colleges of Chicago were founded a century ago on the tenets of providing higher education for the city's working class and immigrant population. The first was originally called the "people's college" and opened in 1911 as an abbreviated baccalaureate program, which grew tremendously, fought off funding woes for a while, then was closed in 1933 as a cost-cutting measure during the Depression. But the outcry from students and labor movement activists (including well-known lawyer and civil libertarian Clarence Darrow) proved loud enough to bring back the college—and two more too. In 1956, Chicago pioneered college instruction via television, broadening the City Colleges teaching reach even further. By 1962, the current number of seven colleges had opened, and later the curriculum was expanded to put a greater focus on vocational education. By the late 1980s, the City College community was more diverse than ever, with students representing 50 countries and more than half of them women. They now offer transfer programs that prepare students for a 4-year college or university; programs of study ranging from architecture to agriculture, hospitality to manufacturing; as well as continuing education, adult education, child development, and more. Visit the website to find out more specifics about each of the seven colleges.

COLUMBIA COLLEGE CHICAGO
600 S. Michigan Ave.
(312) 369-7130
www.colum.edu
Columbia College started small in 1890 and nearly disappeared by 1960, but by that decade's end, several advocates revived the school, which is now the country's largest and most diverse private arts college, boasting 12,000 undergraduate and graduate students. Occupying 27 buildings in the South Loop, this urban educational hub

gives its students opportunities through internships and part-time jobs to experience its world-class cultural neighbors, including the Museum of Contemporary Art, Chicago Symphony, and other arts institutions. Average class size is 17, and more than 120 academic programs offer a range of specialties, including film and video, fashion studies, photography, dance, theater, and music. Showcasing the results of their studies and creativity are the student-based initiatives such as Manifest, an urban arts festival that presents student projects in a public way; and the Shop Columbia store, selling students' work on campus. It's all part of Columbia's intent to give students real-life experience and portfolios to take with them as they begin their post-college careers.

DEPAUL UNIVERSITY
1 E. Jackson Blvd.
(312) 362-8000, outside Illinois (800)
4DE-PAUL
www.depaul.edu
This not-for-profit school dates back to 1898 and is the largest Catholic university in the US (the founding Vincentians still sponsor the school). Today, DePaul attracts a wide-reaching student body of more than 25,000 from all 50 states and 90 countries—it was ranked number 10 in the "Diverse Student Population" category of the 2008 Princeton Review. On its two main Chicago campuses and four suburban campuses, it offers 275 undergrad and graduate programs, the most popular majors being psychology, business administration, public relations/advertising, political science, and biology. The Loop campus is known for its College of Law, where the Intellectual Property and Health Law programs get national attention for their excellence, and for its part-time MBA

program and innovative technology courses, including an award-winning game development program. The largest campus is its 36-acre patch of Lincoln Park, which houses a popular College of Liberal Arts and Sciences; residents who live around the campus often simply say they live "in the DePaul neighborhood." The suburban campuses are located in Naperville, Rolling Meadows, Oak Forest, and near O'Hare. Though students in DePaul's School of Music and Theatre School only amount to about 2 percent of total enrollment, acceptance to the schools is hard to come by, and the talented young men and women who get in make a big splash with several hundred open-to-the-public performances each year. Athletics are also big here, and the DePaul Blue Demons sports teams always rank tops, at least in fan enthusiasm. The athletic teams compete in NCAA Division I, the Big East conference in basketball (men's and women's), soccer, softball, golf, tennis, and more. A bonus for students here: Tens of thousands of alumni establish their careers in Chicago, giving young graduates an amazing resource to begin theirs.

ILLINOIS INSTITUTE OF TECHNOLOGY
3300 S. Federal St.
(312) 567-3000
www.iit.edu
IIT was created in 1940, but the seed that led to its formation was planted much earlier. It started in 1893 with the Armour Institute of Technology, founded by meatpacking mogul Philip Danforth Armour Sr., who was inspired by Chicago minister Frank Wakely Gunsaulus. In what's now called the "Million Dollar Sermon," Gunsaulus claimed that, with a million dollars, he could build a school of higher education for students other than simply society's elite. Armour took the bait,

donated the money, and established his technical school, which offered courses in engineering, chemistry, architecture, and library science. A liberal arts, science, and engineering school on Chicago's west side called Lewis Institute opened a couple of years later, and it was the merging of Lewis and Armour that created IIT. Its numbers are small—only about 7,700 students—but IIT is most definitely a big deal. The architecture program, one of the best in the country, can credit much of its bragging rights to Mies van der Rohe who headed the department beginning in 1938 at Armour and then IIT until 1959. Mies's own creative mark is all over campus, including the College of Architecture's main building, S.R. Crown Hall, which received National Historic Landmark status in 2001, a few years before the entire academic campus was added to the National Register of Historic Places for its many architecturally significant structures. Besides architecture, IIT is highly regarded for its engineering, science, humanities, design, and psychology programs, and its Chicago-Kent College of Law and Stuart School of Business. IIT prides itself on being a front-runner in the realm of technology, so much so that it recently launched an initiative to provide every incoming student with the latest Apple iPad. To learn more about IIT's architecture, see the listing in the Tours chapter.

LOYOLA UNIVERSITY
Lake Shore Campus
1032 W. Sheridan Rd.
(773) 274-3000
Water Tower Campus
820 N. Michigan Ave.
(312) 915-6000
www.luc.edu

Founded in 1870 as St. Ignatius College, Loyola is the largest of 28 Jesuit colleges and universities in the US. It has a total enrollment of just under 16,000 students who attend the 10 schools and colleges, including arts and sciences, business administration, law, and communication, just to name a few. Its Lake Shore campus literally hugs the Lake Michigan shoreline in the Rogers Park neighborhood, which means that after hitting the books, most students make plenty of time to hit the beach and bike path. The Water Tower campus is in the heart of downtown, adjacent to the Magnificent Mile, a dynamic place to learn and live, and close to the Loyola University Museum of Art. Besides its city campuses, it also has a suburban campus in Maywood (708-216-9000) where its Stritch School of Medicine and Marcella Niehoff School of Nursing work closely with the Loyola University Health System. Internationally, Loyola has a center in Rome; it serves as the US host to the Beijing Center for Chinese Studies in Beijing, China; and it features an academic center in Saigon-Ho Chi Minh City, Vietnam. Among Loyola's many diverse alums are two who have risen to pop-culture fame: Bill Rancic, winner of Season 1 of *The Apprentice,* and Ian Brennan, a co-creator and co-producer of *Glee.* Athletics may play second fiddle to academic and religious pursuits here, but the Ramblers are, in fact, part of NCAA Division I sports, and the school is a member of the Horizon League. For more information about the Loyola University Museum of Art, check out the Attractions & Museums chapter.

NORTH PARK UNIVERSITY
3225 W. Foster Ave.
(773) 244-6200
www.northpark.edu

This small school of about 3,200 was founded in 1891 by the Evangelical Covenant Church and relates its education to the Christian faith. Minnesota was actually North Park's first home, providing Swedish immigrants with useful skills and training to succeed in their new lives in America. With an offer of land that was then north of Chicago's city limits, the school moved and began to grow. The very first building was completed in 1894, and this Georgian Revival structure known as Old Main still stands as a campus focal point. Through the years, North Park has expanded its campus to more than 30 acres, including a residence hall, athletic field, state-of-the-art recreation center, and new library. Students appreciate the low student-to-faculty ratio and the choice of more than 35 undergraduate majors, as well as pre-professional studies. An annual campus theme program presents the entire student body and faculty with an open-ended question, such as "What is justice?" About 19 percent of incoming students on a recent poll described themselves as part of the Evangelical Covenant Church, while another 60 percent associated themselves as Protestant or Catholic. North Park's graduate-level Theological Seminary offers four master's degrees, 10 dual master's degrees, 10 certificates, and a doctoral degree. The North Park Vikings compete in NCAA Division III, with both men's and women's basketball teams earning several championship titles.

NORTHEASTERN ILLINOIS UNIVERSITY
5500 N. St. Louis Ave.
(773) 583-4050
www.neiu.edu
What began as a teacher training school in 1867 has evolved into today's fully accredited university with 12,000 students and more than 70 undergraduate and graduate degree programs—its College of Education is still a top choice. Ranked as the most ethnically diverse university in the Midwest by *US News and World Report,* Northeastern is located in the equally diverse neighborhood of Albany Park. Its affordable tuition—it's consistently noted for its high number of students who graduate with little or no debt—makes Northeastern attractive as a place for adult learners too. Its mostly commuter-population base means students are immersed in the city of Chicago and all it has to offer; plus, there's lots of parking available. In addition to its main 67-acre campus, there are three additional locations in Chicago, as well as degree programs in Lake County.

NORTHWESTERN UNIVERSITY
633 Clark St., Evanston
Evanston: (847) 491-3741; Chicago: (312) 503-8649
www.northwestern.edu
Although residents in Evanston often complain that Northwestern doesn't pay property taxes, the school does contribute $6 million in other fees and taxes and supplies its own police force and snow plowers. Besides, Evanston might not have existed at all without Northwestern. Back in 1853, when the initial area was purchased for Northwestern—the school was founded in 1850 to serve the Northwest Territory comprising Ohio, Indiana, Illinois, Michigan, Wisconsin, and parts of Minnesota—the land was simply open country about 12 miles north of nascent Chicago. Evanston was actually named for one of the school's founders, John Evans. And while the facility's founders originally purchased 379 acres of land along the scenic lakefront, today the university comprises just 240 acres on its Evanston campus. Among

its 10 undergraduate, graduate, and professional schools and approximately 16,500 full-time students, its largest population of about 4,300 is concentrated in the undergrad College of Arts and Sciences. Second to that are the 1,800-or-so who beat the competition for spots in the prestigious Kellogg School of Management, typically ranked in the top five in the nation. The accolades are equally outstanding for its undergrad and graduate journalism programs, law school, and medical school. The only private institution in the Big Ten athletic conference, Northwestern has an avid athletic spirit for its NCAA Division I Wildcats who play in eight men's and 11 women's teams and whose football team made it to the Rose Bowl in the 1995–96 season (sadly, they lost). A slew of well-known alumni include Chicago's new mayor Rahm Emanuel, as well as screen stars Zach Braff, Stephen Colbert, Garry Marshall, and David Schwimmer—a testament to the acclaimed theater school whose student productions are often on equal footing with professional ones.

ROOSEVELT UNIVERSITY
430 S. Michigan Ave.
(312) 341-3500
www.roosevelt.edu
Cheered for being one of the more flexible Chicago universities in terms of schedules, Roosevelt has a large group of part-time students who work full time—some students don't even start at Roosevelt until they've worked a bit first, judging by the average undergrad age of 24. There are about 4,400 students divided between full-time and part-time, undergrad and graduate programs at the Chicago campus; another 2,000-plus attend classes at the Schaumburg campus (847-619-7300), which was added in 1996. In

fact, when it comes to area colleges, Roosevelt is relatively young, founded by Edward J. Sparling in 1945. Sparling left his position as president of the YMCA College in Chicago in protest of the school board's demand that he supply a demographic breakdown of the student body. Fearing the board would use the information to limit the number of blacks, Jews, immigrants, and women admitted to the school, Sparling decided he'd start his own independent institution that was open to all. Sixty-two of the 63 YMCA College faculty followed him. They named their school in honor of human rights champion Franklin Roosevelt, who died in office soon after the school was chartered; Eleanor Roosevelt remained supportive throughout her life. The school continues to attract a diverse population to its six colleges and 126 degree programs. The Music Conservatory and Theatre Conservatory are highly regarded, with their performances attended nearly as much by the general public as by the college community. Athletics on campus have recently made a return after a long drought. There are currently six men's and six women's teams of Roosevelt Lakers, who participate in the National Association of Intercollegiate Athletics, with aspirations to join NCAA Division III competitions. Watch for a new addition to its historic Auditorium Building—a center for academics, student life, and housing that will top out at an impressive 32 stories, making it the second-tallest university facility in the country.

UNIVERSITY OF CHICAGO
5801 S. Ellis Ave.
(773) 702-1234
www.uchicago.edu
The digits at this Hyde Park university are impressive: More than 154,000 alumni

worldwide; 85 Nobel Prize recipients, 13 of them faculty; 24 Pulitzer Prize winners; research that has led to more than 3,300 patents filed since 1987; and 211 acres that were designated a botanic garden in 1997. The University of Chicago sure has plenty of fame to its name—and add to all those numbers the fact that President Barack Obama taught here for 12 years as senior lecturer at the law school. Since its founding in 1890 by the American Baptist Education Society (it's a nonsectarian school) and John D. Rockefeller, UChicago (previously referred to as U of C) has always emphasized academics, class discussion (over lectures), research, and strong interdisciplinary studies. In other words, although the original buildings are a traditional throwback with their gargoyle-decked English Gothic–style architecture, the superior education that takes place inside them is innovative, challenging, world-changing, and sometimes controversial. The same academic standards that started the school continue on for today's 5,252 undergrads and more than 10,000 graduate, professional, and other students. The school offers 49 undergraduate majors and has four graduate divisions and six graduate professional schools, all tops in their categories. Modern architectural additions to the sprawling campus have included the Chicago Booth School of Business (in 1943, the university created the first executive MBA program); the futuristic Helmut Jahn–designed library; the Reva and David Logan Center for Creative and Performing Arts; and the Ratner Athletics Center, a 150,000-square-foot facility designed by Cesar Pelli, which is, among other things, the home of several of the school's 19 intercollegiate NCAA Division III teams.

UNIVERSITY OF ILLINOIS AT CHICAGO
601 S. Morgan St.
(312) 996-7000
www.uic.edu

Less expensive than other city options, but no less of a high-caliber experience, UIC is the city's largest university with 27,000 students in 15 colleges, and it has one of the country's most diverse student populations. The original University of Illinois campus was chartered in 1867 in Champaign-Urbana; the Chicago campus formed through the 1982 consolidation of its Medical Center campus—which dates back to 1859—and what used to be called the University of Illinois at Chicago Circle, which began in 1946 at Navy Pier as a two-year prep-type facility for World War II G.I. vets. After completing the two years there, the students could finish their degree in Urbana. When the Navy Pier outpost closed, continuing demand for a public university inspired the opening of a more permanent outpost in 1965 in what's known now as the university's east side of campus. An impressive list of programs includes colleges of applied health science, architecture and the arts, dentistry, engineering, nursing, urban planning, public affairs, and the nation's largest medical school. At UIC, research is given high priority, and that isn't just for graduate students. The Undergraduate Research Experience and Undergraduate Research Assistant Program allow students to start early by working with faculty mentors. The UIC Flames are the university's 18 varsity NCAA Division I teams who compete in everything from basketball to gymnastics, swimming to tennis.

TECHNICAL & VOCATIONAL SCHOOLS

ILLINOIS INSTITUTE OF ART—CHICAGO
350 N. Orleans St.
(800) 351-3450, (312) 280-3500
www.artinstitutes.edu/chicago
Part of a network of more than 40 locations in North America, the Chicago outlet offers two: one in the Merchandise Mart and one at the corner of Lake and Wabash Avenues, featuring the student-run Backstage Bistro. The school offers a variety of year-round bachelor degree programs in fine arts, arts, applied science, and science; several associate degrees are also available.

KENDALL COLLEGE
900 N. North Branch St.
(888) 90-KENDALL (905-3632)
www.kendall.edu
Kendall College is famous for its culinary arts program, but it also offers undergraduate degrees in business, hospitality management, and early childhood education. Founded in 1934, the college currently has more than 2,500 students, with the culinary arts students making news recently when The Dining Room at Kendall College got a shout-out in the first-ever Michelin Chicago guide, making it one of just three US culinary school restaurants ever recognized in a Michelin Guide.

LE CORDON BLEU COLLEGE OF CULINARY ARTS CHICAGO
361 W. Chestnut St.
(312) 944-0882
www.chefs.edu/chicago
The Chicago location of this culinary giant, which got its start in Paris more than 100 years ago, offers associate and certificate programs in culinary arts and baking. Students get plenty of on-the-job training, including at the student-run restaurant called Technique.

NATIONAL LOUIS UNIVERSITY
Chicago Campus
122 S. Michigan Ave.
(888) NLU-TODAY (658-8632),
(800) 443-5522, (312) 261-3057
National Louis started with its College of Education, founded in 1886. It has since added a College of Arts and Sciences, and a College of Management and Business. Besides its flexible day, evening, weekend, and online classes, its class size of generally fewer than 20 contribute to the university's appeal for its more than 14,000 students, 70 percent of whom participate in graduate programs. In addition to its downtown Chicago campus, National Louis has campuses in suburban Elgin, Lisle, Skokie, and Wheeling.

SCHOOL OF THE ART INSTITUTE OF CHICAGO
37 S. Wabash Ave.
(312) 629-6100
www.saic.edu
The list of SAIC's famous alums is impressively long and includes everyone from Georgia O'Keeffe to David Sedaris, Cynthia Rowley to Nora Dunn. And there's good reason. Founded in 1866, 11 years before its partner institution, the esteemed Art Institute of Chicago museum, the school provides multidisciplinary undergraduate, post-baccalaureate, and graduate degrees in all realms of art. The fine arts graduate program was ranked number 3 out of a list of 220 in the US by *US News and World Report*.

HEALTH & WELLNESS

A s you might expect, Chicago has some of the most respected and renowned hospitals in the country. You are never too far from excellent health care, emergency services, and ongoing treatment facilities. The City of Chicago runs several discount walk-in health clinics that serve a wide variety of residents. There are also an amazing number of alternative-care practitioners. Many even take health insurance plans, though others do not, so it's helpful to ask first if that's important to you. While there are too many to list all the options here, we have included two websites that provide a database of doctors of all varieties to help you find the one that fits your needs.

HEALTH DEPARTMENTS

CHICAGO DEPARTMENT OF PUBLIC HEALTH
333 S. State St., Rm. 200
(312) 747-9884
www.cityofchicago.org/health
The CDPH monitors, diagnoses, and investigates health status and problems in the greater Chicago community. It also helps to educate and empower people about health topics; develop health-related policies; enforce laws and regulations that protect health safety; connect people to the health resources they need; evaluate health services; and more. On the CDPH website, you can find Chicago public health information, data, and research. There's also information on neighborhood health clinics, mental health clinics, specific services for sexually transmitted infections, and clinics geared toward women, infants, and children, and other essential public health services and programs.

ILLINOIS DEPARTMENT OF PUBLIC HEALTH
535 W. Jefferson St., Springfield, Illinois 62761
(217) 782-4977
www.idph.state.il.us
With its more than 200 different programs, the IDPH monitors and maintains public health in conjunction with local agencies. Their services cover health-care regulation, health promotion, health protection, men's and women's health, planning and statistical collection and analysis, and preparedness and responses to public health issues.

HOSPITALS

ADVOCATE ILLINOIS MASONIC MEDICAL CENTER
836 W. Wellington Ave.
(773) 975-1600
www.advocatehealth.com/masonic
Part of the 12-hospital Advocate Health Care network in the state, Illinois Masonic was named one of the top 100 hospitals in the country by Thomson Reuters in 2010 and

2011, one of just six in the Chicago area that made the list. The faith-based Advocate grew out of the merging of the Evangelical Health Systems Corporation and Lutheran General Health System. The 408-bed Illinois Masonic is acclaimed for its Level I trauma center, Level III Neonatal Intensive Care Unit, the city's largest certified midwifery program, and its Heart and Vascular Institute.

CHILDREN'S MEMORIAL HOSPITAL
2300 Children's Plaza (Lincoln Avenue and Fullerton Parkway)
(800) KIDS-DOC, (773) 880-4000
www.childrensmemorial.org
A host of awards—including a *US News & World Report* ranking as one of the top 30 best children's hospitals in the country, and 11th out of 75 children's hospitals in America as reported in a survey by *Parents* magazine—testifies to the extraordinary care here. Families from every state and more than 35 countries bring their children here for everything from cardiac care to liver transplantation, gastroenterology to plastic and reconstructive surgery. A brand new state-of-the-art facility is scheduled to open in June 2012 at 225 E. Chicago Ave., on the campus of the hospital's academic partner, Northwestern University Feinberg School of Medicine.

NORTHWESTERN MEMORIAL HOSPITAL
251 E. Huron St.
(312) 926-2000
www.nmh.org
The sprawling Northwestern Memorial campus comprises numerous medical buildings and clinics, testing centers, learning centers, rehabilitation facilities, psychiatric institutes, physicians' offices, and two hospitals, including this one. The other, the Prentice

Women's Hospital (250 E. Superior St.), is a new 1-million-square-foot, 328-bed facility for obstetrics, gynecology, gynecology-oncology, breast and plastic surgery, hematology-oncology, and neonatal intensive care; its birthing center boasts capacity for 13,600 deliveries a year and it's always busy with babies. Overall, Northwestern ranked number-one in Chicago as the metro area's best hospital by *US News & World Report*.

RUSH UNIVERSITY MEDICAL CENTER
1650 W. Harrison St.
(312) 942-5000
www.rush.edu
This academic medical center includes the 676-bed hospital, Rush University, Rush Oak Park Hospital, and an integrated network of providers that combine to make up Rush Health. *US News & World Report* has included Rush in its rankings of the area's best hospitals, and Rush is the preferred medical facility for the Chicago White Sox and Chicago Bulls teams.

SWEDISH COVENANT HOSPITAL
5145 N. California Ave.
(773) 878-8200
www.swedishcovenant.org
Serving Chicagoans for more than 125 years, this academic community hospital is rooted in the Evangelical Covenant Church, but serves a wide range of patients in a wide range of areas, from cardiology to family health, dermatology to weight management. It includes a well-known midwifery program, as well as a sleep and neurodiagnostic center, a back institute, and mental health services. It also offers innovative robotic surgical services, and the Chicago Back Institute for treatment of spine conditions.

UNIVERSITY OF CHICAGO MEDICAL CENTER

5841 S. Maryland Ave.
(773) 702-1000
www.uchospitals.edu

Besides a 541-bed general medicine and surgical hospital, the Hyde Park–based UCMC includes Comer Children's Hospital; Chicago Lying-in Hospital for maternity and women's care; the outpatient Duchossois Center for Advanced Medicine, which houses much of UCMC's diagnostic and outpatient treatment services, along with other outpatient locations around Chicagoland; the top-ranked University of Chicago Pritzker School of Medicine; and the Bernard A. Mitchell Hospital, an adult inpatient care facility that includes the emergency department and several intensive-care units. Atop Mitchell Hospital is a specially equipped medical helicopter that serves the emergency care center's Level I pediatric trauma unit, as well as a burn unit and perinatal unit.

UNIVERSITY OF ILLINOIS MEDICAL CENTER

1740 W. Taylor St.
(866) 600-CARE (2273)
www.uillinoismedcenter.org

More new physicians earn their medical degrees at UIC than any other medical school in the country. Within the UIMC are a 496-bed tertiary hospital, outpatient facility, specialty clinics, and the university's six colleges of health sciences. It's nationally recognized for minimally invasive surgery, live donor transplants, and its high number of National Institutes of Health–funded research grants.

URGENT CARE & WALK-IN CLINICS

CHICAGO CENTER FOR ORTHOPEDICS URGENT CARE

Weiss Memorial Hospital
Third Fl, A Elevators
4646 N. Marine Dr.
(773) 564-ORTHO (6784)

Got a weekend-warrior injury that can't wait? For children and adults, the experts at this walk-in clinic (though appointments are appreciated and encouraged) can see you on Sunday. Really. Hours are 9 a.m. to 1 p.m.

MICHIGAN AVENUE IMMEDIATE CARE

180 N. Michigan Ave., Ste. 1605
(312) 201-1234
www.maicoh.org

In a brand-new facility in the Loop, this no-appointment-necessary clinic sees patients who have acute or nonurgent medical needs. It is a certified yellow fever vaccine clinic and offers pre-travel consultations and vaccines and is popular with students. MAIC also offers X-ray services.

i The City of Chicago website lists mental health centers that often allow visits for free or sliding-scale payment. www.cityofchicago.org—look under Public Health.

NORTHWEST IMMEDIATE CARE

4332 N. Elston Rd.
(773) 754-3500
www.northwestimmediatecare.com

Open 365 days a year, this facility treats patients of all ages, accepts most insurance, and offers services ranging from minor abrasions to coughs to headaches to school physical exams. They also have X-ray, other lab facilities, and a dental clinic, and they can perform ultrasounds and physical therapy. The website lets you check first to see how long the wait time is.

PHYSICIANS IMMEDIATE CARE
Multiple locations
(877) 875-4200
www.physiciansimmediatecare.com
With 16 locations in and around Chicago, these walk-in clinics provide general treatment and care of illness and injury such as sprains, colds, fractures, and flu, as well as occupational medicine and physical therapy services. Other services include physicals for school, sports, and immigration. No appointments are needed, and they are open 7 days a week.

ALTERNATIVE CARE

CHICAGO HEALERS
www.chicagohealers.com
You can rest assured that the MD, chiropractor, life coach, holistic dentist, nutritionist, or any other of the approximately 200 integrative medicine and healing practitioners listed on this website will serve you well. Though a free service for users, the providers listed on the site have gone through a screening process that includes phone interviews, completion of a detailed questionnaire, and referrals. Besides finding the right person for your needs (and reading through their extensive provider profile), you can learn more about each modality, follow practitioners' blogs, subscribe to a monthly newsletter, and find out about upcoming alternative healing-related events, workshops, and classes.

CHICAGO MEDFINDS
http://chicago.medfinds.com
Offering a comprehensive online search tool, Medfinds makes it easy to find an alternative medicine provider of any kind in Chicago (there are versions in nearly 20 cities across the country). The caveat is that the practitioners listed are not ranked or screened in any way by Medfinds, so it's up to consumers to do their own due-diligence in learning more about the person, but it's still a great place to start.

WHOLEHEALTH CHICAGO
2522 N. Lincoln Ave.
(773) 296-6700
www.wholehealthchicago.com
One of the first mainstream centers to bring together a host of holistic healers under one roof, WholeHealth is still one of the best. The integrative healers, who often work together to provide you with the best treatment plan possible, practice in fields including clinical psychology, homeopathy, chiropractic medicine, acupuncture, herbology, and physical therapy. An online resource guide also provides valuable information about ailments, therapies, nutritional supplements, and more.

RETIREMENT

We might not have palm trees or a slew of early-bird specials, but what makes Chicago such a great place to retire is that it is simply a great place to live. Its accessibility via public transportation and its multiple senior services allow retired residents to get around easily and enjoy everything the city has to offer. There's no need to slow down when there are so many things to do at any pace and at any age. You won't miss the palm trees when you can still get to Chicago's many museums, stroll along the lakefront path, enjoy a free concert, or dine at any number of amazing restaurants that open just as early as you need them to, but serve award-winning food from world-renowned chefs. When it's time to take things down a notch, Chicago offers a variety of comfortable housing options that offer care with respect and dignity.

SERVICES & ORGANIZATIONS

Under the umbrella of Chicago's Department of Family and Support Services, the Senior Services Area Agency on Aging conducts assessments for appropriate needs, and disseminates information about the services available. The agency provides for the spectrum of senior residents, from those who may be seeking out continuing education classes to those who need help with day-to-day routines. Services include help finding housekeeping, caregiving, and employment; a shuttle service; legal assistance; and a senior companion program. For more details, check online at www.cityof chicago.org or call (312) 744-4016.

Regional Senior Centers

There are 6 regional senior centers, plus 10 satellite centers. Following is a list of the regional centers. A list of the satellite locations can be found at www.cityofchicago .org.

- 2019 W. Lawrence Ave., 312-744-0784
- 6117 S. Kedzie Ave., 312-747-0440
- 3160 N. Milwaukee Ave., 312-744-6681
- 2102 W. Ogden Ave., 312-746-5300
- 1767 E. 79th St., 312-747-0189
- 78 E. Washington St., 312-744-4550

EDUCATION

Through the City of Chicago, the Lifelong Learners Program partners with teachers from City Colleges of Chicago to offer free weekly class sessions at regional senior centers. Open to residents who are 60 years old and up, the noncredit courses include topics such as dance and art appreciation, budget management, and foreign languages. Credit courses are available for seniors who have already earned their high school diploma or GED certificate. Seniors may register for the classes at the regional senior centers. Upon completion of a session, a special graduation ceremony is held. More information is available by calling (312) 744-4016.

HOUSING

When residents in Chicago are ready to move to housing that provides some living assistance, there are plenty of options. The City of Chicago's website maintains lists of all types of facilities.

Assisted living facilities are paid for with private funds and are for those seniors who want as much independence as possible, but also want the comfort of knowing that care is there if they need it.

Supportive living is meant for low-income seniors who qualify for Medicaid. This option of housing also allows for a great deal of independence.

Nursing homes provide the most wellness care and offer long-term doctor-supervised assistance with all daily routines without needing to be in a hospital. This housing may be paid for privately, by Medicaid, or through private insurance.

For seniors who remain in their own homes, the city of Chicago offers the Small Accessible Repairs for Seniors (SARFS) program to help provide minor safety, security, and accessibility improvements. The services are free for seniors at least 60 years old who meet certain income requirements and are either home-owners or renters living in a 1- to 4-unit building.

i The Illinois Department on Aging has additional information and resources that help seniors navigate everything from health care to volunteer opportunities. Find out more at (800) 252-8966; www.state.il.us/aging.

NUTRITION

The Meals on Wheels Association of America serves communities throughout the Chicago area, providing nutritious meals to home-bound seniors or people with disabilities. They provide home meal delivery, holiday meals, short-term immediate meals to those recovering from hospital stays, and even some typical home modification to make homes more accessible for people in wheelchairs. There are several member programs in Chicago that provide meals to seniors through Meals on Wheels:

- **Community Nutrition Network,** (312) 207-5290; www.cnnssa.org
- **Meals on Wheels Chicago,** (312) 744-2120; www.mealsonwheelschicago.org
- **Senior Services-Area Agency on Aging,** (312) 743-0300; www.cityofchi cago.org/city/en/depts/fss.html

VOLUNTEERING

Keeping actively involved in the community is important, and volunteering is a great way to do that. While many organizations are open to volunteers of any age, Chicago participates in two programs in particular that specifically seek out older volunteers.

The Foster Grandparents Program links seniors with disadvantaged children who lack adequate daily love, care, and attention. Volunteer "grandparents" may simply spend time with the child or help with homework at a school, hospital, drug-treatment center, correctional institution, day-care center, or Head Start program. For more information, call the Senior HelpLine, (800) 252-8966.

With the Retired and Senior Volunteer Program (RSVP) of Hull House/Chicago, the skills and interests of people 55 and older are matched with organizations throughout the city that need qualified volunteers. More than 780 volunteers participate in this program, serving as everything from mentors to nutrition aides to museum guides. For more information call (312) 235-5359.

Volunteer Opportunities

ANTI-CRUELTY SOCIETY
157 W. Grand Ave.
(312) 644-8338
www.anticruelty.org

One of the oldest animal shelters and pet advocates in the city, the Anti-Cruelty Society works to find loving homes for healthy or rehabilitatable dogs and cats. They also help educate the community about compassion for animals, work to prevent cruelty to animals, and provide low- or no-cost spaying and neutering. Volunteers are essential for all components of its mission.

BOYS AND GIRLS CLUB
550 W. Van Buren St., Ste. 350
(312) 235-8000
www.bgcc.org

With its 16 locations around the city, primarily focused in Chicago's most underserved and often most threatening communities, the Boys and Girls Clubs of Chicago offers children ages 6 to 18 a welcoming and safe after-school option. The programs address character and leadership, education and careers, health and life skills, the arts, and fitness and sports. The most common ways to lend a hand include mentoring, helping to run or assist with programs, and organizing supply drives to collect everything from sports equipment to school supplies.

CHICAGO ANIMAL CARE AND CONTROL
2741 S. Western Ave.
(312) 747-1406
www.cityofchicago.org/
animalcarecontrol

It's not the most beautiful way-station for lost and unwanted pets, but it's possibly the hardest-working. This City of Chicago open-door shelter accepts all animals and typically has in its kennels and cages between 300 and 500 dogs, cats, reptiles, rabbits, and more. The 54,000-square-foot facility houses a medical division as well and runs a fleet of 22 vehicles for stray animal pickups. Warning: Volunteering here requires a screening process including finger-printing, not to mention that it might just lead to bringing home a pet of your own.

i For a list of more animal shelters in need of volunteers, check out the Chicago Animal Shelter Alliance, which was formed in 2003 to help effect the greatest impact possible (312-458-9239; www.casachicago.org).

CHICAGO CARES
2 N. Riverside Plaza, Ste. 2200
(312) 780-0800
www.chicagocares.org

Chicago Cares is kind of a clearinghouse for volunteer opportunities across Chicagoland that typically require short-term commitments. They help to organize and lead a wide range of projects appropriate for individuals, community organizations and schools, corporations and groups, and youths. Focus areas of involvement include adult and children's education, environment, health and wellness, hunger and homelessness, senior service, and youth assistance. Chicago Cares runs more than 200 volunteer programs around the city each month and since 1991 has enlisted more than 330,000 volunteers; the annual Serve-a-thon engages in public school improvement projects and involves about 6,000 volunteers alone. The website allows you to search for current projects with volunteer needs or to register for the annual events.

CHICAGO CONSERVATION CORPS
Downtown office: 30 N. LaSalle St., Ste. 200
Neighborhood office: The Chicago Center for Green Technology, 445 N. Sacramento Ave.
(312) 743-9283
www.chicagoconservationcorps.org
A project of the City of Chicago's Department of Environment, this organization partners with other leaders in environmental improvement, restoration, cleanup, and education. Their blog provides a list of upcoming projects, which might include everything from a work day at the Forest Preserves to a "Trash to Treasure" swap.

CHICAGO CULTURAL CENTER
78 E. Washington St.
(312) 744-6630
www.chicagoculturalcenter.org
Help out with the multitude of free events at this landmark Loop cultural institution, lead building tours, answer questions at the information booths or at booths at center-sponsored events, or even assist at the Marriage Court wedding ceremonies here. Besides the chance to meet a variety of interesting people and do something good for Chicago's arts scene, volunteers receive 15 percent off merchandise at the Cultural Center shop.

i The City of Chicago website is a great resource for learning more about volunteer-based organizations in and around the city: www.cityofchicago .org.

ONE GOOD DEED CHICAGO
City Hall, Rm. 406
121 N. LaSalle St.
(312) 744-7135, or call 311
www.onegooddeedchicago.org
Through a Cities of Service Leadership Grant, Chicago began this city-sponsored effort to promote volunteerism by harnessing the talents and knowledge people have and matching them with existing nonprofits that need assistance. Organizations register to become part of this growing network, and people and groups interested in volunteering search the database to find a project that fits. The focus is on high-risk youth, education initiatives, and economic recovery.

PAWS
Adoption Center: 1997 N. Clybourn Ave.; (773) 935-PAWS
Spay/Neuter Clinic: 3516 W. 26th St.; (773) 521-SPAY
www.pawschicago.org
Founded in 1997 and now Chicago's largest no-kill animal shelter, PAWS is famous for its cageless adoption center and its busy spay and neuter clinic. Among other things, PAWS Chicago's 4,000-some volunteers serve in the welcome center, as adoption-center tour hosts or adopter follow-up callers; they keep the animal spaces clean and the animals loved and fed; they ride aboard the new GusMobile spay-neuter van, which is based on the South Side where the largest concentration of Chicago pets are; and they foster pets in their homes until they're ready for adoption.

INDEX